The Fame of Gawa

The Lewis Henry Morgan Lectures 1976
presented at The University of Rochester
Rochester, New York

The Lewis Henry Morgan Lecture Series
Fred Eggan: *The American Indian:*
Perspectives for the Study of Social Change
Ward H. Goodenough: *Description and Comparison*
in Cultural Anthropology
Robert J. Smith: *Japanese Society: Tradition, Self,*
and the Social Order
Sally Falk Moore: *Social Facts and Fabrications:*
"Customary Law" on Kilimanjaro,
1880–1980

The Fame of Gawa

A Symbolic Study of

Value Transformation in a Massim

(Papua New Guinea)

Society

Nancy D. Munn

Duke University Press   *Durham and London*

*Mira Gaw', palatala buki vagara yakamiya
kamweidona. Yagara "Butura Gawa"*

For the Gawan people and especially for

Kaidiriya and Kilay, Tarakuruku and Meri, Moyikebu and Sinteyi, Takavatara and Nameis, Kimada and Toroy, Kiweru, Mutawadiya and Boganuma, Karibew, Toromweya, Weruwa and the late Lolovila, Diwewa, Agata, Gunumora, Tamowaw, Petay, the late Veikway, Bwarowi, Kanamweya and the late Sineibada, Kawraboga, Kataawasi, Yurasay and Niyeta, Ugakina and Nagobwaw, Tanaabwasi and Kwaabwaw, Urisaku, and Tamsibona

Contents

vii

Illustrations

Figures

Foreword

In this very substantial expansion of her Lewis Henry Morgan Lectures, Nancy Munn has amply satisfied the expectations aroused in her listeners by her original presentation, and by her seminars. A brief foreword can do no more than hint at the contexts in which this study must be placed. It is clearly a theoretical contribution of importance to anyone concerned with social and cultural analysis. At the same time, it can be read as an especially fine contribution to the ethnography of a remote corner of our world.

Gawa is situated in the Massim area of Papua New Guinea, an area familiar to generations of beginning anthropology students who have read Bronislaw Malinowski's *Argonauts of the Western Pacific*, though few such students can have fully appreciated the theoretical implications of *Argonauts*. Nancy Munn, with great skill, makes it possible for any reader to grasp her theoretical points and to see clearly how these relate to life on Gawa. Only the best monographic accounts achieve what she has achieved: a masterly integration of her theoretical framework and her rich ethnographic materials.

Some readers will place this account first in the context of the Kula,while others will consider it in relation to the growing literature in cultural-symbolic analysis in anthropology. Its bearing on the work being done on action, value production, signification, space and time, and exchange will engage the attention of others. Certainly, the implications of this work for social theory, and for philosophers enamored of constructed examples, should be noted and pondered.

The very existence of this volume raises a question, in the monograph's own terms, regarding the fame of Gawa: The name of Gawa will achieve an unprecedented eminence – a "spacetime" whose dimensions surely surpass any envisaged by the Gawans themselves. What consequences might this entail?

Nancy Munn agreed to give the Lewis Henry Morgan Lectures while still at the University of Massachusetts, and, after arriving at the University of Chicago, delivered them at the University of Rochester on November 2, 4, 9, and 11, 1976.

ALFRED HARRIS
Editor
The Lewis Henry Morgan Lectures

Preface

In 1976 I was privileged to be invited to the University of Rochester to give the Morgan lectures. This book is the result of a long-term revision and expansion of those lectures.[1] Although not exactly undergoing a "sea change," the original ideas passed through many versions as well as an actual sea journey: a return field trip during 1979–81 to Gawa island, the source of the ethnography for this study.

During my first field periods on Gawa (1973–4, May–July 1975), three general features of Gawan society came to be of special interest to me from the perspective of symbolic analysis: the moral emphasis on food-transmission and the contrast with consumption; the outward focus of Gawans on their relations with other islands and their fame in the inter-island world; and the importance of witchcraft assumptions, especially in public speaking and in connection with the Gawan political emphasis on individual and lineage autonomy. I was particularly interested in developing a model of symbolic process that was able to convey the interrelations between these and other dimensions of Gawan society. About 1975–6 I began to think of Gawan food giving as a key type of value-creating act in a polar relationship with acts of consumption and witchcraft. Posing the problem in this way led me to focus on a more general idea that became one of the core elements of the later argument: namely, the notion of value-producing types of act as a dialectical symbolism of positive and negative value transformations. This elementary notion – combined with an argument developed in examining what I described in a 1975 paper as the "spatiotemporal transformations" occurring through the construction and exchange of Gawan canoes (Munn, 1977) – in turn led me to develop a more general model of value transformation. The original 1976 Morgan lectures constituted the first approximation of this model, although I have substantially changed its terms since then.

It is in connection with the focus on food transmission that Morgan's work acquires relevance to the present study. In his examination of house types among the American Indians, Morgan (1965 [1881]) sought to demonstrate that what he called the "law of hospitality" was connected with communal living in extended, multifamily households and with house structures reflecting this communal order. The presence of the law of hospitality was associated with the "existence of common stores"; and hospitality served as the distributional mechanism of this communally based order that made it possible to equalize subsistence resources beyond the household. "The law of hospitality," Morgan said, "indicates a plan of life among them which has not been carefully studied, nor have its [i.e., the law of hospitality's] effects been fully appreciated" (1965:61).

Morgan regarded hospitality as a moral virtue as well as an economic mechanism, but unlike symbolically oriented nineteenth-century scholars such as Fustel de Coulanges (1956 [1864]) and Robertson Smith (1956 [1889]), he did not conceive of food giving or communal feasts as a means of expressing bonds of social relationship. Similarly, Morgan viewed the house as a material enclosure of the communal group. However, he did not regard the organization of space as an expression of group bonds or social categories as did Coulanges or Durkheim and Mauss (1963 [1901–2/1903]). Indeed, an approach that makes meaning central to the problem of societal process was alien to the paradigm from which Morgan worked (see Sahlins, 1976:58ff.).

The present work examines such matters as food transmission and space from the perspective of a symbolic framework (in which, however, the relationship between meaning and social process is rather different from that posited by the classical Durkheimian tradition). Thus the particular concerns of this study with the Gawan view of the effects of food giving and with the culturally defined outcomes of transmissive acts must necessarily appear at odds with what Morgan meant when he referred to the importance of examining the effects of the law of hospitality. Nevertheless, not only this general theme, but also the more specific one of the relation between equalization and food transmission and between space (and artifacts) and sociopolitical relationships, which were of interest to Morgan, all enter prominently into this study, albeit in very different form.

In addition to focusing on value and action, the model I develop in this book is informed by a long-term interest in problems of cultural space and time. I first elaborated this interest in regard to the Massim region in an unpublished manuscript on "symbolic time" in the Trobriands, written while I was a visiting member at the Institute for Advanced Study, Princeton, in 1972. After my initial fieldwork on Gawa island, some of the ideas very roughly drafted in this manuscript concerning kula exchange as a temporal process and the connection between bodily beautification (as a process "at the interstices of keeping and giving," Munn, 1972:74) and the

Maussian theme of the separation of objects from the "self" occurring in exchange were incorporated in considerably revised form in my 1977 paper on Gawan canoes. A second attempt to view kula as a way of constructing time (by now seen as "spacetime") was developed in a paper on Gawan kula exchange for the 1978 conference on kula in Cambridge, England (Munn, 1983).

My research in the Massim region of Papua New Guinea began in 1972 when I spent about two months in the northeast Massim looking for an appropriate field site. At that time I was able to stay briefly at Kwaibwaga on the Trobriands at the invitation of Annette Weiner, who was doing anthropological research there. From the Trobriands I traveled to southern Woodlark Island (Muyuw), where I stayed for short periods at Guasopa and Wabanuna, whose residents taught me some of the Muyuwan language and extended me their hospitality. I am indebted to Arthur Smedley, then Australian patrol officer stationed at Guasopa, for his aid on Woodlark and for enabling me to obtain permission to travel on a government patrol vessel that went to several islands in the area. The captain of that ship was Faytili, a Dobuan well known in the area as an important "kula man"; I thank him for his help on that first exploratory trip, which introduced me to Gawans and enabled me to stay for a night on Gawa island. As a result of this trip, I decided to attempt to return to Gawa the following year to do a long-term field project.

Since that time, I have spent three research periods on Gawa, all of which were supported by the National Science Foundation; I take this opportunity to express my appreciation to the foundation for this generous aid. My initial work was done during the first two periods, which extended from June 1973 to mid-July 1974 and from late May 1975 through July 1975; the third period, under a separate fellowship, extended from mid-October 1979 to early January 1981. I am indebted to the national government of Papua New Guinea and the provincial government of Milne Bay for giving me permission to do research on Gawa; I am grateful for the courtesy and aid of their officials, especially for the help of the patrol officers in the northeast Massim during my last period of work on Gawa.

Before I began my work on Gawa, David Lithgow of the Summer Institute of Linguistics, who had done extensive linguistic research on Muyuw, kindly made available to me unpublished Muyuw language materials and a brief vocabulary from Gawa. These materials were extremely useful in the initial stages of my research. During my stay in New Guinea, I was assisted by so many people in Port Moresby and the Milne Bay Province that it is impossible to adequately acknowledge all of them. I wish to mention Eileen and Bob Davis of the (British) Voluntary Service Overseas, who were stationed at Kulumadau on northern Muyuw in 1979.

On my voyage to Gawa in 1979, they kindly put me up when I arrived at Kulumadau unexpectedly. During 1979–80 I was isolated on Gawa, and they made special efforts to obtain supplies for me and to make contacts with the mainland on my behalf. I thank them especially for their unfailing sense of humor!

My greatest debt in this research is, of course, owed to the Gawan people. I have tried to express my deep gratitude in the dedication of the book, where I have been able to mention only a few of the many people who helped me. It may perhaps seem strange that, in a book about fame, I have not cited Gawan names apart from the dedication. I have excluded names for two reasons: First, it was necessary to keep some specific statements and certain kinds of information anonymous to protect the informants; second, since some people's names were excluded, I felt more comfortable being consistent and giving no one what might appear to be relatively exclusive mention. All in all, this seemed to me to be the fairest way to handle this problem.

During the 1973 and 1979 field trips to Gawa I lived in houses built for me in two different hamlets, both in the northwestern part of the island. I am indebted to Toroy Tarakwasisi for initial housing in 1973 (before my own house was built), and to both Toroy and the late Baradiy Tarakwasisi for organizing the housebuilding for me in Sipuleiyeiwawa hamlet (also considered part of Gitawatawa). In 1979, when I returned after an absence of four years, Mutaawadiy Imukubay (my "mother") and her husband, Boganuma Tarakulabutu, gave me their house in Kogeta to live in temporarily until a house could be built for me. I am indebted to Weruwa Tarakwasisi, my "father," for organizing the building of my house in his hamlet, Kogeta.

In the dedication I have named a number of other Gawan friends. I should like to comment here specifically on the kind of assistance offered me by a few of these people. Kaidiriya, my "mother's brother," was indeed my kinsman and my most rigorous teacher during both my main trips to Gawa. In 1979–81, he and his wife Kilay continually made me welcome in their hamlet. I am deeply indebted to Kaidiriya for the long, sensitive, and patient conversations that helped me to understand many aspects of Gawan culture, especially kula. One of my first friends on Gawa was Mutaawadiy; her interest in my work and her knowledge and sharp wit were of great help throughout my visits. Another early friend was Kiweru Tarakubay. When I first arrived on Gawa in 1973, no one on the island spoke much English. Kiweru took an interest in teaching me the Gawan language monolingually, and later discussed taped speeches with me in some detail. I hasten to add, however, that many Gawans were pleased to be of help in my initial and continuing language learning. Tarakuruku Tarakwasisi was one of the first senior men of influence on Gawa to support my work. In 1980, I sailed on the canoe that went to Muyuw in association with his kula reconnaissance and minor kula trip in that area. Many other people on Gawa also helped make it possible for me to carry out this study. I apologize to them for not being able to mention their names, and to all Gawans I say *kagatouki kweiveka beisa yakamiya.*

I have also incurred debts during the preparation of this manuscript. The final work on the manuscript was funded by a National Endowment for the Humanities Fellowship for Independent Study and Research (1983–84) and a grant-in-aid from the American Council for Learned Societies (1983). The book could not have been completed without this financial aid.

For friendly support at crucial times, my thanks go to Jean and John Comaroff. I am grateful to William Hanks, Andrew Lass, and Rafael Sanchez for reading parts of the semifinal version of the manuscript; they provided creative inputs when I most needed fresh perspectives. Thanks also go to Terry Turner, Annette Weiner, and to the anonymous publisher's readers of the book for their helpful suggestions. Needless to say, the responsibility for the final version is mine. Finally, I would like to express my appreciation to Professor Alfred Harris, University of Rochester, for his sensitive reading of the manuscript, and for his forbearance and supportiveness during the long preparation of this work.

A note on the orthography

The orthography I have used for the Gawan language is based (with some alterations) on Lithgow (1974). In writing Gawan vowels I have used the following letters (illustrated here with English words that have a similar vowel sound): *a* as in c*u*t; *aa* as in c*a*r; *e* as in k*e*pt; *ei* as in c*a*re; *i* as in k*ee*p; *o* as in c*au*ght; *ou* as in c*oa*t; *u* as in c*oo*l. In addition, following Lithgow, I write *aw* for what is frequently written as *au* (pronounced as in English h*ow*) in the Massim literature; *oy* and *ay* for *oi* and *ai*; and *ew* (final) for *eo* (final). An exception to the contrast between *o* and *ou* is made in the case of the proper name *Ovetu* (Figure 2), where the *o* is pronounced as is *ou* elsewhere. An exception to the use of *aw* for *au* is also made in the case of the proper name *Mwadau*, for which I have retained the map (Figure 1) spelling.

When affixes to a root are indicated, they are set off from the root by hyphens (e.g., *agu-moru*, my hunger; *butu-ra*, its fame; *ta-kamkwamu*, a man who eats excessively; *i-busi*, he or she descends). When a Gawan term is cited without affixes but does not in fact occur independently, I have indicated this by a hyphen in the appropriate initial or final position (e.g., *-busi*; *butu-*) when the term is cited for the first time; however, if the term is repeated, I use a hyphen again only where it seems necessary for clarity (for example, if the word is cited in a separate context from an original citation, or if the hyphenation is relevant or needed for consistency in the context where the term appears). The same procedure is used when, on occasion, a term is cited with an affix with which it occurs regularly in key contexts (e.g., *mapu-ra*, written also as *mapura*, its repayment or return). When Gawan words are not italicized but are used as English loan words, the hyphen is, of course, not shown.

The Fame of Gawa

PART I

Introduction

I

The conceptual framework

This book is concerned with certain types of transformative action through which a community seeks to create the value it regards as essential to its communal viability. I examine these modes of positive value creation in relation to antithetical transformations that, in the perception of the community, specify what undermines this value or define how it *cannot* be realized. These negative potentials are in a kind of ongoing tension with the positive transformations, and in their stronger forms threaten the capacity to produce the desired value and the ideal construction of self and social relation this value entails. In the extreme (which, in the present Gawan case, takes the form of acts of witchcraft), positive value is not simply negated but is subverted and envisioned under the sign of its own destruction.

This dialectical process is shown to be synthesized within the community's attempt to control these negative transformative possibilities. Value creation viewed in this wider sense is a complex symbolic process, both a dialectical formation of the symbolic system of meanings constituted in sociocultural practices and an ongoing dialectic of possibilities and counter-possibilities – explicit assertions of positive and negative value potentials – through which the members of the society are engaged in an effort to construct and control themselves and their own social world. By means of this process *taken as a whole*, a community may be said to act "as an agent of its own self-production" (Touraine, 1977:4).

The focus of this study is the island society of Gawa as I knew it between 1973–5 and 1979–81. Gawa is a small island of some 532 people situated in the northeast section of the Massim region of Papua New Guinea (Figure 1). It is an important link within the well-known kula trade "ring" (Leach and Leach, 1983; Malinowski, 1922; Munn 1983).[1] By means of the complex long-distance arrangements of kula exchange, armshells and necklaces are circulated in opposite directions to form "an intricate time–space–person system" (Polanyi, 1968:12) connecting islands of

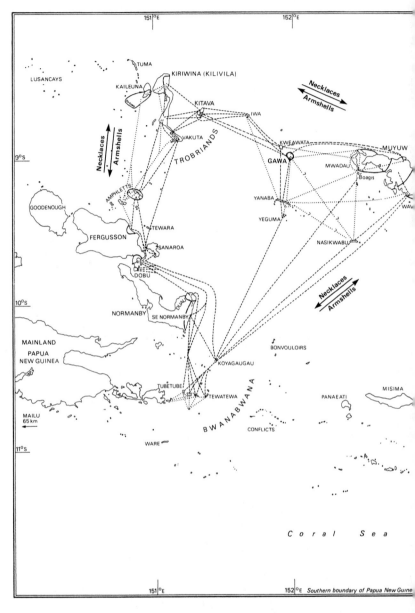

Figure 1. The Massim region of Papua New Guinea showing kula routes in the 1970s. From Leach and Leach (1983:20, Map 1), with adjustments. Based on Woodlark Island (3095) 4th ed., produced by Australian Division of Mapping, 1973.

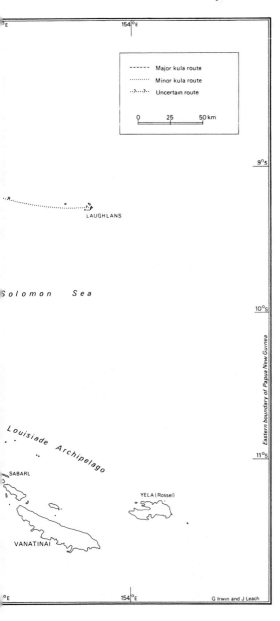

154°E

	Major kula route
	Minor kula route
	Uncertain route

0   25   50 km

9°S

LAUGHLANS

Solomon   Sea

10°S

Eastern boundary of Papua New Guinea

Louisiade Archipelago

SABARL

11°S

YELA (Rossel)

VANATINAI

154°E

G Irwin and J Leach

varying cultures in the northern and southern Massim. For Gawans, the
kula network constitutes the widest regional network of their island world
– one in which they can make connections not only with "consociates"
(Schutz, 1962:16ff.), but also with more distant contemporaries with whom
they have few or no face-to-face relationships.

Gawan society has to be understood in terms of its grounding in this
inter-island world. On the one hand, the community asserts its own *internal*
viability through the concept of its positive evaluation by these *external*
others, expressed in the Gawan emphasis on fame (*butu-*),[2] the renown or
good name of Gawa in this world. On the other hand, fame itself (like kula
shells) can be produced for Gawans only through an initial externalizing
process involving the separation of internal elements of Gawa (especially
garden crops and canoes, which are the produce of its land and trees) and
their transaction into the inter-island world.

In the present study, this regional construction of the Gawan world is
examined as part of the wider process or system of value creation referred
to above, which operates through different kinds of practice to build a
moral dialectic focused in the tension between outward transformation of
self and its negation. My characterization of this process is grounded in an
analysis of types of action, and the practices of which they are components,
seen as culturally meaningful forms. Thus I move from the *overt* forms of
acts – their "mere facticity," in Cassirer's (1953:74) terms – to the "internal
relations" that give them *significant* form and that specify the nature of the
value produced. Methodologically, this move is made through the analysis
and explication of cultural meanings implicated in practices. Let me
explain my notions of meaning and symbolism and some of the premises
behind the particular approach to value offered here.

Some of the underlying assumptions of this study derive from the
varied anthropological approaches at times referred to as "symbolic
anthropology," which presume that theoretical arguments dealing with
sociocultural phenomena must be based on the examination of culture-
specific meanings. As Rabinow and Sullivan (1979:5) have put it, "The
web of meaning constitutes human existence to such an extent that it
cannot ever be meaningfully reduced to constitutively prior speech acts,
dyadic relations or any previously defined elements. Intentionality and
empathy are rather seen as being dependent on the prior existence of the
world of meaning within which the subjects of human discourse constitute
themselves" (see also Bourdieu, 1977:80; Geertz, 1973:5, Ricoeur,
1983:91ff.).[3] But whereas Rabinow and Sullivan's phrasing tends to
suggest that meaning is a kind of container – a static world within which
actors constitute themselves – I argue that actors construct this meaningful
order in the process of being constructed in its terms. This view will be
made clear as I proceed.

I understand "meaning" as a cover term for the relational nexus that enters into any given sociocultural form or practice (of whatever order of complexity) and defines that practice. The anthropological analysis of cultural meaning requires explication of cultural forms – a working through or unfolding of these culturally specific definitions and connectivities in order to disclose both the relational nature of the forms and the significance that derives from this relationality. Although in any given context the concern may be with a particular relation or aspect of meaning, the overall intent of such analysis is to make explicit the more fundamental sociocultural processes and principles entailed in overt types of practice, and to show *how* these processes and principles are embodied within *these* forms.

From this perspective, the terms *symbol* and *meaning* may be taken to be essentially coterminous.[4] "Symbolic" can refer to any cultural form, of whatever kind or complexity of meaning, and to the immediate manipulation and working out of meaningful forms within specific activities. In this view, symbolic analysis is a method that may be applied to the examination of any problem related to sociocultural process. A symbolic study is not substantively restricted (for example, to the examination of myth or ritual or some special, predefined class of objects). Rather, the practices by means of which actors construct their social world, and simultaneously their own selves and modes of being in the world, are thought to be symbolically constituted and themselves symbolic processes. As Ricoeur (1979:101) has pointed out, "It is not only that the symbolic function is social, but that social reality is fundamentally symbolic."

Operating from these general premises, the present study analyzes a symbolism of value production. In this chapter I explain the basic analytic concepts that provide the framework of the study. These concepts first took shape during my attempt to analyze Gawan value production in theoretical terms that took account of the phenomenal or existential form of practices (cf. Bourdieu, 1977:8ff.), while exploring the significance and nature of the value being produced and of certain underlying structures (in particular, what I later call "generative schema"; see Chapter 6) that characterize the value-production process.

In explaining my model of value creation, I have attempted to set out analytically what may be seen as multiple facets of any sociocultural practice and the transformational process of value production entailed in the practice. Since the discussion is a discursive account of aspects that cohere simultaneously within a manifold, the reader may find that at times it turns back on itself.

In sum, the intent of this book is to suggest a more general anthropological model of practice as symbolic process through the examination of a single ethnographic case. Thus in addition to elucidating the Gawan system, the ethnographic analysis moves forth in the spirit of a theoretical exploration in which the particulars of the empirical material become the means of developing an approach relevant to general anthropological theory.

ACTION, SPACETIME, AND VALUE

The point of departure for this study is the notion of a lived world that is not only the arena of action, but is actually constructed by action and the more complex cultural practices of which any given type of action is a part. By *act* I mean simply the operation of an agent (or agents) that has the potential for yielding certain outcomes. "Giving food to specified others" or "carrying out a prohibition on eating"; "receiving a kula shell" or "speaking about kula"; "hacking out a canoe" or "planting a garden" are examples of general types of act. An act's various culturally defined capacities are those aspects of its meaning that specify what an actor can expect from performing it. For instance, for Gawans, giving food to overseas visitors has the capacity to yield not only return hospitality to Gawans, but also, in the long term, the acquisition of kula shells and renown. These outcomes, as I discuss in Chapter 3, depend on the act's capacity to produce another kind of effect, namely, to influence the minds of the overseas visitors so that they will make the desired returns. Effects such as these exemplify some of the significant capacities of a given type of act, but obviously, they are not its only culturally defined outcomes, nor are they assured; they are merely key potentialities or capacities and may, of course, fail to be realized in a given case.

Although the acts and capacities I have exemplified involve desirable outcomes in Gawan terms, the same act could also have more latent capacities that Gawans view as undesirable. Furthermore, when considered in terms of the general process of creating the value essential to community viability, certain key *types* of act are felt to have positive outcomes, whereas others have negative outcomes. I return to this point later.

In the most immediate sense, the value of a given type of act can be seen in terms of its essential capacities or key possible outcomes (whether these be other acts, specific entities or the properties of these entities, or expected subjective effects) such as those exemplified above. These outcomes can be regarded as the particular, substantive value potentials or products of acts. But a product (or the value-producing act) may be seen in another sense as embodying a differential proportion of some homogeneous potency; its value (and the value of the act) can then be expressed relatively in terms of a parameter (the kind of potency involved) along which value is, as it were, "measured" (see T. Turner, 1979b:20, 1984:19, personal communication). Value in this sense is general and relational, rather than particular and substantive. It involves a deeper dimension of cultural meaning implicated in the substantive value products and acts (and their various interrelationships with each other) – one that can be explicated and defined through the methods of symbolic analysis previously mentioned. Thus neither the nature of this value (the kind of potency that is relevant) nor the particular forms it takes are to be assumed; rather, they are induced from the cultural material.[5]

In the present study, analysis of Gawan practices led me to develop a notion of sociocultural spacetime[6] as the relevant potency and value parameter. I argue that in the Gawan case, value may be characterized in terms of differential levels of *spatiotemporal transformation* – more specifically, in terms of an act's relative capacity to extend or expand what I call *intersubjective spacetime* – a spacetime of self–other relationships formed in and through acts and practices. The general value of an act or practice is specified in terms of its *level* of potency, that is, what I sum up here as the relative expansive capacities of the spacetime formed. I first explain my notion of spacetime, using as the primary example a particular Gawan exchange practice, although other kinds of social practices could, of course, illustrate my point equally well. Explanations of what I mean by *spatiotemporal extension* and the rationale for my description of this spacetime as *intersubjective* follow.

SPACETIME

Let me refer again to my example of Gawan hospitality to overseas visitors, considering it now as part of a nexus of acts (and outcomes) forming a more complex Gawan practice. As Chapter 3 explains, a Gawan giving food hospitality to an overseas visitor initiates the possibility of entering into a particular kind of reciprocal transaction with the visitor. The spacetime that can be formed by this act (and of which the act is also a component) entails connections between two men from different islands; involves these men in occasional, repetitive (but indeterminately timed) travels to each other's island homes; engages the possibility of return food hospitality at an unspecified later date at the current visitor's home, and so forth. Initially, it is apparent that these acts constitute a mode of spacetime formed through the dynamics of action (notably, giving and traveling) connecting persons and places.[7]

Such practices also involve certain crucial subjective aspects (or subjective "acts") such as those of remembering. For example, the reciprocal giving of food between the two men is expected to yield mutual influence between them (one's gifts are the means of moving the mind of the other or making him remember the giver) and this influence can be seen both as a productive capacity or product of the acts of giving, and as a subjective dimension of the spacetime formed that is a condition of its continuing operation. Moreover, in certain crucial cases, Gawans emphasize the importance of remembering as the means by which acts occurring at a given time (or spatiotemporal locus) may be projected forward and their capacities retained so that they may yield desired outcomes at a later time (see Chapter 3). In other words, a spacetime may involve certain critical subjective dimensions that are among the constitutive factors in its formation. Similarly, certain types of act might be expected to yield negative subjective states such as anger, which could destroy the possibility of producing a desired outcome (and hence of creating a given spacetime), or which might yield instead a spatiotemporal order of subverted relations involving acts of witchcraft (Chapters 9 and 10).

A third aspect of a spacetime derives from the qualities or properties of certain entities involved in a given set of practices. These entities consist of material (for example, Gawan food, canoes, and gardens) or nonmaterial (for example, fame) media and products of agents' acts, and, as well, of the bodies of agents themselves. For instance, the medium of cooked food in the example of Gawan hospitality to a visitor has certain spatiotemporal properties of significance to Gawans, such as relative lack of durability. This feature contributes to the mode (and, as we shall see, the value level) of the spacetime created. A given entity itself may be considered a condensed spacetime, and may be analyzed in order to give a fuller account of the wider intersubjective spacetime in which it operates in a given case, or as in Chapter 4, to discuss certain qualities of things relevant to the argument. Gardens, for example, in Gawan terms, constitute an interior spacetime whose ancestral stones must be maintained in place so that the land will be heavy, an attribute necessary for the retension of reproductive capacities from one garden to the next; separation of the stones from the gardens dissolves this spacetime (Chapter 4). Most important in the argument is *bodily spacetime* (to be discussed in the section "The body and the signification of value").

In sum, an intersubjective spacetime is a multidimensional, symbolic order and process – a spacetime of self–other relations constituted in terms of and by means of specific types of practice. A given type of act or practice forms a spatiotemporal process, a particular *mode* of spacetime. Defined abstractly, the specifically spatiotemporal features of this process consist of relations, such as those of distance, location (including geographical domains of space), and directionality; duration or continuance, succession, timing (including temporal coordination and relative speed of activities), and so forth.

Thus, it is not merely as Giddens (1981:30) has put it, that "time-space relations are . . . constitutive features of social systems," but additionally that the "situated practices," which in Giddens's terms make up these systems, themselves *construct* different formations of spacetime. As I have argued elsewhere (Munn, 1983:280), sociocultural practices "do not simply go on *in* or *through* time and space, but [they also] ... constitute (create) the spacetime ... in which they 'go on.'" In this sense, actors are "concretely producing their own spacetime."[8] On the one hand, these practices generate particular spatiotemporal forms (i.e., different modes of intersubjective spacetime); on the other hand, as people actively engage in these practices, they form this intersubjective spacetime in immediate experience. In this latter respect, a mode of spacetime defines a form in terms of which the world is experienced by the agents whose actions produce it. However, as I discuss later, not only do the agents produce their world in a particular form, but they may also be seen as producing themselves or aspects of themselves in the same process.

VALUE AS THE RELATIVE EXTENSION OF SPACETIME

A given *mode* of intersubjective spacetime (such as the example given above) can be understood as having a particular potency or value *level*: namely, what I have referred to as the relative extension of the spacetime. In general terms, *extension* means here the capacity to develop spatiotemporal relations that go beyond the self, or that expand dimensions of the spatiotemporal control of an actor. I speak then of the capacities of acts and practices for yielding certain levels of spatiotemporal transformation, but I do not of course mean by this that Gawans speak about spatiotemporal value or control over spacetime in the abstract; rather, as I have stated, this general value is implicated in types of act and practice. The way in which Gawans do talk about their practices is part of the evidence on which my own argument – that, in the Gawan case, spacetime may be used as the significant value measure relevant to understanding the creation of the experience of community viability – is based.

For instance, as previously indicated, Gawans are concerned with their ability to develop relations outward into the inter-island world. In the example of hospitality practices, it is of considerable importance to them that the connection being created goes beyond Gawa and that, through the transaction of food on Gawa at one particular time, one can produce for oneself the possibility of gaining something beyond that time, and from beyond Gawa itself (for example, the later hospitality of the current visitor on his own island). Conversely, if Gawans do not give hospitality in food to overseas visitors, this level of spatiotemporal extension of the self cannot be generated. Gawans are concerned with the relative capacity of certain acts or practices to create potentialities for constructing a present that is experienced as pointing forward to later desired acts or material returns. Practices that constitute the Gawan actor in terms of inter-island relations form a greater "extension of self" and of the actor's spatiotemporal control than those involving intra-island relationships.

On the other hand (to pursue the example further), food hospitality to overseas visitors in itself entails less expansive spatiotemporal control for Gawans than the level made possible in inter-island kula shell exchange. The creation of this apparently lesser value level is nevertheless a precondition of the more expansive (kula) level, and the mode of dynamic entailment between them is characteristic of the way Gawans formulate crucial value-producing practices (Chapters 3, 4, 6).

Although I have drawn here on inter-island food transmission to exemplify my argument, various kinds of acts, practices, and the spacetimes they generate are dealt with in the more concrete arguments of this book. For instance, in some contexts I consider a coordination of actions to create a synchronous spacetime that transcends the otherwise fragmented spacetimes of separate categories of actors (see especially Chapters 4, 8, 9, and 10). Thus, when Gawans sail on a major kula competition, all the canoes should sail at the same time (Chapter 9). For Gawans, this synchronization or spatiotemporal coordination of canoe groups into a single fleet is a consensual formation that implies agreement within the community and among the sailors about the performance of the competition, the time of sailing, and so on. (Viewed in another way, the intersubjective spacetime formed – the synchronized sailing group – has agreement as a crucial subjective dimension of the relationship that it defines between the actors.) If one or more canoes sail at different times (some go ahead of the others), the success of the venture could be endangered and some misadventure such as a death could occur. The coordinated spacetime of the fleet transforms the disparate spacetimes of each canoe of travelers to an expanded level that contains the desired potential for success in the venture. But the fragmentation of the fleet involves a negative value transformation or a failure to achieve this more extended value level (more will be said later about negative value).

These points lay out a rough framework of notions about value levels and spatiotemporal transformations. I would stress that what I sum up in any given case as a greater or lesser expansion of spacetime is based on Gawan symbolism and draws variously on the different dimensions listed above (acts, entities and aspects of subjectivity) that are entailed in a particular spacetime. A final example may help to reinforce this point. In Gawan marriage exchanges (Chapter 6), an artifact such as a named canoe can not only be transacted sequentially by internal and overseas recipients (making what Gawans call a "path" that goes overseas), but it can also develop historical memorability as a unique artifact so that it may be remembered long after it has disappeared; these factors, among others, give the mode of intersubjective spacetime formed in the canoe trans-actions a greater level of spatiotemporal expansion than that created by the annual internal transmission of the anonymous, relatively perishable yam harvest from a woman's kinsmen to specified affines (a repeatability made possible only by the replanting of old seed yams that must die in the reproductive process, and in which the duration of the medium is not transcended in its memorability as a unique object).

NEGATIVE AND POSITIVE VALUE

In speaking of relatively greater or lesser capacities to expand spacetime, we may also distinguish negative value transformations: namely, the "contraction" of spacetime, or the failure to expand it; and, more radically, the subversion of positive, relatively expansive transformations, as in Gawan witchcraft, where significant value reversals occur.

I argue that certain broad types of Gawan act are fundamental symbolic operators of positive value transformation and its negation. As my use of the example of Gawan overseas food hospitality may perhaps suggest, these consist respectively of the separation of food from the self (the transmission of food to *others* to consume) and its negative polarity, the incorporation of food in consumption.[9] Although the symbolic relation between food consumption and transmission is obviously more intricate than the notion of polarity suggests (see the discussion of Chapter 3), for the present it is sufficient to refer to it in this way to convey a generalized paradigm of value creation in terms of key acts. For instance, if Gawans eat a great deal instead of giving food to overseas visitors, they fail to create the kind of overseas expansion of self made possible through hospitality. Instead of outward, self-extending acts, their acts are, in effect, self-focused, since they involve the incorporation of their own food and, in Gawan terms, the "disappearance" of the food and thus of any further potentialities it may have for positive transformations.

Whereas food transmission is able to generate further, more potent levels of positive value for Gawan actors, consumption is the pivot from the production of negative value to the radically negative or subversive value transformations of witchcraft (since witches are typified as consumers and their prime food is the dead). That is to say, consumption is the center of negative transformations: On the one hand, consumption of food cannot in and of itself produce positively transformative value; on the other hand, consumption by witches goes beyond this negativity in actually destroying or subverting positive value.

Gawan witchcraft constitutes a subversive intersubjective spacetime in which the spatiotemporal control level of one actor (the witch) expands to destroy the positive spatiotemporal control capacities of others. Witchcraft is not simply another mode of value production, but a hidden world of its own, with a specific construction of being that dissolves and disorders the overt, visible spatiotemporal order of Gawan existence, crystallizing a latent, negative significance, and even subverting the apparent positive value potentials of transmissive acts into negative, destructive value.

The witch is the prototypic consumer, but in the intersubjective spacetime formed by witchcraft, this consumption marks, as will be seen, a radical *expansion* of the witch's intersubjective control (rather than a *contraction* of control) that destroys the other: Witches make people ill, kill them, and consume the dead. Subversive value consists in the destruction of the ordinary spatiotemporal world and its embedded positive value potentials through the radical spatiotemporal expansion of control of one agent (the witch). Another plane of reality with different basic framing spatiotemporal coordinates emerges (see also note 8). Within the value processes of this hidden underworld, the positive value of spatiotemporal expansion is itself reversed (see Chapters 9 and 10).

INTERSUBJECTIVITY

As Giddens (1979:55) has observed, "The notion of action has reference to the activities of an agent, and cannot be examined apart from a broader theory of the acting self." In using the phenomenological term *intersubjective*[10] to characterize the social spacetime formed in practices, I wish to emphasize certain features in my model concerning the relation between the category of action (practices) and that of the experiencing subject, that is, "the acting self." In general, I take the view that agents not only engage in action but are also "acted upon" by the action (see Sartre, 1966:426; cf. also the "action approach" to sociology of Touraine, 1974a, 1974b, 1977). In this respect, my position is related to certain Marxian-influenced and phenomenological concepts of practice, as well as to certain symbolic approaches within anthropology (most notably, those referring to ritual action).[11]

The term *intersubjective* combines several implications relevant to my argument. First, it reflects my concern with types of practice and their component acts as forming self–other relations and the constructions of self or *aspects* of self that are entailed in these relations. From this perspective, the mode of spacetime formed in a given type of practice is also a formation of the actors' selves (as well as of the specific self–other relations by which these selves are being defined). As indicated in my previous example of Gawan overseas hospitality, the Gawan who gives food to his overseas visitor creates a particular relation with another, one in which he attempts to move the recipient's mind so that at a later time this man will make (it is hoped) similar or perhaps additional, even more desirable gifts to the Gawan. The selves of the Gawan and the recipient are being constructed in this process, each in terms of the action and the relation to the other it entails. We may take the Gawan as an example. In giving food to the other to eat, he constitutes himself as a generous person (in certain respects superordinated to the recipient; see Chapter 3). He also becomes defined in terms of the view of himself he is attempting to create in the other, and ultimately by the action of the other toward himself as revealed later when he goes to visit this man overseas.

Of course, in any given case, we have to conceive of any *particular* actor's self as also being already founded in ongoing sociocultural processes (including any premises about the nature of self prevalent in the community). However, I am not concerned with this here. My point refers simply to the general principle that practices not only form particular types of social relation but also, coordinately, the actors who engage in them. To borrow a phrase of Heidegger's (1982:161), the self "reflects itself to itself from out of that to which it has given itself over."[12]

From this perspective, the spatiotemporal value transformations effected in given types of practice can be viewed as transformations of the value of the actor's self. In producing a given level of spatiotemporal extension beyond the self, actors produce their own value. Such value transformations become most apparent when we can identify in the cultural evidence symbolic value products of action that clearly relate to the self-constitution of the actor and also typify the level of transformation characteristic of a given spacetime. For instance, through entering into overseas hospitality relations, the Gawan actor's name as a man of hospitality (and eventually of eminence in kula) may come to be a medium of circulation beyond his own person and island home. "Becoming known" is the rendering of the action process as a whole in a discourse that positively defines and evaluates the self of the actor (see Chapter 5). Similarly, the name of Gawa as a community achieves this circulation and eminence through the actions of its members (most notably its men, although women also have a critical part in this process).

Thus intrinsic to the value-production process is the evaluative rendering of the self by significant others. Fame is both a positive value product (an outcome of certain positively transformative actions) and an evaluation of the actor by significant others. Similarly, the reverse evaluation of defamation is an outcome of certain negatively transformative actions, most notably in the present argument, acts of witchcraft (Chapter 10).

Of course, fame (and its negative form) are not the only value products that crystallize the value of actors and of a given spacetime. In fact, the properties of fame as Gawans conceptualize it, must be understood as part of a more comprehensive set of qualities that are crucial signifiers of spatiotemporal transformation in Gawan symbolism and that are embodied in various media (see the next section).

Nevertheless, the notion of fame crystallizes the concern of this study with the complex nature of the "otherness" of the other who stands apart from the self of any given actor and yet, by this apparent separateness, becomes the organizing processual field of each self – the ground upon which, within social process, the self is experientially constituted. From this perspective, social relationships can be seen as engaging the actor's perspective on an outside other that implies a perception of the other's perspective on the self. As Sartre (1966:319) has expressed it: "Consciousnesses are directly supported by one another in a reciprocal imbrication of their being." Indeed, what anthropologists sum up as "exchange" and "witchcraft" are among the fundamental kinds of practices formulated in ways that turn on this basic phenomenological structure.[13]

Finally, the use of the term *intersubjective* to describe the kind of spacetime dealt with here gives expression to the point noted earlier that (culturally constituted) subjective states are a critical dimension of a social spacetime. In this respect, the term may be taken in its most literal sense to indicate that the social relations formed in any mode of spacetime are to be understood as involving relations between the subjectivities of actors. Certain subjective states such as consent, refusal, happiness, or anger, or a state in which one category of actor is felt to be hiding his or her true intentions vis-à-vis others (see Chapter 10), may be crucial to the value of different spacetimes. In these respects, value transformations involve transformations of subjective states.

In sum, calling the spacetime generated by practices *intersubjective* emphasizes the notion that constructions of actors' selves (or aspects of them) and subjective attitudes are entailed in the social relationships of a given spacetime.

THE BODY AND THE SIGNIFICATION OF VALUE

Thus far I have been concerned with the value generated by types of acts and practices. However, a key part of my argument concerns the way this value is signified through specific qualities that characterize such components of practice as the body, kula shells, fame, and other entities previously noted. I argue that these qualities (and the relevant entities) exhibit in themselves – that is, "iconically" (see Peirce, 1955:104ff.) – the transformative value of acts and modes of spacetime.

The term *sign* is used here in a more specific sense than *symbol*. As discussed earlier, I employ the latter as a term to convey the intrinsic meaningfulness of all cultural forms. My use of *sign*, however, has a more specific function within the argument. Here it refers to a condensed marking or "appresentation" (see Schutz, 1962:294ff., on Husserl's concept) that is part of a more comprehensive whole and conveys some fundamental aspects of that whole. In the present study, I am referring to certain embodied qualities that are components of a given intersubjective spacetime (the "more comprehensive whole") whose positive or negative value they signify. I call these qualities *qualisigns*, adopting the label (as I have also adopted that of "icon") from the philosopher C. S. Peirce (1955:101; see my Chapter 4).[14]

The specific Gawan qualities that provide the most salient value signifiers form a cluster of polarized elements focused primarily in motion (speed vs. slowness or stasis); weight (lightweightness vs. heaviness); and light (light vs. darkness). They also have certain associations with directionality (for example, upward vs. downward movement) and particular geographical locales (e.g., land is slow or heavy and the sea is swift or buoyant). In addition, they are redolent of gender associations, a feature that becomes critical to the analysis when the symbolism of certain aspects of male–female relations enters into the discussion of value production and signification.

My argument is that certain media – in particular, the body and other important elements (such as Gawan canoes and kula shells, which can be shown to have bodily and anthropomorphic associations in Gawan symbolism) – exhibit qualisigns of the positive or negative value generated by acts, notably by acts of food transmission (and other acts involving constraints on eating) and consumption. For instance, if eating excessively rather than giving to overseas visitors is said to yield nothing but sleep rather than the potentials engaged by food giving to visitors (as suggested in the quotation cited at the beginning of Chapters 3 and 4), then sleep is being taken in this instance as a qualitative conversion[15] of the actor's body, a value product of the act of eating (as directly contrasted in this instance with giving). As shown in Chapter 4, this motionlessness entails, in Gawan symbolism, a negative value form of the body, a contraction of the body's own spacetime.

Certain outcomes can therefore be considered icons of the acts that produce them – in other words, they can be said to involve iconic signs of the spatiotemporal value transformation (positive or negative) generated by the act. Since the body takes on qualities that express the value of the intersubjective spacetime produced, this *bodily spacetime* serves as a condensed sign of the wider spacetime of which it is a part.

In focusing on the intersubjective aspect of the process, we may also see this form of bodily being as a particular construction of the actor's self and the defining self–other relation of which it is a part. From this perspective, the intersection of the problem of value signification and that of the constitution of the subject becomes apparent. Thus in the previous example, sleep is a negative form of the actor's being-in-the-world: the self takes on an experiential form of being that epitomizes failure to move the minds of overseas visitors and so engender future potencies accruing to the self. Fame, on the other hand, can be shown to condense spatiotemporal qualisigns of value that engage precisely the reverse mode of being or construction of the actor and self–other relations (Chapter 5).

In Chapters 6–8, I analyze what I see as a basic template or underlying structure for value production and signification in Gawan symbolism. There I argue that the connection between particular food-related acts and specific bodily qualisigns forms a systematically elaborated causal-logical nexus that regularly emerges in Gawan value symbolism (Chapter 4). This structure of value production and signification informs marriage and other exchanges where the crucial signifying media are not always the bodies of actors, but may include objects of exchange such as canoes and kula shells. I examine the bodily or actor-related significance of such objects, thus developing the Maussian problem of the identification of persons and media of exchange (Mauss, 1968) within this more general theoretical framework of action, value production, and signification.

HIERARCHY, EQUALITY, AND VALUE

Obviously, any study of fundamental value processes in a community cannot ignore the complex problem of the way in which the society formulates the interplay of hierarchy and equality. I now explain the way in which this problem is implicated in the present model of value creation.

Underlying the notion of general value as a relative potency entailed in given types of acts or practices is the assumption that value involves a hierarchizing process (in the present instance, the development of relative extensions of spacetime or spatiotemporal control). But this process is itself encompassed by certain governing cultural premises relating to the creation of hierarchy and equality. In the Gawan case, these premises specify as fundamental the relative autonomy and equality of persons and of the minimal collective units constituting the basic bodily and social identity of persons (i.e., the lineage with which one is identified by blood). These cultural premises (initially set out in terms of the Gawan concepts in Chapter 3) create the underlying moral-political problem of contemporary Gawan polity: namely, that to generate and maintain positive potency within their community, Gawans must mediate between these overriding assumptions about the relative autonomy and equivalence of all persons and the hierarchizing that appears to violate these premises. Integral to the processes that mediate these tensions is the necessity of maintaining the autonomy of the individual will and at the same time constraining this autonomy within more encompassing relations.

These mediations are considered in different forms and contexts (see especially the discussions in Chapters 3, 8, 9, and 10). For instance, what in my view is the basic hierarchizing act – food giving – has sacrificial dimensions that compose within it a mediation of the interrelated dimensions of hierarchy (the incrementation of potency by the donor) and equalization, on the one hand, and of the autonomy of the will and viable self–other relations, on the other. Similarly, certain kinds of reciprocities compose another mediating mode well known to anthropologists, in which the hierarchizing of one set of actors relative to others in a given type of act can be reversed in the act's reciprocal (see Chapter 8 for a notable case in the exchange of Gawan entertainments). On the other hand, for reasons that will be made clear later, food consumption (in contrast to food giving) cannot *in itself* (i.e., within the form of the act) create or initiate mediation, although it is necessarily part of practices that do (see Chapter 3).

The modes of intersubjective spacetime formed through persuasive Gawan acts such as food hospitality or certain kinds of speech contrast with those formed by acts of witchcraft (which rest upon secret threats and force) in terms of the capacity to mediate or manage the moral tension created by these antitheses. For instance, the former mediate but do not violate the autonomous will attributed to both actors (the persuader and the persuaded), but the latter expand the spatiotemporal control of the autonomous will of one actor (the witch) by destroying the autonomy of another (the victim).[16] Whereas witchcraft constitutes the negative subversion of this problem – the inability to create mediation at all – this subversive process is more complicated than my simple example suggests. In general, the witch (and acts of witchery) can be viewed as a complex symbolic condensation of the moral-political problem engaged by this oppositional tension in its most destructive, unmediated form (Chapter 9). This negative symbolism can be posed, as we shall see, against the similarly complex symbolic mediation formed by acts of influence and epitomized in the generous "man of influence."

When witchcraft comes to the fore in Gawan experience (as in contexts involving long-term illness or death, or some possible threat to life), Gawans must then reconstruct the affected relations in terms that positively mediate these contradictions. This reconstruction is not done by publicly identifying the witch, but by bringing into play persuasive modes of action (notably speech[17] as well as the transmission of certain comestibles), which attempt to subordinate the autonomy and dominion of the witch (or the actor's self in its form as witch) to the influence of the other (see Part III, especially Chapter 10).

The mode of working out the tension between hierarchy and equality, and between the autonomy of each person's will and self–other relations defines in the most encompassing sense the differentiation of positive and negative value. On the one hand, I have discussed value as relative potency: in the Gawan case, the relative capacity of acts or practices for expanding the spatiotemporal control of actors and the community as a whole. What I have called *general value* is specified by reference to relative potency. On the other hand, one may ask what makes a given potency viable in terms of the culturally defined moral-political prerequisites of the society for the construction of a communal order. In this latter sense, the positive or negative value of a given type of act or practice is defined by reference to governing premises about the appropriate and possible relations of power that pertain in the society. Whereas the nature of value transformation is constrained by this moral-political problem, the problem in turn is embodied in the relevant transformative practices and is worked out within them as an aspect of the value transformations – that is, as a critical component of the positive or negative value that is being generated.

CONCLUSION: COMMUNAL VALUE

Having set out the the basic analytic terms of my model of value transformation, let me now sharpen certain points made at the beginning of this chapter about my concept of communal value (i.e., the value a community regards as essential to its viability). This value can be understood in two senses: one more limited and the other more comprehensive. In the more limited sense, actors create communal value through effecting positive value transformations. As I have suggested, these transformations combine relative increment or control of potencies, defined in terms of some general parameter of cultural significance, with the capacity to mediate fundamental contradictions in the community's moral-political premises. My thesis in the Gawan case is that these transformations consist of expansions of intersubjective spacetime or spatiotemporal control entailed in varying symbolisms, which coordinately mediate the antitheses of hierarchizing and equality, on the one hand, and autonomy and social encompassment of the person and lineage group, on the other.

However, positive transformations are dialectically formed in tension with negative, or negative-subversive transformations (in the Gawan example, the contraction or failure to expand spacetime, or the destructive subversion of intersubjective spacetime in witchcraft). The operation of this dialectical symbolism – including the explicit manipulation by the community of the relations between positive and negative transformative capacities in order to produce the former and negate the latter – yields communal value in its more powerful, comprehensive sense. As I attempt to show in this book, it is through this process that the community creates itself as the *agent of its own value creation*. Thus, only by examining the production of positive value as part of a wider dialectical system can we discern the processes through which this most essential form of communal value creation takes place.

2

Gawa in the 1970s
An ethnographic overview

Gawa is a heavily forested atoll of about 7.6 square miles rising out of the sea to some 400 or more feet along the "encircling coral wall" (Seligmann and Strong, 1906:356) at its edge.[1] In 1979–80, some 532 people[2] lived on Gawa, their hamlets stretching across the top of the island below the coral cliffs, and aligned for the most part along or just off a central path running from the northwest harbor at Ovetu in a southeasterly direction across the island (Figure 2). Except where the land is cleared for hamlets and current gardens, the top of the island is covered with young trees, bushes, and ground cover that is dotted with the remains of old yam and taro gardens and is traversed by many small paths.

The cliffs and upper slopes are forested with many large trees, some of which provide timber for the seagoing canoes of great beauty that Gawans specialize in producing. In a small part of the shoreline, rocky ledges extend down to the sea, but most of the island is rimmed by beaches, some of which are major harbors where Gawans build their canoe sheds and visitors from other islands may camp while on Gawa.

In 1979–80 there were 46 named hamlets (veru)[3] on Gawa, classed into the five traditional neighborhoods (see Figure 2). Most hamlets are geographically distinct units, but some are laid out contiguously with few visible demarcations. Hamlets range in size from one to five or six households, and may include a domesticated pig or two, dogs, and some chickens.

The spatial organization of hamlets is not uniform. Within each, the residences (bwara), cookhouses (bulatum), and closed yam houses (bweima) with a lower sitting platform are variously laid out. In some hamlets, residences face each other in a more or less concentric arrangement, whereas in others they are more loosely, sometimes more linearly, organized.

Gawans feel that a hamlet should be kept clean of refuse, weeds, and small stones; thus it forms a domesticated, controlled space, delineated

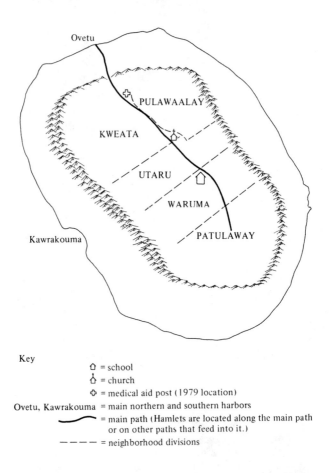

Key

                 ⌂ = school
                 ⚐ = church
                 ✚ = medical aid post (1979 location)
Ovetu, Kawrakouma = main northern and southern harbors
              ━━━ = main path (Hamlets are located along the main path
                             or on other paths that feed into it.)
           − − − − = neighborhood divisions

Figure 2. Sketch map of Gawa showing relative locations of different neighborhoods (not to scale). Adapted in part from *Gawa, sheet 9280* (Edition 1), Series T601, Papua New Guinea.

from the surrounding bush. Although the initial work of clearing a hamlet area is primarily a masculine responsibility, the daily responsibility for maintaining cleanliness lies essentially with women, who sweep (*-katanay*) the hamlet with coconut-spine brooms and take out small stones and weeds (*-takud veru*). Maintaining this clearing is thus part of the activity of daily life. We shall see its relevance to other cleansing procedures later (Chapter 4). The open space in front of the houses or in the interior of the hamlet is known as the *baku*, a term that is not often used, however. The cleared hamlet area as a whole is called *veru*; this widely used term specifies a place of human habitation and may also denote the island as a whole.

There is a graded differentiation between the clearing that is one's immediate home and the increasingly overgrown area extending away from it. Distinctions are made between the shady hamlet edge (*tadew*), where people sometimes sit and chat, and the bush (*yousew*) just beyond, where refuse may be thrown and where some say that witches (*bwagaw*) may come and stand, attracted to human habitation and food. The edge of the yousew may be distinguished from the space beyond as *ou-dadara yousew* (at the side of the yousew), and beyond this is the general area of bush or forest (*naawoudu*, or *wa-naawoudu*, in the forest).

Gardens (*bagala*) are also cleared from the bush. Like most other New Guineans, Gawans practice a form of shifting cultivation. Yam gardens tend to be cleared in areas bordering the hamlets, but like taro, yams may also be planted on the lower slopes of the cliffs. Since taro requires moister soil, it is planted further out in the bush, although some taro may be planted in the yam gardens.[4] As in the case of the hamlets, the initial tasks of clearing are performed primarily by men; however, the burning off is a stage in which women play a prominent role.

A network of paths (*keda*) in varying states of use crisscrosses the island, connecting hamlets and gardens and in some cases leading down the cliffs to different beaches. In contrast to the hamlet clearings, the openness of the main thoroughfare across the island and to the northern and southern harbors is maintained by collective community work, ordinarily organized under the authority of the elected Gawan councillor.[5]

The top of the island is thus a pattern of hamlets, gardens, and paths cleared out of a surrounding bushland. This region of the island is essentially an interior area, for the most part out of sight of the sea. Standing on the cliffs (*koya*), however, one may look out onto part of the great expanse of brilliant ocean that surrounds the island. If a returning Gawan canoe is expected, children keeping watch from the cliffs send up a shout as soon as they first sight it, a tiny speck as yet far out on the sea. Adults then gather there to watch its approach as they prepare to go down to meet the travelers. The high cliffs, like the beaches below them, are medial locations where the sea becomes part of the immediately apprehended Gawan landscape and the island becomes incorporated into the surrounding seascape with its implications of other places and islands at a distance, or out of sight of Gawa.

Gawans move back and forth between the upper and lower levels of the island, going regularly to the different beaches. A beach has two basic areas – the interior edge (*kwadew*), where there may be trees and bushy areas that provide shade for sitting, and the sandy beach bordering the sea (*unamata*). The whole area may also be called *unamata* – the main location of sand (*kelekel*) as against the soil (*pweipwaya*), which characterizes the interior. The island as a whole, however, may also be called *pweipwaya* in contrast to the sea (*bwarita*).

The beach is the scene of various activities that fix its significance in Gawan experience. Gawan men and boys fish off the beaches from small canoes, or with nets on the reefs. Women and girls dig for crabs that live in the sandy areas of the beach or further inland. Gawan women do not fish or sail in the small canoes. People also regularly wash in the sea, and Gawans obtain most of their drinking water from parts of the reefs where fresh water emerges from underground springs.

In contrast to human beings, who live on top of the island, canoes (*waga*) are housed on the beaches. As some Gawans once said to me, a canoe "goes into the sea, washes, and then returns to its house on the beach" (see Munn, 1977:41). The building or renewal of the canoe shed (*bunatora*) is part of the standard series of major jobs in canoe building.

In building a canoe, Gawans haul the roughly hewn canoe hull and strakes from the steep cliffs down to the beaches for construction. On important work days, the beach is the scene of large, festive gatherings. Similar gatherings on the beach occur when Gawans return from a voyage, on mornings of a canoe departure, or on the arrival of overseas visitors. On such days people gather with supplies for travelers on their journeys or with gifts for departing visitors. Just as the beach is the home of the canoe, so it is the domain of transiency – the port of departures and arrivals or Gawan returns from overseas journeys. Visitors (*bwabwali*) may camp here during their stay, or Gawans occasionally sleep overnight on a late evening return from a journey, or in preparation for departure.

THE REGIONAL CONTEXT

Contemporary Gawan life involves a frequent coming and going of canoes from other islands of the northeast Massim sector, as well as canoe journeys by Gawans to visit these neighbors. Visitors come to Gawa for various reasons: In addition to those special voyages undertaken primarily for kula exchange, they may arrive to attend Gawan community entertainments, to obtain kula shells and other goods to bedeck a new canoe, or to acquire Gawan garden produce in return for other comestibles in which the visitors' homelands specialize. Visitors also come to sound out Gawans regarding possible kula exchanges and arrangements regarding the passage of shells along partners' common "paths" (*keda*), to request pigs for their own kula competitions or to meet other internal obligations, to weep for the death of close kinspeople or kula partners, and so forth. Whatever the particular purpose of these visits, they generally involve some talk

Plate 1. Gawa looms on the horizon as a Gawan canoe returns from a minor kula trip to Yanaba.

between partners about their kula. A few kula shells may also be casually transacted, kula shells thus passing between islands apart from major kula ventures.

Gawans themselves travel to other islands for these or similar purposes. For instance, they sail to Muyuw (see Figure 1) for extra supplies of betelnut and for sago, which does not grow on Gawa, or to Yanaba (in Gawan speech, Yaraba) for additional coconuts. They also travel to these islands to attend sagali soy memorial rites (cf. Malinowski, 1922:489ff.). On occasion, they go north to Iwa or Kitava for the entertainments there. These and other interactions between Gawans and their neighbors are part of the dense connectivities between the different islands through which a common world is created.[6]

The Trobriands form the northwest bounds of this Gawan consociative network that stretches south to Yeguma and southern Muyuw (and may be taken to include Nasikwabu, with which interaction appears somewhat less common). With the exception of Nasikwabu and Boagis, all the peoples of this region speak a language belonging to what Lithgow (1976) has called the Kilivila family; Gawans understand and can often speak these languages.[7]

The most frequent overseas contacts are with the nearer southern islands and with neighboring Kweawata. The regularity of inter-island contacts diminishes as one goes north into what Gawans call Ugawaga (the islands to the north, between Gawa and the Trobriands). Gawans and Kweawatans – whose home islands are within sight of each other – visit on a casual basis, although Kweawatan men tend to journey more frequently to Gawa (especially for church visits) than do the former to Kweawata. The two communities do not kula with each other; rather they compete for shells from other islands (see routes in Figure 1). Gawans kula directly with Iwa and Kitava, but whereas visits from Iwan canoes are not uncommon, Kitavan canoe visits are less frequent and more likely to be confined to community kula ventures. Trobrianders, on the other hand, do not ordinarily sail to Gawa on indigenous canoes, although they may occasionally come by government or trade vessels traveling in the area. Although Gawans do not kula directly with Trobriand communities, they maintain relations of mutual visiting and hospitality with their indirect Trobriand partners: When Gawans travel northward on a kula journey to obtain necklaces, they usually visit in Kilivila, often traveling with Kitavan canoes. Similarly, in the southeastern region, Gawans do not kula directly with southern Muyuwans, but close visiting relations – much closer than with the Trobrianders – are maintained with them.

Going southwest within the kula circle into the regions Gawans call *Raramani* (primarily the Bwanabwana islands) and Duau (eastern Normanby), or Dobu island and its environs, we also leave the kilivila language area. Face-to-face relations do not simply drop out, however; rather, contacts become less frequent and less multiplex in form. Gawan interaction with these people depends largely on contacts made on islands other than Gawa, as visits from these islanders to Gawa on their own inter-island journeys are relatively rare. Thus Gawans may meet Dobuans on the Trobriands or visitors from the southwest on Yeguma, whose residents themselves travel to these southwestern regions, but Gawans themselves do not sail their canoes to these places, and a visit of a single canoe from the Bwanabwana islands to Gawa is a comparatively rare event. The island world increasingly sheds its density of interaction as one leaves the regions into which Gawans sail.

I have referred (Chapter 1) to these more socially distant peoples as Gawan "contemporaries" rather than "consociates" (see Schutz 1962:16ff.), because their face-to-face relations with Gawans are minimal and few Gawans have ever seen these peoples' own home communities. Nevertheless, their indirect kula relationships with Gawans keep them firmly within the horizon of Gawan concerns and continuously implicated within the dense core of Gawan consociative networks. In this respect, they differ from peoples such as those of Misima and Goodenough, who are outside the kula circle. The latter fade beyond the social horizon within which lies a world of common structures (at the minimum, kula), ongoing mutual implication, and intertwined events.

THE DALA AND THE KUMILA

All Gawan land, including beaches and paths, is parceled out into named, owned (tara-wagara) land tracts. Small, matrilineal, exogamous groups called *dala* are the land-owning units.[8] Land inheritance and administration, however, are specified in terms of individual men (or women if there are no men). More than one man of a dala may have been allotted some land tracts that he administers (kareiwaga),[9] although only one – the informal dala head (guyaw) – is regarded as the dala administrator of the lands.

There are some twenty-four dala groups currently living on Gawa.[10] Dala range in size from one or two to some seventeen adults.[11] Like the land tracts, dala are named (although names are not necessarily well known by others). Within the dala, genealogical relations between living members can usually be traced only to the grandparental generation of the speaker. However, a common ancestress connecting all members is presupposed.

The dala forms the core of the individual's social self. As I discuss in Chapter 6, it grounds the bodily person in pre-given, transbodily being through bonds of bodily substance (notably by blood) to other, living and dead, persons.[12] Thus the central reference of the important term *veyo-*, which can be glossed as "kin," is to people of one's own dala.

Gawans conceive of themselves as essentially an island of immigrants. Except for one Gawan dala that is said to have emerged from a hole on Gawa, all extant dala are said to have come from elsewhere, entering Gawa from different islands, at different times. Of the current Gawan dala, thirteen are regarded as having arrived at different times from Muyuw; the remaining ten dala are said to have come from Kitava (6), the Trobriands (2), Iwa (1), and Kweawata (1). There are no standardized concepts about the sequence of these arrivals, although there are individual opinions on the matter. Some dala, moreover, are very recent arrivals, as Gawan men occasionally marry women from other islands. Dala are not connected to each other by any temporal formula such as the notion of dispersal from an earlier common location or genealogical segmentation of a previous unity, which introduces the idea of differentiation out of an original whole. Each dala has separate origin traditions (leliyu) frequently referring to its arrival on Gawa and acquisition of lands. As temporal formations of identity, dala are thus defined as essentially independent ancestral units. Special kin (veyo-) bonds between dala are created through variable affiliative processes involving food giving and related aid. These affiliative (-ka-veyora, create kin)[13] relations can sometimes lead, over time, to the fusion of dala, and are usually, but not always, formed between groups of the same overarching category known as the kumila. However, the kumila does not connect separate dala through the notion of a common ancestor.

As I discuss more fully in Chapter 4, the dala is physically represented in the land by stones expected to remain when the land is not being gardened. A few contemporary hamlets also have dala stones (see Chapter 4, note 8). Key garden stones mark the boundaries of dala-owned land tracts and cannot be moved. Thus the dala constitutes a differentiating, segmenting principle of Gawan land.

The exogamous social category kumila categorizes dala at a more comprehensive level. Each dala belongs to one of the four named kumila (Kulabutu, Nu-kubay, Nu-kwasisi, Malasi).[14] Although the kumila does not embody a temporal horizon involving reference to a single origin, the term veyo is usually applied generically to all dala of one's own kumila.[15]

In terms of spatial associations, a contrast may be drawn between the dala identification with Gawan land segmentation, involving the fixity of stones within the land, and kumila identification with the four winds. Gawans emphasize that just as there are four winds (Bwalima, east; Iyavata, west; Bwoumata, north; Youya, south), so there are four kumila. In addition, each kumila is associated with a particular bird (although currently Gawans appear to place somewhat less emphasis on the bird associations than do some of the societies to their south).[16]

The connection between the winds and the kumila is not merely conceptual. It is directly constituted in bodily activity during sailing when men call in the wind from the appropriate direction, addressing the (female) winds by their kumila label in special chants. The kumila structure is thus experientially oriented in terms of the winds, and is most directly associated with inter-island travel (although Gawans are also concerned, of course, with the wind directions on Gawa itself, for example, when they are planning a canoe journey, awaiting seasonal shifts, or expecting rain). In their connection with the winds, the kumila divisions are identified with motion across the fixed terrestrial order as the winds come from beyond Gawa,[17] and with the sea that embeds islands in the possibility of travel and inter-island relationship, rather than with land segmentation and boundary fixing within Gawa island.

The kumila categories thus appear to be connected with the formation of a wider regional, extra-Gawan spatial order in experience. This emphasis is consistent with the fact that the kumila define basic veyo relations with persons on other islands. From Gawa to the Trobriands there are four kumila with cognate labels; although Muyuwans have eight kumila, the names of four are cognate with Gawan terms, and Gawans subsume the other four as dala groups under appropriate Gawan kumila rubrics. Although some Gawans have immediate dala kin on other islands, it is only at the kumila level that any Gawan can find veyo in all the main communities with which Gawans interact.

Significantly, a Gawan's first attempts to establish overseas exchange partnerships generally focus on veyo – that is, kumila kin (unless they have immediate dala relationships in that place). Kumila kin are a man's expected point of entry into partnerships, because with them he can activate the general aid expected of a kinsman. Furthermore, *veyo* serves as a general term for kula partners (irrespective of specific kumila identification, which may then entail a more particular kin designation). In sum, the kumila appears as an inter-island, encompassing category of social identity, one that serves to generalize kinship connection across the region.

THE WINDS AND THE SEASONAL CYCLE

In being identified with the winds, the kumila are associated secondarily with a binary temporal cycle of the seasons, and seasonal activities. When the wind is called in by its kumila name, the season with which the wind is associated may be evoked. The four winds form a two-part temporal cycle in which the north and northwest winds bringing the rainier phase are paired as (*nube-*) "friends of different kumila," in contrast to the opposite pair of friends, the south and southeast winds, which bring the drier phase. This pairing defines the seasonal cycling of the "wind year" (called *Bwalima* after the easterly wind)[18] between the *Iyavata* (west wind) phase and *Bwalima* (east wind) phase.

Somewhat unexpectedly, the Bwalima, during which the yam harvest takes place, is regarded as the season of *moru*, "famine" or "hunger," and Iyavata is the phase of *mariya*, "plenitude." According to some Gawans, the rationale is that during the wetter phase of Iyavata, breadfruit, gwadura nuts, and other fruits ripen more or less sequentially so that when one is finished, another is usually ready for gathering and eating. Conversely, after the yam harvest, yam supplies soon tend to become short, and fruits do not ripen sequentially.

In addition, the relative dryness of the Bwalima period associates it with famine. Thus, in the wind chants, dry south and east winds (in contrast to the winds from the north and the west that travel laden with gwadura nuts and other foods) carry nothing on their journey: "they bring famine; they sail without anything in their canoe." The treatment of the wind year as a cycle between famine and plenty is consistent with another view Gawans hold in which garden foods are said to come from the north and travel south; conversely, famine is usually said to come from the south and west –

directions that are identified with Normanby and Dobu – and to travel northward.

Although Gawans do not emphasize the seasonal implications of the kumila apart from the wind chants, the use of the kumila to form paired cyclic relationships (different, however, from the particular pairs of the chants) is pronounced in community entertainments (see Chapter 8), and the contemporary form of the kula competition (see Chapter 3). Thus the kumila principle organizes dualistic, cyclic activities on the more comprehensive plane of the community, in contrast to the dala, which is focused in intracommunity segmentation engaging ancestral continuities.

GARDENING, DAILY ACTIVITIES, AND GENDER DIFFERENCES IN WORK

Among their daily activities, Gawans give gardening priority over all the others; ideally (although not always in practice), gardens should be tended each day. Other important activities may even be seen as taking one away from the basic work in the garden. Nevertheless, daily activities generally involve different projects relating to the moment, such as the various jobs entailed in canoe building, preparations for particular feasts, or the collection of resources for a major exchange, as well as less specialized activities such as fishing.

Daily work (*wotet*) is planned by each person or nuclear family. Similarly, a person's participation in any wider group arrangements for work depends entirely on individual decision. An overall pattern of the days has been set, however, in that Gawans have adopted the (Mission-introduced) European workweek: No one gardens on Sundays (reserved for churchgoing and visiting), and Saturday is the standard day for individual fishing and beach activities (although men also fish during the week).

Both men and women garden. The basic social units of gardening activities are a husband and wife and their immediate family. Hamlet groups frequently have some plots in a single garden, but members also garden elsewhere. Decisions about planting, garden location, and the like are made essentially by men (whose work of clearing and fencing or organization of that work gives them the basic control and ownership of the gardens), although women may sometimes have plots in independent gardens that they arrange on their own, and may also have their own plots in a garden. A man does not necessarily garden on his own dala land, although some of his gardens in a given year are usually made on his own lands.[19]

Although gardening decisions are individually made, yam gardening is the source of a regular cyclicity in which clearing, planting, and harvesting are roughly coordinate across the entire island. People should harvest yams about the time that the Pleiades (*pulipulimatara*, many-eyed) are seen in the early morning sky, start planting soon after (i.e., roughly in June), and finish planting by the time the Pleiades may be seen in the evening skies (about October-November).[20] In fact, in my experience most clearing did not begin until July or August, but planting was completed in October at the latest. Yams are harvested in March (*kuvi* yams) and April (*teitu* yams), and any major community feasts requiring large piles of raw yams are scheduled after the harvest. Yam gardening thus entails a communal time in contrast to taro gardening, whose cycles, as one might expect, are not coordinated. Taro stalks harvested for daily consumption must be replanted regularly (perhaps a week after harvesting); moreover, taro gardens may be cleared and planted in either Bwalima or Iyavata.

Although men and women work in both the yam and the taro gardens, there is some feeling that taro gardening is more basic to women's gardening activities. Yam gardens involve heavier work (e.g., in the planting and in the setting up of the yam sticks), and are more typically masculine garden work. For instance, when there is community-coordinated group work on the yam gardens, men organize by neighborhood to do the basic clearing, fencing, and planting, and to prepare the yam poles. Women are formally asked to help with the burning off, but not, for the most part, with the planting (although ordinarily women also plant and harvest yams). These different gender associations of yam and taro gardens, although not strongly marked, are consistent with the differences between the two with reference to the community-wide time noted earlier, since men control activities involving more comprehensive spatiotemporal coordinations. At the same time, we may note the lack of sharp gender distinctions in connection with gardening.

Although men and women may leave the hamlet to carry out their daily projects, not infrequently working together in the gardens, women's projects are, on the whole, more sedentary than those of men. Women more often stay in the hamlet watching children and watching the hamlet (although men will also do this on occasion). Similarly, although the initial gathering of materials for mats or skirts (or sometimes for roof thatching) takes women to the bush, the actual production involves the sedentary work of plaiting (mats) or stripping fronds (for skirts), which women usually perform while sitting in the hamlet. Women may also be found in the cookhouse in the late afternoon (after a day in the gardens, or after harvesting vegetables there) preparing the evening meal. With certain exceptions,[21] cooking is exclusively feminine work, and the one that, for Gawans, most typifies feminine activity.

Masculine daily activity is characteristically less sedentary, taking men more frequently to the outer domains of Gawan space. We have seen that men fish and sail. The contrast between male and female activities on a canoe illustrates women's relatively sedentary role: When women sail, they must sit quietly while the crew works; on returning to Gawa, they cook for the sailors in payment for the travel service. Men also do the major jobs of canoe building on the cliffs and beaches whereas women cook in the hamlets or on the beach to feed the workers. In addition, men hunt in the bush with nets to catch any wild pigs that might have been spotted, and only men and boys climb trees (for example, to obtain coconuts and betel), or go hunting for the occasional flying fox, possum, or bird. Although both men and women own pigs, it is the men who capture and kill domestic pigs for feasts, and who do the initial roasting, baking, and cutting up of the meat. Just as male activities control a wider spatial domain than feminine work, these activities also tend to be more mobile and energetic, and to involve men in handling the mobile elements (fish, pigs, canoes, etc.) in the environment.

Artifactual procedures that create spatial domains, "carving out" the space or creating bounding structures, are confined to male activity. The initial clearing of gardens and hamlets, the building of houses and canoes are all essentially masculine activities. Men also manufacture nets for capturing fish and pigs from unbounded or undomesticated spatial domains. In contrast, women make clothing, as well as mats that may be laid between the body and the ground, house floor, or wooden bed, or be used to protect the body from rain and cold. Furthermore, as the cooks, women prepare food for bodily consumption. Thus women's typical productive activities tend to focus on somatic space, whereas men's activities engage them in the construction of extrasomatic space – in preparing new domains of human activity and bounding them. We shall see that these spatial differences between masculine and feminine activities are important to the understanding of value transformation examined in this study.

THE HAMLET

A Gawan hamlet is a socially close and relatively autonomous grouping. It may contain two types of residence: that of the family and that of unmarried youths. The family residence is typically the home of a married couple and their young children, and foster children. A hamlet may also have a house for an unmarried teenage boy (*tawalata*) made available to him for courting.[22] A family residence usually has a separate cookhouse, but a cookhouse is sometimes shared.

There is at least one yam house in a hamlet. A married man has his own yam house when his responsibilities become large enough to require it, and his paternal and maternal kinsmen decide to help him build one (ordinarily

after a few years of marriage). Otherwise he and his family have their own
compartments in the yam house of a more senior man of the hamlet. A
senior married woman may also have her own yam house if her husband
chooses to build one for her, but more typically, yams from her garden
plots will be stored in a compartment of her husband's house. In addition
to his own and his wife's produce, a man's house may store the produce of
other men (or sometimes women) of his hamlet, as well as yams acquired
at harvest from affines (see Chapter 6). Yam houses are named according
to the dala of the owner, each dala having only one yam house name,
which may be instantiated, however, in more than one house (in the same
or different hamlets).

A hamlet also contains its dead. Those buried in the hamlet are ideally
but not exclusively members of the dala of the hamlet head (taraveru,
hamlet owner or head). Nowadays, graves are usually placed at the edge or
on the side of the hamlet, but not centrally, owing to the injunctions of the
government and the church. Gawans are usually reluctant, however, to
bury kinspeople at any distance from the cleared hamlet area. As one
woman suggested to me, to do so is to treat the dead like animals, putting
them in the untended area of the bush. It is as if one expelled the dead
from the humanized space of the hamlet. The hamlet thus represents
premarital and marital life stages and, like Massim hamlets elsewhere,
attempts to maintain the dead within its domestic space.

Each hamlet has its male head or owner (taraveru), most commonly, the
senior man of the hamlet. Through its taraveru, the hamlet is identified
with a particular dala. Ideally, the hamlet should be built on this man's dala
land, but if built on the land of another dala, a kula shell and pig payment
must be made to the owning dala to secure rights over the land.[23] If
payments have been made, members of the headman's dala may be buried
in the hamlet land without further return, but if not, the dala owning the
land may (at its discretion) require payment for the burial. Similarly,
payments must be made to a dala head and his dala if he permits a member
of another dala – for example, the spouse of one of the hamlet's residents –
to be buried in his hamlet land.

Each dala may be represented by one or more hamlet heads, but the key
hamlet of a dala is the hamlet of its recognized guyaw (leading man, man of
high standing). When a dala is represented by more than one hamlet, these
are (with exceptions) usually fairly close to each other, and in some
instances contiguous. With some exceptions, the garden lands owned by a
dala are in the vicinity of the hamlet of a dala's guyaw. The ideal basic
model entails the identification of the dala and the dala guyaw with a
unitary hamlet space. The independence and equality of each dala and its
guyaw is closely linked in Gawan thinking with the spatial segmentation
and independent equality of each hamlet (see Chapter 3).

The residence of married couples in a given hamlet, or with a particular hamlet head, is not, however, determined strictly on principles of matrikinship. After marriage, a young man may reside with his father (*tama-*) or foster father; a mother's brother (*kada-*) of his own dala or a dala of his own kumila; or his wife's father (*yawa-*), if the latter is influential and wishes to keep his daughter in his hamlet. In each case, co-residence involves support of the senior man, who in turn makes certain resources available to him.[24] Unless a young man has early established a special support relation with another senior kinsman or close dala affiliate whose heir (*mapu-*) he expects to become, he is most likely to reside with his father until the latter's death, or until he (the younger man) arranges a relation with another senior man. On the father's death, a man may move to a dala kinsman's hamlet or make other choices, depending on exigencies, including that of setting up a new hamlet. Creating a separate hamlet of one's own is part of a process of asserting a certain autonomy and equality with other hamlet heads (*i-guyaw* – becomes or attempts to become a man of standing). Gawan hamlets are small in part because of this strain toward independence, although other reasons such as conflict can lead to the fission of larger hamlet groupings.

THE HOUSE

The Gawan house is the bounded arena of social space within which the most intimate care and protection of the person takes place. It is also the locus of transitions into life and death. Houses vary considerably in their internal structure, but a typical arrangement involves an outer room for visiting (*kwowukweda*) and an inner room (*tatoma*) for sleeping and the storage of personal possessions, a distinction thus being made between private and relatively public space. The inner room may have wooden platform beds (*keba*) at the back with an area for a fire underneath. When these structures are present, they betoken an important use of the house in the creation of a warm protective surrounding for a woman when she is giving birth, and until she and the new baby first come out (*-sakapu ou murakata*).

When a woman becomes pregnant with her first child, the couple moves back temporarily to the woman's parents' or foster parents' hamlet if, as is usual, they have been residing elsewhere. The woman's parents and their bilateral kin, with the help of the young husband and his parents and kinspeople, build a house for the birthing. Like all housebuilding, this one is primarily a male responsibility. (It will be recalled that it is essentially men who construct bounded – and, as we see here, protective – spaces; in the present context, women are those protected by these masculine constructive acts.) The child is to be born in this warm, dark house, the mother sleeping on the bed at the back while being heated from the hot, cleansing fire built beneath.

When the mother and baby first come out of the house, she and the baby must be protected from the cold (e.g., her head must be covered and she wears her pregnancy cloak) so that bodily covering is substituted for the protection of the house, as she moves into relatively external, open space. Various food and sexual prohibitions also obtain until the child starts to walk (note the emphasis on motion as a significant point of transition).[25]

In this case, as in other curative contexts, heat and the creation of an enclosing house are crucial parts of the attempt to maintain life. But when a person dies, he or she must also be laid out inside the house for one night so that an appropriate burial can be performed. As we shall see later (Chapter 7), this is a medial phase in which memories of the living person are evoked. Similarly, when mourners live in the house of death after a burial, they are the living representatives of the dead (see Chapter 7).

Thus the house is the domain of bodily transition into being and of the dissolution of being. These remarks may serve as background for additional points about interiority and motion to be discussed in later chapters.

CROSS-HAMLET RELATIONSHIPS AND PREMARITAL YOUTH

The familial residences and the prefamilial, bachelor houses do not simply represent different intrahamlet statuses and stages of a life and domestic cycle, but also different types of cross-hamlet bonds and modes of association.

Courting youths form a distinctive peer group. Those who occupy this status together at any given time are *metabouwen* (age-mates) to each other. Gawan adults accord the group a distinctive internal authority (*kareiwaga*) of its own, allowing the young people considerable freedom, while carefully monitoring the particular lovers (*nube*) with whom their children are involved at any given time, and evaluating the work attitudes of the various young people.[26] Marriage can take place only if the girl's parents supply the foodstuffs necessary to establish marriage (see Chapter 6).

A youth usually enters this age group by about twelve or thirteen, that is, about puberty, and is married by or before the age of seventeen or eighteen (boys usually being somewhat older at marriage than girls). Once married, Gawans are supposed to put aside the relatively irresponsible life of their youth: An individual couple is detached from the courting group and its new social bonds are defined in terms of responsibilities engaged by affinal relationships. Gawans sharply contrast this youthful stage of their lives and that of married life. After marriage, one's age-mates of the opposite sex should not be mentioned in the presence of one's spouse, and relationships formed in this period are relegated largely to the past.

The distinctive life of youths is conveyed by the expression *i-rarore-s*, "they wander around," which suggests their relative freedom from the responsibilities of married couples, and their enjoyable activities beyond the confines of hamlet and garden. Since the group itself includes all the Gawan young people of that time, it forms a community-wide peer group that is not segmentally defined.

Although less regular garden work is required of a youth than a married adult, Gawans point out that night (*bogi*) is the appropriate time for young people to gather together, make assignations, and wander where they wish; in the daytime (*yam*), however, they are expected to work. Night is thus a time phase associated with youthful activity, whose characteristic entertainments involve dancing and singing. Sometimes a youth or a group of young people sitting in one of the young people's houses may sing late into the night. Larger gatherings usually take place either in the large hamlet area of the church, or in the hamlet of the sponsor of an organized entertainment (*kayasa*, see Chapter 8). In addition to the youths, younger children may sometimes play together into the night, especially when there is a full moon. Thus while married adults sleep in the family houses, children and young people may romp.

A feature of youthful behavior during this phase is emphasis on the elaboration of a Gawan speech genre called *seibaw*, which is a form of joking or teasing that combines friendliness with self-assertive aggressiveness and may have sexual overtones. Since it creates a joking atmosphere that also displays the aggressive control of the user over language, this type of speech may also be used by men in kula activities where language skills are a critical means of persuasion (Chapter 3). Its elaboration in courtship is connected with the development of persuasiveness in order to acquire sexual favors.[27]

The patterns I have described for the Gawan courting period have the familiar transitional features of *rites de passage* with their separations and reversals. Thus the residential shift to the bachelor house; the transient identification with a group defined as age-mates; association with a spatially unbounded kind of activity (wandering), and with special activities at night rather than during the ordinary working day, and so on – are all well known indicators of transitional social phases. The fact that we do not have here the more familiar kind of passage rite in which adults exert rigorous control and effect the radical subordination of initiates is significant. Instead of hierarchizing processes explicitly shaped by the authority of adults who impose regulation from the outside through direct control over initiates' bodies, Gawan transition emphasizes the relative autonomy of the youths while adults watch from behind the scenes, exerting covert influence on their children, but interfering directly only in cases of radical misbehavior. The overt emphasis is thus upon the exercise of relative autonomy and a youth's own persuasive powers, while the constraining influence of the adult operates as a covert control regulating this autonomy.

MARRIAGE AND MARRIAGE EXCHANGES

Partly because of the relatively small hamlet size, Gawans usually marry outside their own hamlet. Although marriages may take place between families living in neighborhoods at different ends of the island, most marriages connect less distant hamlets. Inter-island marriages also occur, but marriage within Gawa (especially for women) is preferred. There is, however, no general principle governing marriages in terms of residential grouping.

On the other hand, a person must marry (-*vay*) outside his or her dala; all sexual relationships within the dala are *sivasouva*, "incest." As I indicated above, the kumila is also exogamous, but an occasional case of intrakumila marriage occurs. In addition, children of men of one dala should not marry because they are opposite-sex siblings (*nu–ta*)[28] to each other. The same principle applies more weakly to children of men of one kumila if the dala relations are close.

At the present time on Gawa, there are no positive marriage principles operating as a standard model, or a consistently held ideal that defines affinal continuities over time through repetitive marriages between dala or kumila. Although people recognize other dala with whom their dala has frequently intermarried in the past, marriages are not typically treated as reconstituting or aimed at reconstituting past marriage links between dala (or kumila), or as creating the potential for future links between the same dala (or kumila) groups. Rather, Gawans frequently say, "We marry without rationale (*sabwamu*)." Although the marriage of a man or woman into his or her father's dala (i.e., bilateral cross-cousin marriage) occurs occasionally, and may sometimes be used for political purposes, there is no standardized preference for this type of marriage. In fact, some people feel negatively about such marriages, and Gawan views are more complex than I can discuss here.

A marriage establishes an affinal link between bilateral kin of each partner, and between people of four *key* dala: namely, the paternal and the maternal dala of *each* spouse.[29] In discussing affinal exchanges, I shall speak summarily of each partner's kin, signifying the bilateral kin of each (which can include foster kin).

Affinal connections are established through exchanges between individual kinspeople of the marriage partners. Each marriage is thus the medium of a complex of exchanges between persons on both sides who may reside in various Gawan hamlets and neighborhoods. The goods consist essentially of garden produce (*teitu* and *kuvi* yams and taro, *wuni*, which Gawans summarize as *karu*) and pigs (*bulukwa*) from the woman's side; artifacts including canoes, kula shells, and such items as European cloth and knives, and in the category of edibles, fish, from the man and his kin.

The marriage exchanges in which these items figure are various, but the key *buwaa-* exchanges define the marriage as such. In later chapters, I analyze the latter as basic transformational processes. In the present context, I provide some necessary background for this analysis, illustrating the way in which these exchanges form dyadic networks of connections across hamlets.

The essential core of the buwaa exchange is the harvest of raw garden produce (yams and taro), given individually from the garden plots of particular kin of the wife to kinspeople of the husband, and returned on an occasional basis by kula shells and canoes. The people figuring in these buwaa partnerships may change somewhat over time and are not an entirely closed set of individuals, but a core of persons remain in these relations as long as the marriage continues, or until one of the donors in a partnership dies.[30] A man refers to the comestibles transmitted from his wife's kin as *his* buwaa, and a woman refers to the shells and canoes from her husband's kin as *her* buwaa. Gifts of both types taken together are *buwe-si*: their (the couple's) buwaa. The couple, however, are forbidden to consume the food themselves, and both types of goods must be transacted via them to others. Thus each married couple localized in a given hamlet becomes the node of a number of dyadic relationships that involve persons residing in different hamlets and neighborhoods.

Figure 3 exemplifies these connectivities, showing relationships mediated through a couple (1, 2) residing in Hamlet A, of Utaru neighborhood. Six dyadic relationships (comprising persons residing in nine hamlets) are shown. Note that the relationships are actually established between married couples, although one member of the couple is the immediate partner. Thus, (3) and (3a) are the foster father and mother of the wife (2). They give buwaa (garden produce, and the like) for their foster daughter (2) to the foster parents (4, 4a) of the husband (1). Technically, the father of the woman is making the gift, for men are the prototypic food givers for women in marriage exchanges, but the wife (in this case the foster mother) frequently identifies herself or sometimes is identified by other women as a donor with her husband.

The immediate recipient in this case is (4), the foster mother of the man (1); she is also his own mother's full sister, and lives in a hamlet of Utaru neighborhood, where the nodal couple also reside. Both she and her

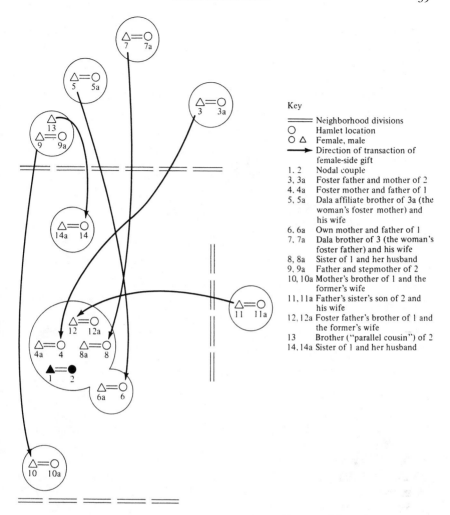

Key

===== Neighborhood divisions
O   Hamlet location
O △   Female, male
━━▶   Direction of transaction of
         female-side gift
1, 2   Nodal couple
3, 3a   Foster father and mother of 2
4, 4a   Foster mother and father of 1
5, 5a   Dala affiliate brother of 3a (the
         woman's foster mother) and
         his wife
6, 6a   Own mother and father of 1
7, 7a   Dala brother of 3 (the woman's
         foster father) and his wife
8, 8a   Sister of 1 and her husband
9, 9a   Father and stepmother of 2
10, 10a Mother's brother of 1 and the
         former's wife
11, 11a Father's sister's son of 2 and
         his wife
12, 12a Foster father's brother of 1 and
         the former's wife
13   Brother ("parallel cousin") of 2
14, 14a Sister of 1 and her husband

Figure 3. Interhamlet *buwaa* relationships focused in one nodal couple.

husband are regarded as those who "eat" (*kam*) the food (see Chapters 4 and 6); the return (for instance, kula armshells) comes from the man's foster father and goes back to the woman's foster father. The woman's own father (her mother was dead) gives buwaa for her, which in this case, goes to the husband's mother's brother (10 and his wife). Immediate recipients of the food gifts from the woman's kinsmen (i.e., the partners on the husband's side) may be either men or women; in the latter case, the female recipients' husbands are then responsible for acquiring the return buwaa gifts.

Although Figure 3 shows the couple (1, 2) as the node of exchange relationships constructed by virtue of their marriage, this couple is itself engaged in exchanges by virtue of the marriages of still other couples. Similarly, each of the marital couples shown in partnerships in Figure 3 are themselves the nodes of buwaa exchanges, as well as being engaged in buwaa exchange relations other than those mediated by this nodal couple. Thus each spatially localized marriage "fixed" in a given hamlet domain is matrixed in a network of marital transactions of goods across hamlet domains.

Although the married couple is the basic unit in buwaa relationships, the man is the key, originating donor. Thus I consider further the types of kin for whom he typically gives buwaa, especially the food-giving relationships between a man and a woman. These relationships generally involve more than just the buwaa gift since they include produce from the man's gardens that can be eaten by the couple concerned and which is therefore not transacted beyond them to the husband's kinspeople.

A man typically gives food for one or more of his female dala (or dala affiliate) members, and for his own or foster daughter(s) – members of his wife's dala in the first descending generation from his own (or of another dala whose daughter he is fostering). Men typify the food-giving relationships to their dala in terms of the cross-sex sibling relationship, treating the relationship as intragenerational, although actually they may take up responsibilities for other types of female dala kin. In addition, they may establish food-giving relationships with women of other dala, who are frequently, but not necessarily, of their own kumila. Establishing such realtionships is referred to as "creating a sister for oneself" (*i-vaga nu-re-ta*).

The wife's relation to the women for whom a man gives garden produce is important. A man calls all the women of his dala for whom he gives this produce *agu-gamagali*, (my person).[31] A man's wife speaks of her husband's gamagali as *her* gamagali, thus identifying with him. In this sense, a wife is giving buwaa to her husband's gamagali.[32] The asymmetric structure of the identification indicates the male centering of food transmission in marital exchanges; at the same time, the common term marks the unity of the couple, and the joint part of the wife in her husband's transactions.

Food thus goes out from a man (with his wife) in one direction and it comes in to him via his wife or son's wife. It will be noted that when a woman is designated as the immediate recipient or consumer of buwaa produce for the marriage of another couple, the direction from which a man (her husband) receives produce is consistent with this directionality: That is, he is acquiring it *via* his wife. On the other hand, when a man is the immediate recipient-consumer of buwaa, he is acquiring produce given for the marriage of a dala kinsman (or structurally parallel kinsman), in this sense, through his *kinsman's* wife.

Conversely, male goods are transacted by a man to (via) his wife or his son (and son's wife) rather than his sister and daughter. Similarly, a man *receives* these goods via his sister (or other dala kinswoman) and daughter (or foster daughter) rather than his wife – that is, from those types of female kin to or for whom he gives food.

The binary directions of a man's transactions for women (prototypically, sister vs. wife) encode the fundamental opposition between the two types of cross-sex relationships: a man and his sister (marked by the reciprocal *nu–ta*) and a man and his wife (marked by the asymmetric terms *-mwara*, husband and *-kwav*, wife). Gawans explicitly contrast the two. Physical contact is prohibited between cross-sex siblings, and specific prohibitions are placed on entry into each other's houses once the age of sexual courting has been reached. Reference to the sexuality of one member of the pair in the presence of the other is prohibited. These and related patterns of separation form a spatial separation between the pair that contrasts with the spatial identification (the sharing of a single house, and the physical bond of sexuality) that typifies the marital pair. Although the bodily unity of one-dala siblings (the prototypic sibling relationship) is based in internal, blood relationships, that of a married couple is based in their external sexual contact, and their reproduction of children (see Chapter 6). The difference in mode of bodily relationship is conveyed, for example, at the death of one marriage partner when the other lies all night embracing the corpse in the mourning house, while the cross-sex sibling and other dala members can only enter the house intermittently to wail (Chapter 7).

The pre-given identification of cross-sex siblings is that of an undifferentiated whole – an a priori sameness of blood – rather than the unity of two separate, incomplete parts. Thus, opposite-sex siblings must be made separate through prohibitions against contact, whereas, conversely, marriage makes separate persons into a differentiated whole of complementary parts. We shall see later that in Gawan thinking the marital relationship appears as the epitomizing form of a social totality.

SINAVARAMA

In addition to exchanges of goods, affinal relationships are formed through work responsibilities. Each member of a married couple is *sinavarama* – a source of work help – to the spouse's parents and their immediate dala kin. The most important sinavarama relationships are with spouse's parents (including foster parents) and spouse's siblings. This aid is activated in contexts requiring collective work beyond the household or hamlet bounds (e.g., fencing operations for a large garden, fishing and cooking at canoe-building feasts, and so on). A critical function of the male sinavarama is in distributing food at feasts of which his affines, such as his wife's brothers or father, are the proprietors. Only men publicly distribute food (see Chapters 3 and 8).

In contrast to a female sinavarama, a male sinavarama is obliged to bring his own kinspeople (and their spouses) to work for his affines. This difference is part of the asymmetry in the male- and female-side marriage gifts. A man receives work support from the direction in which he sends garden produce (via sisters and daughters) and is the node of additional work support for his own affines, who give produce to him and his kin. This gender asymmetry of obligations is also consistent with other differences in gender roles already described: It is the male sinavarama who draws in additional workers within and beyond his own hamlet, that is, beyond himself.

THE COMMUNITY

As is typical of New Guinea societies, the Gawan community as a whole lacks any superordinate center of control, but there are some relatively senior men of greater community eminence and influence than others;[33] these men have strong kula reputations. Although men and youths of all Gawan dala participate in kula (their common participation itself being a part of contemporary Gawan egalitarianism), kula provides a medium for defining hierarchical differences between men (see Munn, 1983). Among the many adult men of good standing who are active in the community, men of special eminence are key figures in the organization of community-wide activities such as major community entertainments, special community garden work, and the calling of public meetings on matters relevant to the community at large (see Chapter 10).

Gawans also distinguish two separate complementary spheres of knowledge and authority (*kareiwaga*) based on control of the most powerful gardening (including weather) magic (*mega*), on the one hand, and magic for curing and control of witches (*bwagaw*), on the other.[34] The most influential experts or specialists in these domains are community functionaries who use their power to "care for" (*-yamata*) the community at large (see Chapter 4).[35] Such men are also generally major or at least substantial figures in kula.[35] Whereas the leading Gawan garden experts are concerned with the fertility of the land, the curer or witch-controlling specialists focus on the state of health of the human body. The combined control over witchcraft (*bwagaw*) and curing derives from the Gawan view that all long-term illness and all deaths except for those of the very old are caused, in the final analysis, by witches. As I have previously indicated (Chapter 1), this premise is fundamental to the Gawan moral-political process (see Part III).

To these two complementary kareiwaga of community-wide importance may be added that of the two major reciprocal community entertainments (*kayasa*) regularly performed on contemporary Gawa: most notably the Drum (*kupi*, also called *wousi*, song, and *kalibomu*, referring specifically to the night dancing) and the Comb (*Sinata*). (I shall refer to the former as the Drum dance.) The Drum dance belongs to a dala of the Nukubay and the Comb to a dala of the Nukwasisi. Performances of each entertainment are held in the hamlet of the guyaw of the owning dala (see Chapter 8).

In fact, there are more than two such major entertainments known on Gawa, with at least one being ascribed to each of the four kumila, but the major entertainments of the other two kumila have not been performed within living memory. Nevertheless, Gawans emphasize that each kumila has a key entertainment and even younger informants can outline the lapsed entertainments (the Model canoe, *Kulabutu*, and the Fishing, *Malasi*).[36]

The continued theoretical adherence to the four-part model is significant. The four entertainments mentioned, like the kumila between which they are divided, can be seen as forming the model of a totality. As one Gawan pointed out to me, two are performed in the hamlets (or on the top of the island) and two on the beach (and there are also other, concomitant sea–land oppositions). In theory, the totality should be constituted in experience through the sequential and reciprocal performance of each kayasa (cf. the identification of the kumila with the seasonal wind cycle).

Thus according to one senior man, in the past the four entertainments enabled each kumila to exercise alternate control over the major resource distribution involved in the organization of the entertainments so that each remained equal. The current cycle is less satisfactory in this respect, but as we shall see (Chapter 8), the two current entertainments have taken over the totalizing function and the kayasa cycle remains fundamental to the construction of the islandwide community order.

In addition to these traditional kareiwaga are those pertaining to the government, the United Church, and the school.[37] Each of these spheres also has spatial representation on Gawa (the government through the medical aid post as well as the hamlet of the current councillor; see Figure 2), and each constitutes a particular sphere of authority with community functionaries. The elected government councillor who represents the concerns of the provincial government on the island, may or may not be a man of eminence in the indigenous context, but government-related matters such as cleaning the main paths, building medical facilities, and so on are his kareiwaga. Similarly, the elected members of the school committee may be young men, but school matters are their kareiwaga, and other people (including more senior men) should listen to them on school issues. Each of these three kareiwaga, like the indigenous kareiwaga, is a particular, limited sphere of authority that does not give its functionaries any communal control beyond this sphere. Gawans incorporate these new authorities into their community on the fundamentally acephalous (separate and equal) terms of the indigenous order.

KULA EXCHANGE

In 1979–80 some 118 Gawan men and youths were engaged in kula in varying degrees. A boy begins his own kula transactions about the time he enters the courtship phase. He may obtain a small first armshell (*mwari*) or necklace (*veiguwa* or *soulava*) from a senior kinsman on Gawa (a mother's brother, father, and so on) with whom he then transacts a return shell, or from a man on another island, particularly one of his own kumila whom he has helped while visiting during kula; the latter may then give him a shell and become his first overseas partner. In either case, to obtain a shell the boy has had to aid his senior, doing what the latter requests. A youth may also establish kula relations with members of his peer group on other islands, using the relatively small shells obtained from one of his senior kinsmen to initiate transactions. (For additional commentary on apprenticeship and matrilineal inheritance of kula partnerships, see Chapter 5.)

Kula paths (*keda*) of partners (of varying degrees of extension and durability), are made by the travel paths of shells. A man of standing in kula generally has built three to four relatively stable partnership paths. But paths should be thought of as dynamic processes rather than fixed sets of relationships; however, I cannot go into the complexities of their formation and their relation to shell movements here. At any given time, many paths of partnerships may not complete the entire ring[38] and other completed paths may have atrophied; but the unidirectional, sequential movement of each type of shell and the bidirectional continuity governing the overall movement of shells around the islands create a closed "circularity." This structure is the enabling principle of an indefinitely reproducible circulation.

Gawans do not manufacture kula shells on Gawa, although they may alter them to improve their appearance. The two directions from which shells come into Gawa (necklaces from the north-northwest and armshells from the south-southeast) divide the inter-island world into two sectors: the former, Gawans identify ultimately with Dobu, and the latter with Raramani (notably, the Bwanabwana islands to the south). It will be recalled that the paired winds (north-west and south-east) similarly divide Gawa's inter-island world on an asymmetric model. Moreover, both dualisms as they enter into the formulation of Gawan experience do not simply define static, binary wholes, but rather form totalities through motion (as they travel from one direction toward another) and through cycling (exchange or seasonal alternation). (On kula and the totalizing of the inter-island world, see Chapter 6.)

Some shells enter Gawa defined as the personal possessions (*-vavaga*) of particular Gawans, who can then make all decisions regarding their disposition. Shells regarded in this way are classed as the *kitomu* of the owner[39] and are received initially in return for certain restricted types of services or goods; for Gawans, the most important source of kitomu is their own artifact specialty, canoes, whose southward trade nets them (among other items) kitomu armshells coming from the southern recipients of the canoes. The significance of kitomu is discussed in Chapter 6. Here we may merely note that when a Gawan puts his kitomu on a kula path, the shell of opposite category finally returned for it as its equivalent becomes his kitomu, and the first shell is reclassified as *murikura* to him – that is, as a shell that is not his personal possession (but that may have become somebody else's, presumably that of the relatively distant partner who located the return shell). Most of the shells a man transacts are murikura, and he may or may not regard them as someone else's kitomu.[40]

When Gawans sail on major kula ventures, shells numbering in the hundreds may come into Gawa at once, but even the more adroit do not often obtain as many as ten named shells. These trips are group sailings involving the Gawan community as a whole, or at least more than one canoe. The most important of these group sailings is an *uvelaku*, a community-organized kula competition in which a formal winner is established (see Chapter 3).

Although kula is built upon individual partnerships, it is also the central means by which the Gawan community engages with other communities on a sociopolitical level, competing with some to acquire shells from others. Gawans are not concerned simply with the state of their own personal kula, but also with that of the community as a whole. Thus when a man brings back a famous shell to Gawa, its presence there contributes not only to his own fame, but also to the fame of Gawa in the inter-island world.

PART II

Food transmission and spatiotemporal transformations

3

Food transmission and food consumption
The basic dialectic of value transformation

[When someone eats a lot of food] it makes his stomach swell; he does nothing but eat (*-kam*) and lie down (*-masisi*, lie down/sleep); but when we give food (*karu*) to someone else, when an overseas visitor eats pig, vegetable food, chews betel, then he will take away its noise (*buraga-ra*), its fame (*butu-ra*). If we ourselves eat, there is no noise, no fame, it will disappear (*b-i-tamwaw*), rubbish, it will default. If we give to visitors, they praise us, it is fine. If not, there is no fame; Gawa would have no kula shells, no *guyaw* (man of high standing), no kula fame.

Gardens and kula are what make a man a guyaw. Whoever has gardens, overseas visitors come and eat there all the time. They say you are a guyaw. [Later] they will come and give you armshells and necklaces. Your fame will spread. The garden "pays off" (*peyola*, has a big yield). The thing "ahead" is the food (*karu*). The kula is "behind" [i.e., dependent on the garden food]. You cannot feed the visitors if you have no food.

A Gawan man's explanations of passages from public speeches, 1974–5

As in many societies, Gawans treat food giving as the basic form of generosity. Generosity (*lalasi*) and selfishness (*mulamola*), connote opposed bodily actions of releasing and incorporating or retaining for oneself. Thus the generous person may be described metaphorically as "wide-handed" (*karatanay yama-*), which suggests an opening of the hand (*yama*) that gives (*-seik*), whereas a selfish person is one who continually holds back things requested by others (*-kayus*, refuse something, keep or protect),[1] reserving them for him- or herself. The selfish person, as one Gawan put it, "does not give to people, he or she eats." The basic descriptive label for a greedy person is, in fact, "one who eats" (*-kamkwamu* with a male, *ta-* or female *na-* prefix).[2] A selfish individual (or a person perceived after the fact as having behaved in that way) can be bewitched by a piece of food caught inside the chest, which causes the illness. This illness illustrates the internalizing effect of the selfish act with its central connotation of taking or holding back toward one's own body rather than releasing to others. The most extreme act of holding back is incorporating; food that is caught inside the body, in turn, epitomizes what is not only consumed, but also cannot be released.

49

Conversely, the generous person gives food to others to eat. In this respect, it is significant that the term *kam*, "eat" has a causative form *-vaakam*, which means "feeds, gives to another to eat." Vaakamu is a fundamental means of achieving influence with others by regularly nourishing them with food. For example, a man gains rights over his own or a foster child and builds influence with a child as it grows up, by acting as its *-vaakam*.[3] When the child is a baby, he may pre-chew food for it, and taking it out of his own mouth put it directly into the baby's mouth. This transaction is a paradigmatic instance of food giving as the separation of food from one's own body for incorporation by another. The structure of food release and incorporation as an action cycle directly connecting the bodies of donor and recipient is given prototypic significance in this context.

When a man or woman who has regularly fed a child grows old, the child in turn should care for this person – for instance, by giving daily food when the latter is ill (cf. Weiner, 1976:125). The long-term outcome of this food giving is thus a return of bodily care to the original donor at a time when he or she requires the kind of help that has been given to the recipient in the past. This spatiotemporal cycle inherent in the vaakam relationship points up the difference between nourishing one's own body (eating) and giving food to another to eat.

A similar principle is expressed in the first Gawan quotation at the beginning of this chapter. In this commentary, the outcome of eating one's own food instead of giving it to overseas visitors is described in terms of its immediate effect upon the body of the consumer, which is nothing but bodily swelling and the sleep of surfeit. The food itself is destroyed, losing its capacity to produce anything else for the consumer. The comestible and the fame, its potential product, disappear (*i-tamwaw*). Conversely, giving food away to overseas visitors for their own consumption is perceived as initiating a spatiotemporally extending process – an expansion beyond the donors' persons and the immediate moment, and beyond Gawa island – as visitors take away the favorable news of Gawan hospitality. In this way food (*karu*) is converted into fame (*butu-*), an extrabodily component of the self (see Chapter 5), with attendant implications involving kula and the development of guyaw leadership to be discussed later.

The Gawan's commentary thus conveys the spatiotemporal value transformation embedded in the dialectical process of acts of food consumption and transmission. Whereas consumption directs food "immediately" into the body, reducing the duration of the food and destroying its potential for yielding anything in the future, the transaction of food away from the body can produce further positive value products that themselves transcend the body of the donor, and in this instance, are seen as going beyond Gawa itself. The dialectical tension between the two types of act is itself the processual matrix defining the basic significance of each. As I discussed in Chapter 1, this tension is fundamental to the Gawan system of value production, forming an underlying meaning process operative in multiple contexts.

The second commentary quoted at the beginning of the chapter is obviously related to the view expressed in the first quotation and makes a point generally emphasized to me by Gawans regarding the means by which men build political standing. That is, to become a guyaw, a man must be a good gardener so that he can dispense food to overseas visitors. The latter will then regularly come to visit him because of his generosity. In effect, these overseas visitors are viewed as those whose decisions to release kula shells govern a man's advancement. It is they who "say you are a guyaw." From this perspective, it is only through an external reflection of the self – what amounts to a favorably appraising "look" coming from the outside other (Sartre, 1966:346ff.; see also Leroy, 1979:185) – that Gawans can define their own guyaw. This grounding of self-definition in the appraisal of the other is fundamental to Gawan value transformation.

Since a guyaw is "one who feeds visitors," it is significant that a man who is strong in kula (*ta-kurakura*, a kula man) can be figuratively contrasted with one who is weak by calling the latter "a man who eats" (*ta-kamkwamu*) or saying simply that he eats but the other man kulas (*i-kurakura*). Conversely, one may say that a man who eats without reason (*sabwamu*), who doesn't work (*wotet*) in the gardens or in kula (also called *wotet*, cf. Damon, 1978:60) and give food to visitors is *to-b-ei-kam*, "a man who would eat." Such a man "has no name" (*yaga-ra*), – that is, he is not known abroad – an attribute that epitomizes the negative spatiotemporal transformation of self–other relations involved.

But the relation of eating and kula is more complex than this opposition of social categories would make it appear. This complexity becomes illuminated when we consider that kula visits to other islands are times when Gawans enjoy the reciprocal hospitality of their hosts. Indeed, eating the foods served on other islands is one of the pleasures of kula. However, kula activities proper are centered in speech (*livala; livalela kura*) in which a man attempts to persuade his partners or others to release desired shells, talks to partners about shells on his paths, and listens (*rega*) to the kula talk of others. As part of these activities, a man goes around to see and admire kula shells, and learn their names and histories. In general, he attempts to increase his knowledge about shell identities, locations, and transaction histories with the ultimate aim of incrementing his own kula skills and abilities to obtain desired shells. Thus kula speech[4] – an important medium involved in "working" one's kula – is a productive activity yielding shells and the knowledge necessary to obtain shells.

Eating, on the other hand, although an important part of the visit, does not yield shells. Indeed, one of the devices a Gawan might use to persuade his partner to release a desired shell is to refuse to eat at the latter's home until the shell has been "thrown" (*lev*, throw, release) to him (see Chapter 4 for a consideration of the demonstration of constraint in acts of "not eating").

This distinction of productivity between kula activities centered in language (speaking and listening) as opposed to eating, as well as the connection between them in kula, is sharply conveyed in standard ritual insults called out jokingly to recipient men at the distribution of food in a kula feast held on Gawa before a major competition (*uvelaku*). One such insult goes: "You don't kula, you go along 'emptily' (*sabwamu*), you only eat."[5] The term *sabwamu* refers to the idea that something lacks an "inner seed," is empty, or without reason. The point in this case is that nothing is achieved, no kula shells acquired that transcend the particular context of the action and that can be brought back to Gawa; rather, the recipient returns to Gawa empty-handed, for he only consumes.[6]

This type of insult is part of a rhetorical context in which food recipients are supposed to shout out the names of shells that they claim they will obtain during the coming kula trip. In fact, these assertions are not expected to be truthful; the claims are rhetorical. In the midst of food distribution, and a coming kula trip in which men will hope to eat well at the homes of their partners (and are indeed dependent upon their hosts for adequate food supplies), the dialectical relation between eating and kula is brought into focus. On the one hand, the requirement that men make rather grandiose claims draws Gawan minds to what goes beyond the present context and is emphasized as the real aim of the coming trip: the acquisition of the (nonconsumable) shells. On the other hand, the satiric insults crystallize the underlying dialectical tension that unites the two activities of eating and kula. The former is defined as purposeless and unable to surpass the moment of the action itself – as failing to create anything with further potential or yield – the other as productive, and capable of extending spacetime (creating something that goes beyond the immediate moment and locus of action, and thus beyond the body of the actor, and that yields an object that itself condenses potentialities for further transactions).

At the same time, the hospitality in food from partners on other islands is regarded as a reciprocal return or replacement (*mapu-ra*) for one's own hospitality; in this sense, it is a positive value product of one's own food giving. I shall return later to inter-island transactions in food hospitality to examine these matters further. For the present, the main point is that what is uppermost in this context is the notion of consumption as a nonproductive, self-focused act rather than as an aspect of the exchange process linking kula partners. Like ritual insults in other contexts (see section on "remembering") these insults and their accompanying boasts bring into the present (here, the uvelaku feast) a focus on the future (*wunikougwa*, [the time] ahead) and on the acquisition of value products that themselves "contain a future," by reminding food recipients that eating in itself has, as it were, no future.

Let us turn back from the problem of consumption to that of food transmission. Whereas food-giving to overseas visitors is at the base of a man's ability to create successful kula relations for himself, a woman may become a *guyo-vira* (*guyaw*-woman) by her generous cooking for visitors, aiding her husband in his kula endeavors. But since she does not directly transact kula shells and create partnerships herself,[7] she cannot acquire the fame created by handling shells with their long-term, extended circulation beyond Gawa. This level of self-transformation is confined to men. She is nevertheless extremely important in the persuasive process – both to her husband (who listens to her opinion and whom she aids in making himself influential with his partner), and to her immediate dala kinsmen, who may also be concerned with her opinion and for whose kula partners (as well as for her husband's) she may make mats and skirts. Finally, she is important to the partners of these men (especially those of her husband) who try to persuade her to view them favorably so that she will agree to the transmission of desired shells.

The role of women as cooks rather than direct kula transactors is connected with a more general position women occupy in the public transaction of food. In contexts of collective, public food giving, as at mortuary transactions or entertainments, it is men who determine the distribution. In this public context, men rather than women perform the acts of dispensing food, separating it from the self.[8] The fact that female activities are typified by cooking and the preparation of food for consumption is a feature that in certain respects associates women with eating rather than with the giving of food. This feature emerges most strongly in the context of witchcraft (see Chapter 9). One should not, however, stress it at the expense of the transactive significance of cooking, for the latter involves women at the very center of the transaction of cooked food, as they prepare the food for others to eat. What should be emphasized in general is that the part women play in value production associates them closely with the medium of comestibles, especially garden produce, a feature that is critical in the position of women, and that of the female gender principle, in the transformative process.

As indicated in Chapter 2, yam and taro gardens are central to Gawa's subsistence and affluence. Although other edibles are used in major transactions, yams and taro typify garden produce (*karu*) for Gawans, and they are the core of major transactions in comestibles – pigs (*bulukwa*) and fish (*in*) occupying more specialized positions.[9] Moreover, although both yams and taro appear in these contexts, yams – which, as I have pointed out, all Gawans harvest roughly at the same time and which are storable for several months after harvest – are considered somewhat more important for major transactions. Of the two varieties of yams that Gawans plant, *kuvi* and *teitu*, the former produces fewer but larger tubers to the planting and is more highly prized for major transactions, including raw food gifts or immediate hospitality to kula partners.

When a family harvests its yearly yam produce, it separates the produce into three groups: Yams of intermediate size, by far the greatest proportion, go into seed yams (*yagougu*), some of which can also be eaten during the year; a second group is put aside for daily consumption (*karu*) – these are yams that are damaged, relatively small (*gouwa*), or of medium size. A third group, the largest and best yams of the harvest, are put aside for visitors (especially a man's kula partners), or for special transactional obligations (e.g., community entertainments, special marriage gifts for women, etc.). Yams of the latter category (*karagira*; *karu*) may be referred to figuratively as *youd*, a term meaning "things" or "goods," which is not ordinarily used for comestibles.[10]

The reference to yams as *youd* indicates that they are not just ordinary comestibles, but can yield something more. Gawans sometimes contrast food unfavorably with more durable goods because of its short time span and the fact that it disappears (*-tamwaw*) in bodily consumption and must be continually replenished. However, it is as if yams set aside for special transactions are able, in certain respects, to exceed this limitation.[11]

Although the comestibles used in hospitality for visitors or other major transactions are not, of course, confined to yams, the harvest classification encapsulates the basic dialectic of consumption and transmission, and the changed potentials of food in transmissive contexts. The procedure of categorizing yams introduces differentiated spatiotemporal potentials into the harvest, as Gawans set into separate piles, yams for the next planting and reproduction of the garden; yams to be used up for immediate or daily family consumption; and yams to be reserved for later transaction to others. Whereas seed yams go to reproduce themselves and the gardens – and thus to maintain the harvest cycle itself (see Chapter 4) – and yams for daily consumption go to produce the bodies of the producers, those set aside for visitors and major transactions (where they will be transmitted raw, *gagayata*, rather than cooked, *minumenu*) go to produce something other than themselves, and something beyond the persons of the producers. It is this latter category that represents the portion that Gawans set apart from the processes of reproduction and immediate subsistence to "work upon [their own] work" (Touraine, 1977:25) and so become active in their own positive value transformation.

MODES OF INTERSUBJECTIVE SPACETIME:
HOSPITALITY AND KULA EXCHANGE

Reciprocal acts of hospitality between Gawans and their overseas partners have the capacity to create a particular mode and value level of intersubjective spacetime in the island world. I now consider in more detail aspects of the spatiotemporal structure of this hospitality and its articulation with that of kula shell exchange.

As we have seen, when a Gawan man goes to another island to visit, his kula partner(s) (*burawura*) in that community will be responsible for feeding him and offering him general hospitality, just as *he* is responsible for *them* on their visits to Gawa. In addition to cooked foods eaten during the stay, hospitality includes gifts of raw produce to be taken back to Gawa, as well as aid in obtaining pigs on request (*kerasi*). Women's skirts, mats, Papua New Guinea money, and other such goods may also be considered part of the overall relationship, but these gifts are more specialized elements of the basic food-giving relationship.[12] As I have pointed out elsewhere (Munn, 1983:289), this reciprocal hospitality "continues as long as the partnership irrespective of whether shells are 'thrown' between [the partners on a given visit].... As one man said: a Gawan can throw a shell to a partner one year and then not throw [shells] ... for a time, but he will still eat at that man's home."

The overseas hospitality relation is one example of a form of transacting for which Gawans use the general term *skwayobwa*. A distinctive feature of skwayobwa is that it involves reciprocal transacting that is not temporally specific to a particular end (see Munn, 1983:289). Skwayobwa continues without the assumption of closure (-*kous*, finish) effected by an equivalent (*skwera*, square or -*bod*, level) reciprocation in any given "moment" of the relationship.[13]

Comestibles are the core of skwayobwa, although as in overseas hospitality, other items may be involved since the term connotes an ambience of regular aid. Although certain elements within the overall hospitality relationship between partners are subject to an accounting of equivalence (notably that of aid in obtaining pigs), the visiting relationship itself is of the "ongoing" skwayobwa type. This kind of repetitive process, an exchange lacking sharply defined spatiotemporal units of debt and debt closure, is essential to the continuance of the kula partnership.

Thus Gawans regard this hospitality between men as the foundation (*wouwu-ra*) of the kula relationship, because without it partnerships cannot be maintained. The term *wouwura* means "its foundation," or "originating cause." It thus carries the spatiotemporal connotations of being "below" (at the base) and "prior to" something else, as well as being the potentializing source out of which the latter emerged. As one man suggested to me, the wouwura of kula is the gifts regularly made to one's partner who later remembers (*i-raruway*) this skwayobwa by giving a kula shell. I shall have more to say of the notion of remembering later; here, we may note that skwayobwa has the potential to extend a man's spatiotemporal control by acting upon the mind (*nano-ra*) of the other so that in the future he remembers and is thus influenced to give a kula shell (itself the sum of still further potentials for spatiotemporal extension).

Skwayobwa is closely related to another type of transaction called *pokala* that is well known from Malinowski's (1922) account of Trobriand island kula. Gawan pokala are gifts consisting of noncomestibles (such as money, cloth, tobacco, or relatively low-quality kula shells) made with the aim of acquiring a particular kula shell, or to affect a specific transaction. In this sense, pokala is temporally specific, and connected with a particular transaction, a feature that some Gawan informants used to distinguish it from skwayobwa. Moreover, pokala is not ordinarily reciprocated.

However, Gawans occasionally use the term *pokala* in a broad sense to cover all ongoing gifts and aid they give to their partners: In the context of relatively enduring relationships, the line between the two types of transactive process appears blurred. Similarly, skwayobwa may be used as the generic term covering attempts to obtain specific shells in the context of an ongoing partnership. Indeed, Gawans sometimes say they do *not* pokala their partners; rather, pokala in its narrow sense of a particular payment, is made to persuade a *nonpartner* in the absence of previous persuasive gift giving. Skawyobwa, in short, is perceived as a temporally generalized process through which a store of influence is built up between partners.

Considering skwayobwa in terms of its central component of food giving, we may say that food giving has a potential for yielding kula shells, but comestibles and shells are not directly exchanged as equivalents or as payments (*meyisa-ra* or *mapu-ra*, its return, replacement)[14] for each other. Rather, the exchange of comestibles in hospitality is the *dynamic base, and condition which underlies kula shell exchange between partners*. Food giving generates the mutual influence through which transformation to another value level (and mode) of inter-island spacetime – namely, kula shell exchange – can be effected.[15] As will become apparent in later chapters, this double-tiered structure of transactive nexuses with repetitive acts of food giving as the creative base of the process is a model that in variant forms is fundamental to Gawan value transformation.

Food skwayobwa and kula transactions involve systematic differences of spacetime. I shall briefly outline some of the more obvious of these differences here. Hospitality takes place most regularly between immediate kula partners (*burawura*) on each side of ego (i.e., in each kula direction) with whom he transacts shells directly (see Figure 1). Somewhat less frequent, but also important, are hospitality relations with partners just beyond these (for instance, at Sinaketa in the Trobriands, or in southern Muyuw) with whom he does not legitimately transact shells directly. These men are one's most immediate *muli* with whom, men say, a man visits on his kula travels, and by whom he is "fed." Visits to burawura and muli are not restricted to major kula journeys, but, as indicated earlier (see Chapter 2), may also take place on other casual journeys. Visits to muli, however, being somewhat more distant, are more likely to be confined to major kula trips, at least in the north.

In hospitality relations, transactions of comestibles and other goods are limited in inter-island space. Restricted to inter-island consociates, they create, moreover, dyadic or closed exchange relations between the two participants in any given case (cf. Damon, 1978:130). If partners formed relationships with each other only in terms of skwayobwa, each dyad in which a man participated would constitute an isolated intersubjective spacetime of repeated reciprocities with its own internal timing of transactions relative to his other hospitality relations; but there would be no formal connection (or potential for connection) between these separate spacetimes. The structure would be similar to that familiar from Lévi-Strauss's (1949) model of restricted exchange.

Although kula shell transactions also entail dyadic exchange units, in that a man and an immediate partner exchange shells of opposite categories,[16] these transactions are not restricted exchanges or closed spacetimes. The shells that the two men transact travel beyond them, and these travels may be sequentially followed and defined in any given instance as the path (*keda*) of a shell. Thus a connective overlay is constructed that opens up the intersubjective spacetime of a man's different burawura (and immediate muli) relationships, creating implications and connectivities that transcend them.

For instance, if a northern Woodlark man A gives a Gawan man B an armshell, which B gives northward to a Kitavan man C, and C later gives to D of Sinaketa, then B's respective, separate dyadic relationships with A and C are brought into spatiotemporal relationship with each other via the travels of the shell; in addition, the burawara relation of C and D is brought into a specific relation with C–B and B–A (and so forth) through the mediating travels of the shell. Although this provides only a minimal, simplified model of the process to which I am referring, it makes the point that each dyad is matrixed in a more comprehensive spacetime created by the capacity of shells to form linking paths that transcend any given pair of transactors, and any particular transaction between them. Moreover, it will be noted that for any given transactor, the shells do not merely have the capacity to connect those different dyads in which he participates (i.e., his burawura relations), but they also link these with others in which he is not a direct participant (e.g., A–B and B–C, with C–D);[17] of course, *some* of these latter connections are also outside his consociate network and consist of people with whom he may never interact at all (see Chapter 2).

Without going in any great detail into the complexities of kula structuring processes, I suggest simply that the example points up a central characteristic of kula spacetime: namely, that the travels of kula shells create an emergent spacetime of their own that transcends that of specific, immediate transactions. This spacetime may be thought of as that of circulation in contrast to such transactions as those of skwayobwa or any other similar action system in which the movement of media does not create an emergent order of spatiotemporal structuring involving *named*, detachable media that take on a circulatory life of their own. As indicated in Chapter 2, kula circulation entails a bidirectional process of shell movements in which any given shell may travel around the area in such a way that it can potentially return to any community or person who handled it at some previous time, and continue around beyond that community in an "endless" unidirectional circulation.[18]

This general cycling is formed, however, in terms of discontinuous transactions that begin with an opening or starting shell (*vaga*) and should end eventually with a squaring or closing shell (*gulugwalu, kudu*), although shells may also default (*toubu*). Transactions have to be renewed with further transactions (new vaga), in order to generate continuity. The timing of renewals is complex, and a lineal temporality or chaining of transactions one after the other does not necessarily take place. For instance, in long-term transactions, one or more intermediate starting gifts (called *kurarera* and other terms by Gawans; cf. Campbell, 1983a; Damon, 1983a:333; Malinowski, 1922:98, 355–7) may be given at different times after an initial vaga has been transacted, but as subordinate components tagged to the first transaction. These shells are also vaga in the sense that they create their own debt and spatiotemporal cycle (each one must eventually be reciprocated), serving to renew initial starting gifts on a path of partners, or contributing to the establishment of a new partnership path. A given vaga transaction may actually finish before or after the closing of one or more of its subsidiary transactions. Similarly, a named shell may return to the same island community on a *different* transaction (to different men) before its closing equivalent has been received in a previous transaction (to other men).[19] Hence the timing and duration of transactions is dependent upon the various contingencies of the circulation process and need not take the form of a "linear succession"; we have rather to deal with a complex interplay of the incommensurable spacetimes of different transactions than with any homogeneous spacetime defined by determinate calendric frames (cf. Bourdieu, 1977:105).

Discontinuities also occur in individual partnerships; as indicated in Chapter 2, these partnerships do not necessarily form continuous circuits (-*parat*) around the ring at any given time.[20] Since shells establish or maintain partnerships as they travel, partnerships may be transient and never complete more than a sector of the area of possible circulation. Similarly, completed, long-term paths may atrophy if they do not have shells (most importantly, starting shells that create debt) traveling on them. Thus partnerships are not fixed relationships, but are grounded in and constituted by discontinuous transactions and shell circulation. The capacity for creating an unending circulation in the overall kula process is predicated on creating particular transactions with endings. For any individual kula man, keeping his kula continuous and strong requires that he engage in acts of both closure (equalizing), and debt renewal (the creation of increment, hierarchizing; see Munn, 1983).

The circulation that characterizes the overall capacities of shell movement reacts back upon the calendrics of kula travels, requiring a loosely coordinated scheduling across the islands. I shall use this feature to give a simple example of the spatiotemporal coordinations of experience and the contributions to the construction of a common inter-island world that emerge from the circulation of kula shells. A central contingency affecting major kula sailings must necessarily be, of course, the locations of large shell collections and of specific, high-ranking shells at any given time. Gawans must watch where shells are, and when and where they move; this watching includes a concern with areas outside of Gawan consociation as well as within, and can be seen as part of the construction of a form of coordinated kula timing across the islands.

In January 1980, one man explained to me that the Yeguma people had recently traveled south to Raramani for kula shells and that the southern Muyuw would be waiting for them to come back; after this, the southern Muyuw hamlets could go to Yeguma to obtain armshells. Once the southern Muyuwans had obtained their shells, then northern Muyuwans could travel south to bring back armshells to their hamlets. After this, Gawans could then sail to northern Muyuw to obtain armshells. He thought that perhaps about the same time, representatives of the Raramani peoples would visit southern Muyuw to obtain necklaces currently in those hamlets.

As it turned out, Gawans went for necklaces before armshells (for reasons too complex to detail here, but which included the fact that northerners had themselves obtained large shell collections from the west by the time Gawans were able to travel) and the particularities of the sequence my informant projected were not worked out precisely, owing to the complexities of kula politics. But the general point remains the same: the circulatory travels of kula shells engage a loosely coordinated major kula sailing or visiting calendar in which one community's major sailings are contingent upon and relative to those of others across the region in which shells circulate.

Such wide-reaching inter-island coordinations of expectancies and events engaged through the regulatory power of kula circulation are not, of course, implicated in skwayobwa relations. In addition to the fact that skwayobwa relations are strictly dyadic and confined to consociates, one must note that although the goods involved may in some instances endure beyond the immediate transaction context, the core of the relation is in edibles, which will sooner or later be consumed. Even when the hospitality gift has a longer-term potentiality than cooked food, Gawans do not treat any further transactions in which it may occur as forming a path that connects future transactors of the item with previous ones. Thus such goods or produce do not in themselves enable the particular transactions of any pair of actors to be surpassed and generalized.

In contrast, kula shells are named, their travels followed around, (-kikura) and their material enduring. As one Gawan said: Kula shells "don't die" (gera b-i-kariga) or "rot" (gera b-ei-pwas). This durability is commensurate with their power of circulation. Another man pointed out in a public speech: Kula "never finishes" (gera b-ei-kous); "it never disappears" (gera b-i-tamwaw); "it goes around time and again" (tuta tuta b-i-taavin). In sum, in contemporary kula we have a highly generalized process that transcends the actor and the immediacy of any particular transactional "moment" to create its own regulatory dynamic. I discuss the significance of this generalizing process for the constitution of self in Chapter 5.

SUBJECTIVE CONVERSIONS AND REMEMBERING

I have pointed to the fundamental persuasiveness inherent in food-giving acts, particularly in those at the foundation of kula exchange. This aspect may be considered a subjective potential or conversion power of an act – its capacity for affecting actors' attitudes or intentions.[21] These subjective potentials are necessary mediating aspects of any transformation cycle, marking the fact that the process is intersubjective in the primary sense of forming or attempting to form a specific kind of relation between the minds (nano-) of actors. In any given case, the capacity of an act to yield the desired subjective conversion is, of course, uncertain.

To convey the notion of persuasion Gawans use such expressions as "makes" (-vaga), "turns" (-katouvira), or "carries" (-kouw) his or her "mind" (nano-ra). A person whose mind has been affected in this way "agrees" (-tagwara and other terms)[22] to act according to the desires (magi-ra, or yawu-ra, his or her wants)[23] of the person who has moved his or her mind. If a period of time is involved, such a person may be said to remember (-raruway) a donor and the latter's gifts (see discussion of "remembering" later in the chapter).[24] Among nonverbal acts of persuasion, it is, of course, not only food giving that acts persuasively but the giving of material goods in general. Although food is the basic nonverbal persuasive medium, the transaction of a kula shell is also a mode of persuasion aimed at generating the agreement of others to send other shells back to the transactor (see Munn, 1983).

Through the hoped-for subjective outcomes of his acts, the donor in effect reconstitutes himself in the mind of the other, thus transforming his own level of control beyond himself. Clearly, however, the evidence of these control capacities and of the positive view of the donor taken by the other, lies only in their objectivation through his acquisition (sooner or later) of whatever was desired from the recipient, or of some objective token of that desire. Regularly demonstrating his ability to objectivate these desired subjective outcomes, the actor climbs (*i-mwen*) – raising his own standing or value by coordinating the mind of another with his own (gaining consent) and creating, as it were, an external agent of the self. This uncertain process may be viewed as the basic generative unit of the long-term transformational cycle by which a man ultimately constitutes himself as guyaw. The capacity to regularly demonstrate such subjective outcomes is systematically developed in kula exchange, and is crystallized in the symbolism of fame.

It is, of course, in its capacity to create subjective conversions that a transmissive act ultimately works to yield further productive potentials for the donor; by the same token, it is the medium's power in the subjective realm that gives it productive capacities, extending its life, so to speak, through an entailment of outcomes that transcend the moment of transaction and of the recipient's use or consumption. The Gawan emphasis on such subjective conversions is illustrated by their notion of remembering (*-raruway*). Remembering has a double aspect: The gift should not only make the recipient remember the donor so that he subsequently repays him; but also, most notably in kula, the donor must remember his *own* transactions in order to stimulate, if necessary, the memory of the recipient. Gawans emphasize memory in relation to gift giving in both these and wider senses.

Remembering enters in as an important dimension of the process when transactions are not *immediately* closed and when they do not involve the closure of a *previous* transaction. We have seen that Gawans refer to closing acts as "finishing" (*-kous*) a transaction or sometimes metaphorically (especially in kula) as a "dead person" (*toumata*) (cf. Campbell, 1983a:216). Closure, like consumption, has negative spatiotemporal capacities, even though it involves a desired equivalence. (I return to this point in connection with kula later.)

The sense in which a skwayobwa process may be seen as being converted into remembrance is illustrated in the following case, in which the long-term process is later expected to yield transactions of another (more expansive) spatiotemporal level.

A little girl living in another hamlet from her young brother (a boy of about seven), sent him a basket of chestnuts when these nuts had ripened in the 1980 season. He and his father immediately made the appropriate token return of a basket of yams. (Such reciprocal giving, initiated by the girl, would probably be repeated in future years.) The boy's father told me that when his son grows up the boy may then "remember" and give the girl yams for her marriage gifts to her husband's kin. He pointed out that this type of transaction may be carried on between children who count themselves as cross-sex siblings (*nu–ta*, see Chapter 2) but live in different hamlets (i.e., this type of gift maintains connection between residentially divided siblings, or in some instances may create sibling relations not already defined).

It will be noted that the boy's token return gift of yams to the girl is of the type appropriate from a male sibling in a marriage gift, thus prefiguring the possible form his return could take in the future if he remembers the little girl. Moreover, the intersubjective spacetime constituted through her initiation of the skwayobwa transaction of chestnuts and yams (which links the girl and her immediate family in one hamlet to the boy and his family in another hamlet) may eventually lead to an even wider and more enduring nexus of relationships should the boy indeed remember her later with marriage gifts. In that case, he and his kin would be connected not only to the girl and her kin, but, as indicated in the previous chapter, to her husband and *his* kin, a nexus that could last until the death of the girl or her husband. Thus the transformation of spacetime initiated by the girl's gift could then be transformed onto a still more expansive spatiotemporal level involving affinal linkages.

Gawans frequently connect remembering to transmissive acts in a more general way. For instance, they speak of remembering people as the regular donors of certain kinds of gifts, or of remembering them in terms of and because of what they gave. This memory may be associated with the hands (*yama-*) that hold and make the gift. For example, when someone who has made such gifts has gone away, the recipient might think sadly of that person as "hands that gave." At a person's death, mourners may refuse to eat certain foods because the deceased gave them these (or other) foods to eat, or for buwaa marriage gifts. They do this in memory of the deceased. Conversely, gifts are an essential sign that a person has remembered one, and one's previous gifts. Giving may generate a recipient's remembrance of the donor or be a sign that a previous recipient has remembered one. The memory to be induced by the donor in the recipient (as for instance in the example of the little girl's gift to her brother) projects the recipient's mind toward the future (*wunikougwa, ahead*), in this way extending the transaction (the past) and the particular media involved beyond themselves and holding them, as it were, in the form of an ongoing potentiality that is not finished. This type of memory may culminate in objectifying acts, which, as the finalizing outcomes of earlier transactions, synthesize the long-term past within the ongoing present for both donor and recipient (see Munn, 1983). By remembering, one keeps the objective medium or act from disappearing.

Given the circulating character of kula, Gawan notions of memory in the context of kula exchange make these ways of constructing spatiotemporal connectivity especially explicit. In contrast to a gulugwalu closing gift, a vaga[25] initiatory gift must be remembered by the recipient both as a debt to its donor and – when further transacted – as a shell for which others are indebted to him as a donor, and for which he expects a future return. Thus when a vaga shell is transacted, it should be converted into the memories of both recipient and donor as a debt (*buki*, book) in order eventually to be reobjectivated as a gulugwalu.[26] But when a gulugwalu is transacted onward (to the next person on the path to whom it is owed), the donor can forget (*-lumlev*, from the root, *-lev*, to release or throw away), because the transaction is finished; nothing further is then entailed in it beyond the immediate objectivation of one's control capacities, and the demonstration to partners of one's ability to meet a debt. In contrast to the vaga, the gulugwala is a man's *vavaga*, his "possession" or acquisition to which he is entitled. It has already been made. As one man put it: "We don't remember a gulugwalu; it is a dead person" (*gulugwalu gera bi-ta-raruway, toumata*). It will be noted from this, that the completion of a kula transaction has both positive and negative aspects, for closure (equalization) is expected and necessary as the objectivation of the potential entailed in a vaga, but it also ends the subjective conversion process – the intersubjective nexus of remembering – which the vaga has set up. If there are no further unfinished transactions on a given path of partners, or no new vaga started when the gulugwalu is returned, then the path itself will disappear (see Campbell, 1983a; Damon, 1983a; Munn, 1983).

As long as a vaga shell of medium or high rank that has passed through a man's hands (or that of a man whose kula paths he has inherited) has not received its matching return, it is important that he remember its name and routing regardless of the length of time since its transaction; in this way he is able to follow (*-kikura*) it, keeping it from disappearing or defaulting even if the initial Gawan transactor is dead. In order to awaken (*-vaguri*) this long-term debt, the claimant sends a shell of the same type as the original vaga (for example, an armshell if the original was an armshell) to the final recipient of the earlier shell, or to his heir. This person is usually on the far west or south side of the ring. In doing this the claimant must send along the information that he is calling for (*douw*) the shell of the previous transaction (*levabogwa*, the old or earlier, *-bogwa*, throw), referring to the latter by name. For instance, he should say that he is calling for Manutasopi, if Manutasopi was the original shell that is to be matched. This new vaga is called the "revivifyor" or "awakener" (*kalamamata*); as a new objectivation of the old debt, it is intended to remind (-*katabogwa nano-ra*, literally, make his mind past) the defaulter of this long past shell transaction, and persuade him to send the claimant an appropriate return. To be persuasive, the claimant must show that he remembers the old shell by using its name in referring to the new transaction (*levavaw*, new or more recent throw).

Verbally as well as through the movement of the new shell itself, he reawakens the dormant past (*mutabogwa*) within the present (*nagera*).[27] If the debtor's mind is moved by this transaction, he will send the return, but if not, more shells may be required to reactivate the debt and obtain closure. I shall have more to say of the notion of awakening later. Here we may note its connection with motion (the movement of a shell) and with the attempt to create a reciprocal "remembering" joining self and other.

Whereas in the above example the focus is on the memory of the creditor (by means of which he is then able to revive the memory of a debtor), in other contexts emphasis may also be placed on the debtor's memory. When a vaga is being thrown to a new recipient, the donor may insult (-*karawouw*) him in order to "spark his stomach" (-*yik nuwa-ra*) so that he will be reminded that the current gift has a future entailment, and be aroused to make a quick return (whether of an equivalent shell or of another vaga that will continue the present transaction). Stereotypic insults used in this context generally refer to such matters as the weakness of the recipient in kula and his inability to make appropriate returns, but the speaker may remark as well upon actual incidents in which the recipient has failed or has deceived his partner, and warn him against further behavior of this kind. Milder warnings may also be made when the partners are on good terms. Thus the recipient is defined negatively (treated as if he were descending, *busi*, or low, *ou-taginaw*) just at the moment when in fact he is climbing (-*mwen*) through the acquisition of a desired shell. Conversely, the donor is directing attention to his own control over the situation by asserting the kula inferiority, deceit, or lack of control of the recipient, just when he himself is in fact losing control over his shell. In this liminal moment, the shells are quite literally "betwixt and between" the two men, and the donor's certain physical control over the object is being converted into what is only an uncertain control or influence over the mind of the other. It is possible that his shell could disappear rather than produce an actualization of the potential entailed in his act.

The same sort of procedure is a standard part of the Gawan community entertainments in which the feast givers jokingly chastise recipients as they hand over to them the huge conical piles of raw yams that mark the close of the vaga performance of an entertainment cycle. The reciprocating entertainment is owned by the recipients and will begin sometime later at the latters' discretion. I discuss this chastisement in some detail in

Plate 2. An eminent Gawan kula man receiving armshells from a young man of a Mwadau island (northern Muyuw) community who has inherited the kula of the Gawan's recently deceased partner (see Chapter 5, n. 5). The fine armshells in front of the Gawan, who sits in a respectful position listening with a lime spatula in his hand as he chews betel, have just been released by the donor. The donor in this case only mildly harangues the Gawan, warning him that he (the donor) will treat the Gawan in the future in exactly the same way that the latter treats him: For example, any deception or failures to make shell returns on the Gawan's part will be matched by the donor. The woman and child watching are relatives of the Mwadau man.

connection with the entertainments (Chapter 8), but here we may note that as in the kula case, the stated aim of these jokes is to make the recipients remember their debt to the donors.

In these examples we can see clearly the sense in which an attempt is being made to transform intersubjective spacetime positively, as recipients in the process of acquiring kula shells or food are directed to project the current experience of receiving in terms of their future, reciprocal giving. In effect, the appropriate extension and synthesis of time (the capacity to draw the present forward into the future and later, the future and past into the present) and the coordinate extension of spatial control in the connection of self and other, can only occur through the conversion of the objective gift into subjective remembering. In this way it will not disappear but will be retained as a potentiality within the ongoing present and at some later time (and place), can be converted again into objective reciprocating acts. If memory fails, however, transactions and their media will simply disappear and spatiotemporal connectivities cannot be generated. This is well illustrated by the following case in which the notion of remembering was used rhetorically in admonishing Gawans for an apparent lapse in taking up responsibilities necessary to prepare for a future kula competition.

In 1980, the death of an eminent kula man interrupted preparations for the initial feast preceding an uvelaku kula competition. The current sponsor of the uvelaku, an influential man of the Nukwasisi kumila (see Chapter 2), had, however, previously arranged to bring in some trade-store food for the feast. Because of the death (and for other reasons I do not discuss here), he decided to distribute the food simply by giving it to Gawans to eat at a public gathering. But this feast was not the uvelaku; nor was it a payment for group work. Rather, it was given, as Gawans said, "emptily" (sabwamu) – without any specific rationale – so that its consumption was not justified by any creative project, or anything Gawans had done.

Concerned by this situation, a man of the Nukubay kumila that was cosponsoring the competition spoke to the assembly, addressing himself specifically to the cosponsors. "You Nukubay," he said, "we all have authority over (kareiwaga) the uvelaku.... You remember; if not, someone should tell me. I think you don't remember. If you remembered, when D. returned [with the trade-store food for the uvelaku feast], the senior Nukubay men and the Nukwasisi would have made a decision (kareiwaga). I think we [Nukubay] may sink into the sea.... Today, whoever runs the feast, will give us food and we eat [i.e., without rationale]. I think you don't remember. ... it is our 'book' (debt). I certainly remember our book. The man who died[a] [owed] a whole lot."[28]

The speaker continued, pointing to the fact that in the last (1978) uvelaku, kula partners on the northern island of Kitava had given several pigs to the previous uvelaku sponsors (guyaw of the other two Gawan kumila who had cosponsored the earlier uvelaku). At the current uvelaku, therefore, the sponsors must obtain pigs from their own Muyuw partners (i.e., their partners for armshells) to make a return to the previous sponsors for the pigs from Kitava that the present sponsors had eaten.

In this case, the speaker reminds Gawans (especially the cosponsors of his own kumila) that the food now being eaten is, in fact, the food for the uvelaku, and that it is being consumed without being used to reciprocate the previous uvelaku feast (a vaga for which the current sponsors were to make return). The speaker treats the baseless consumption of this food as a failure to remember the debt. In fact, as we shall see in connection with one of the stereotypic jokes used at entertainment finales (Chapter 8), forgetting may also be described metaphorically as "eating."

The structure of the uvelaku competition is significant in understanding

---

[a] The deceased was an important kula man of the Nukubay kumila.

the spatiotemporal implications of the speaker's statement. The contemporary Gawan uvelaku is organized in terms of a moiety-like, community structure in which men of two kumila form a single sponsoring and cosponsoring cohort, while a senior kula man of one of the opposite two kumila is to be the main winner. The latter and others of his cohort are the key immediate recipients of the uvelaku feasts and receive the prizes of money, food and other items for which, in the case of a vaga uvelaku, they become indebted to the sponsoring cohort. If a vaga uvelaku has been performed for incoming necklaces, then the later reciprocal uvelaku must be for armshells, and vice versa; for any given transaction the opposed pairs of Gawan kumila are articulated with the opposed kula directions.

Similarly, the debt between the two cohorts draws in part on their inter-island partnerships in the two directions, and involves comestibles (notably pigs) received at the time of uvelaku visits. In the present example, the debt of the Nukubay and Nukwasisi to the Kulabutu and Malasi sponsors of the northern uvelaku in 1978 included pigs consumed on Kitava that were provided by the Kitavan partners of the latter sponsors. This part of the debt should be repaid to them by pigs received from the partners of the Nukubay and Nukwasisi *in Muyuw* on the occasion of the next uvelaku visit. The unremembered debt thus involved not simply local, but also inter-island connections and events on different islands.

In short, forgetting the debt entails a breakdown in a particular spatiotemporal process connecting members of the Gawan kumila pairs to each other, to their kula partners on other islands, and to the opposed shell directions of the inter-island world; similarly, the previous northern uvelaku visit remains unreciprocated by its appropriate future southern conversion. In effect, the immediate situation (which it will be recalled is occasioned in part by the death of a major kula man – a disruptive, fragmenting factor in kula paths and activities) makes it seem as if these linkages, and the positive intersubjective transformations they entail, are falling apart. The negative transformation of the Gawan community and the selves of its members is aptly rendered in the act of eating up the uvelaku feast, and the speaker draws attention to the negativity implicit in this action by connecting it with its mental correlate of forgetting.

GAWAN CONCEPTS OF MIND, WILL, AND DECISION MAKING

These considerations of the subjective potentials of food transmission and their negation in consumption lead us to consider further the grounding of the process of persuasion and consent in Gawan concepts of mind and will. Gawans regard decision making, intention, and cognition as being located in the mind (*nano-*). The mind is said to be in the forehead, (*daba-*) or sometimes in the throat (*kayo-*, neck, throat).[29] As in our own usage, "mind" refers not only to the locus of mental functions but also to the notion of a cognitive state or viewpoint. Thus Gawans speak of "his or her mind" (*nano-ra*) to refer to a person's view or opinion. The related term *-nanam* is the general label for cognitive acts (thinking, thinking about) and in its nominal form may also refer to "thought or viewpoint" (*kara-nanams*, his or her thoughts on something).

Like the Trobrianders and Muyuwans (see Damon, 1978:75; Weiner, 1976:217, 1983:695) Gawans emphasize the intrinsic hiddenness of another person's views or intentions, an uncertainty expressed in the phrase "we do not know (*-kakin*) his (or her) mind." One cannot know another's mind because it is inside the body (*wo-ra*) and thus invisible (cf. *-kin*, see, *-kakin*, know). Although intentions are made known and overt through signs such as speech and other acts, these signs (especially those of speech) could themselves be deceptive as they only indirectly mediate the hidden mind of another; pretense and deception (*katudew*), subjects of some concern to Gawans, are always possibilities. All action goes on within the underlying framework of these presuppositions, but acts of reciprocal long-term transmission are the major means of mediating this problem so as to form over time, some experience of trust or reliability (*-nanamis*).

These notions of uncertainty in intersubjective relations are themselves inseparable from the Gawan political formulation of the person as an independent locus of decision-making powers (*kareiwaga*). The important concept of *kareiwaga* refers to both the act of deciding, or a decision, and a legitimate sphere of authority or decision making. In different contexts, *ra-kareiwaga* may specify "his or her decision" or "his or her sphere of authority" (see Lamphere, 1971:95 for a very similar concept in another egalitarian society). It is ultimately one's own kareiwaga as to whether one refuses (*-pek*) or consents and "listens" (*-reg*) to another's requests.

This assumption refers to young children as well as to adults. Both may be persuaded to work (for example, by the expectation of appropriate material payment or of being fed at the workplace), but whether they consent or not is their own kareiwaga. For instance, if a man wants workers for a major canoe job, he must gain the consent of others to work for him. They signify their willingness simply by coming on the appointed day of work. Although kin obligations and other factors may enter into a person's decision as to whether he or she will help or not, the decision itself is up to the individual. I have occasionally heard some men complain about the recalcitrance of young men who, they say, do not want to do the necessary canoe work, but are preoccupied with their own interests and cannot be persuaded to come. Thus each person (male or female) is felt to be the locus of an essentially autonomous or sovereign will – a decision-making power – that is seen as the ultimate basis for action.

This notion of autonomy also holds with respect to the group that forms the immediate collective matrix or social identity of the self, that is, the matrilineal dala; and in addition, the residential hamlet group, which, as we saw in the previous chapter, has certain close associations with the dala. Although a dala may be represented by more than one hamlet, each dala has at least one hamlet headed by its current leading guyaw, and tends to be most explicitly identified with this hamlet; moreover, each dala with its own guyaw leader is regarded as autonomous with respect to other dala. A guyaw of one dala does not have the right to kareiwaga members of another; his own dala forms the limits of his kareiwaga. Similarly, an individual residing in one hamlet does not have the right to go into another hamlet and make demands of its people or its head.

The hamlet and the house are matrices of self-identification that are defined as relatively autonomous with respect to any external control. The hamlet represents, in principle, an inviolate or autonomous space that is the sphere of authority of its owner (*taraveru*; see Chapter 2). Within the hamlet, the fundamental center of a resident's own kareiwaga is his or her house. Although the (typically male) family head, or the unmarried youth in the case of a bachelor's house, is the ultimate repository of this centering control, each adult member of a household has a similar kareiwaga. Each household and house is a relatively autonomous locus, the sphere of an independent kareiwaga, just as is each hamlet. For instance, in one case, a youth being chased by the irate owner of coconut trees from which he had been stealing escaped into his own house. The man chasing him, a senior man from another hamlet, could only stand on the path outside the hamlet and berate him and others in the hamlet who were listening circumspectly, some sitting at their doorways or inside their houses.

Similarly, if a person comes to another's house and tries to hurt or scold a visitor in that house, he is showing that he does not fear or respect (*-kore*) the householder. The householder has been violated.

As one woman explained to me, "[this person] hasn't 'made my forehead', [i.e.] he or she doesn't respect or fear me (*gera i-vaga daba-gu, gera i-kore-gu*). [If] today I . . . sat in my house, and another woman came to chat with me, should anyone come and hit the woman I was chatting with, I think I have no forehead (*gera daba-gu*). The woman who came is my responsibility (*gura-pakura*) . . . the woman who came is my kareiwaga. Later when she has gone out along the path you [can] go and hit her; I will make no trouble. My house is my kareiwaga."

The house provides a protective bounded domain of social being (see Chapter 2). Just as the agent can act within it to assert autonomy, so the house itself is the artifactual form of that assertion, an extrabodily model of autonomy, which as a material enclosure coordinately exerts constraint against entering upon outsiders, and defines the exclusiveness of the residents.

In the above example, the expression "I have no forehead" is used to convey the idea of lack of respect for the speaker's kareiwaga. Similarly in public meetings, when men are exhorting Gawans in regard to some issue, they may on occasion point to the autonomous decision-making powers of each individual and dala, by emphasizing that "the kareiwaga is in his or her forehead" (*kareiwaga ou-daba-ra*); or "the guyaw is in his forehead, the guyaw is in his hamlet" (*guyaw ou-daba-ra guyaw ou-veru*). The first phrase refers to the individual as the ultimate source of decision-making power. The second phrase conveys the autonomy of each dala guyaw relative to any other (and thus refers to dala autonomy) and by implication ("the guyaw is in his hamlet") to hamlet autonomy. This latter phrase connotes the multiplicity of decision-making centers on Gawa – the fragmentation of the community into autonomous loci of the operation of the will – no one component having the right to stress superordination over any of the others. Thus the *superordinative* dimension, i.e., the guyaw element, has its locus in the individual, the dala and hamlet segments, rather than in any single representative of the whole, and is held *equally* by each part, no one part being guyaw (climbing) above the others. For this reason, Gawans call themselves *guyoraba*[30] (or *guyoreb*) – a label that signifies, according to informants, that there is no single guyaw on Gawa. Gawans use this label to contrast themselves with the northern Trobrianders whom they perceive as supporting a system where one dala guyaw (that of the Tabalu of Omarakana; see Malinowksi, 1922, 1935; Weiner, 1976) is superordinate (see Chapter 10).

As we might expect, emphasis on consensus in the decision making necessary for organizing collective activities is an integral aspect of this egalitarian, fragmenting construction of power relations and authority so familiar in New Guinea societies. I shall have more to say of consensus as a mode of constructing both the self and the collectivity when dealing with witchcraft (Chapter 10), but here some briefer comments are warranted. Since the notion of consensus consists of a collective consent, which in Gawan thinking should be unanimous, it creates the experience of a structure of unity out of the fractioning of control. The following account summarizes what one man explained to me in connection with the organization of canoe building:

In deciding whether to build a canoe, a man goes and asks all his dala kin (including women as well as men). They look over the food situation to see if there will be enough provender for the feasts and feeding of the workers that are integral to the construction procedures. If the food potential is sufficient, they are likely to agree.

If one person doesn't agree, it can't be done. If they go ahead despite the refusal of this one person, the canoe might get a hole in it because one person is angry (*kavikura*) – i.e., it is as if the person refusing had bewitched (*bwagaw*) the canoe.

This example of the necessity of consensus in collective action points also to the fact that segmentary autonomy and the equal weight of each person's kareiwaga underlie not only the key legitimate political process of persuasion and consent, but also the essentially illegitimate political process that subverts them, that of witchcraft. In a given collective activity, the failure to recognize the will of a single person could lead to some failure or disturbance in the venture owing to his or her anger; conversely, one might perceive the failure of a given venture as a sign of the disagreement of one person who has bewitched the enterprise, and thus acted in a way that, as we shall see later, actually negates the very consensual procedures and assumptions that justify the anger.

Persuasion and consent are the legitimate means of hierarchization for they entail the recognition of the other's equal kareiwaga as part of the process of attempting to assert one's own kareiwaga, and to achieve one's own ends. Although persuasion and consent are diffusely operative in everyday life, they are clearly the central *modus operandi* of kula. From one perspective, kula consists of the continual performance by each man of acts of persuasion and consent. On the one hand, a man is subject to the autonomy and equality of others whose agreement he must obtain by persuasive means in order to receive (starting) shells and "climb." Being subject to the other's kareiwaga in the persuasive moment of kula action, he is in this respect subordinate to the other, and subject to the principle of the latter's essentially autonomous equality as a locus of decision-making power. On the other hand, in refusing to release vaga shells, a man exercises his own kareiwaga, making decisions to whom a shell should be given or when and how it should be passed on.[31] But the necessity for releasing the shell at some time, to someone, requires recognition of the persuasive powers of the other to whose power the donor becomes subject just when he exercises his *own* decision-making powers to release the shell. This transformative intersubjective process thus mediates hierarchy and equality, yielding a positive formation of self through which over time a man can become, with maximal success, a guyaw – that is, hierarchization requires a man to engage in acts that *mediate* hierarchy and equality. Even so, this incrementation of personal value is subject to possible witchcraft. As Read (1959:430) has pointed out in examining societies elsewhere in New Guinea, there is a certain "tension generated" by the contradiction between the equalization of persons, on the one hand, and the building of personal strength or influence, on the other. In fact, in Gawan society *any* perceived incrementation of one person's value vis-à-vis others is subject to the possible anger of another who sees it as a violation of his or her own equality (see Chapter 9). This negativity is thus itself implicated as a latent potentiality of positive transformative acts – one that, however, may or may not be activated.

In sum, in using persuasion to gain his ends, a man has to work by means of the other's kareiwaga, his powers of decision making, attempting to affect the latter's decision in any particular instance without coopting or alienating and appropriating these powers themselves. This essentially positive construction of intersubjective relations is nevertheless underlaid with the subversive potential of witchcraft that alienates the other's decision-making powers. Secretly aiming at the death of the other, the witch attempts to "cancel" the latter's "externality" (Hegel, 1967:233) to the witch's own kareiwaga.

Returning to the symbolic transformations generated by food transmission, we can now review their significance in terms of the regulation of the wills of donor and recipient. To do this, we must consider more carefully the place of consumption in this process. If "food transmission to others to eat" is so fundamental to the positive construction of self, then it would seem that in the scheme of significances, eating is more than either the simple reciprocal or polar opposite of this act.

Although the documentation will not emerge fully until later, it is perhaps sufficiently evident from the present discussion that it is precisely food consumption that is felt to involve the most fundamental kind of satisfaction for the individual actor *as an autonomous involuted being*. Eating is a basic cultural model of the self-focused form of personal being that cannot initiate positive intersubjective transformations, but that is nonetheless the ground on which positive transformations operate – that they require and presuppose. Indeed, on Gawa, it would seem that food is a basic medium on which the conflicting perceptions are focused that Lévi-Strauss (1969:496) centers in women in his study of marriage exchange. One may paraphrase Lévi-Strauss's idea here in terms of food. In the context of the present argument, it is the same food (rather than the same woman) that may be perceived "under two incompatible aspects: on the one hand, as the object of personal desire, . . . and on the other, as the subject of the desire of others."[32] From the first perspective, food excites the desire to eat; from the second it is the means of persuading others to agree to one's own will and ends. But one must also add a third, hidden dimension: As "the desire of others," this food is also perceived as subject to possible theft (*veraw*) or witchery – closely associated acts that negate one's own will and capacity to create positive value transformations.

Thus food transmission operates on the self-focused desire of the donor as a sacrificial, separative act that, in effect, accommodates the other's desire to eat (in this sense recognizing the latter's will), while at the same time expanding the donor's own will and intersubjective control through basic persuasive means. Positive value, as Simmel (1971:48) puts it, "is the issue of a process of sacrifice." We shall see more of these sacrificial dimensions in later chapters.

But although the consumer of food received from another acquires, as it were, "the sweet object of desire," this consumption of *someone else's food* implies that the self-willed autonomy typified in eating is being constrained by an element of heteronomous limitation. Whereas the donor's will is limited by, so to speak, "the temporal and delaying mediation of a detour suspending the accomplishment or fulfillment of 'desire'" (Derrida, 1972:8), and hence is subjected to a concern with the desire of the other, the food recipient's will (which is expressed in the overtly self-focused act of eating) is not detoured in achieving its end; rather, it is limited by being brought into the political domain of the *donor's* will. The autonomy of both donor and recipient appears encompassed in the constraint of the other, and the self of each is formed in terms that embody the "tension between self-willedness and self-constraint" (Burridge, 1975:92, 94). Although the terms of this transformative process are asymmetric (for the consumer, as we have seen, cannot extend his or her spatiotemporal control through the act of eating, but literally consumes it by consuming the medium of potency within the action), this asymmetry is resolved of course in the reversal of acts for each actor that completes the exchange cycle, and conveys equality in its most ideal form for Gawans.

One may see, therefore, that the act of food transmission is the starting point for a positively transformative process, but the act of eating cannot itself be such a starting point. Thus we may understand why in feasts for canoe building, for instance, each participating Gawan family brings to the workplace a basket or more of cooked produce that is not for its own consumption. At the end of the day, the baskets will be collected, laid out on the beach, and distributed so that each contributor will get the food of someone else. In such contexts one therefore operates in terms of a model of positive value production even though immediate consumption is a necessary part of the procedure: through the procedures of food collection and redistribution each person becomes at once food donor and recipient. No one may eat his or her own food, but everyone gives food, and everyone eats food that comes from another.

4

Qualisigns of value

Gardens, food, and the body

> By considering the body in movement, we can see better how it inhabits space (and moreover time) because movement is not limited to submitting passively to space and time, it actively assumes them, it takes them up in their basic significance.
>
> Merleau-Ponty, 1962:102

At the beginning of Chapter 3 I cited a Gawan commentary that envisions consumption as producing nothing but sleep, a bodily state that the speaker contrasted with the kula shells and fame producible through the overseas transmission of food. On the face of it, this comment connecting eating and sleeping may seem unremarkable; as I shall show, however, it reflects an underlying nexus of meanings that are important in understanding value transformation on Gawa.

In this chapter I examine the relation between certain bodily states and acts that separate food from or identify it with the bodily being or self of the actor. Acts of separation include not only food transmission, but also food prohibitions and limitations on the quantity of consumption (eating only a little), which we shall see are related acts in the value-producing process. I argue that in the symbolic system, positive or negative value transformations involving food are systematically conveyed in certain key bodily qualities. As explained in Chapter 1, I call these qualities "qualisigns," drawing on Peirce's (1955:101) term and his view that qualisigns are icons: that is, they exhibit something other than themselves *in* themselves.

My general thesis is that these qualisigns characterize bodily spacetime in terms of a complex of polarized quality clusters that signify the positive or negative value transformations – the levels of intersubjective spacetime – effected by the acts. In subsequent chapters, shells, fame, and other elements will also be examined with respect to this qualisign system. In fact, an account of these qualities, which derive from the basic engagement of the body in the world, is necessary not only to an understanding of the nature of fame, but more generally to the way value is signified in exchange processes.

Underlying the reference to bodily torpor in the Gawan commentary referred to above is a general Gawan conception that excessive eating makes the body heavy (*mwaw*) and slow (*mwaw-utu*). Sleep is directly associated with heaviness in such contexts as the Drum dance (Chapter 8), where it is opposed to dancing in which the body exhibits lightweight buoyancy (*gagaabala*).

The term -*masisi*, which signifies the action "lies down" or the state "is lying down" and which connotes "sleep," not only conveys a dormant state of the body, but also has particular associations with the house, an interior domain of space. Sleep is appropriate to night and not to the daytime (see Chapter 2). A person who regularly lies down inside his or her house during the day is either reprehensibly lazy or in need of protective care (as in the case of women who have recently given birth and must stay inside the house), or is weak (-*gweya*) from illness or old age. Unless a person is ill or very old, he or she should be up and about during the day, going to the gardens, or about his or her work. Indeed, the term for a lazy person, *na/ta-bagumata*, means literally "one whose gardens (*bagula*) die (-*mata*)," for gardening is the pivotal activity carried out on a daily basis.[1] In these respects, the Gawan view is similar to that summarized by Panoff (1977:18) for the Maenge: "Activity is considered as the first of virtues and passivity as the social defect *par excellence*." Lying down and sleeping involve a minimization of social activity and of the physical space controlled by the body – an eclipse of bodily motion and vitality.

Sleep, fainting (-*kaburamata*), and death (-*mata*) have certain parallels. In the latter two states, the *balouma*[2] spirit or life essence that is inside (*wa-nuwa-ra*) the body becomes separated from it and may move (-*rarora*) in the external world unseen by others, whereas the body itself is motionless or lifeless. Although the separation of balouma and body is not a necessary concomitant of sleep, it may also occur during sleep. Thus the balouma of a witch may be moving around in the bush when the witch's visible body remains asleep.

When a person faints outside the house or hamlet, people hurry to carry the inert body of the person back to the hamlet, and into the house to be cared for. The immobility of the body, and the protective confinement and minimal space of the house contrast with the wandering of the balouma outside in the bush. Similarly, the balouma of a deceased person wanders in the bush when the corpse is still in the house during the preburial rites and just after burial. Thus when the balouma moves invisibly apart from the body, the latter is in a phase of disintegration, itself empty and inert, controlling only a minimal spatial domain.

In previous chapters I have discussed the importance of the house as the primary protective and controlled physical space in connection with a person's kareiwaga, with the pre- and postnatal care for a woman and her newborn baby, and with death. Just as the house is the regulated interior space into which one is born, and which provides a mediating location between the interiority of the mother's body and the exterior world outside the house (a world into which the baby and its mother move only in carefully regulated stages), so also it is the location of the last phases of life – the domain of dying, the final repose of the deceased before burial, and of the secluded mourners who represent the dead after burial. Both of these transitional states are phases of weakness when mobility is constrained or the body inert. In general, the house is the domain of physical space that marks the least extension of the person in spatial control and that in a number of contexts is associated with the body in a prone or otherwise in an immobile position.[3]

The kinaesthetic relation between weight and the timing of movement is clearly conveyed in the terms for slow motion and heavy weight themselves: *mwaw*, "heavy," and *mwaw-utu*, "slow" or "taking a long time." Illness, for instance, is a slow, heavy state of the body, when a person has "found his or her heaviness" (*i-ban kara-mwaw*). The expression connotes sadness or grief, and one may speak in relevant contexts of *kara-mwaw* or *i-mwaw nano-ra* (his or her mind is heavy) to convey suffering.

Old age has similar connections with slow motion. Its stereotypic image is that of a person walking slowly with a cane; as a phase of weakness in which one moves around less easily, and takes more time to do things, the body in old age approaches the pole of motionlessness expressed also in sleep, illness, and death.

Slowness also has important connections with the notions of difficulty and recalcitrance. When something is hard to do or to obtain, it is tight (*kasay*) – in effect, difficult to move from its position. Hard work is *kasay*, and in this respect it is also slow, requiring more time to do. Similarly, a kula shell that takes a long time (*tuta vanon* as against *tuta papun*, a short time) to obtain – for which one has to make many journeys, or to work for several nights on a single visit – is tight. Likewise, the person who is refusing the shell is tight, or recalcitrant. Gawans stereotype kula necklaces as being harder to obtain than armshells and thus as moving more slowly. Necklaces are tight in contrast to armshells, which are easy or loose (*pwapwasa*) and move more quickly (Munn, 1983; see also Chapter 6).[4]

Whereas slowness or heaviness is an undesirable spatiotemporal state of a person's bodily engagement with the external world, speedy activity (*naanakwa*) and buoyant lightness (*gagaabala*) are the opposed qualities conveying in different contexts the body's health, or youthfulness, and the feelings of joy (*mwasawa*) or well-being that go with these states. As suggested above, speed is also associated with soft-looseness or ease of operation and acquisition. In addition, these two qualities have significant connections with slipperiness (*damwalili*). For instance, boiling food makes it slippery so that it goes down swiftly; for this reason, boiling is forbidden in those contexts in which there is an emphasis on limiting food intake.

In general, Gawans place considerable emphasis on the desirability of getting things done swiftly, or at the appropriate time rather than lagging behind – a standard that, not infrequently, they feel that they fail to meet. For instance, in the preparation of food for feasts, people might complain that the work is being done too slowly, and consequently, the distribution at the end of the day is too late.

Whereas heavy, prone bodily states have their epitomizing physical locus in the interior, bounded space of the house, speedy movement is epitomized in activities on the sea. The sea is itself a buoyant, mobile domain of inter-island travel where the body is brought into direct experiential relation with the wind-propelled motion of the canoe (see Chapter 2; see also Malinowski, 1922:107). Gawan magic images this canoe motion as flying (*-youwa*) (see Malinowski, 1922:130; Munn, 1977:50). Canoes must be swift and lightweight – qualities that canoe spells are intended to ensure – and this emphasis is also reflected in friendly rivalry over the relative speed of canoes. The connection of speed with flying further conveys its upward (*wa-nakayouwa*) directionality, which contrasts with the downwardness (*ou-taginaw*) of heavy, slow states of being.

Sailing is also associated with youthful vitality. On a canoe younger men climb the rigging, doing the work that requires the most exertion, while more senior men steer and give instructions. The retirement of an old man from kula is frequently expressed by reference to the fact that he no longer sails.

As we have seen, sailing is essentially a masculine activity, although women are in no sense excluded from sea travel and may sometimes sail on kula trips as well. But unlike men, Gawan women express little joy in sailing, and it is a common view among both sexes that women tend to get seasick on canoes. This domain of space with its dynamic quality is essentially masculine in its gender connotations, in contrast to the interior space of the house with its feminine connotations. As I discussed in Chapter 2, masculine activity in general tends to be more mobile and to regularly engage a wider spatial domain than that of women; in particular, it is more directly associated with the sea and external domains of Gawan physical space. Thus, according to one man, land (*pweipwaya*) is feminine (*vavira*) because it stays in one place, whereas the canoe is masculine (*taw*) because it travels.[5] Similarly, fish (with which canoes may be metaphorical-

Plate 3. Men and boys hurry to draw a returning Gawan canoe to shore. The pandanus sail is just being lowered, but canoes usually drop the sail while further out at sea.

ly equated in some magic) is the masculine gift in routine marriage exchanges in which cooked garden food comes from the woman's kin. A consideration of the significance of gender associations is reserved for later chapters.

If we think of body-house and body-sea as representing domains along an axis of extension from the self, they can be located respectively at the relatively interior, unextended or static pole, and at the relatively exterior, self-extending or dynamic poles of being. The former involves a bounding off of the person from others and the outside that marks a minimal extention of social being and identity, whereas the latter involves the breaking down of social boundaries as in travel, and the creation of social connectivities rather than boundaries. Furthermore, speed and buoyancy entail an expansive spatiotemporal control: Body tempo is fast (less time is taken) and, in effect, the body energetically "goes beyond itself" forming active relations with the physical world outside itself. Slowness and heaviness, on the other hand, entail a winding down of activity, a contraction or negative transformation of the body to a level of spatiotemporal integration in which it does not form a dynamic inter-relationship with the external, physical world.

That lightness and speed convey a state of bodily exuberance and energy that can be described as a kind of bodily surpassment is succinctly expressed in certain Gawan spells (*mega*) for encouraging children to walk early.[6] Gawans encourage a child to stand up and walk as soon as possible, often giving it pleasurable inducements – for example, by helping it to move along a string tied between two supports while drawing a bright flower playfully ahead of it. Emphasis on dynamic mobility and development of bodily independence thus occurs early in childhood. In the spells for early walking, the child is described as going ahead (-*kougwa*) of a very fast-crawling sand crab. That is, the child is supposed to be faster than the crab. The image conveys the idea that the child will walk both early and fast.

These spells also assert that the child climbs one tree and jumps to another, a hyperbole connecting speed with *upward direction* and *forward leaping*. A number of spells, including those for early walking and some curing spells, involve hitting some relevant entity so that it is startled (*sibarutu*), gets up and hurries away. For instance, in curing spells, the illness is treated in this manner, and as the illness hurries speedily away, so also the sick person becomes lightweight (well). In the walking spells, the body of the child is supposed to be lightly hit in a similar manner so as to become buoyant and mobile. In sum, in these spells the body's capacity to move ahead of, away from, or above something else – or to change from a previous state of slowness by moving away from something that then becomes a marker of that earlier state, a measure of new-found mobility – provides the imagery of speedy lightness.

Returning to the Gawan commentary with which I began, we can now see the symbolic nexus that defines the significance of the bodily state said in this case to be produced by eating one's own food instead of giving it to overseas visitors. Sleep is not merely an outcome of the act; rather, it constitutes a contracted bodily spacetime that *exhibits in itself* the negative transformational value of the act that produces it. The body's lassitude here becomes an icon of the negative intersubjective spacetime created by consumption as opposed to transmission of one's own food. The actors do not simply destroy the food, thus producing it in a negative value state, but also, coordinately, they produce their own bodies and persons in a negative state of heaviness and stasis, or contracted spatiotemporal control.

The iconicity illustrated in this simple example is in fact part of a more ramified system in which a logico-causal connection is made between qualisigns of tempo and weight (and other related qualities yet to be discussed) and acts of eating (or not eating). I now consider the symbolism in which states of the body and states of the garden are treated as being in a symbiotic relation linked through acts of eating. As we shall see, qualisigns of tempo and weight exhibit the value of both garden and body as a differentiated order in which operations affecting the state of one part of the order affect that of the other.

THE HEAVINESS OF THE GARDEN AND
THE REGULATION OF EATING

In contrast to the sea, with its mobile, slippery and buoyant upward-moving qualities, the land is felt to be heavy and tends to be identified with a downward direction. The necessary positive quality for productive garden lands reverses that for the human body: Gardens should be heavy; land or a garden that is lightweight is empty and unproductive. Like the body, however (and unlike the sea), the land can lose its essential potency. Thus certain kinds of contact between elements of the shore or sea and the land can effect negative conversions of the garden. In some destructive garden spells a person might perform because of anger, or to demonstrate power, elements associated with the sea that are brought into the land drain the land, making it lightweight. For instance, a ritualist could call a long-necked crane (also a metaphor for a canoe) from the seashore into the garden to eat the crops, and so empty the garden. The fact that the spell uses an act of consumption to deplete the garden, has as we shall see later, wider implications.

The heaviness of the garden is not maintained simply by the crops rooted inside it, but most importantly by stones (*dakula*) that epitomize both heaviness and durability. Stones are hard (*matuwo*) objects that remain inside the land irrespective of whether it is being cleared, burned off, and planted that year or whether it has returned to bush.[7] The most important stones – those that should remain in the land and become visible again when a garden is cleared – mark boundaries and corners of land tracts, junctures of major plot divisions or the center of a given garden. As I pointed out in Chapter 2, boundary stones mark the limits of dala ownership (or an individual member's limits of control) and must not be shifted.

At least one stone or stone cluster in a garden may contain the spirit (*balouma*) of a dala ancestor.[8] This stone may be referred to as "the guyaw's stone" (*kala-dakula guyaw*). As one young man pointed out to me, indicating a large stone at the boundary of a newly cleared garden, *nano-ra n-i-seis* (it has a mind). Stones that contain a balouma should be approached with circumspection; they should not be touched by garden tools during work, or moved. If any boundary markers are shifted, the soil is angered (*kavikura*), and, as one man put it, "Its body becomes cold" (*i-rourun wo-ra*).[9] Plantings in the garden will then have no yield because "the men of old (*tamumoya*) have left their position" (*kaba-ra*, resting place, long-term, traditional location). Whether or not land is being gardened in any given case by members of the owning dala, its continuous reproductive potency is an aspect of the dala in its terrestrial objectification, and is directly identified with the bounding and fixity of land parcels.

When a tract of land is not being used, it may be metaphorically described as being asleep while planting awakens it (*kalamamata*)[10] much as a kula shell may reawaken an old debt that has remained unpaid from the past (see *kalamamata*, Chapter 3). Planting requires the use of some part of the material substance of a previous harvest (for instance, taro cuttings or seed yams) so that renewal involves the generation of the "new" from some part of the "old" (cf. Leenhardt, 1947:62f.). This mode of developing spatiotemporal continuity is directly reflected in the label *tabu-na* (grandparent), which Gawans use to refer to the old, wrinkled seed yam still remaining on the new growth, because, I was told, it is "wrinkled like an old man" (cf. Damon, 1983b:312).[11] As the means of a substantive, reproductive mode of renewal, the garden land and plantings constitute a form of spatiotemporal continuum that may be contrasted with that of shell circulation (although, as we shall see in Chapter 6, an interesting approximation of the reproductive mode is developed in certain operative features and metaphoric definitions of kitomu shells).

Thus stones embody the heaviness of the soil as an enduring potential productivity immobilized inside the matrilineal dala land across the transient tillage and planting of the gardens. This interior heaviness contains a potentiality for the future plentiful growth of plantings – that is, for the introduction at planting of a rooted movement (motion within a bounded space) involving not only the swelling of the tuber, but also the upward growth or climbing and spreading out of foliage. In the case of yams, motion includes the downward extension of the yam tuber and its roots from the eyes (*mata-ra*) of the seed yam, as well as the upward growth of the yam vines; when the latter have wound around the yam sticks, the plants are in their lightweight phase. For taro, the eye at the juncture of the large leaf and stem must open in the unfurling leaf, a growth process referred to metaphorically in one taro spell as being like the wings of birds spreading out in flight.

The heavy, enduring immobility of stones is thus a prerequisite of both the tight rootedness of the tuber (the wouwura of the plant) and the sprouting, upward growth or mobility of the plant's foliage, for it holds these capacities as latent resource potentials within the soil. Although Gawans themselves did not say this to me, one may perhaps conjecture that the upward plant growth in the garden is analogous to human vitality and mobility, and the heavy stones are analogous to the dala base or wouwura of each person in the continuity of the dala (see also note 11).

One illustration of this basic model of the garden as a productive spacetime is a type of crop magic called "stone." The magic requires a bespelled stone wrapped with certain leaves to be buried in the land after clearing or at planting.[12] Before burying this object the ritualist spits ginger onto the leaf wrapping to heat up the soil or make it "aggressive" (-*gagasisi*) so that the crops sprout and multiply. The bespelled leaves themselves belong to plants that are said to have many small multiple seeds that resemble the desired food plenty. The leaf-wrapped stone combines the properties of vital growth and heaviness – the heaviness being held inside the surface leaf wrapping with its qualities of sprouting and multiplicity.

One spell used with this object shows the basic spatiotemporal model particularly clearly. Like many Gawan spells, this one has three parts: a *wouwura* (foundation, see Chapter 3), trunk (*tapwara*), and top (*dabwara*) (cf. Malinowski, 1922:433). The wouwura usually (but not always) names a foundation element (*kaputurara* or *wouwura mega*) that is the key power agent called on to be identified with the speaker or to supply its properties to the target of the spell (Munn, 1976). This element may sometimes be explicitly connected with the ancestral past or with the establishment of a continuity between past and present. The tapwara frequently applies desired properties to the target through a series of parallel phrases involving a single type of act, and the dabwara concludes this process (see Tambiah, 1968:191ff.); but the speaker should return to the power base, the wouwura, in performing the spell. The relevant "stone" spell is a good example of this particular paradigm. A translation of part of it is as follows.[13]

Wouwura

Tudava [male ancestor], Malita [female ancestor]
Stays on my shoulders, "spell word" [no meaning]
Stays on my buttocks
Malita stone [in bush] food
He "tudava" [i.e., Tudava creates] food.

Tapwara

I make sprout/multiply my garden I make sprout/multiply,
My garden-markers I make sprout/multiply,
My tree roots [-at] I make sprout/multiply,
My hamlet area*a* I make sprout/multiply....

Dabwara

[Reiterates pattern of tapwara referring to fruit trees.]

The wouwura names two ancestors associated with the gardens, Tudava and his female counterpart Malita. Tudava is equated with Gerew, the ancestral creator who traveled from the Trobriands across the northeast region to Woodlark (see Damon, 1983b:321; Malinowski, 1935, v.1: 68ff.). Tudava/Gerew established the Gawan garden layout that requires the orientation of stones and garden plot dividers (or paths) so that the sun always travels across them diagonally rather than coinciding with the paths. Without this ancestrally fixed orientation, the garden will die because if the sun travels along the garden paths (plot dividers), its "eye" will be "closed." The sun has to spread out sufficiently over the garden to make it grow; if its route coincides with the dividers, it will, according to one explanation, go through and never return, or according to another, hit the "eye" of the garden (stones at the juncture of stick dividers or, in the ideal model, at the center of the garden) and so be closed.[14] Just as the eye of the taro must open, or root growth must extend from the yam's eyes, so the sun's eye must also open on the garden to create motion (growth, awakening).

Thus Tudava is the ancestral agent of both the appropriate light and mobility in the garden (the motion of the sun's daily travels and garden growth) and the fixity of its internal structure that is connected in part with the presence and positioning of stones. (The association of light with motion and the experience of waking as against sleep will be discussed later.) The appropriate light and mobility, however, are dependent upon the proper arrangement of stones and dividers in (or on) the soil.

In the spell, the terms *Tudava* and *Malita* also denote the stones referred

a This spell may be used for the matrilineal stone of the speaker in his hamlet as well as stones in his gardens (see note 8).

to above that are to be bespelled and buried in the land. In addition, these terms are used more widely to refer to certain specific types of stones. Tudava/Malita as stones and ancestral persons make the food (*i-katudava karu*). Furthermore, in the wouwura, the speaker's body is being identified with the ancestral persons-stones who are the active source of this creative potential. The identification occurs at once through the agency of *the speaker* – that is, by means of his own speech, which performs the identification by stabilizing the ancestral heaviness of growth potential on his own body – and coordinately through the growth-stabilizing agency of *the ancestors* who stay on the body of the speaker. Attached to his body, or as an aspect of his person, they then create the food.

Through this procedure, a complex agency, a model of the ancestral past as retained productivity in the ongoing present, is constructed. In this respect, the spell operates as a special case of the actor's construction of self, one in which the actor reconstitutes himself with the qualisigns of value required for the targeted object world external to himself on which he is acting.[15] Yet, in effect, this world is no longer external to himself, as he acquires the properties of the media by which he makes it. The subsequent tapwara and dabwara sections of the spell then proceed from the foundation of this productive agency – the "I" who has been created in the wouwura section – to apply sprouting and plenitude to the garden. The term that I have glossed as "sprout/multiply" (-*vapoula* in the spell) is -*poulu* (or, reduplicated, *pulapoulu* denoting bubbling in ordinary speech and in other spells), and connotes both upward motion and plurality.

In sum, the productive model of the stone as agency, which carries in it the potentiality of synthesizing past and future within the present – of renewing a reproductive spacetime – is established in the wouwura, itself the initial segment of the verbal sequence, and associated with origins, foundations, and priority. From this establishment of agency, the vitality of growth then emerges in the second and third parts. As in all spells, the speaker should conclude this one by returning to the wouwura, thus repeating, in this case, the construction of the productive agency or stone source with its intrinsic potential for creativity. In effect, by returning to the wouwura base, the speaker returns to the capacity for constituting a future out of the past.

After the spell is spoken into the leaf wrappings, the stone is then placed in the land. We can now see that this object itself has the topology of the spell: In the material medium, the verbally prior wouwura is translated, in effect, into spatial "inside" (as the stone itself is put inside the land) and the ginger-heated leaves simulating sprouting, translate into spatial "outside."[16] Moreover, this object spatially suggests the future crop in the garden – with the roots or tuber inside or underneath the ground and the leaves growing upward to the outside. It will be noted that the heated leaves suggest the warming of the soil, in contrast to the disruptive cooling that conveys the soil's "anger" when the stones are moved, and makes the soil infertile. It would seem that the leaf-wrapped stone both contains and models the spell that precedes its planting, and the planting of crops or the growth process supposed to follow after planting.

This ideal value model of productive continuity in the land may also be reversed by evil magic that makes the food disappear by taking away the potentializing stones that weight the land, and thus contracting or destroying the type of potentiality for renewal that becomes possible through gardening. We shall consider this sort of reversal shortly, but first it is necessary to examine certain integral connections that are made between the relative plenitude of the garden (its positive or negative value state) and the state of the human body with respect to eating.

The Gawan term *moru* refers not only to food shortage (a bad harvest, a state of famine, or the phase of the year felt to be short on varied resources), but also, when prefixed by a possessive pronoun, to hunger. *Agu-moru* denotes in general "my hunger" or "food shortage," but more specifically, "my hunger for vegetable foods" (as against *agu-vikeya*, my hunger for fish). The opposite of *moru* is *mariya*, a state of plenty. However, this term is not used to denote sufficient food consumption – the latter being referred to simply by terms for enough (*deisa*) or full (-*kalawta*, also applicable to the garden and other containers). In fact, *mariya* as a general state of food plenitude is, as I shall argue, *contradicted* by a bodily state involving considerable consumption. On the other hand, hunger and famine do not contradict each other, but for reasons that are not as straightforward as one might think. It is not only that if there is no food in the garden, people will, of course, be hungry. But causality also runs in the other direction: If people are hungry all the time and so want to eat a great deal, they will eat too much and deplete the gardens quickly. The garden becomes "hungry," as it were, when people hungrily eat too much.

Many Gawan taro and yam spells that are aimed at ensuring a plentiful harvest include a passage asserting that the people eat only a little. For instance, the spell may say that the food is dry (*raburabu*) or the throat is tight (*kasay*) so that the food does not go down quickly and people eat only a little (*tutana*). Similarly, the spell may state that the food is vomitted: that is, people are soon satisfied – in effect, their tight throats reject the food – so that they consume only a little, and much remains. Thus the food is eaten up slowly. This slow eating corresponds to the tightness of the food in the ground. So, for instance, when one woman found some food distributed at a 1974 communal work feast rather bitter, she remarked that one of the current community garden specialists (see Chapter 2) must have bespelled it, making it unattractive so that people would not eat a lot (see Young, 1983b:183 for a similar view on Goodenough Island).

The same rationale is behind the rule that during communal, islandwide rites for ensuring plentiful gardens, people must not boil any of their food. As I pointed out earlier, water makes the food slippery and so it goes down quickly. The aim is to control consumption – to make people feel they have eaten enough when they have eaten only a little – so that the gardens will remain heavy and become plentiful with growing crops. One must remark, however, that underneath this constraint on eating is precisely the concern that people eat well; and that they also be able to give food to each other to eat, to feast, and to demonstrate prodigality with visitors. This can only occur, however, if they eat only a little. It is not only therefore, as Young (1983:183) has stated the paradox for Kalauna, that "on the one hand, 'food is good to eat,' but on the other 'it is good *not* to eat food'"; but additionally, on Gawa "not eating good food" is defined as a *condition* of "abundance in good food to eat," and conversely, abundance in food implies that people do not greedily eat a lot (see also, Malinowski, 1935, v. 1:277f.; Tambiah, 1968:201f.).

To put this process in reverse – to create negative rather than positive value transformations – one may, for example, take the stones out of the land through destructive spells that make the land *lightweight*. As one Gawan man explained to me: "If the soil is lightweight, the food disappears. If the stones stay and weight the garden, the people won't eat a lot of food. But if the stones leave, the people will eat a lot of food and there will be famine."

The point here is not simply that by making a state of moru in the gardens one is making people hungry. But it is also that in taking the stones out of the garden, one is making people want to eat a lot, and from this insatiable hunger a state of moru ensues in which people are hungry because the gardens are empty.[17]

Making the garden lightweight actually disintegrates it as a productive spacetime, detaching its essential growing potential, and so destroying its power for reproductivity. Its lightness is a qualisign of this emptiness or negative value. This negative transformation of spacetime also applies to the human body, which assumes, however, the reverse qualisigns:

When people are famished, their bodies are heavy (*i-mwaw wa-wes*). They don't garden or wash or do anything but sit and sit. They are listless [as in illness], and don't stand up. The person [who performs magic for taking stones from the garden] sits and sits as the sun goes over the hamlet and at night sleeps sitting with his head bent over.

The spell referred to in this comment is one that makes the sun scorch the land; it may be contrasted with the spell for garden productivity discussed above, in which the land is vitalized with warmth. The negative spell begins with the phrase "malita, buttocks," thus naming the ancestral personage or stone also called on in the positive spell. But here its citation (along with that of another stone) signifies that the ritualist, having taken these stones out of their appropriate marking position in the land (which my informant illustrated by showing an appropriately laid out garden and a stone being taken from a central intersection of boundary markers) is sitting on the stones, and hiding them.[18]

The further constitution of the ritualist's own body in terms of qualities expressing listlessness follows: For example, the speaker asserts, "My 'leaning against' [is] a post-for-leaning"; there then follows a phrase in which he describes his body turning in place in coordination with the sun's daily motion and relentless presence:

> The sun rises, I turn around,
> I "give my back to" the sun;
> [The sun] goes down, I turn around,
> I give my cheek to the sun.

The sun's movement is thus encompassed by the motionless body of the ritualist. Reversing the productivity and future potential of the garden by moving the garden stones out of position, he converts the *vital* heaviness of the past into the heaviness of *moru* simulated in his own body. His body (at once hiding the stones, and taking on their heaviness) then *immobilizes* the sun's daily motion, just as he has *mobilized* the stones, taking them out of their proper resting place. The result of mobilizing the stones in this case is that the sun overheats the land rather than making the land cold; but the effect in either case is infertility. Both the bodily and the garden spacetime created is one that, so to speak, has no future, no extending motion. But the garden in this state of moru is lightweight, whereas the body is heavy.

To sum up: hunger produces hunger. When food flows swiftly into the body (insatiable eating that makes the body heavy), it flows swiftly out of the garden. When stones or food leave the garden, producing a state of moru and making the garden lightweight (empty), the body becomes heavy with hunger; the body and the garden are coordinately produced with reverse qualisigns of heaviness and lightweightness, signifying their spatiotemporal contraction and value emptiness. The result then is that eating too much in fact yields eating too little and the two extremes both yield the qualisigns of negative value transformation (bodily heaviness). On the other hand, moderate, controlled eating in which food is dry and goes down slowly (that is, the throat is tight) implies productive, tight planting and the retention of stones in the garden; conversely, tight planting implies controlled eating. These coordinate features characterize a state of *mariya* or plenitude on Gawa and correspondingly, of bodily fitness and buoyancy, a spatiotemporally extended value state of the self.

From this perspective, *mariya*, a state of abundance, entails more than simply an experience of food plenty. It connotes a world in which there is an abundance of food remaining external to the body, and in which there is always more than what one requires for one's own immediate consumption. Since people want to eat only a little, plenty remains (and conversely, since there is plenty, people have not eaten a lot). This attempt to create the experience of excess entails the model of self-constraint – the separation of food from the self – which, as I argued in the previous chapter, is fundamental to the creation of positive value in Gawan society.

We can understand in related terms the rhetorical image that Gawans (like Trobrianders, see Malinowski, 1935, v.1:227) sometimes use to convey the ideal form of mariya: Food, according to this image, should be so plentiful that much of it is never consumed at all but rots (*-pwas*, cf. *pwapwas*, soft) outside the body as an iconic token of the state of mariya – an excess of food external to the body that one need never use up at all. Rotting suggests here not so much spatiotemporal dissolution as an *extension* of spacetime. As the polar opposite of food shortage, the image conveys a transcendence of the termination and closure effected by consumption, combined with the sense of having totally satisfied the desire for consumption. But creating satisfaction at a level that makes this abundance possible implies, as we have seen, that Gawans have limited this desire. Thus the figuring of prosperity as excess would seem to be an icon of this striving to surpass the self – that is, of the attempt to mediate the closure or "using up" that is the outcome of eating and the conservation of food that results from relative abstinence.

Indeed, the model of excess is especially important, as we might expect, in connection with Gawa's overseas hospitality. For visitors to be able to eat their fill, and yet to see at the same time that there is plenty left over – that there is so much food that it is rubbish on Gawa – is an ideal image of their community that Gawans would like to have broadcast overseas. Through such hospitality the fame of Gawa "will go on high" (*b-ei-ra wa-nakayouwa*) as visitors return to their homes with news (*buragara*) of Gawa's impressive abundance. When Gawans themselves go abroad, the community so graciously treated can hardly fail to satisfy their visitors with equal hospitality in order to convey their own potency. Beyond this, the impressiveness of Gawan hospitality in food has a positive effect on their receipt of kula shells, for as we have seen, kula is grounded in the transformational power of food giving.

From this account, we can also begin to understand why it is an insult that defames Gawa (*i-busi butu-ra*) and arouses shame (*-mwasira*) to gratuitously tell outsiders that Gawa is in a state of moru.[19] We shall see further why this is so when we discuss witchcraft, for the latter, the sign of subversion in intersubjective relations, drains abundance, the essential form of positive transformative potential, and thus defines a negative state of the Gawan self.

A state of abundance on Gawa is then a precondition for producing the more extended, inter-island modes of spacetime, just as for each person, abundance in the garden (the result of vital, energetic work) is the enabling condition of the capacity to positively transform the self through transaction. In effect, the bodily constraint conveyed in "eating only a little" (with its appropriate qualisigns of bodily buoyancy and health) defines the precondition for further positive intersubjective transformations; as a mode of separating food from the self, it can be seen as an icon of these potentialities. Furthermore, this lightweight, vital state of the person is interconnected in Gawan symbolism with the maintenance of a long-term reproductive potential in the land, a mode of generating spatiotemporal continuity that entails keeping things inside or fixed in place (weighting them down, and bounding them, as it were, rather than making them circulate as in kula). The concentrated image of this power is the *dakula*, and it is, of course, no accident that matrilineal continuity and identity are formulated in this model.

COORDINATE TRANSFORMATIONS OF BODY AND PLACE IN CURING AND HAMLET-PLANTING RITES

To illustrate the way in which some of the interrelationships I have been discussing in this chapter may be created in a concentrated form in immediate experience, I shall briefly examine a community curing that Gawans perform when they feel afflicted with widespread physical malaise or with the threat of illnesses.[20] This rite exemplifies, on the one hand, the experiential constitution of qualia as relationships between the individual's body and physical space in a particular context of activity, and suggests how a given activity itself may formulate these relationships; on the other hand, the rite also condenses the symbiosis between value transformations of the body and those of the productive land and the crops.

The curative part of the rite is a communal activity called *Bibira*, the aim of which is to cleanse the island and the people by sending away illness. Conjointly with this curing and cleansing, Gawans perform activities that focus on the fertility of the land, and are part of another agricultural rite. Although they may therefore be performed separately from the Bibira, it is also clear that they simply represent another related aspect of the whole procedure. The core of the rite takes one day and consists of sending illness away from the island, cleansing the body, performing curing ablutions with spells, and closing the hamlets and island off from illness. Coordinately, bespelled leaves and grasses are planted in each hamlet so that food will stay on Gawa, the hamlets be made hard (*matuwo*) and the people eat with moderation. I shall outline the basic events of the rite as I participated in it in the rainy season of early 1974 when Gawans felt that there was a considerable amount of illness on the island.

The cleansing began just before dawn in the southeast residential neighborhood where some of the community gathered along with the current leading garden specialists (see Chapter 2) and their helpers, to start the noisy rush across the island that was to chase the illness out of house and hamlet along the central path and down to the northwest beach. Proceeding from hamlet to hamlet, the people shouted and beat on the houses in order to startle (-*sibarutu*) and thus awaken the illness, making it emerge from the houses to be chased along the path to the beach. As the procession went along, it increased in size until almost all the community had joined in, led at a fast pace by its leader, the senior garden specialist, who swept the path with a broom of bespelled leaves as he went. Apart from the leading curer and one of the garden specialists who remained behind to make magical preparations, those who remained in the hamlets were primarily the ill or incapacitated and the old; all others descended to the sea.

The procession descended the cliff just as it was getting light, and emerged on the beach. People washed in the sea, scrubbing their faces clean with leaves freshly bespelled on the beach by a number of men who were reputable curers. At this time, a little model canoe was prepared and sent away to the northwest with appropriate spells spoken over it. On it sailed the sickness that was being expelled from Gawa to the Trobriand Islands where (according to all the spells for this procedure) it would land under the bed of the head of the chiefly dala of Omarakana and from there be sent on northward out of the immediate island world.

We can see from this brief account how the bodies of the actors take on the desired qualities of body tempo – the expansive control of spacetime entailed in speedy movement – both in the swift passage across the island to the sea and the purificatory washing that submerges the body in flowing water. This energetic expansion of spatiotemporal control is precisely the reverse of the bodily state in illness, hunger, and sleep. In fact, since the activity begins at dawn and awakens not only the illness but also the people, it is a "waking up," and "putting into motion." While the procession is proceeding roughly in the direction of the rising sun, northwest to the sea, the weak remain behind in the hamlets, to be treated later by curers when the revitalized and cleansed people return. Thus the action polarizes the sea-beach and house-hamlet, the former becoming the locus of vitalizing activities of motion and the latter the locus of those left behind, of weakness and immobility.

It will be noted that this procession, led by communally recognized men of influence, transcends the fragmenting kareiwaga of each hamlet space by drawing people out of their hamlets and mobilizing their bodies into an attuned collective sweeping of the path as they travel through the hamlets and down to the sea. It would seem that in this collective, common activity, the participants' spatiotemporally coordinated action actually embodies their singleness of purpose and common agreement or consensus. This point is quite in keeping with certain Gawan views about collective work and the signs of consensus (see Chapters 3 and 10).

Moreover, the day before the curing, Gawans had worked together, at the behest of the organizing leaders, to clean the paths in preparation for the next day's activities. This made the paths *murakata* – clear and free of entangling weeds or wild growth that might snag the illness so that it would stay around rather than swiftly depart from Gawa; such wild growth would also impede the procession.[21]

As noted above, the ritual leader carries a bespelled leaf broom. We have seen (Chapter 2) that ordinary, coconut-spine brooms are used (especially by women) in the regular sweeping of the hamlet area, a procedure that is part of the means by which the hamlet is kept clean and clearly marked off from the unmanicured bush. In the ritual, the leading communal garden specialist (with the people behind him in procession) sweeps through the hamlets, bringing people out of their homes beyond the bounded hamlet space to clean the path that connects the segmentary hamlets to each other and to the sea. The movement embodies the power to mobilize collective action that moves across the hamlet units.

The island space and the human body are thus coordinately reconstituted in the procession. The "movements and displacements," as Bourdieu (1977:90) has suggested, "make the space [one might add 'time'] within which they are enacted"; but they also "make" the body's own spacetime as they do so (i.e., the body becomes lightweight and fast). This motion in turn is synchronized with (and by) the rising sun so that the body, land, and sky form a unified spatiotemporal order; similarly, qualities of light, and its expanding upward direction, are brought into experiential synthesis with the body's movement toward the sea and with the cleansing of the body at dawn. Thus the immobile land itself becomes infused with the potentiality of movement. In this respect, we may be reminded that within the static heavy garden the motion of growth also requires the appropriate travel of the sun spreading across the garden; and planting awakens the dormant land, creating motion.

The washing (-kaakay) that climaxes the procession to the sea is also connected in other ways with the sweeping of the land. At this time, the body (especially the face, regarded as the locus of individualized identity) is cleansed – a process that Gawans regard as the essential prior act in procedures of beautification, but that is also an ordinary part of daily ablutions. In this washing, the face is scrubbed by the bespelled leaves as people bathe in the sea. Through this cleansing the body's dirt (*bikibiki*) or hiding darkness (*bwabwaw*) is converted into *pwapwaakaw*, light or whiteness and visibility, and clear brightness (*murakata*). Like the island paths and hamlets, the surface has been cleansed of grit and brought into the open (*ou-murakata*). Similarly, the cleansing and smoothing of the land through sweeping has made it possible for people to move quickly from place to place, and for the sickness to rush along without being stopped by impediments that keep it from leaving Gawa. In effect, the autonomous divisiveness of each kareiwaga – each hamlet and each person – is opened up and people are formed, as it were, into a bodily agreement, an intersubjective spacetime in which the hiding darkness, dirt, and illness have been expelled.[22]

After the washing was finished in the late morning, the people returned casually to their individual hamlets. Some of them decorated themselves to parade along with the curers and their aids as they proceeded from hamlet to hamlet performing curative spells on the bodies of those who were ill, washing some in bespelled coconut juice and providing beneficially bespelled white, sweet-smelling coconut scrapings for all the people to rub on their bodies.

At the same time that these bespelled substances were being applied to the body in order to send out the heavy illness, curers were also driving two bespelled, forked stakes into the sides of a path flanking the point of entry into each hamlet; the stakes would snag or pierce the illness should it attempt to return.[23] By this means the cleansed state of the hamlets was assured by eliminating the possibility of the return of the illness that would negate the previous outward motion. In short, the qualities produced by the extension of spacetime created in the initial transformational process were then to be held within each hamlet. Similarly, on a later day, the principal curer and his assistant went down to the beach and walking around Gawa set up stakes to protect the whole island. This protective closure is supposed to last for an indefinite time after the rite, but it can be broken, and then the rite should be performed again.

Whereas curers administer to the ill (heavy) body to make it healthy (lightweight), and to the cleansed hamlet to close out the illness and retain its cleansed state, the garden specialists administer to the potential productivity of the land to make the food heavy within it. Traveling with the decorated parade, they plant bespelled grasses and leaves in the hamlets in order to hold the food tightly within the land (equivalent to making people eat slowly and moderately) so that there will be a state of plenty on Gawa. It was explained to me that in doing this, the specialists warm (*-teviyayi*) the hamlets. The latter, people said, are like the children

Plate 4. A garden specialist plants bespelled leaves next to a house post during the Bibira rite.

of the garden specialists who take care of them as one cares for children. This procedure also makes the hamlet hard (*matuwo*) so that crops growing in the gardens won't spoil. Thus garden specialists care for the gardens where crops grow by caring for the hamlets where people live; and they care for the hamlets (and the people in them) by caring for the crops.

Similarly, they foster the lightweight vitality of the body by attempting to assure crop fertility (regulating food consumption).

By means of the procedures of both types of specialists, both body and land are coordinately constituted with qualities that signify the new value level – the positively transformed intersubjective spacetime – which now characterizes Gawa and the selves of Gawans.[24]

FOOD TABOOS AND BODILY QUALISIGNS

Limited consumption can be viewed as an act intermediate between unregulated eating and food transmission, on the one hand, and between eating and food prohibitions, on the other. A consideration of the connection between qualisigns and the limiting of consumption thus leads to an examination of food taboos. Both the regulation of intake and prohibitions on eating mark the act of eating in an essentially negative, moral obligatory mode (see Lyons, 1977:823ff. on the "deontic" mode). This is even more marked in the case of prohibitions than in the case of the notion of limiting intake, as the former clearly infuse any context to which they apply with the "hortatory negative" (Burke, 1961:20ff.).[25] At the same time, we shall see that they involve, as Gell (1979:133) has suggested in another context, a process "whereby the ego both recoils from the world in constituting itself, and is simultaneously drawn back into the world in accomplishing its projects."

In some contexts, Gawan food prohibitions (*boumiya-*) are directly associated with food transmission. All major, formal transmissions of comestibles are accompanied by explicit taboos on the key donors' consumption of any part of what they transmit. Such acts of eating are *bwaboum* (forbidden). Similarly, the particular individuals most directly involved in initiating such a transaction may be forbidden to eat any edible returns from it. In these contexts, it is apparent that the taboos mark the donors *as* donors, restraining them from being consumers at all in the transaction, and so explicitly emphasizing the polarization of the two acts.

One of the most important contexts linking the food taboos and food transmission is marriage exchanges of the type called *buwaa-*, which I outlined in Chapter 2. As indicated earlier, in these exchanges both the woman and her husband (the nodal couple in the transaction) are forbidden to eat any of the comestibles coming from individual kin of the woman. Gawans consider it shameful (*mwasira*) to break this rule. An individual thought to have eaten the buwaa given for his or her marriage is likely to be described as greedy, that is, "one who eats" (*na/ta-kamkwamu*). Or as one woman said (referring in this case to the male partner in a marriage): "A man who eats the buwaa from his wife's people 'has no mind' (*ta-nagouwa*). The wife says to him: 'I give you food to give your [kinspeople].... [But instead] you eat the taro. What a mindless person you are!'" On the other hand, the particular kinsperson of the husband who receives the food is the one who is specifically referred to as obtaining the right to eat it (i.e., to consume it himself or herself as well as at his or her discretion, to share it with others). This recipient (with his or her spouse) is thus the rightful consumer.

In the Gawan statement above, the woman speaks of herself as giving food (from her kinsman) to her husband. It will be recalled (see Chapter 2) that this gift is referred to as "his," that is, the husband's, buwaa; conversely, gifts from the husband and his kin are the wife's buwaa. Although from this perspective the wife is a donor vis à vis her husband, and the husband vis à vis the wife, the two are also viewed as a couple whose unity is marked especially in the common food taboo. As one man put it: "A man gives a woman a canoe [for example] and a woman gives a man food. It is called their buwaa (*buwe-si*); the man and his wife [literally, 'with his wife'] must not eat; it is forbidden."

Since the woman and her husband are both forbidden to eat the food, they are marked as a unit in relationship to it, and as such they are food donors who must mediate the food to others rather than consume it themselves. In the dyadic relations between the individual affinal kinspeople or couples (originating donors and recipient-consumers), the nodal couple as a unit is "the third element, which offers a different side to the other two, and yet fuses these different sides in ... [its own] unity" (Simmel, 1950:135). Coordinately, the unity of the couple is being matrixed in the more encompassing relationship of the affinal donors and recipients. This extended transactive structure has certain similarities to the ternary prerequisite of kula (see Young, 1983c:395).[26]

As the couple is also forbidden to keep any of the occasional goods returned from food consumer to donor, the husband and wife must continually be the media of gifts they do not keep for themselves. Their part is to transmit or yield up their buwaa – to be recipients who do not keep or consume. Thus they objectify in themselves both the sacrificial constraints epitomized (as I suggested earlier) in food giving, and the ideal potentiality or continuity of the intersubjective process formed through the buwaa food transmission. In effect, they embody its character as nonconsumption or as not finishing – as a "potentializing" process created by separating comestibles from the self.

It would seem, then, that the taboo'd position of the nodal couple conveys what food transmission (or transmission in general) is about: namely, not consuming or finishing something oneself. The mediating actors do not simply extend the number of links in the transactional nexus or provide the fulcrum of the wider relationship between affines: They also introduce an iconic model of the transformational process into the process itself. The taboo on eating and keeping makes each couple into an iconic embodiment of the actor *as* donor (nonconsumer) and thus of the transactional process as ongoing potentiality for positive self-transformation or spatiotemporal extension of the person's control beyond the self.

No pronounced connection appears in this context between the keeping or breaking of such prohibitions and the qualisigns of value discussed above. However, one man explained to me that in certain other contexts in which food received cannot be eaten by the immediate recipient, but must be distributed to others, the food is also called this recipient's *buwaa-ra*: It is "forbidden to his mouth" (*wado-ra bwaboum*); eating it, my informant said, "will make the mouth heavy" (*b-ei-mwaw wado-ra*).[27] According to this man, buwaa of this sort consists essentially of payments in comestibles and betel to a specialist in return for his magic, or gifts in raw comestibles to a man from his kula partner (*buwaa-ra veiguwa* or *buwaa-ra mwari*, the buwaa of the necklaces, or of the armshells). These forms of buwaa appear to involve contexts in which speech (spells or kula speech) is a critical potency. Eating negates this potency (i.e., it makes the mouth heavy), an outcome that is consistent with the dialectical relation of kula speech and eating discussed earlier.[28]

Connections between the value qualisigns and the breaking of food prohibitions also appear systematically in certain other contexts. For example, a man who is the main skilled builder of a particular canoe is prohibited from eating the edible returns from the transaction of the canoe because they will weaken him or make him tired (*bw-ei-nanisi wa-wo-ra*) and therefore unable to do the skilled work of cutting another canoe. In this context, breaking a food taboo is felt to deplete the vital energy necessary for building further canoes.

Observation of food taboos is critical to the production of desired bodily qualities in certain contexts involving beautification. Gawans prohibit eating before any bodily adornment (*kay-bubura*) in which spells for beautification are used. Sometimes these prohibitions are in force for the entire day of the adornment. Such prohibitions also occur in conjunction with the painting of canoe prowboards with *or without* spells. As I have shown elsewhere (Munn, 1977), decoration of the canoe prowboards is metaphorically identified with human decor and canoes have anthropomorphized properties (see also Chapter 6).

In both contexts, food prohibitions affect the capacity of the decorative acts to create beauty,[29] a state of the body epitomized in the qualities of light or visibility, whiteness and brilliance in contrast to darkness or shade (*bwabwaw* or *bwaw*, dark; *daduba*, shade), as I discussed in connection with the curing rite. The basic principle is that if the decorators or the person being decorated eat during the day of the painting or before the taboo is appropriately lifted, the work will appear dark or dirty (*bikibiki*) rather than light. Light in its multiple aspects is the central qualisign defining visible beauty. Conversely, darkness signifies the negative conversion of the body to ugliness. Breaking taboos that separate food from the body endangers the capacity of the decorative operations and the materials they add to the body to create beauty or to effect the desired bodily conversion.

PREGNANCY RITUAL, FOOD TABOOS, AND LIGHT

To exemplify the connection of food taboos and light I shall consider certain aspects of the pregnancy rite that is optionally performed for a woman during her first pregnancy (see Malinowski, 1929:211ff.). In this rite, a woman's paternal[30] and affinal kinswomen (the female matri-kinswomen of the father-to-be) are the key persons in charge of decorating the woman; her own matrilineal kin prepare the feast that is part of the return for the decoration, and that will be consumed once the decoration is finished and taboos are lifted.

The paternal and affinal kinswomen each prepare a fine white cloak of stripped and dried banana leaves for the woman to wear during her pregnancy, and decorate her to aid in a swift birth. The cloak protects her belly from the eyes of those who might be jealous of her pregnancy and the reproduction of her dala, and bewitch her, thus creating difficulty in childbirth or loss of the child. However, the cloak is also part of the beautification procedures that, as I explain shortly, make her *more* visible.

On the final day of work on the cloaks, the women are forbidden to eat. Women told me during the 1974 rite that I observed (and from which my account is derived), that if they ate, they would darken the young woman's facial appearance (*b-i-dadubura magi-ra*) and the bespelled facial designs (*soba*) of glowing black resin and white lime that they would paint on the following day; in general they would deface her brilliant beauty. At that time, food taboos would be in force for the girl as well as her decorators and for any other women attending the rite (including myself), all of whom must also decorate themselves. The regulated bodily state of *all* participants is necessary to ensure that the decorative process will yield its appropriate bright effect.

The girl was decorated on the southern beach (the beach nearest to the hamlets of her maternal and patri-kinspeople) in the early morning light. As in the curing rite discussed above, the women arrived on the beach just as light was dawning. The decorative procedure included basic operations characteristic of Gawan adornment, which always begin with washing, usually in the sea. The girl's hair was then trimmed and her eyebrows shaven;[31] her skin was oiled with heated coconut scrapings, which have an attractive sweet odor and give an overall glowing visual effect to the skin. Designs (*soba*) in black resin and white dots were painted on the face; decorative red kaloma shell earrings (which are given by a male kinsman) were attached *over* her dark tortoise shell earrings (which may come from women) used for daily wear; two kula necklaces from her father's kinsmen were put around her neck and arranged under each breast (shells from her husband's kin would also have been appropriate if available). Her two new over- and underskirts were put on and neatly trimmed. After more coconut oil was rubbed on her face and body, betel nut was mixed in a bright red paste and applied to the mouth. The betel substances for the designs and the coconut had all been bespelled, but such substances may also be used in less regulated contexts without bespelling. The overall effect of this painting should be *kaakata*, "sharp" or "piercing" and "brilliant," rather than *babeita*, "blunt" and "dull."[32] Finally the cloak made by women of the father's side was held over the girl by the two chief affinal and paternal women, laid around her shoulders as she stood facing the sea, and then trimmed. This cloak would be worn until food taboos were lifted and then the cloak prepared by the husband's kinswomen put on for daily wear. A red frangipani flower was put in her hair as the decorated women moved in procession back to the hamlet.

It will be noted that the necessary preparatory basis of the additive procedures is a cleansing that scrapes off the body's dirt before a brightening substance like coconut oil can be added; similarly, hair and skirt trimming is an important part of the aesthetic procedure. Skirt trimming is a regular part of the procedure for women's ceremonial decor in all festive contexts (but hair trimming is not). Shell decor (variously arranged), decorative skirts for women, or bright, clean cloth laplaps for men are part of the standard decorative practices for major events. Most men no longer wear earrings, but the decorative attachment of red shell earrings (made out of kaloma shell derived originally from inter-island trade, and associated with kula) over earrings of tortoise shell is standard for women; the fact that the resultant layering places the shell given by a male kinsman *over* the darker shell that may have a female source is significant (see especially Chapter 6). We may also note in this connection that the male-linked earring is more temporally specialized to a particular event, whereas the female-linked shell is worn on a daily basis.

The betel stain on the mouth and the red frangipani had to be removed before the young woman could eat on her festive return to the hamlet. If she ate with the bespelled cosmetic on her mouth (bringing food consumption and beautification into direct contact), her skin (*kalevi-*) would turn dark and visibly diseased (*kurikuri*, skin sores). Eating as internalization is antithetical to the cosmetic process, which gives an expansive quality of sharp brilliance to the body that intensifies visibility and presence.

The mouth is also, however, the point at which the contradictory significance of beautification as seductive, self-focused modification of the body is concentrated and most available. The red (*bwaabweila*) betel nut juice is an erotic substance – both the color (represented also in the red flower) and the juice itself are explicitly seductive in their connotations. As we might expect, Gawans like most other peoples, make metaphoric equations in certain contexts between eating and sexual intercourse. These apparent contradictions in beautification are taken up later.

A special rite lifting food taboos was also performed over the girl, since spells had accompanied all parts of her beautification. As she sat inside her house on return to the hamlet, a stick with a piece of cooked taro on one end was rotated around her lower leg and then thrown out of the house to signify the release of the taboo. The spell spoken to lift the taboo instructs the skin disease and darkness to "descend" from her body. This procedure, a standard Gawan means of releasing food taboos in other contexts as well, enabled her to eat again without darkening her beauty.

The properties that produce the overall quality of light are, in particular, the oiled cleanliness of the skin and the contrastive coloring of red, white, and black applied to the head and facial area. The significance of color is complex and I do not intend to examine the problem in detail here. I will note simply that although red and white are the chief colors connected with light, a dark component is part of the total contrastive effect. The well-known red, black, and white color triad (Turner, 1967:59ff.) thus gives the brilliant clarity of contrast that Gawans emphasize (Munn, 1977). In the context of adornment, red and white have particular associations with the dynamic, moving light of lightning; a person of unusual beauty can be described as "shining like lightning" (*i-kavikawra*, literally, "he or she lightnings"). This expression applies especially to men, and relates to their association with the sea.[33]

It will be useful at this point to review the bodily significance of light as conveyed in the term *murakata*. We have seen that a critical connotation of this term is "outsideness," and that when used with a locative prefix it denotes this spatial position. A common usage is "Let's go outside" (*ou-murakata*) meaning in a characteristic context "outside the house"; a basic contrast is made between the dark, shady inside (*wa-nuwa-ra*) of a house and the light outdoors. Temporal connotations are also implicit in the connection between murakata and daylight (*yam*, day), as opposed to darkness and night (*bogi*).

As we have seen, the appropriate time for ritual washing is the morning, and in these contexts it takes place ideally at dawn as the sky turns to rosy pink and the sun rises. In such contexts, participants may be up in the dark and travel from the hamlets down the steep paths to emerge on the seashore just as light is breaking. In washing, the process of making the face and body murakata as against dark and closed (*-taboda*) has a very specific sense that connects the light that comes from the external world with whiteness emerging from the removal of darkness from the skin. Light in this second sense is revealed from inside the covering layer of dirt (see the discussion of the curing rite earlier in the chapter). Spells for washing may refer to the "breaking" or "bursting open" (*-taavisi*) of the face as it becomes clean and white (see also Malinowski, 1929:366). Similarly, the rough dark skin (*kalevi-ra*) of a vegetable should be carefully shredded (*-visi*) or peeled (*-kwali*) off to make it appropriate to serve to guests or for other special occasions. These skins are dirty (note that it is the skin that has been in direct contact with the soil), whereas the inner part is white or clean. These procedures should be compared with the sweeping and smoothing of the hamlet area, and of the paths in the curing ceremonies discussed above. In these respects, washing (scrubbing with leaves and cleansing with water, itself a medium of light and motion), brings out the light from within: The interior becomes external and the externalized whiteness of the body is directly connected with light from outside, the whole process being concentrated in brilliance.

Darkness, the negative qualisign of the body can be understood as a contraction or internalization (hiddenness, disappearance) of the person, reminiscent of sleep and death, which as we have seen, have associations with the interior space of the house and the time phase of night (see also the blackening of the body in mortuary rites, Chapter 7). Obscuring darkness is also the quality of the witch, or of dangerous spirits of the dead (*balouma*, also *aruwa*) who may hide in the coverings of dark clouds on the sea.[34] Conversely, light dynamically extends the body, integrating it into the wider world, making it outside or sharply visible, and connecting it with external sources of *moving* light such as the sun or lightning. During the night, the equivalent light source is the moon, which is important in nighttime *dancing*.

It is apparent from the accounts of the curing and pregnancy rites that light and cleanliness are integral to bodily motion. In these respects, beautification as a process of bringing brilliance to the body and its reciprocal of making the body (with special emphasis on the face as the locus of identity) more visible to others constitute a spatiotemporal extension comparable to that of speed and buoyancy; in fact as we have seen, it emerges in activities where these mobile qualities are stressed.

In the pregnancy rites, additional connections between the qualisigns of light substantialized in body decor, and those of weight and tempo are an important aspect of the rite, one of the central aims of which is to aid the girl in giving birth quickly. For this purpose, at her washing, the girl is given a drink containing bespelled leaves to make the child slippery (*damwalili*). The girl herself is being made lightweight in this procedure since when a woman is pregnant she is said to be heavy. According to one man, the magic also releases any witchery that might make her ill during pregnancy, and in this respect also heavy. Thus one aim of the procedures is to work against any heaviness induced by the negative attitudes of others. Similarly, the white cloak both hides the woman's belly from prying eyes, so that negative attitudes are not aroused, and is also part of the procedures intended to arouse positive attitudes, giving her the surface visibility of a cleansed state with its potential for successful, speedy birth.

Failure of the beautifying operations would reverse the desired swift, easy birth that makes the mother lightweight. Breaking food taboos can thus be seen as yielding heaviness as well as darkness. The fact that it is women representing paternal kin of the woman and the child who are attempting to create this dynamism in her body, and not her own matri-kinspeople, is an important feature. As we have already seen, men are identified with vital mobility and external domains of space. It is thus the essentially masculine potency of mobility that is being mediated to the woman by her paternal and affinal kinswomen.

BEAUTIFICATION, PERSUASIVENESS, AND FOOD TABOOS

The synesthesia of color or light and body tempo is also demonstrable in other contexts where food taboos are important to the positive outcomes of beautifying activities. The painters of the red, black, and white designs on canoe prowboards should ideally be unmarried youths, for more senior men are stereotyped as slow and ugly, whereas younger people are supposed to be vital and beautiful. Should the painters eat on the day of the painting, it is said that they would darken the boards, for "eating makes the body heavy and slow" (Munn, 1977:48). Magic is not necessarily performed on the paints, and the painting is entirely casual, but in order to produce the desired qualities on the canoe boards, painters themselves should exhibit these qualities in their bodily being.[35] Indeed, the boards themselves, like the human body, must be washed in the sea and scrubbed before being painted.

Similarly, a man who eats when preparing armlets of leaves bespelled in coconut oil to adorn himself for kula, is not only likely to fail to persuade his partner to give him the desired shells but, as one man pointed out to me, will darken the shells themselves, thus destroying their desirable smooth glow. Further identification of the ritualist's body with the shells is exemplified in certain washing and bloodletting spells[36] for kula in which a man may speak of a slippery fish leaping up and turning toward (-touvira) him. Slapping and slashing his body with the fish (an image of bloodletting) he acquires qualities of slippery buoyancy making him so attractive that the partner gives swiftly. The fish is identified with the shells themselves, and with the partner's swift giving (the slippery fish slapping and turning toward the ritualist): Thus the partner's mind turns toward the hopeful kula recipient. As I have pointed out elsewhere (Munn, 1983:285), "The Gawan's ability to move the shells is in this way being identified with his ability to form himself in terms of their ideal qualities, or to become beautiful like the shells."

As this last point illustrates very well, vital beauty is the persuasiveness of the body – the visible aspect of the immediate person that may attract admirers, who in relevant contexts may be favorably inclined toward a person and so moved to yield up desired goods. For instance, a spell used for the flower worn in the pregnancy rite spoke of people standing and admiring the red flower worn by the girl, which is compared to a bright red fish hung in display on the cave of a house. Beautification is crucial in kula, not simply in the elaborate form of bespelled preparations, but also in ordinary preparations without bespelling when men wash and anoint themselves, putting on their best attire as they go out to visit their partners (see Guidieri, 1973, on impression management in kula). For youths, adornment to enhance their own youthful beauty is a medium of sexual persuasion; as the essential model of seduction, sexuality is carried over metaphorically into relations with kula partners.[37]

In adornment, persuasion takes the form of visible qualities of the body – "the sensuous and emphatic perceivability of the individual himself," as Simmel (1950:340) has put it – through which "the eyes of others [are led] upon the adorned." On Gawa, light or sharp brilliance as the pervading quality of beauty is indeed the surface amplification of the body, providing the "arena" of a person's "being-for-himself and being-for-the-other" of which Simmel (1950:339) speaks. Adornment persuades not by detaching some desirable material thing from the self and giving it to the other (to satisfy the other's desire), but by making one's own desirability visually available to the other – in this sense, as a "gift" in virtual form only. In this respect, the beautified person persuades by exhibiting his or her persuasive potency as a visible property of the self.

Certain contradictions inherent in this intersubjective formulation are expressed in the Gawan handling of compliments (teleway). If a beholder expresses admiration of a person's beautiful appearance, Gawans expect the recipient to pay for the compliment with a material gift to the admirer. Admiration can be referred to by a phrase – i-yageiga nano-ra, "it [the beauty] makes the [admirer's] mind bad" – in which the feelings of pleasure and possible envy appear to mingle, for the person admired possesses something especially desirable that makes him or her climb relative to the beholder. The compliment itself gives expression to this situation, for through the compliment the admired recipient climbs. Thus as a sign of the subjective conversion of one person's beauty into another's admiration, the compliment requires its return payment – a separation of material goods from the admired (see Munn, 1977:49, regarding a similar process for canoes). In this way, equivalence is restored by a further paradox: In effect, the self-focused component of beauty is released, and the self-transcending significance of beauty completed, as the person is compelled to detach something from him- or herself, that is, to give.

If we consider the spatiotemporally extending qualities of beautification as light and motion, we can see that eating negates or reverses the externalizing direction of the self implicated in this process: The actor consuming food internalizes and destroys positive value potential within the body rather than displaying it on the body surface, making it available to the perception of others and conveying his or her potent vitality. The presence of the food taboo marks this dialectic, and the qualisigns of dark-ugliness that are supposed to emerge if the taboo is broken, specify the negative transformation or contraction of body spacetime brought about by this negating act.

It is significant, then, that some of the decorative qualities that characterize the positive value form of the body can signify negative value conversions of the garden. According to some informants, human beings are forbidden to decorate themselves with sweet-smelling herbs or coconut oil before going into the garden, and a similar taboo prohibits the consumption of certain foods that might redden the garden: For example, sand crab should not be eaten before entering the garden because the shell is red when cooked, and this might redden the leaves of crops and kill them. One man explained such prohibitions by saying that the locus (*keba*) of human beings is "above" (*wa-nakayouwa*) whereas that of the gardens is "below" (*ou-taginawa*). "Dark soil," he said, "befits the garden, but it dirties the human hands. When we come out of the garden, we wash."

CONCLUSION

In concluding, I wish to draw together certain points made about the spacetime of the land or garden. In this chapter we have seen that gardening (with its central productive acts of planting) creates a spatiotemporal expansion through plant growth and multiplication by means of immobility or containment (tight planting, and maintenance of the immobility in stones) rather than release. In the land, slow-heaviness is the precondition or base – the *wouwura* in its full temporal and spatial senses – of motion or growth. These acts and the garden as their media are in turn logicocausally connected in Gawan symbolism with acts that regulate incorporation and its destructive consuming and self-focused implications. In effect, tight planting is equivalent to a negation of, or imposition of constraints on, eating. Whereas the immobility of the garden, as condensed in its stones, appears from one perspective simply as the opposite of bodily mobility, from another perspective, the antithesis of both mobility and immobility is *unregulated eating*, which negates or releases the positive immobility necessary for productive growth. From this latter perspective, immobility is the *base or precondition of mobility*, and the garden as its paradigmatic domain is set apart as a distinctive form of spatiotemporal potency. The domain of immobility is both opposed or contradictory to the mobile order and a necessary precondition of it.

We have, then, two poles of spatiotemporal potency. If *stones fixed within the island's land* can be taken as the concentrated media of the one, then kula shells that form an inter-island circulation can be seen as the concentrated media of the other. As we have seen, stones assure renewal and long-term spatiotemporal continuities through internal fixity and an unchanging continuity of substance across different gardens, particular garden plantings and growth, and gardening years. Kula shells, on the other hand, are the most expansive of the circulatory media that create what I have suggested is "an emergent spacetime of their own" (see Chapter 3) by means of release and mobility, that is, by the continuous changing (exchanging) of shells in inter-island transmission.

Perhaps the stones, some of which are also named, might be viewed as creating their own emergent spacetime in the form of a permanent storage of resource potential *inside* the land. The transcendent internalized continuity of resource storage in stones is the reverse of the shell circulation kept track of or followed (*kikura*) by Gawans across the seas and from island to island.

Although the garden is the paradigmatic domain of immobility, we have seen that the basic formula of the relatively immobile base as precondition for motion is also reiterated within it. Therefore certain analogues may be noted between the relation of stones and rooted crops to growth and extension (a form of mobility) in the garden, on the one hand; and the relation of skwayob hospitality in comestibles (focused in garden crops) to kula exchange, on the other. It will be recalled that in the previous chapter, I argued that skwayob to overseas visitors – with its specific mode of ongoing spatiotemporality producing in itself a lesser value level of spatiotemporal extension than kula – is nevertheless the *generative base* of kula. The significance of these analogues will emerge more fully in the discussion of marriage exchanges in Chapter 6.

5

Fame

His fame traveled around, it made shell returns;
The armshell Iyoyai traveled to Dobu,
It was exchanged for Rapweata necklace on the Raramani islands
   of the Buduwakwara sea.
                    A woman's fame chant for her brother, recorded 1973

The value states of the body examined in the previous chapter can be ordered on a scale of symbolic distance, or levels of expansive, spatio-temporal control, from a contraction of bodily spacetime (sleep, weakness, death) involving identification with the interior, bounded and dark space of the house, and marking a diminution of capacities for positive intersubjective transformation; through the active expansion of bodily spacetime, in effect beyond the boundaries of the body itself as in youthful health and ordinary vital, energetic daily activity; to the intensified image of this expansion in cosmetic adornment by which the body (and especially the face) is "opened" and, as it were, extended in light. Light, in turn, is the arena where the body's visibility is formulated in terms of the visible light deriving from the world external to the body, and the body's motion is identified with the external, slippery and buoyant domains of water.

But we may also put fame (*butu*-)[1] on this scale of self-constitution, viewing it as an enhancement that transcends material, bodily being, and extends beyond the physical body but refers back to it. Fame is a mobile, circulating dimension of the person: the travels (*-taavin*) of a person's name (*yaga-ra*) apart from his physical presence. In fame, it is as if the name takes on its own internal motion traveling through the minds and speech of others.

PERSONAL NAMES AND SHELL NAMES

All Gawans have more than one name (usually at least three or four) acquired within the first year of life from both parents and other kin on the mother's and father's side. A set of names usually includes at least one deriving from the ancestral names of the mother's dala, but other names may be more idiosyncratic. At any given time, however, one of these names is generally more widely known than others by the community at large and is in more regular use, whereas other names seem to drop out of general usage altogether, or are used by only a few people.[2]

The names by which prominent Gawan kula men are known appear fixed in community usage, but it is possible that the names by which they are known in other parts of the kula area could vary in some places (see Damon, 1980:290, n.9). In my experience, however, the most outstanding kula men from other islands, and it would seem, Gawa as well, appear to be widely referred to in the kula area under a single name.

Within Gawa, each member of the community is identified by a distinctive name that does not overlap with that of other *living* members of the community. In the case of dala names, the person whose dala name one holds must always be dead. Beyond the island, however, a Gawan may sometimes know of another person (generally not more than one) who shares his or her personal name (-*veriyesa*, namesake, person with same name as ego). The broad emphasis, however, is on the name as a carrier of the unique identity of the individual; within the island, this means there should be only one living instantiation of a personal name at a given time.

Proper names are regularly used as terms of address and reference. But by and large, Gawans (including children as well as adults) do not like to mention (-*kataga yaga*-) their own names, although there is no prohibition on doing so. Most people I questioned could not explain this reluctance, although some said they felt ashamed (*mwasira*) to mention their own names. However, one important kula man, himself fastidious about not mentioning his own name, explained to me that a person's name is for *other* people to use, not for the person himself. Although his was the only explicit statement I obtained of this view, its basic tenet is borne out in the more general attitudes and usages of the community. Thus it seems accurate to suggest that the uniquely identifying personal name is that aspect of the self that is felt to be rightfully lodged in the speech or use of *others* in contradistinction to the person named.

Face and name are the two centers of an actor's personal identity. In the context of overseas relationships, Gawans distinguish knowledge of one's name from knowledge of one's face (*magi-*), saying that when a man is widely known there are places where the people may have "never seen his face," but they "know his name." A man's name can become known and used well beyond his particular face-to-face contacts because of his kula transactions, and the travels of named and especially well-known shells he has obtained and passed on.[3] It is said that one's name travels with the shells (see also Damon, 1978:43), since people will hear about a man and mention his name in connection with successful transactions.

When a shell travels on beyond a recipient, arrangements must be made for its further movement, and its paths sorted out; thus a given transactor's name will also enter into the sequences of names a man must know in order to enter into these negotiations. Shells are followed (-*kikura*) by means of such sequenced name lists that represent the paths of persons through whose hands (*yama*-) the shell traveled on one or more transaction cycles. The news (*buragara*) and discussion of a shell's travels in other communities noises a transactor's name abroad.

In contrast to a man's face, his name is an identifying token referring back to him, which can travel beyond his immediate locus not only to other consociates whom he may see at some other time, but also in its maximal extension to contemporaries in kula who never see his face. As I have pointed out elsewhere (Munn, 1983), fame in this sense is created through the handling and passage of shells: It is a product of transactional processes. References to shells and a man's butu may be treated interchangeably. When a man receives a named kula shell (primarily a vaga, opening gift, but also a gulugwalu, closing gift), it is his butu; Gawans say that his butu "climbs" or "goes all around" (-*taavin*; also -*touvira*, turns back). Thus butu reflects "a man's capacity to 'move' his partners to accede to his own will" and points to the potentiality for future transactions that a man acquires with the shell (Munn, 1983:286). Through continuing shell transactions a man's name is, in effect, regularly on the lips of distant others. "I am a guyaw," one man explained to me, "they [i.e., other islanders] speak my name."

Conversely, a guyaw also knows (-*kakin*) names of distant kula men, and will have developed sources of information through his important partners extending across the widest kula area. The information required for intellectual mastery includes not only knowledge of the paths of shells (sequences of movement in terms of persons' names and relevant locations) involved in his unfinished transactions and the earlier paths of these shells, but also such matters as the current possessors of high standard kula shells; the potential onward routing of these shells so that a man might consider strategies for obtaining them if he wishes; and related information needed to work (-*wotet*) his own kula.

This knowledge, with the resources in partnerships necessary for it, is built up over time through continuing transaction, and is itself necessary to the developmental incrementation (climbing, -*mwen*, as against descending, -*busi*)[4] of a man's fame. The knowledge a man has of the transactions of distant others and the knowledge these others have of him and his own shell transactions, mutually entail each other, as over time a successful man transacts more shells and shells of better quality. By means of such ongoing transactions he builds up a long-term circulation that is the external objectivation and medium of his own internal knowledge and others' knowledge of him. Men say that when a man of kula fame dies, his name is widely spoken, for he is known in every place, and his death will affect a large number of transactions and kula paths.

In contrast, young men who are just starting out in kula are not usually widely known;[5] their names do not go beyond their own consociate partners. Relationships at this stage are temporally shallow, and their transactions relatively short term. Neither do young men have a wide knowledge of others and of shell locations in the inter-island world. For the most part, youths lack the spatiotemporal extension of self entailed in the circulation of names that characterizes the successful kula man.

However, human names could not circulate in this way were it not for the naming of shells, for it is obvious that shell paths could not readily be followed if the shells were unnamed. It is precisely because the lowest-ranking category of Gawan shells are *not* named that, as Gawans point out, they are likely to "disappear." Ranked just above this nameless grade are shells that Gawans think of as having generic rather than personal names.[6] Informants said that if these shells rise in value as they circulate, they will be given more specific, personal names. Although the names of middle-range shells are thought of as personal rather than generic, Gawans recognize that they might have more than one exemplar. However, only one of these exemplars is regarded as the true (*mokita*), original shell of that name. At the very highest level, among the most famous shells, names should have only one instantiation – this very uniqueness being a mark of their high rank.[7] There is thus an ideal correlation between having a unique name and being widely known.

At one end of the scale we have, therefore, shells that cannot circulate in verbal form apart from their own material circulation because they lack verbal identity tokens and so cannot readily be kept track of; these shells tend to disappear and be forgotten. At the other end of the ranking scale are the most famous shells, which circulate in verbal form as unique names and are known and talked about all over the ring. These latter shells are ideally old (*mutabogwa*) or with certain exceptions, regarded as old, and epitomize to Gawans the temporal durability and spatial extendability produced in long-term circulation. Such shells are like eminent guyaw; indeed, it is ordinarily only guyaw who transact them.[8]

In these respects, names are not simply the verbal tokens of shells that make it possible for the latter to be linguistically known and followed apart from the immediate location of the shell at a given time. But in addition, the shell-ranking scale models the process of becoming famous in terms of the acquisition of a name and the increasing exclusiveness of its application. In this sense, the ranking scale depicts the process of becoming known, as one of increasing uniqueness, an increasing capacity to be identified and spoken of in one's specificness. This entails a spatial and temporal expansion of knowledge of the shell. The shell model of the process of becoming famous or climbing is thus an icon of the same process for men (see Munn, 1983).

SPEAKING AND LISTENING

The expansive spatiotemporal construction of self that is developed through kula has also to be considered in connection with transformations through language processes in another sense: namely, those of speaking and listening. I have already commented on the importance of speech as a persuasive medium and defining action in kula (Chapter 3). When a young man who wishes to advance in kula is starting out, he must not only develop his own kula speech skills, but also listen to the discussions of more senior men, learning the path histories, metaphors, names, and so on, pertinent to kula.

But as we have seen, listening is an act that in relevant contexts also carries the connotation of consenting to the requests of others. Gawans emphasize that one of the first prerequisites of advancement for a young man is that he listen (-reg, -kabikawra) to the requests of some senior man on Gawa (typically a matri-kinsman, but also a father), aiding this person and working for him, so that the latter in turn agrees to give him various goods, trees, magic, and so forth. A young boy who works for an older man of his dala or kumila may in this way become apprenticed to him in kula; by this means, he can both inherit some or all of this man's kula paths (with occasional exceptions, kula paths are matrilineally inherited), and as well, be able to back up this inheritance with knowledge of the senior man's paths and shell transactions. This youth becomes known to his senior's immediate partners and others as he travels with him on kula as a junior helper. Thus one man, now a major figure in Gawan kula, told me that his butu began to go around when he was a young boy, as one who "listened" to a particular older man; men from other islands then recognized him, and said that perhaps he would be the replacement (mapu-ra) for the older man when the latter died. The recognition of other islanders who come to know a youth personally and speak about him – and the initial extension of spatiotemporal control that this implies – is the reciprocal of a young man's subordination to the senior man to whom he listens.

Whereas young men should listen both to kula speech (livalela kura) and to the kareiwaga of a senior man, the true guyaw is one who not only commands kula speech, but who also speaks up in large public meetings of all kinds, including kula meetings in other island communities.[9] These men are men with names (ta-ka-yagei-sa); without such men, Gawa as a whole has no fame. Younger and less influential men are less likely to speak up in large inter-island meetings out of fear of making mistakes in the presence of older men who know the paths. One man suggested that younger men

Plate 5. A senior man of kula eminence speaking to Gawans at the Drum dance entertainment (see Chapter 8).

will "keep quiet" in public, speaking only privately in very low speech (-*makom livala*) to their partners; but when men have obtained kula shells of high standard, they can speak up in public (*livala ou-murakata*) for "the tusk of a wild pig has hit their foreheads (*bo-i-wey dabe-s kalavat*)." This metaphor means, according to my informant, that the guyaw is as strong (*tawatora*) as a powerful bush pig with a large tusk who is not afraid to come out into the cleared area of residential space because he knows that people respect or fear him (-*kore*, see Chapter 3). The strength to be able to speak out openly in this open or central area (*baku*) of the hamlet (which is associated with public speaking in contrast to the house interior or the hamlet margins where more private or casual speech takes place, see Chapter 2) itself derives from the extended control over spacetime that the guyaw concentrates into himself through kula. This concentration is epitomized in his butu, the attribute of his identity that entails an enhancement of his own name through its affirming use by distant others.

Thus in the descriptive epithet of the pig cited above, the term *kalavat*, used by the speaker to denote "pig tusk" (ordinarily, *doga*), here refers metaphorically to a first-rank kula shell. It is the sharp power of the shell-tusk[10] that has, as it were, impressed itself from the outside upon the forehead of the guyaw, enabling him to bring himself and his speech *ou-murakata*. In this respect, it should be recalled that in stereotyped phrases denoting the individual kareiwaga or decision-making authority, reference is made to the forehead (see Chapter 3); and that the most prominent location of the mind is in the forehead with the alternative locus in the throat, also associated with speech. It is as if the shell-tusk has hit his mind or kareiwaga, so that the extending sharpness of his authority is figured as coming from the outside onto the body surface.

This way of figuring the acquisition of power is reminiscent of the imagery of the kula spells cited in the previous chapter in which the hopeful kula participant speaks of hitting and slashing himself with brilliant fish that are equated with the kula shells he acquires; the beauty thus being imprinted upon his own person from the outside is also the capacity to move the other (see also Munn, 1983:285f.).

FAME, DECORATION, AND BEAUTY

These points bring us to a further consideration of the relation between fame, decoration, and beauty. Just as senior men possess butu as, in effect, a spatiotemporal extension of the self, but in Gawan stereotypes of age lack bodily beauty, so younger men who are just beginning their kula possess bodily beauty, but lack butu as an attribute. But as one kula spell aimed at spreading a man's renown makes clear, it is fame that decorates the guyaw. In this spell, the guyaw's head is decorated with feathers (typical masculine decoration for dancing) which are a metaphor for his kula necklace:

> Whose feathers? the feathers of the guyaw
> They hear echoing sound, the Raramani people take it away....

The decoration (*bubura*) that the guyaw has put on, his head-feathers and necklace, creates an echoing sound that spreads south and is heard by the Raramani people, who in this way know of him. One may suggest that fame is metaphorical body decor that ramifies as sound beyond the body. Kula shells, the material medium of this butu, are themselves an enduring form of decor that have their locus apart from the body and Gawa itself in inter-island circulation. As media of circulation that come from the outside world, shells epitomize the matrixing of the individual and the Gawan community in this external order. We may turn briefly then to consider the sense in which shells function as adornment.

When necklaces and armshells arrive on Gawa, they may both be applied to "self-decoration" (A. & M. Strathern, 1971), but in somewhat different ways. Armshells are typically hung in the vestibule or outer room of a man's house where people who visit may see and admire them. When hung in this way, they should, if possible, be arranged by rank so that the highest-ranked shells are nearest the door, and *most visible*. Necklaces are not displayed in this way but are ordinarily kept in a personal basket with one's precious possessions, or are frequently given to kinswomen (wives, daughters, sisters' daughters, etc.) for daily wear.[11] Women do not wear armshells, although they are not prohibited from doing so. But whereas armshells typically decorate the outer room of the recipient man's house (and thus his hamlet), necklaces typically decorate the female body, a feature consistent with the classification of armshells as male, and necklaces as female (see Chapter 6).

Both types of shells may, however, be worn by men for various ceremonial purposes, but necklaces are more frequently used in this way.[12] A man may wear his own shells, but a relatively senior man is more likely to give them to a younger matri-kinsman, son, or son-in-law to wear. However, it is women in particular who are given necklaces to wear on a daily basis or for ceremonies such as the finale of the dance entertainment, or, as we have already seen, a first pregnancy rite. According to one woman, when a woman wears a man's necklace, she becomes the "decoration" of her kinsman (who could be a father,[13] mother's brother, husband, etc.). Women decorate with necklaces, she continued, and become the fame of the men, just as a new canoe (*yeiyay*), decorated with kula shells by overseas kula men, becomes the fame of the builder. Although the women's beautification displays their male kinsmen's kula prowess, it should be kept in mind that it also decorates *them*, attaching the positive qualisigns of value to the women's own persons.

Moreover, women compose fame chants called *butura* that celebrate a man's kula acquisitions, telling of the journey in which he obtained the shells, and other related events. These chants name the shells that a woman composer has worn, or that have been given to her and her kinsmen from her husband as part of her buwaa marriage gift; or they may name shells received by a matri-kinsman, who is usually in a food-giving relationship to the female composer. Women may also compose chants that name and celebrate a new, finely decorated canoe in which the kinsman sailed, as well as the shells thrown for the new canoe, which may be placed on its carved ends for display. Such chants spread a man's fame not only by naming the kula shells received, but, in addition, the canoe in which he sailed when he received them; these chants are also regarded as the butura of the canoe and usually refer to its decorated beauty (see Chapter 6).

Thus women's butu chants spread the fame of men who have honored (-*kaves*) them, "naming" the men by naming the kula shells and canoes identified with them. In these contexts, women are the others who transform the selves of the male actors by converting the latters' particular acts and material acquisitions into a verbal discourse that circulates apart from them, the artifacts, and the relevant momentary events. At the same

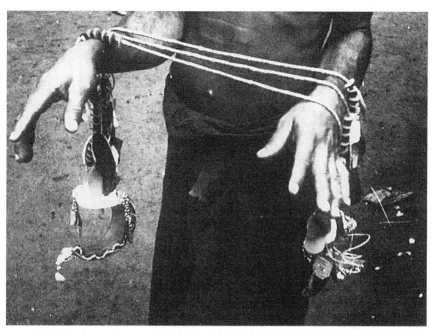

Plate 6. Muribikina, a high-ranking kula necklace on Gawa in 1980.

time that their chants are about fame and its processes, they also make famous what they chant about (cf. Redfield, 1975:32).[14]

There are certain parallels between this process of *verbal* publication by the other, which characterizes the essential structure of fame, and the material mode of self-display by which the media of influence a man acquires are demonstrated on Gawa in his beautification of another person. When shells are lent out to be worn by someone else, the owner's self-decoration is, in effect, detached from him and made public by another. The shell refers back to the owner, adorning him through his capacity to physically adorn another. In this respect, the wearer becomes the publicist of the donor's influence, as if she or he were mentioning his name.

Just as shells decorate the person, they themselves are decorated with attachments to the armshell or necklace string. Gawans regard these attachments as necessary to the beautiful appearance of the shells. Although the essential characteristics that determine the shell's standard are contained in the properties of the core shells (and the shells themselves have beautifying properties of color and light),[15] Gawans place considerable emphasis on maintaining the attractiveness of the decor, and may use this procedure in an attempt to seduce recipients into attributing a higher rank to the shell (see Campbell, 1983; Munn, 1983).[16] In the case of the armshell, the conus shell is the core – referred to as the "body" (*wo-ra*) (with a "back" and "forehead" – the surfaces of the shell – and an "anus" and "mouth" or "tooth" – the larger and smaller apertures, respectively) (see also Campbell, 1983b:231ff.). The decorative, beaded ovula ovulum shells attached to it are called *kara-loubu*, a term meaning "its shell decor," which may be used to denote both the decorative shell attachments of canoe prowboards (Munn, 1977:49) and shells when used to decorate the human body. Extending beyond this colorful *unmoving* attachment are the mobile attachments of shell pieces, nutshells and other elements that make a jingling sound as the shells are handled or carried. Gawans comment that these latter attachments are noisemakers (*buragara*, noise, news). The necklace also has decorative attachments to the "trunk," some of which also act as delicate noisemakers.

The communicative significance of these jingling elements has been expressively described by Campbell (1983b:236) in an account of Vakutan (southern Trobriand) kula:

It is at night that the vast majority of shells are relinquished.... The man who succeeds in winning a kula valuable away from another does not, according to etiquette, carry his own valuable away. Instead, a colleague picks it up and takes it to the beach. As the carrier makes his way to the boats the sound of bwibwi [noisemaking elements] informs others in the village that someone has succeeded in kula. In response to the sound of bwibwi, villagers will call from the dark to inquire for whom the carrier walks. The success of the man who won a valuable spreads through the darkened village with each step of its carrier. Chiming of the bwibwi triggers off additional conversation around small fires scattered throughout the village about the man's kula, the valuable's keda [path], how many times it has been around the ring [and so forth].[17]

In sum, like a person, a shell has a body (the center of its rank), an attached material decor that adds a seductive intensification of beauty to that of the body, and a noise (mediated by part of the added decor). The decor extends the body in space and the mobile decor makes a sound that ramifies this space – as if putting it into motion – so that what may be out of sight may nevertheless be heard.

FAME AS A MODEL OF INFLUENCE

We have seen that kula fame can be understood as the conversion of concrete shell circulation or of particular transactions in shells into an oral circulation of the names of men and shells. In the sense that names circulate via shells beyond the possible travels of persons, this verbal circulation is an exponential aspect of the emergent spacetime of kula.

Since the verbal identity token, the name, can relocate the person and the shell he has transacted in the mind of another who may then know of him and positively evaluate him irrespective of whether he has ever seen him or not, a man's becoming known is also a subjective conversion, like his immediate influence with a partner (see Chapter 3). But although a man's fame may act as a factor affecting his influence in a given context, fame itself is obviously a different order of phenomenon from influence.

To explain this difference, it is necessary to briefly review the notion of subjective conversions discussed in Chapter 3, looking at it now specifically in the context of kula exchange. Whether a shell a man receives is a starting gift or a finishing gift, it is a manifestation of his persuasiveness – his ability to turn the mind of the donating other, or to make the latter remember him. In the case of a *gulugwalu* (closing gift), the relevant influence was generated at some previous time by the transmission of a shell *from* ego to the current donor, and the present shell is the material demonstration or objectification of the influence previously generated. On the other hand, if the shell is a starting gift, it is a new or a renewed materialization of ego's persuasive capacity vis à vis the donor. As a *vaga*, it also contains potential for establishing influence with another recipient (and indirectly with additional recipients of the path it may subsequently take) when ego acts as donor, transmitting the shell onward to a man in the kula direction toward which it is moving. In this sense, evidence of an actor's influence in the immediate past as a recipient and his potential for initiating future influence as a donor are embedded in the vaga shell, or more strictly, in his acquisition and holding of the shell. Although a gulugwalu shell does not contain for any given recipient further potentialities in the same transaction cycle, shells as circulating media can be understood in general as objective embodiments of previous and future subjective conversion processes connecting transactors and recipients.

Fame, however, is a different order of subjective conversion. To include it in the model we must introduce a third party observer outside the immediate transacting parties, or in addition to the categories of transactor and recipient necessary for a simple model of persuasion. This third category of actor represents the other who hears about the transaction. As Leroy (1979:185) has recently put it in a trenchant statement adapting Sartre's notion of the witness:

To announce that exchange is triadic is simply another way of saying that it occurs in the presence of others, and that these can condense into a single, anonymous third person who is anyone and everyone in the culture. He does not even have to be present for his influence to be felt; imagination and memory may represent him. Indeed, his importance is in representation, not action. Through his unifying glance, donor and recipient understand their act to be a part of a wider public reality.

In Gawan images of kula fame, the virtual third party is the distant other who hears about, rather than directly observes the transaction.

One man said that if a man travelled northward to Iwa and Kitava on kula, and received necklaces at these places, his name would "turn around" (-touvira), going back southeast to reach the Muyuw people who would hear about his achievement. In this account, the name travels in the reverse direction from the Gawan, but in the same direction as the necklace he has obtained; travelling apart from either, it provides the knowledge which Muyuw men can use in arranging future transactions. Similarly, in the hyperbole of one kula spell, southerners who hear of a Gawan's receipt of a necklace rush to sail northward to Muyuw (presumably to obtain the shell). The movement of the shell to the Gawan thus generates the further motion of names (verbal information) and this in turn is seen as stimulating still further movement on the part of distant kula participants.[18]

A similar theme appears in a woman's fame chant which refers to a Gawan kula trip for armshells. A free translation of the end of this chant goes: "They [the sailors on the boat][a] admired the armshell called Tera Iwa; on the boat Poreta they gave me my name, 'One who wins murikawa' [armshell of the top standard]; my fame is put into the boat, oh large shell and a shell of muridoga standing [middle standard, good quality] they see in my hand, they [the sailors on the boat] see. They take away my fame to Inos [a kula man] in the town of the white people [Alotau on the mainland]; oh muridogu, the shell called Nutura they [the sailors] see in my hand" (see also Munn, 1983:286ff.).

In the first example, the transactor's name, and that of the shell he has acquired, travel to the distant others who hear about him and his shell acquisition. Thus converted into a nominal form, their identities and the new locus of the shell circulate to distant others. In the second example, the shells are identified with the Gawan recipient who holds them in his hands (see Chapter 3, on hands as the holders of goods, and gifts), and in whose boat they are put. The admiration of the sailors is then, in effect, spatiotemporally extended into the spreading of the recipient's butu to a distant kula man in Alotau who later hears about the Gawan's *coup*. The chant draws attention to an expanding trajectory of intersubjective transformations of the person, moving from manual possession or bodily identification with shells that engage the sailors' admiration of them as attributes of the recipient (they call him a winner), and outward to the admiration and knowledge of an interested, distant third party who is not present.

In general, fame can be described as a positive subjective conversion effected by a particular transaction, which derives from the outside cognition of a distant other external to the transaction. Whereas an

[a] The chant refers to a trip made on a trawler, rather than the more usual Gawan mode of canoe travel. Similarly, the chant refers to fame acquired in Alotau, the capital of the Milne Bay Province.

immediate transactor, or the particular event, starts one's fame (as, for example, when Gawan visitors take back news of the sumptuousness of Gawan food gifts, or the sailors admire the Gawan recipient's armshell), fame itself must be a process that goes beyond this relative immediacy, as the Gawan images cited above suggest. This third party other favors the transaction in a positive fashion with his notice, giving it a known, favorable identity, an existence beyond the immediacy of the act, and the spatiotemporal location of the transaction.

From another perspective, the spatiotemporal control exerted in the immediate transaction of a shell – the capacity for influencing the mind of another that is demonstrated in the transaction – produces a reverberation that further extends that influence in spreading awareness of it to others who objectify it as knowledge. In doing so, they give it a potentiality for affecting their own kula acts. This is suggested in the example cited above: Southern kula people who hear about a transaction in the northern area rush to travel north on kula because they know the Gawan's acquisition means that he has acquired a shell that he can then transact in their direction. This rhetoric is a straightforward rendering of the idea that fame extends a man's immediate influence on the minds and actions of partners to *distant* others. In this sense, fame depicts or models influence – that is, the influential acts of any actor – as being the *potential* for influence on the acts of a third party other.

In sum, fame can be understood as a coding of influence – an iconic model that reconstitutes immediate influence at the level of a discourse by significant others about it. Fame models the spatiotemporal expansion of self effected by acts of influence by recasting these influential acts (moving the mind of another) into the movement or circulation of one's name; this circulation itself implies the favorable notice others give the person – hence the latter's "influence" with them. Acts are thus matrixed in a discourse or code that refers back to them. As iconic and reflexive code, fame is the *virtual form of influence*. Without fame, a man's influence would, as it were, go nowhere; successful acts would in effect remain locked within themselves in given times and places of their occurrence or be limited to immediate transactors. The circulation of names frees them, detaching them from these particularities and making them the topic of discourse through which they become available in other times and places.

Since fame is the circulation of persons via their names in the realm of other minds (or in the oral realm of the speech of others), it typifies the capacity for subjective relocation and positive reconstitution of the self that is fundamental to the transaction process. As virtual influence, fame reflects the influential acts of the actor back to himself from an external source. Indeed, through it, the actor knows himself as someone known by others. As one Gawan said to me: "I am a guyaw; they speak my name." It is through fame, then – the fact that he is known by others – that a man may come to know *himself* as a guyaw.

By the same token, it is in Gawa's perception of itself as having fame (and thus as the home of men of fame) that the community knows itself as being strong – as able to create positive value or generative potency for itself. The climbing fame of Gawa (*butura Gawa*) constitutes a sign of the positive value state of the community and its internal transactive potentialities. Later we shall see that when Gawans fear that the viability of Gawa and its immediate projects are being threatened by witchery, speakers in public meetings may rhetorically appeal to the importance of Gawan fame and overseas standing, and to the subversive effects of witchery upon it, which result in defamation and shame.

PART III

Exchange and the value template

6

Marriage exchanges as value transformations

If we have no sisters, we go down. Women lift [a man] up (*i-rupe-s*), he climbs on high. Without a sister, one is down below. She gives us necklaces, armshells, canoes.

Gawan man discussing marriage exchanges, 1975

In Chapter 4 we saw a causal-logical nexus emerge in a variety of Gawan contexts between operations on food (the separation of food from, or its identification with the actor) and certain qualities of the body. I argued that in this symbolism the state of the actor's body exhibits the level of spatiotemporal control effected by the action, iconically signifying a positive or negative transformation of value.

I have described this nexus roughly as involving "logico-causal" relations. The whole relational nexus can be seen as entailing "ordering functions" (Tyler, 1978:242ff.) of causality, sequence, and likeness, as well as a dialectic of binary opposition (positive vs. negative value). The meshing of the first three functions is critical: The qualitative state or mode of being is both the outcome of the act, and also an icon of it. Furthermore, it is in this iconicity that the value of the act is concretized or given form. We may think of the entire nexus as an underlying causal-iconic formula formed in the potentializing model of action, which engages dynamic tensions between negative and positive value in the process of self and self –other formation.

I shall call this relational nexus a *template* or a *generative schema* to carry the sense of a guiding, generative formula that underlies and organizes significance in different overt symbolic formations or processes, and that is available as an implicit constructive form for the handling of experience (cf. Ardener, 1978:106, who speaks of "template structures" to convey a somewhat related idea). I suggest that this form is the dominant Gawan schema or template for constructing intersubjective relations in which value is both *created and signified*.

In this and subsequent chapters, I argue that this template governs three key Gawan exchange cycles: those of marriage, mortuary exchanges, and community entertainments – each of them forming a particular mode of intersubjective spacetime. I attempt to show in what sense the template formulates positive value models that mediate hierarchy and equality, through examining the structure of the cycles of spatiotemporal transformation entailed in the particular exchanges and the component media of the exchanges.

THE SPACETIME OF BUWAA
MARRIAGE EXCHANGES

A Gawan marriage is initiated by a gift of baskets of cooked garden produce (taro, sweet potatoes, yams if available) from the young woman's maternal and paternal kin to the kin of the young man. The homes of the parents or foster parents of each member of the marital pair provide the centers for the collection (the woman's parents) and redistribution (the man's parents) of the food. This transaction (*kalawodeli*) signals the consent of the woman's kin to the marriage. It is paid for collectively on the following day by gifts from each of the young man's kin who has received a basket of food (and thus accepted the marriage). The man's payment (*takola*, see Malinowski, 1929:89; Weiner, 1976:186) consists of nonedible goods, many of which are now externally introduced tradestore items such as knives, cloth, or western clothing; Papua New Guinea money; and more rarely a kula shell.[1] Each basket should be paid for with at least one item plus an additional item for the betel nut topping on the basket. The takola closes the immediate exchange but this whole short-term transaction converts the casual sexual liaison of the courtship period into the ideally enduring relationship of the marriage (-*vay*) in which the partners live together, and the bond between the couple is matrixed in the bonds between the two sets of kin (see Chapters 2 and 4).

Since the cooked garden food is the initial gift, signaling the consent of the woman's kinspeople, this food giving is the act that transforms the sexual relationship from relative temporal and spatial transiency, with a comparatively limited and only informal involvement of additional kin (most notably the parents)[2] into a localized, ideally long-term relationship that entails extended connectivities beyond the couple and via them to Gawan kinspeople on each side. Moreover, the donor source and distribution of the food baskets to different recipients defines the initial set of key affines who are to be linked in dyadic relationships of long-term buwaa gift giving as well as other kinds of affinal exchanges (see Chapters 2 and 4). The spatiotemporal transformation initiated by the cooked food gift (and its immediate payment) thus brings into being long-term cyclic exchanges that are expected to last as long as the marriage (whether terminated by divorce or the death of one of the spouses), or until the death of one of the partners to the exchange.

The initial exchange also models the basic *directionality* of the subsequent formal buwaa exchanges in which, as indicated in Chapter 2, raw comestibles (taro and yams on a regular basis, and pigs when required) are transmitted from the woman's to the man's kin, whereas kula shells and canoes are the essential noncomestibles from the husband and his kin.[3] It is the part of the female gift centered in raw garden produce that forms the most important core of the buwaa from the female side, and that concerns me here.

Like directionality in kula shell movements, that of the female and male affinal gifts cannot be reversed, but unlike the former, these affinal directions do not encode the relative geographical locations of exchangers. Rather, geographical location enters into this directionality in a different way through the respective connections of each set of media with internal and external poles of the Gawan world. Although the essential female gift is garden-based produce with its source in the interior pole, kula shells come into Gawa from the outside as media of inter-island relationships. On the other hand, we shall see that canoes occupy a complex medial locus in the land–sea trajectory: they are seaward relative to garden produce, constituting a medium of sea travel made, however, from the trees of Gawan bushlands (see Munn, 1977).[4]

Both yam and taro buwaa are transmitted raw at their harvest. But since taro has no uniformly scheduled planting time, transmission occurs any time the donors' designated plots for particular recipients ripen. In the case of yams, however, we have seen that there is a Gawa-wide scheduled planting period, and a single annual harvest occurring between late March and May. Yams are the more public buwaa gift, and Gawans have some tendency to regard them as more important, although taro also has considerable significance (see Chapter 2). I shall limit my commentary to the yams as epitomizing the basic principles of the buwaa garden gift.

A man designates one or two plots in his yam gardens for each woman to whose husband's kinspeople he is giving yam produce. Whereas the donor plants the garden (sometimes with aid from the recipient consumers of the yams), the harvest is *always* done by the recipients and their aids. As one woman explained, they work because they eat – that is, it is theirs to eat, even though (as indicated earlier) they may not actually consume all of this food themselves.

Since the recipients return a portion of the harvest to the donor's yam house as seed yams for future planting of the buwaa of the woman involved, the transaction can be reproduced at the next harvest from the yams of the previous harvest. The recipients decide on the portion of the harvest that is returned, doing the sorting at their own yam houses, and then taking the seed yams back to the donor to be stored in a separate compartment of the latter's yam house. Thus at harvest small groups of people may be seen harvesting yams in the gardens of certain of their affines, and later informally visiting with them at yam houses in their (the donors') hamlets.

Since the timing of this event is determined by the repetitive yam harvest cycle, the mode of continuity that characterizes the affinal buwaa transaction replicates the repetitive, cyclic reproduction of gardens. Moreover, just as yam gardens in general are reproduced by seed yams from the previous season, so yam buwaa as a transactive category is also reproduced from seed yams of the same buwaa in the previous season. In this respect, the buwaa yam gift, like yams in general, is renewed through substantive continuities – a production of the new out of the material of the old. As we have seen, the stones of the garden condense this spatio-temporal mode of creating enduring potentiality. The affinal harvest maps this kind of temporality into a transactive form.

Moreover, the temporally generalized rather than specialized character of the harvest giving is on the order of other skwayobwa relations with their core in the transaction of comestibles (Chapter 3). Just as skwayobwa in cooked and raw food is the base of influence on which kula exchange is built, so the transmission of the raw produce from the women and their kin in the affinal context is the dynamic source of influence that yields them kula shells and canoes.

These kula shells and canoes from the husband's side are occasional rather than regularly timed gifts, pinned to no particular schedule, and not necessarily repetitive. The timing of kula shell gifts is dependent on the complex contingencies affecting a man's kula shell acquisitions, which, in turn, derive from the spacetime of kula and its circulatory mode of continuity rather than the reproductive mode of the gardens. In addition, both canoes and shells belong to categories of durable goods that have unique identities. A canoe (like kula shells above the lowest ranks) is always named, and long remembered by its owner-builders and its affinal recipients. Thus men of the female side convert their nameless, and perishable but temporally repetitive gifts of raw garden produce into temporally specialized, but relatively enduring and personalized (individually memorable) artifacts from the husband's kin. The particularized identities of these durable artifacts introduce additional expansive potential into the transformational process, as I comment on later, especially in connection with canoes.

Unlike kula shells, which are transmitted between individuals, canoes are collectively owned by a dala. They are built by a man and his dala, with additional work–aid from affines (especially sinavarama and their kin, see Chapter 2) and other members of the wider community. A canoe can be built only when a man and his dala feel they have sufficient gardens to support the major feasts and the feeding of the workers, which are intrinsic to the construction process. Each man should give his wife, and through her, one of her kinsmen, at least one canoe built by *his dala*. The husband himself may be the chief builder, or the builder may be another man of his dala who is a recipient of yam and taro harvest produce from one of the wife's kinsmen.

Men may sometimes compete for a desired canoe by attempting to give more food than another man – making special produce payments and building up a strong food-giving relationship with a relevant dala member of the husband. An extra gift of food may also be given by a man from his gardens on receipt of the canoe. If two men giving buwaa for a woman both want the canoe, the one who does not receive it may be given a kula shell instead to allay any resentment he might feel. But whatever decision is made, the husband's dala are persuaded to give a man a canoe only through the latter's food giving. However, the canoe (as also any kula shell gift between affines) is not, strictly speaking, repayment for the food, although labels like *mapura*, "replacement/return," or *meyisara*, "payment," may be applied loosely to it. Rather, the produce gift is the wouwura or base of the canoe – what makes it move or generates its path (*keda*). As one man explained, the expression *ra-kidakeda waga* (which can be glossed "the canoe's pathway") means the base of the canoe, "the food we give our sisters" (*karu ta-seik na-dei-ta*), which makes their husbands' kinsmen *consent* to transmit the canoe. The canoe must subsequently be paid for by its recipients, since the produce does not pay for the canoe, but moves it.

The transmission of buwaa kula shells is also built on food giving. A kula shell is typically transmitted between individual men linked in a buwaa relationship. Thus it is given as part of the reciprocation for produce from the kinsman of a female affine (or sometimes of a wife's female affine).[5] The donor generally derives the shell (which is never of the highest standard, but usually a named shell of an intermediate or relatively low rank) from one of his own inter-island paths. This shell should be a *vaga*, although it may also be a shell that is his own possession, that is, his *kitomu* (see Chapter 2). In the latter case (unlike the former), he has no debt for the shell to a man from another island. In either case, the affinal recipient uses the shell as vaga to transact on one of his own paths or to establish a new path of partnerships, sending it along in the appropriate direction whenever he decides to do so. Gawans call transactions of this kind "home kula" (*kura veru*).

A shell may be transmitted by being carried from the hamlet of the donor to that of the recipient and hung on the latter's house or yam house, where it may be displayed for a time. It should yield an equivalent gulugwalu return at a subsequent time – ideally at the next sailing for shells of the opposed category after its transmission onward – but the actual period of the debt is uncertain, and it is not entirely uncommon for shells given as buwaa to default.[6] When the return is made, it goes back to the original Gawan donor, who in turn should send it back on the kula path that was the source of the original shell, if the latter was not his kitomu. If the shell was his kitomu, he may use the return as he wishes. In either case, the second shell squares the original and technically closes the transaction between the two men.

It is possible, however, for such a transaction to become a more enduring intra-island segment of the two Gawans' kula relationships. If this occurs, a unitary inter-island path may then be built out of parts of what were previously different paths of partners belonging to different Gawan men; or a single enduring path may be created de novo by the travel of the original (and then subsequent) shells linking the inter-island contacts of these two men. Some men build strong relationships with one of their food-giving affines by embedding the relationship in an ongoing kula path so that buwaa shells may continue to be passed between them. Such a sustained kula bond then has a repetitive temporal form – one that is not timed, however, by the harvest schedule of edible produce, but by the complex, uncertain and multiple exigencies of kula. As in ordinary inter-island kula, the capacity to continue relations through long-term transactions that ideally do not finish is a sign of the strength of the relationship (in this context, between affines) and reflects back favorably on a man's standing, as well as providing each man with an additional source of kula shells in the partnerships or path segment of the other.

But whether the kula transaction between affinal partners is continued or not, the general principle is that the harvest transaction has the capacity to transform the affinal relation internal to Gawa into the more extensive and encompassing inter-island spacetime of kula, where it becomes a (Gawan-internal) segment of a kula path. A transformation of spatiotemporal level is thus effected from a cycle based on the garden harvest which involves only consociates connected in a closed set of affinal intra-island relationships, to an inter-island cycle in which affinal consociates become bound up in the more expansive circulation structure of kula.

In return for his harvest giving, then, a man is obtaining a named artifact that engages a more comprehensive expansive level of spatiotemporal control. In fact, an astute man who has a number of kinswomen for whom he gives food (as indicated earlier, typified as "sisters") can enhance his kula and his general dala standing.

One man suggested to me that another (whom I will label A) had "carried off the decision-making authority (i-kouw kareiwaga)" of his dala – even though this authority had nominally passed to his mother's brother, a more senior man – because A had a number of sisters through whom he received kula shells and so established new path relationships for himself. In this way *A* incremented the kula that he had already inherited from his mother's mother's brother. As a result, my informant said, *A's* name "climbed." In actuality, *A* was also a very astute kula man who had managed to gain control of part of his less effective mother's brother's kula. However, my informant's point was that *A* made the most of his affinal relationships to enhance his status. (We might note in passing the implication that a man must be a strong gardener in order to do this.)

Another informant explained that if a man wants to raise his own standing in kula, he may do so by making special gifts in raw garden crops and a pig to his "sister." This will "make the name of his sister rise." As a result, she wants this man to climb in kula; telling her husband of the gifts, she asks him what kula shell he will give this "brother."

These views concerning women's participation in the exchanges are summed up in the comment that heads this chapter. The intervening women to whom a man has given food (his *gamagali*, as noted in Chapter 2) are viewed as the immediate source of the man's ability to rise. Women frequently refer to themselves as the givers of the returns from their husbands or husbands' kinsmen. By giving a man shells and canoes it is *they* who lift him up. Similarly, the transmission of harvest produce from the woman and her kinsmen to the husband and his kin is the originating base or wouwura that effects the object conversion from food to kula shells (and canoes), that is, the initial spatiotemporal transformation.

If we recall the argument of the previous chapter concerning the relation between personal adornment, kula shells (named, memorable artifacts) and a man's name, we can see that what the food donor receives are the media containing the qualisigns of a new level of control potential: the hierarchizing status increment available through kula. Food is, in effect, converted into one's name, the adornment or expansion of self entailed in the spacetime of kula shells and kula exchange. *Rather than being an equivalent of what has been given, the reciprocation is precisely the sign of nonequivalence or increment; it is an objectification of the donor's positive transformation of self, the new potential or influence he achieves by the food-giving act.* The hierarchy of the reciprocal exchange cycle is thus embodied in the product and exhibited in its qualisigns of positive value. Nevertheless, *equivalence* is expressed within the kula segment of the transactions in the return of an equivalent kula shell of the opposite category by the initial shell recipient. I shall return to this problem of the hierarchy and equivalence of objects later.

THE CANOE AND THE
AFFINAL EXCHANGE CYCLE

I turn now to a more detailed consideration of the canoe in the marriage exchange cycle. Elsewhere (Munn, 1977) I have outlined the canoe exchange trajectory and some aspects of the spatiotemporal transformation it entails. Here, I reconsider the problem from the perspective of the present argument.

As I have pointed out, canoes are owned by the building dala. They are transmitted by the chief builder either to another man of his dala (who then usually gives it to *his* wife and her kinsman) or to the chief builder's wife and so onward to the latter's kinsman. Sometimes a canoe is given directly overseas to a recipient on another island, and in this case it travels without an intervening in-Gawa affinal segment of its exchange path. Most canoes, however, are transmitted on affinal paths (which may include one or more marital couples for whom it is given as buwaa) before going overseas to Muyuw or Yanaba on their southerly journey.

The directional transaction of canoes as they move into the inter-island arena is a part of the multiple associations that connect them in Gawan thinking with kula exchange. Canoes must be transacted in the direction from which armshells come because the latter (and *not* necklaces) are the key durable goods acquired from final recipients that will travel back (usually through middlemen) to become the kitomu possessions of the building dala. Canoes therefore travel in the direction of necklaces being transacted for armshells in kula. In fact, in speaking of canoe transmission (both within and beyond Gawa), one says "He kula'd his canoe" (*i-kura ra-waga*). Canoe exchange must, in this sense be viewed as part of the inter-island kula system (see also Macintyre, 1983:216ff.).

Further connections between canoes and kula derive from the fact that canoes both carry and, as we have seen, are adorned by kula shells. Canoes themselves have various important identifications with the human body and its beautification in adornment. These identifications suggest that the affinal reciprocation of canoes for produce, like that of kula shells, is a particular formulation of the underlying cultural template noted earlier (the nexus between bodily or body-related qualisigns and operations involving food), even though overtly it may appear otherwise. These points will be amplified shortly.

A canoe is handed over to a particular male recipient by taking a piece of canoe lashing (and sometimes mats, skirts, and a kula shell)[7] to him in his hamlet. The lashing stands for the canoe. The recipient then acquires the right to sail the canoe to his own dala beach or the beach that he and his hamlet members use for their canoes. This man is now the captain (*tarawaga*) of the canoe and as long as it is in his possession has final control of matters pertaining to its care and use. As captain, he determines not only who may sail in the canoe, but when and where it sails, despite the fact that the canoe still belongs to the original building dala (who usually use it to sail with the new captain and the latter's own people on kula), and all payments for it will go back to them. As canoe captain, a man also increments his own reputation overseas as he becomes known as the captain of a particular canoe. In short, receipt of a canoe entails an extension of the recipient's spatiotemporal control based on the mobile-transportive capacities of the product.

This extension of control also occurs in connection with the exchange of the canoe, since the current captain has the right to determine the next recipient of the canoe and when he will transmit it – that is, he gains control over its onward motion in forming an exchange path.[8] He may decide to give it to his wife and one of her food-giving kinsmen, or to transmit it overseas to a man on another island. If he chooses the latter, he can use the canoe to strengthen his overseas influence and his name in the inter-island world. If, on the other hand, he chooses to make a gift to an affine, he reciprocates food gifts from this man made in virtue of his own marriage and so strengthens his standing with his own wife and affines. The canoe itself then continues along through these internal affinal links; most frequently (but not always – see the next section, and Munn, 1977, Figure 2D), it is transacted overseas after being given as buwaa for one or two marriages, and within one to two years after construction.

But canoe names are widely remembered despite the canoe's departure from Gawa; and so also are the names of the canoe's Gawan and external recipients. Classic canoe names belong to the dala of the builder, and may also be names of bushlands owned by the dala, the location of trees from which canoes can be built (see Munn, 1977). Like named kula shells, canoes have paths that are remembered as sequences of individual names reflecting the onward journey of transmission. Although canoes therefore "circulate" in the sense in which I have used the term (see Chapter 3), the spacetime that is constituted through the transaction of the canoe does not achieve the same emergent order of circulatory autonomy as that of kula (Chapter 3), for reasons that will become clear shortly.

CANOE PAYMENTS

Each Gawan canoe recipient must make a lengthy series of return payments to the canoe-owning dala.[9] These payments are regarded as returns for the canoe work and are distributed accordingly by the owning dala.[10] Neither the chief canoe builder nor any of the couples for whom the canoe and its payments are classed as buwaa may eat from these returns. These returns consist primarily of the edible fruits of trees – raw fruits, nuts, and coconuts – with the additional payment of one or more pigs and a large cooking of taro pudding by each recipient and his kinspeople. Raw garden crops are not part of the payments.

There is thus a change in the kinds of comestibles given by the women's kinspeople to pay for the canoe. Instead of garden produce, fruits from the tops of trees predominate, a feature that seems to suggest an iconic relation between the payment and the canoe (also a tree product), as well as an increasing masculinization of the exchange cycle.[11] There thus appears to be a closer connection between the canoe and these conversions than in the case of the canoe and the basic harvest gifts.

The other items (the live pigs and taro puddings) not only mark the increasing ceremoniousness and specialization of the canoe payment in contrast to the basic harvest gifts, but also suggest the shift from female- to male-centered media, or from stasis to motion. Taro pudding is the one context in which men are the main cooks of vegetable food. Whereas women boil the taro and then pound it into soft patties, only men scrape the coconut, squeeze it into water boiling in the large clay cook pots, and throw the taro patties into the foaming broth; they then stand stirring the mixture with large paddles until it reaches the right consistency. Women do the preparation of the taro, performing that part of the procedure that is both primary and more sedentary; men, on the other hand, actually make the pudding, performing the standing, more energetic part of the work. Thus taro pudding, in contrast to ordinary taro cooking, not only constitutes a masculine activity, but is internally organized in a way that engages the female activity at the base, as it were, whereas the male activity actually creates the pudding and is involved with motion (men stand and stir the foaming froth).[12] Finally, we may note that in contrast to the harvest crops, pigs are individually named, mobile creatures, with certain identifications with human beings (see Chapters 8 and 9). Thus, although the return canoe gifts from the female side affines are comestibles, there has been a significant change in the qualities of these comestibles that introduces elements of masculinization and motion.

Although there is an approximate sequence in which all these payments should be made, only the payment of about one hundred coconuts (*samaka*) tied in pairs to a pole has any really firm position in the sequence and a scheduled time of presentation. This pole should be given the day after the canoe lashing has been handed over to the new recipient as public confirmation of the canoe's transmission. Other payments of fruits and nuts will then be made sporadically by each recipient and his kinspeople whenever their trees are ripe and sufficient produce available from them. The process of completing each sequence for each donor generally extends over several years, frequently continuing after the canoe itself has departed from Gawa on its southward exchange journey.

In sum, unlike the repetitive, homogeneous harvest gifts, the affinal canoe payments consist of a series of different categories of tree produce, and the series of payments from each recipient ends without renewal when all requirements have been met. However, the one canoe (or canoe path) can generate at least one, and frequently more than one, long-term sequence of different kinds of returns; these returns move from each recipient to the original builders, traveling from the former's hamlet at different times to the hamlet of the builder. Thus it is as if the canoe's unitary travel has an expansive, multiplicative capacity to yield additional spacetimes of sequential (but nonreplicating) transactions.

In contrast to the harvest transmission, each type of canoe return is presented in a festive parade of women and men from the hamlet of the canoe recipient where the resources have been collected and prepared for transport, to the hamlet of the chief canoe builder where they are distributed by the latter to kinspeople of his dala and kumila and others who worked for the canoe. The transmission is thus publicized, and the cross-cutting hamlet relationships that it defines are formally marked (in contrast to the notable lack of formal markedness in the harvest contexts).[13]

I have already considered the occurrence of interhamlet processions at the widest community level in the case of the curing rite (Chapter 4). Other parades in addition to those connected with canoe payments involve the festive carrying of goods from one hamlet to another, or across part of the island. These parades involve decorative, public display of the items being transported, and frequently some beautification on the part of participants. Such parades usually move with vitality, and in the most festive contexts may be accompanied by the blowing of conch shells to announce the brightly decorated and happy procession of carriers. Although canoe parades are less decorative than some others and body decoration is less emphasized, participants nevertheless move along smartly in bright display of their gifts.

We have seen in connection with the curing rite some of the significance of such collective processions across fixed hamlet segmentations. When goods are carried in processions, they display the strength to bring together within a single transaction – conveyed directly in the unified line of the procession – resources that are donated by individuals and are brought in from different hamlets to a collection point. Since people carry this collection in a linear array, the act of giving is itself displayed as a unitary process of traveling across fixed bounds.

Formal parades combine human mobility and the spatial connectivities of paths. It is as if the "linearity" of the path receives its human coordinate in the linear sequence of paraders: People and geographical space are aligned to constitute together a spatiotemporal form, a path in its fullest spatial and temporal sense of a "passage." I stress these points in relation to the canoe because this artifact is in all respects one that epitomizes passage. As an artifact, it is of course a vehicle of sea travel, and in its mode of transmission it creates a memorable path of recipients that eventually extends overseas (see Munn, 1977). In contrast, the garden produce that is at the base of this movement is relatively static in its qualities, and connected with the interior heaviness of the garden. Karu, as one man said, is "heavy" – like the garden, it is "down below." Just as the canoe epitomizes passage in these ways, so, also, it would seem that this processional mode of making canoe payments (as, in some respects, the payments themselves) exhibits the spatiotemporal value transformation occurring in the shift from the level of the harvest produce to that of the mobile canoe.[14]

Let us return to the structure of the canoe exchange path. A notable feature of this path is its capacity to travel beyond the trajectory of the harvest buwaa given for one nodal couple, and be given as buwaa for two or more couples.[15] In moving beyond the basic marriage exchange unit, the canoe gives a single, concretized form to the unmarked overlapping that occurs between some of these exchange units; or sometimes it creates such overlapping connections as people make new buwaa relationships in order to obtain the canoe. This is illustrated in Figure 4, which also shows that when the canoe traverses more than one nodal couple, thus realizing the continuity implicit in a given set of overlapping, buwaa food-giving units, it is specifically women who form the enabling links along which it moves.

For example, in the case of the canoe Kaigwayagwa (Figure 4a), the food given by the man *R* for his sister went to the woman *S* as the immediate recipient who could, with her husband, eat the food. *Ka* was also giving food for his sister *S* that *Y*, her husband's dala kinsman, could eat. A canoe was given from this dala (specifically from *Y* who gave it to *K*) to the woman *S* who gave it to her brother, who in turn gave it to his wife *I*; *I* then gave the canoe to *R*, the man mentioned above. Two buwaa-giving units are thus reflected in the passage of the canoe.

If the immediate recipient of *R*'s food (i.e., the ostensible consumer) had been a man rather than the woman *S*, then, given the direction of canoe movements (from husband to wife and not vice versa), *R* could not have obtained the canoe by this route. However, he could have received another canoe from the (hypothetical) male recipient (let us say, built by the dala of *Ka*). If he then sent the canoe overseas as in the actual case, only one marriage (or one buwaa-giving unit) would have been "traversed" by this canoe before it left Gawa. Of course, *R* would also have had the option of giving this canoe to his wife and so onward to a man who had given buwaa for her to be eaten by *R*'s sister *I* (an option he might also, of course, have exercised if he had so wished, in the present case). To use a non-Gawan metaphor, it is as if women are the "runners" along which canoes slide across exchange units.

Thus women are not only the interstitial recipients through which canoes move initially across different dala or between male captains, but they are also the means of extending canoe paths and increasing the length of a canoe path within Gawa. It is, however, the named canoe, the gift from the male side, that moves.

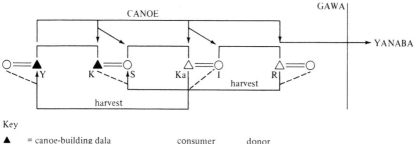

Key

▲ = canoe-building dala
R. I = siblings (1 mother)
Ka. S = siblings (1 mother)
K. Y = siblings (parallel cousins)

a The path of the canoe Kaigwayagwa

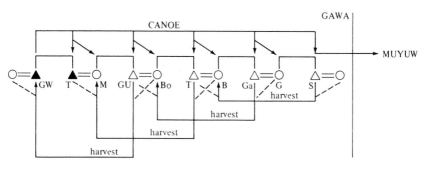

Key

▲ = canoe-building dala
S. G = siblings (1 mother)
Ga. B = siblings (1 mother)
T. Bo = mother's brother – sister's child (different dala of 1 kumila)
Gu. M = siblings (1 mother)

b The path of the canoe Kalopay

Figure 4. Canoe paths.

The sequence of affinal payments made for a canoe by each recipient man does not go back along the path from one canoe recipient to another until it finally reaches the building dala. Instead, each payee makes his gift directly to the building dala. Ordinarily some members of this dala have been receiving buwaa produce as consumers from the particular canoe payee, but when the canoe is transacted on an unusually long internal path, this may not be the case. In Figure 4b for example, S gave food for his sister G for which her husband's sister was the designated consumer, but not anyone of the builder's dala. However, S, like all the other recipients made the appropriate series of payments directly to T and his dala. Thus the canoe's expansive potential makes it possible for a dala to receive direct payments from people whose food buwaa they do not consume. Although the degree of expansion of this particular canoe path does not seem to be common (see Munn, 1977, Figure 2D), the transacting principles for canoes nevertheless contain this potential.

As I have indicated, the canoe path also extends overseas through the agency of the final recipient (not the building dala). When a canoe transaction has been arranged overseas, the canoe itself sails back captained by its recipient and carrying initial returns (foods and condiments in which the recipient community specializes)[16] in its hold. This gift, called *kayvaga-waga* – "starting gift for the canoe" – goes to the canoe-owning dala and is distributed as payment for the canoe work. An armshell given at this time from the canoe recipient will be transacted by a man of this dala (the chief canoe builder if the canoe is not his buwaa) who may eventually decide to treat it as his kitomu should there be a default on the kitomu shells expected for the canoe as final gifts from the ultimate recipients. Otherwise, any return for it should be transacted back to the new canoe recipient.

It may be recalled that in the original transfer of the canoe to its first Gawan recipient, a kula shell of *either* category could go *from* the building dala to the canoe recipient. But in the overseas part of the passage, the movement of the kula shell is reversed, and the shell category is determinate, for the canoe moving into the inter-island world will eventually be transacted against armshells coming north as it travels south. Conversely, within Gawa, the canoe and kula shells go in the same rather than opposite directions (i.e., they are both marital gifts from the *man's* kin).

Not only does a determinate geographical rather than simply gender-based (marital) directionality take over at this juncture, but in addition, the transaction ordinarily takes place directly between two men, without the female mediation intrinsic to the intra-island sphere. The Gawan segment of the canoe path is now being resituated "within a sequentially ordered interisland space [time] like that created by a kula path. Unlike the latter, however, the canoe path does not establish partnerships that [can be continued] ... beyond the single exchange ... [nor can it] create a closed cycle of transactional movement" (Munn, 1977:45). Thus the spacetime of a canoe path cannot be renewed (either within Gawa or in the intra-island order), and in this sense its extension is linear rather than circular, for it only transects a segment of the kula area. The return for the initial canoe gifts is made whenever the overseas recipient comes to sail the canoe back to his home community. Then the canoe builders, those who transacted the canoe southward, and all recipients of the kaivaga waga payment bring gifts of produce to repay the kaivaga waga and farewell the canoe. These returns are called the canoe's departure gift (*kala gala-waga*). The term *gala* denotes "removal to another place" as when people leave one place for another, and departure gifts are similarly made to people leaving Gawa. Indeed, a woman of the canoe-building dala may sit and wail on the beach as the canoe sails away. For although the canoe might return again, sometimes carrying part of its further returns in its hold, it now leaves Gawan physical possession forever.

Although additional edibles are paid for the canoe, the two types of durable good that mark the finale are pots (*walata*) and kitomu armshells.[17] These items are expected from the most distant final recipients of the canoe, usually southerners in the Raramani region of the Massim where the canoe's path ends, and may take several years or more to arrive on Gawa; this timing may be longer than Gawans would like, but they are dependent, in this respect, on the middle men and final recipients.

In theory, the initial Gawan recipient of all overseas returns is the last Gawan captain who transacted it southward, not the canoe-building dala. The former should then transact all returns back along the internal canoe path to the canoe-building dala. In fact, this sequencing (as against direct return) is not, in my experience, actually carried out, but the emphasis Gawans place on it is significant. For these goods, the nominal mode of payment has now shifted in accord with the more typical path transmission of the inter-island kula pattern, and ideally each canoe recipient should be treated as a recipient and transactor of the inter-island returns.

When pots and kula shells from the final southern recipients of the canoe arrive on Gawa, the canoe builders acquire a new level of inter-island transactive potency in the objects of the kula shells. These shells become their kitomu and are ordinarily distributed to men of their dala. Whereas pots are typically distributed to the dala women or the wives of dala men, and remain on Gawa, the kula shell kitomu may, at the discretion of the Gawan recipient, move out again into the inter-island world to strengthen the latter's kula.

The cooking pots, which condense more limited spatial control capacities, represent the female input of cooking into the manufacture of the canoe. The two types of durable return factor out masculine and feminine work. Moreover, they have the effect of separating out aspects of the canoe artifact itself so that in the form of its final artifactual conversions it no longer constitutes the same synthesis of male and female dimensions as that which, as we shall see, characterizes the canoe itself.

It is, however, the kitomu shells and not the pots that actually square the canoe transaction and close it. The sense in which canoes and kula shells are equivalents may already have been implied, but a fuller discussion can be taken up only after considering the artifactual properties of the canoe and its relation to the human body. For the moment, we may note that we have now reached the close of the affinal cycle beginning with the harvest

Plate 7. Kitomu armshells that have just arrived on Gawa hang in a canoe shed
as visitors and Gawans sit talking.

gifts from the women's kin. But this is not the end of the canoe cycle. Just
as the harvest gifts are the wouwura of the canoe, so the canoe is now
regarded as the wouwura – the generative source – of any kula transactions
built upon an original kitomu from that canoe.

As indicated in Chapter 2, these particular shells do not remain the
Gawan owner's kitomu when they enter kula. Rather, the necklace defined
as the matching return of the armshell becomes his kitomu; subsequently,
the equivalent armshell return for the necklace becomes the Gawan
owner's kitomu, and so on. Although one may continually change the
particular shells that instantiate one's kitomu rights,[18] the current kitomu
instantiation and *all the transactions and instantiations started by the first
kitomu have their wouwura* (base) *in the originating canoe.*

A kitomu thus has a *leliyu* – that is, a historical discourse relating to
origins – which consists of the paths (sequentially ordered names of
transactors) it has traveled from the time of its acquisition by the dala. The
man handling the current kitomu will usually remember this leliyu and the
name of the canoe that is its wouwura as well as other relevant details (for
example, the name of the canoe builder, and its original path, and final
recipient, etc.). In this way, the canoe can become part of a historical
discourse in which it is the origin point of kula exchange cycles. By

means of its name, it is now bound in an ongoing fashion to its kitomu conversions and, in effect, *objectified* in them. Yet in its own form it has disappeared.

Not all kitomu put into kula are successfully reproduced. Like other shells, kitomu can default (*-toubu*) and be lost.[19] Moreover, some kitomu are alienated by owners to pay debts in kula, or to obtain non-kula goods. Nevertheless, canoes that Gawans have long since traded southward, and that may indeed have rotted long ago, may still be objectified in their kitomu form within Gawan kula exchanges. Thus the nonreproducible canoe path that created a terminal mode of spacetime traversing intra- and inter-island space is transformed into the more comprehensive spacetime of kula circulation that has a power of reproducibility not available within the canoe path. In this process the canoe itself is converted into a historical memory that maintains a physical presence in its renewable kitomu objectifications.

To summarize, I have suggested that the affinal exchange cycle that involves canoe transmission, like the cycle involving the reciprocation of a kula shell, is lifted up on the dynamic base of produce–transmission, as are the affinal food donors themselves. This base is a repetitive process for the length of a marriage; it is timed by the harvests and has its locus in the internal space of Gawan gardens and hamlets. The transmission of produce from the woman and her kin in a marital relation puts the cycle into motion, as it were, yielding durable objective forms that have the capacity to circulate beyond the level of extension that characterizes the horticultural base, and constituting a spacetime not timed by the harvest cycle, one eventually regulated by the complex contingencies of kula exchange. The canoe cycle is more complex than the kula exchange cycle, involving the intermediate conversion of the canoe, which although itself being an object that is transacted out of Gawa never to return – an object that may indeed, eventually rot – can nevertheless produce kula shell kitomu that come back into Gawa from the outside but can be circulated as enduring reembodiments of the canoe in kula exchange.

This expansive power, which has its source in the harvest gift, models the initial surpassing of self created in the transmission from the female side which, I have argued, lies at the foundation of the transformational process and is its fundamental dynamic. In the mobile object of the canoe, the female side affines receive an icon of the value they have produced for themselves. In practice, this may consist, for example, of a control over inter-island travel and an increment to their standing with overseas communities. But in another sense it is as if they receive a name, or themselves in the form of a named, decorated object. On the other hand, the husband's kin receive as final payment, the increment of value – the new level of potential or influence generated by their canoe transmission –

that is condensed within a kitomu shell. For kitomu have an even higher, more comprehensive level of mobility and continuity (i.e., a greater control over spacetime) than the canoe the dala originally built.

Yet this kitomu return is a sign of equivalence that closes the transaction, just as a kula shell of opposite category to that originally given finishes the affinal transaction in that type of cycle. However, before examining this interplay of equivalence and hierarchy in the finalization of the affinal cycle, it is necessary to consider the complex associations between the canoe and the human body, and some aspects of the relation between these associations and the work of canoe manufacture. This account is necessary to an understanding of the transformational processes and formation of value I have been describing; we shall see that what emerges draws on the same generative schema in another context.

CANOES AND THE BODY

The connection between canoes, the human body and body decor of which I spoke earlier, may be considered in terms of three dimensions of the canoe: the canoe materials – specifically the wood of the hull and the outrigger (but especially the hull); the canoe as a finished artifact; and the transportive capacities of the canoe. In general terms, the overall pattern is as follows. The fundamental wooden materials are metaphorically identified with internal bodily fluids. The most marked connection is one found elsewhere in the Massim (see Berde, 1974:90ff.; Bromilow, 1912:420) between the red wood (*kousiray*, a term also used as a synechdoche for the canoe as a whole) of the hull and blood (*buyay*), which is the body's maternal component and the essential medium from which Gawans say the fetus is formed.

The completed, decorated canoe, especially the prowboard area, is heavily anthropomorphized. In the Gawan view, the canoe projects the image of the ceremonially decorated person, especially a youthful man (see Munn, 1977:47ff.). Similarly, the surface, individuating facial appearance of the person, should ideally connect him or her to *paternal* kin. The canoe itself, as a beautified vehicle for carrying people and goods, can be seen as providing something like an external surfacing of the person within which people arrive on other islands. This function is most significant, as I have already suggested, in kula when a man's persuasive image is so critical. From this perspective, the canoe is itself a kind of body decor, a resurfacing of the body by artificial means.

I begin with a consideration of the identification of the canoe woods cut from trees on Gawan land, with body substances. This identification is made in the historical dala narrative (*leliyu*), which treats the origin of canoe making as indigenous to Gawa. Knowledge of the core of this narrative is widespread on Gawa, although it belongs to only one dala, the originators of the canoe, whose dala name, *Tatatus-pweipwaya*, "The ones who hollowed the soil,"[20] refers to the key feature of the story. I have synthesized slightly different versions of the relevant part of the narrative in the following shortened account and commentary:

Men of the Tatatus-pweipwaya dala, wishing to go sailing, attempt to build a canoe. But instead of hollowing out a log, they hack a long hollow in the ground (*i-tatatu-s pweipwaya*) and make the prowboards from rocks. (These rocks, and what is taken for the hollow, can still be seen on the lands of this dala.) They keep on working and working, month after month, year after year, while food and water supplies run out. A dala sister (who has recently given birth to a child) has been cooking for the canoe building; she looks around and sees that the men have finished the gardens, water supplies, coconuts, etc. (or in another version, she simply grows tired of cooking for the unending canoe work). Going out to investigate, she calls to the workers: "Hey you men! Where is the canoe?" When they show her the hollowed trench and piles of soil, she says "What canoe is this? You are hollowing the soil!" According to one version, she says, "That's no canoe, it won't sail on the sea!" Going to the bush, she takes blood (*buyay*) and white discharge (*naw*) from her genitals, smearing "her redness (*bwaabweila*), her blood" on one tree, and her white discharge on another. The former, the *kousiray* tree, furnishes the red wood for the hull of the canoe; the latter, the *vayoru* tree, provides the white wood for the outrigger log. In another, less common variant, she applies both her substances to the kousiray tree, whose deep red wood is rimmed by a white strip next to the bark. She then calls to the men and shows them the appropriate materials for building a canoe. They work quickly to make the canoe, and are soon ready to sail.[21]

In the narrative, the dala sister is cooking for the workers, while the men do the actual construction work, a role complementarity that reflects the contemporary Gawan world where, as indicated earlier, women do the cooking for both the daily work and the larger feasts involved in canoe construction. Their participation is absolutely necessary for any canoe building to occur. Thus, the *consent* of the men's female dala kin and wives to aid in this way is a vital prerequisite for canoe construction to take place (see Chapter 3).

However, according to the narrative, the men are quite unable to manufacture a canoe until a woman shows them the mediating raw materials necessary to make a vehicle that can be detached from the land, be completed, and so be able to travel on the sea. On the surface, the narrative involves a familiar type of reversal: A woman rather than a man has the necessary knowledge for canoe building, which is a masculine skill. Indeed, the men are so ignorant (a focus of considerable humor in the story) that their canoe construction is interminably *slow* and cannot be speeded up to reach any conclusion.

But from another perspective, this is not a reversal at all. It is simply another formulation of the basic spatiotemporal cycle that we saw in the analysis of the transformational form of affinal transactions. Movement, or the extension of spatiotemporal control, is initially generated through the female gender principle. Just as the affines on the female side make affinal gifts of *garden produce* to the male side – gifts that are the wouwura origin of the mobile canoe – so a dala woman is the originating source of the *land-based raw material, wood*, which enables men to create a canoe. Similarly, just as the women for whom a man has been giving produce (one's *gamagali* – typified as dala sisters, see Chapter 2) are those who give a man canoes from their husbands, so it is the dala sister in the story who gives her brothers the knowledge of canoe making. As the informant I cited earlier said: It is women who "lift up" men. In the canoe narrative, the woman (in an abstract sense, the female principle) is the wouwura of the spatiotemporal transformation achieved by masculine canoe work (in the abstract sense, the male principle).

The productive knowledge held by this dala woman derives from capacities drawn from her own *body* or person that give men the artifact-making ability to work on *wood*, and make a sailing vehicle.[22] A woman thus freely initiates the conversion from her own internal bodily substances to an external medium by separating these substances from herself to make something apart from the body that can then itself be separated from Gawan land and move on the sea (Munn, 1977).

The identification of the wood as raw material with the fluid bodily substances is central to this model of transformation. Gawans identify the red kosiray wood as feminine because it is bloodstained. Blood is not only the key substance in the definition of the maternal bonds of dala members, but it is also the basic medium forming the fetus – in effect, the material out of which the fetus is made. When a child is conceived, the woman's blood is said to coagulate (*i-kabi*) within her to form the child. The white outrigger wood, on the other hand, is explicitly male, an identification established through its smearing with the woman's *naw*. The term *naw* denotes both seminal fluid and female discharge (note the similar use of a single term in the Trobriands, Malinowski, 1929:339f.). Thus it conveys the masculine as against the purely feminine element in the process, suggesting the male element mingling with the female in sexual intercourse (although my informants did not specifically make this latter point).

Both the male and female substances that mark the woods with bodily sexual-reproductive substances come from the woman who, according to a narrator of the Tatatus-pweipwaya dala, could instruct the men only because she had recently given birth. With respect to bodily reproduction and basic material resources, it is women who encompass the male and female principles, and their potency – the capacity to create spatiotemporal potential itself – is the encompassing power.

In sum, in the origin narrative, the female potencies make possible the spatiotemporal level entailed in the capacity to create and finish the canoe with its vital mobility, the qualisign of bodily transcendence (Chapter 4). The canoe itself can be viewed as the reified condensation of this capacity of the body. As "prime movers," women themselves do not make the canoe. Rather, they continue to provide the cooking that is the enabling work for the fabrication that must be accomplished through masculine work upon the appropriate raw materials. In contrast to canoe construction, the essential female occupation of cooking is largely sedentary. It yields an edible product that goes to energize the bodies of the male workers, and to ensure their willingness to aid in canoe construction, but does not in itself produce a durable artifact that transcends the bodies of workers and the production context itself. Energetic masculine activity, on the other hand, does the job of separating the raw materials from the land (men chop down the trees, prepare the timber, and log it down the Gawan cliffs to the sea) and shapes them into a specific (named) artifact with a capacity for motion.

The two versions of the wood marking noted in the narrative summary above may also be considered in these terms. The standard version connects the male and female dimensions to the two complementary units of the canoe: the hull, of which the basic component is the hollow log keel called *waga*, the term for the canoe as a whole; and the outrigger log (*kabalay*), the external addition that balances the canoe on the water. The female wood becomes the dominant unit, the basic carrier of people and goods, while the male wood becomes the attachment to this core without which the canoe cannot, of course, sail on the sea.[23] The two parts together form the necessary complements of a totality.

In the second, less common version, however, the white peripheral marking of the red wood used for the hull is the male portion. When the canoe strakes are first being cut, one can see this narrow strip along the vertical edges of the planks. Here, too, the red female part is basic (the dominant color of the wood) and also interior to the relatively external male portion. This complementary ordering may be compared with that in the finished canoe where the decorative surfacing of the prowboards and the extrinsic beautifying attachments (such as the canoe staffs and shells) give the canoe a predominantly male gender marking (as will shortly be discussed; see also Munn, 1977:49).

The red wood of the finished hull is, moreover, entirely covered by a protective whitewash made from a coral seaweed. Gawans do not, to my knowledge, give a gender-linked interpretation of this feature, but the wash is described as the canoe's "coconut oil," which, as I indicated earlier, men and women use to make their skin glow in ceremonial decoration. Its effect in this context is to overlay the red raw material with a protective, surface beautification so that it becomes an interior property of the whitened canoe.[24]

These remarks on the relation of male and female substances to the canoe may be amplified by examining the key male contribution to the child's body in reproduction. Gawan notions of conception tend to be relatively vague about the specific contribution of the man to the initial formation of the fetus, although the necessity of sexual intercourse for conception is clearly recognized by both men and women. Although a few people remarked that the male *naw* (seminal fluid) mixes with the female blood in forming the child, and one woman suggested that *if* the male semen does mix in this way it makes the child large, the overwhelming emphasis is simply on the congealing of the blood to form the fetus.[25] The immediate cause of this process remains unclear, and apparently not of great interest, and the man does not make a specific contribution to any particular inner substance of the person.

The main male contribution to the child's body is not an internal bodily substance, but an aspect of bodily surface. Unlike blood – which is the very premise of existence and defines the self in its given, dala identity – this male component is contingent, and not an a priori given. Ideally, a child's face (*magi-*, a term that also denotes appearance) should resemble its father's (cf. Malinowski, 1929:204). Gawans recognize that a child may sometimes appear like its mother or other matrikin, as for instance, a twin sibling; but remarking on such a likeness is considered painfully embarrassing for the individual concerned, since it means that he or she has taken after the mother (*i-kapiteika magi-ra ina-ra*). On the other hand, it is highly appropriate to comment on a person's similarity to his or her father (and resembling a father's kinsperson is also acceptable).

At a child's birth, its father's kinswomen have the primary responsibility for the bodily care of the child in the birthhouse, whereas the new mother is cared for primarily by her own maternal and paternal kinswomen.[26] The child's paternal kinswomen, especially the father's mother or other women of the father's dala (all typically *tabu* of the child), should press the child's nose with fire-warmed hands (a procedure called *-yagi*) in order to give the nose the *sharp, narrow shape* that is deemed most attractive. This procedure also aims at *strengthening* the child, and one woman suggested that an additional aim was to make the child look like its father.[27]

The essential point is that the father's and father's kinswomen's contribution to the body of the child is contained in these ideas of the external formation of the child's body. Thus the sense in which the child should possess bodily properties that come from the father is expressed in ideas of particularized surface form rather than generalized, homogeneous substance. This form pertains to the child's individualized personal appearance rather than to an interior body fluid that connects the child in an undifferentiated way to its mother and other members of its dala. These ideas about the body connect the paternal contribution with a formative action that suggests parallels with the male role in canoe building in which men construct female-marked raw materials (homogeneous substance) into a named, shaped artifact.[28]

We may note then that it is especially in that aspect of the body that most specifically identifies the person as an individual recognizable to others, that he or she should not look like dala kin (the matrilineal blood self, interior to the person), but if possible, like the father (the relatively external, paternal other). Whereas the child's bond to the mother is an intrinsic one of material substance and continuity, the ideal relationship to the father is one of likeness to someone extrinsic to one's own bodily self.

If the father's kin indeed think that the child looks like him, he or she can become the *kiyay* of the father's dala when the father dies. The term *kiyay* refers to any material object a person receives as a personal inheritance from another that serves to remind him or her of the donor when the latter dies. Thus one man glossed *kiyay* in English as "memory." Just as the kiyay heirloom extends the relation between persons beyond death by means of a durable medium of memory apart from the mortal body, so the child as kiyay of the father's dala continues the relationship between a deceased man and his own dala, by means of a likeness – a medium detached from the dala's substantive unity of blood, but mirroring one of its members in appearance. Thus one Gawan woman suggested that the father's kin may then go to visit their deceased kinsman's child to look on the face that reminds them of him. The kiyay link between the child and its father's dala (which mediates the two dala only as long as the child is alive), parallels the relation *within the body* of facial appearance to bodily substance. Facial appearance inscribes the *transcendence or surpassing of the body* and interior self *upon the body*; it is the domain of relationality to the other or to an extrinsic, external order (cf. Turner, 1980:116).

But if appearance is the bodily domain of relation to the *external* other, so blood is the domain of a person's relation to *the other who is the interior self* – matrilineal kin and ancestors to whom one is interiorly and substantively bound by blood. Whereas the intersubjectivity mapped into the body by the paternal element entails an expansion of bodily spacetime of the kind we have seen developed in externalizing processes of beauty and motion, that defined by blood bonds is formed through interior connections between the bodies of persons across the generations. This latter mode of bodily spacetime, created and reproduced through the substantive, material linkages and reproductive potentials of blood thus has certain parallels to the heavy interior spacetime of the land and the different gardens cleared on it (see Chapter 4).[29] The body is (to use Devisch's, 1981:35 expression) the "medium of the pre-given relating being" in the very specific sense that this "relationality to the other" is doubly embedded in its physical being both *within* the self (the internal other), and in the external connection of self and other.

It is significant therefore that Gawans prohibit touching the blood of dala kin (and to a lesser extent, kumila kin as well). This prohibition becomes apparent not simply in the case of ordinary wounds, but most notably in bloodletting. Gawans frequently let blood (-*gweili*) to relieve certain illnesses and feelings of malaise, and for special occasions when certain spells are used to make the body especially lightweight, as at the beginning of the Drum dance entertainment.[30] When blood is let, it may be smeared on the face of someone outside the dala and kumila of the patient, but it is forbidden to paint it on a member of one's own dala or kumila. Payment in edibles or condiments (betel nut) is made to the person painted with this blood, which then becomes part of a material exchange between the person whose blood is let and the one on whom it is smeared. If the person letting blood is a man with a child, it is not uncommon to see the blood painted on the latter.

The Gawan explanation for this prohibition on touching a dala kinsperson's blood is simply that these people are one's own blood kin. Two women explained that blood is given "inside" from the mother and is what makes the child in the womb, while the father, they said, doesn't provide any such internal element. It would seem that to smear externalized blood on the skin of a person with whom one is identified by means of this same interior substance is both to negate the interiority of the relation (as the interiorized other who is the self becomes, in effect, shifted to the arena of the external other) and to negate the relationality of the body surface as the arena connecting self and the external other typified in relations between ego and his or her paternal kin.

A similar sort of negative transformation (although in reverse) seems to be implied by saying that a person looks like his or her matrikin. For in the latter case, the ideally interstitial surface – the arena where the person surpasses his or her bodily being – is again being turned into a space that connects ego to the interior level of intersubjective being with which he or she is *already* substantively connected from the past (at the base); at the same time, the very interiority of these connections is being denied. The result in both cases is a negative transformation of a person's bodily spacetime, in which ego is treated as if he or she were dislodged from both types of intersubjective relations and axes of self-expansion whose interconnection forms the self as a totality.

Thus we can see that the same type of totalizing model is being formed in the body; in affinal exchanges through interchanges of goods apart from the body; and then again within the canoe itself as an artifact. In all these contexts, the female potency initiates the extension of spacetime as the wouwura or enabling principle of the male potency; the latter may then yield further levels of spatiotemporal control beyond the capacities of the internal base. In each case, moreover, the male potency is the source of configured, identifying form or of named artifacts: Thus the female potency is converted into individually memorable value products that are potentially media of historical memory.

CANOE ADORNMENT AND CANOES AS ADORNING PRODUCTS

The bodily significance of the canoe has so far been left incomplete in order to consider the body itself. This significance is complexly embedded in the form of the canoe, and I can give only a brief account here. Canoes are beautified by means of carved and painted prowboards, staffs, strings of white shells, pandanus streamers, and other means. They are connected with human beautification not only in concepts about the adorning forms (for example, canoe staffs are compared to men's feathered headdresses used in dancing, and shell attachments may be equated with kula shells decorating the human body), but also in the similarity of beautifying procedures and elements (for example, prowboards, like the human body, are washed before being painted; and pandanus streamers are used in body decoration and for dancing). As we have seen, canoes are also decorated with kula shells received on major kula voyages, as some of these are hung on the canoe.

Anthropomorphism is projected onto the shapes of the canoe's prowboards and the finials; overall, the canoe visually connotes to Gawans the beautified person, especially masculine beauty (Munn, 1977). Anthropomorphism is also carried in metaphoric allusions to human activities surrounding the canoe, which treat such activities as the canoe's own desires. For instance, canoes may be said to "want to drink" when their putty is dry and Gawans plan to moisten it. Or it may be said that the canoe is "hungry" to obtain kula shells (i.e., for shells to be acquired by the sailors on a given kula trip and so carried in its hold). In addition, a canoe's "nose" (the ends of its bow and stern carved in the shape of a pigeon) may be said to "smell" the land.[31]

Various features contribute to the canoe's image of dynamic "sharp" potency. For example, the red and white colors and brilliance of the canoe's prowboards, which, as indicated earlier, should be painted by youthful men and boys only, tend to evoke associations with the essentially male-linked lightning rather than the internal substances that are associated with the woods. Carvings on the prowboards and finials not only involve some representations of birds, but in addition, the basic carving

Plate 8. The decorated prow of a canoe, showing the strings of shells, staff, and streamers. Part of the whitewashed hull appears at the right. The anthropomorphic aspect of the prow can be seen in the figure formed by the finial and the vertical prowboard. The finial may be metaphorically described as the head or hair; it is lashed to the "neck" of the vertical prowboard. The prowboard is the chest (the outer curve) and the shoulders (the inner curve).

motif (a meander and spiral-like shape) connotes the buoyant qualities of birds, and is part of the thematic of motion, which in various ways is built into the form of the canoe.[32] These connotations of upward speedy motion and brilliant light mesh with the anthropomorphic renderings ascribed to these parts of the canoe.

Although the beautified surface and pole extensions give the canoe a generally humanized quality, the decorated canoe may be more specifically compared to a young man who has put on his decorative regalia. One man explained the maleness of the canoe by pointing out that it sails on the sea and "makes a path" like kula shells while women stay at home: "The canoe goes, carries, brings [things] back; it makes a path." Thus the completed, functional and decorated canoe with its male connotations encompasses the interior female dimension, the kousiray wood out of which it is made. This female dimension is not lost, however, and its interior, but crucial, relation to the encompassing male dimension may also sometimes be expressed in such notions as the view that the canoe can be called "mother" (*ina*) because it carries produce in its (interior) hold.[33]

Finally we may reiterate that a canoe, as the medium *within* which Gawans travel, and in which they first arrive on non-Gawan soil, is itself a resurfacing of the person. Just as men going on kula should decorate themselves and present the best impression possible to seduce their hosts into releasing shells, so also the canoe that carries them should be beautified. An unattractive canoe may even be regarded as antithetical to one's kula chances. The canoe thus becomes an external decor – one whose humanized properties reflexively connote those whom it decorates. As external decor, the canoe is part of a man's "impression-management" in kula, and carries the qualisigns of positive self-transformation, conveying to foreign hosts the persuasive potency of the travelers.

In sum, it has become apparent that throughout – from its core resource to its completed form – the canoe encodes its producers in itself. From interior to exterior, it is an artifact identified with the human body, which makes it. This production includes inputs of both male and female producers who, through their differential levels of potency create the extended level of Gawan spatiotemporal control embodied in the canoe. Although the female input both in the present and in the origin account is the cooking of garden produce that energizes the bodies of the workers, the female power in the past also gave the canoe its basic raw materials that men then and now shape into a mobile artifact. Thus the canoe not only gives artifactual form to the body, but also to the gender hierarchy, and the basic transformative processes in which, as we have seen, the primary formulation of the body as a condensed totality of self–other relations is grounded.

GENDER, EQUIVALENCE, AND HIERARCHY IN MARRIAGE EXCHANGE CYCLES

It should now be apparent that the buwaa exchange cycles are one formulation of the causal-logical nexus between body-related qualisigns and operations on food, which I have suggested is a fundamental Gawan template for organizing processes that generate and signify value. The male gift embodies the qualisigns of the transformative value of separating food from the self, created by kin of the female side. The latter obtain this embodiment of value: an expanded, spatiotemporal control and material condensation of motion, which is the outcome of their transformative act, and which objectifies the persuasive effect of their food giving on the minds of their affines. They then gain the right to control and transmit this higher level value product to others, thus constituting themselves as part of a more expansive inter-island nexus that they create. *In this iconic sense, I suggest, the canoes or kula shells received may be seen as "value forms"[34] of food transmission (not simply of the medium food), which exhibit the food donor's capacity to transform intersubjective spacetime to a more encompassing, expansive level.*

Whereas this primary part of the affinal exchange cycles is hierarchical and gives explicit form to the incremental power in the act of food transmission – the second part of the cycle constructs an equivalence that closes the cycle. Yet, as we shall see, the modes of closure for both canoes and kula shells involve a mingling of equivalence with notions of hierarchy.

I shall begin by examining closure in the canoe cycle. As indicated above, two types of durable objects – pots and kitomu kula shells – are the key returns at the end of the overseas exchange. However, only the kitomu are regarded as equivalents that close the cycle. The pots nevertheless are important, since they pay the women. As durable artifacts for cooking they are, in fact, material condensations of the particular contribution of women to the manufacture of the canoe. Unlike food itself, however, they are noncomestible, manufactured goods coming from the external inter-island world; in addition, some of them may be given personal names. In this respect pots convert the women's work into a more enduring spatiotemporal form; indeed, like kitomu, they may become objects of personal inheritance (i.e., *kiyay*), and thus media for remembering past owners. Although pots appear to separate the female from the male aspects of the canoe and the canoe work, an element of male-associated significance thus remains.[35] The question of the differential gender components of the two types of canoe payment will be taken up later.

It is, however, the several armshell kitomu that are given in payment for the masculine work of canoe building that are the true equivalents for the canoe. Armshells and canoes are described as *kakaloula*, "mates" or "appropriate marriage partners" to each other. Objects that are kakaloula are a pair that, like men and women, may marry (*-vay*). The relational logic implied is what Jakobson (1939:273, cited in Holenstein, 1976:123) has called "contrary opposition," in which a necessary connection exists between the opposite members of the pair. Each one therefore both excludes and includes or co-implies the other (Holenstein, 1976:122, 124). The ground of such pairing is a whole in terms of which the categories mutually implicate each other: "The contained elements [the oppositions] are very distinct, and nevertheless, their distinction is developed within a unity that is the rationale of their distinction" (Pos, 1938:76, my translation). Or, put even more sharply, "The unity of opposites is always formed by a concept that implicitly contains these oppositions in itself" (Pos, 1938:246; see also Dumont, 1979:809ff.).

The Gawan model specified in the notion of marriage and the husband–wife (-*mwara* and -*kwava*) pair defines what is clearly, in Gawan thinking, the epitomizing nuclear form of a differentiated social whole. Gawans use this model quite widely apart from exchange contexts, to represent the idea of a totality formed through the necessary, complementary relationship between the parts.[36] In direct contrast to the cross-sex sibling relation (see Chapter 2), a marriage creates a bodily, sexual relationship between a couple who also work together to produce sustenance on a daily basis, thus forming a reproductively viable unit. We have already seen (Chapters 2 and 4) that in marriage exchanges, a man and wife tend to operate as a unit (i.e., as donors, mediating recipients, and consumer-recipients). As discussed in Chapter 4, the mediating nodal couple is the focus of food prohibitions on consumption of the buwaa food, and as such represents the principle of connectivity and the capacity for value transformation in those exchanges.

When viewed in terms of the husband–wife pair (and the more general male–female contrast this entails), the model consists of an asymmetric polarity with a hierarchic differentiation implied (see Dumont, 1979:81off.). However, when considered in terms of the relation of marriage between the polarities, the opposites are *implicitly* subsumed as identical, symmetrical terms (i.e., marriage partners),[37] each equally necessary to the constitution of a whole. From this latter perspective, each replicates the other, and the marriage relation as such encodes the equivalence of each part in the constitution of the whole (cf. Turner, 1985:368).

A dual significance of asymmetry and symmetry also emerges in the application of the notion of *kakaloula*. For although the notion is characteristically explained in terms of the marriage between male and female, exchange pairs cited as kakaloula range from asymmetric to symmetric complements. The latter include, for instance, food (*karu*) as the kakaloula of food; bananas for bananas, and so on.

In the symmetrical cases, equivalence is overtly specified by the repetition of (exchange of) objects of identical category, although in any given context, asymmetric dimensions may be conveyed in the polarization of the actor categories, or other related features of context (as, for instance, in the mortuary exchanges discussed in Chapter 7). In asymmetric cases, however, the equivalence of exchange objects appears only at a more general, implicit category level that defines them (like the overtly symmetric objects) as "replicated instances" (Turner, n.d.: 64) of the whole. It is asymmetric cases that are of particular interest here.

The most notable asymmetric complements to which the marriage metaphor is stereotypically applied are kula shells. Armshells and necklaces "marry" each other when shells of equivalent rank are exchanged as gulugwalu (cf. Malinowski, 1922:356). As one man put it to me, the "lover" (*nube*) of a shell is one that may be transacted against it, but is not its equivalent in standard and thus travels as a starting shell requiring a return (see Chapter 3). The true (*mokita*) mate is the marriage partner, the equivalent that finalizes the transaction. However, in a general sense, the two object categories, the necklaces and armshells, marry each other and are cited as *kakaloula*.

Similarly, canoes (which, it will be recalled, travel in the exchange direction of necklaces) and armshells, not pots, are kakaloula to each other. Thus one man likened the pots to *gimwali*, a purchase or immediate payment that he contrasted, in this instance, with the kakaloula relationship of armshells and canoes.[38] Furthermore, as I have indicated, canoe transacting is classed as kura, and the canoes themselves have a variety of associations with kula shells. From one perspective, then, canoes and armshells are kura. They share certain inter-island transactive capacities, and together they form a totality, as do necklaces and armshells. Put in general terms, this totality consists of the inter-island spacetime defined by the two opposed kula directions of movement and their polarized media. Like necklaces and armshells, canoes and armshells constitute complementary polarities of this inter-island whole, and their exchange is kura, a totalizing process that translates one spatial pole into another (as each opposed element travels in the direction and into the domain from which the other comes).

The fact remains, however, that there is a greater degree of asymmetry between canoe and armshell as kakaloula than between necklace and armshell. Apart from their obvious object differences, a canoe, unlike a necklace, does not circulate repetitively, but forms, as we have seen, a linear, nonrepetitive path that travels only a fraction of the ring. In this sense, the canoe with its directional transactional movement creates a different spatiotemporal mode of kula spacetime, one of lesser transformational value that defines a more limited part of the totalizing process.

In fact, as shown above, the exchange of canoes for armshells effects a transformation *across* these different value levels of kula spacetime. Plotted in terms of the spatiotemporal transformations occurring as one moves from garden produce to canoes and kula shell exchanges, canoes appear not simply as intermediate artifacts in a sequence of goods in the affinal exchange cycle, but more significantly, as spatiotemporal intermediates between the internal spacetime of Gawan affinal exchanges and the maximal circulation of kula armshells and necklaces in the inter-island world. The exchange of canoes for kitomu armshells defines both a break or closure (equivalence) and the creation of a potential for further positive transformation to a more comprehensive spatiotemporal level (hierarchization) for Gawan kitomu recipients. Put in another way, the exchange equivalence of armshells and canoes defines a *juncture* of the hierarchizing process: It constitutes both a *closure* of the low-level cycle (food/canoes–canoe paths) – the end of the affinal canoe exchange and its inter-island extension – and coordinately, the creation of a potential for the maximally encompassing spatiotemporal control level of shell exchange (*lack of closure*). This liminal character of the exchange, which involves the combination of the apparent antinomies of equalizing closure (implying discontinuity) and increment (implying potentiality and continuity), is precisely the key exchange characteristic of kitomu, the special property category instantiated in the armshells acquired for the canoe. What Gawans obtain for their canoe is, in short, an object that can both finish (equalize) and start or potentialize (increment, hierarchize).

Let us review briefly some features of kitomu. Kitomu is a property relation instantiated only in kula shells. A shell that is not ego's kitomu (but may be someone else's) is his *murikura* or *tetala*, that is, a shell that is not his own property. A man (frequently in consultation with other dala members in the case of important shells) has the right to do what he wants with his kitomu, including keeping it at home; withdrawing it from kula circulation (or placing it *in* circulation), and attempting to retrieve it from its current kula holder if in his view it has been wrongly transmitted; using it for the transaction of certain goods other than kula shells (for example, pigs, magic, cash), and as a debt-free shell for the cancellation of long-term debts in kula, as well as for other social purposes. It is notable that the most preferred immediate use for kula shells received for canoes appears to be to put them into kula.

In typical kula transactions, a man transacts the shell in which his kitomu rights are instantiated to an immediate recipient *without* transacting the rights themselves. Kitomu rights over a shell are not released until the owner receives from someone along the path an equivalent shell of opposite category that is to become his kitomu. Since a kitomu instantiation is exchanged for another instantiation of the same kitomu – a kitomu for a kitomu – the exchange understood in this sense is symmetric (see Damon, 1980:282; Gregory, 1982:344). This sort of symmetric exchange of kitomu may also occur in other contexts apart from inter-island kula paths. For example, in Gawan mortuary rites, a man married to a woman of the deceased's dala may sometimes give the dala a kitomu that the latter will return by means of a kitomu of the opposite category at the death of someone in the original donor's dala. In these contexts, asymmetry enters in only with respect to the category instantiation (necklace vs. armshell).

But kitomu may also be exchanged asymmetrically for a variety of non-kitomu items; in such cases they also effect closure, irrespective of whether these items are regarded as the kakaloula of kula shells or not. In these instances, the kitomu owner alienates the kitomu rights from himself, losing the level of spatiotemporal control it represents. For example, a man may indicate to his sister that he will make her and her husband the special gift of the contents of a yam house if her husband gives him a kitomu. A crucial difference between this gift and that of the buwaa transaction is that there is no return kula shell expected from the food donor to finish the transaction and close the debt. The kitomu from the husband squares the exceptional food gift. As a result, the new recipient of the kitomu can use it as a starting gift on a kula path to begin a cycle that has *no connection* with the previous transaction. (Similarly, if he wishes, he may use it in another quite separate asymmetric transaction, exchanging it for some other non-kitomu item.) *As a debt-free acquisition, the kitomu condenses the capacity to close transactions with the capacity to open new ones.* As one man pointed out, "Kitomu is never finished: It is always vaga for you."

What the spatiotemporal powers that characterize kitomu represent when operative in kula (apart from the capacity to pay off debts) is the power to generate new inter-island exchange cycles out of closed vaga-gulugwalu cycles without having to depend on others for an additional vaga shell to start this new cycle. Thus when a man receives the equalizing kitomu for his original kitomu, he now has in his hands a potential vaga for a separate, new transaction produced, as it were, directly out of the previous transaction.

We see then that when a dala receives kitomu for its canoe, it does not simply acquire the potencies embedded in ordinary *murikura* kula shells. The kitomu initially operating to close the canoe exchange cycle, and coordinately to create the potential for a new opening transaction on the more expansive spatiotemporal level of kula, also condenses in itself a further potential: namely, the capacity to both close (equalize) and start (hierarchize) *future cycles* in the context of kula exchange. This synthesizing power is the key spatiotemporal increment concretized in kitomu; from it flow other potencies, such as the kitomu's capacity to strengthen or harden (*matuwo*)[39] a man's kula paths, attracting other shells and partners to his paths (see Damon, 1983a:326ff.; Weiner, 1983:161), or its capacity to be exchanged for a shell of higher rank (Munn, 1977:46).

But this spatiotemporal power of kitomu is itself predicated on the fact that kitomu are personal possessions of the individual and his dala. The nature of kitomu rights is perhaps most directly represented in a man's right to withdraw his kitomu from kula circulation or to alienate it at his (or sometimes his dala's) discretion. The basic premise is that rights over kitomu are embedded in the individual kula actor (or the actor and his immediate dala) and not in the relation between self and other constructed in kula exchange. For instance, the immediate partner who transacts another man's kitomu may regard the shell as his *tetala*: It is his to take care of (*-yamata*) for the kitomu owner. This man's rights derive from his relation to the kitomu owner. He is forbidden to alienate the shell and should listen to the owner's advice in transacting it onward. As opposed to kitomu, tetala are grounded in the self–other relationship of kula partnerships and path continuities.

The relative autonomy entailed in the kitomu principle enables a man to circulate his kitomu within kula, continually *separating it from himself*, while at the same time *keeping his kitomu for himself* (as represented, for instance, in his right to withdraw it from circulation). This dialectical synthesis of keeping and giving objectified in kitomu is the condition of its similar synthesis of the spatiotemporal capacities of finishing and poten-tializing transactions. The power of kitomu lies in its unique condensation and in this sense its transcendence of a fundamental antinomy of Gawan value transformation.

The principle of possession that underlies these synthesizing capacities is illuminated when we consider two fundamental metaphors that convey the matrilineal significance of kitomu, namely, "navel" (*pwaso-*) and "stone" (*dakula*). These metaphors reveal condensations of further polarities; they will also bring us back again to the particular relation of kitomu and canoe. As noted earlier, kitomu (and most especially canoe kitomu) are matrilineally inherited, and we have seen that the dala as a group (including, one should note, the women of the dala) may be concerned in decisions regarding the transaction of important kitomu. As I have indicated, kitomu have a *leliyu* (historical tradition). As one man said, one can refer to kitomu as *kiyay* (heirlooms): "We leliyu kitomu" (i.e., discuss their long past travels). Similarly, he said, one can "leliyu" land, referring to matrilineal ancestors (*tabu*).

The reference to the kitomu as one's navel identifies it in terms that may be used to convey the immediate physical bond of mother and child, and dala members.[40] The transmission of a kitomu to another (whether in kula, as the recipient's tetala, or otherwise) can thus be stated in terms of the Maussian model of possession and exchange: Ego has "rendered to another what is in reality part of his ... substance" (Mauss, 1968:161). It seems paradoxical that it is precisely in a type of object over which one has rights of alienation that the Maussian concept of the substantive bond between transactor and medium is most applicable, but this is precisely the point: What one possesses as an aspect of the self is subject to only one's own kareiwaga, just as the dala itself has its own kareiwaga not subject to determinations by other dala.[41] Nevertheless, as with the other enduring dala possession, land, the ideal for kitomu (especially canoe kitomu) is to maintain them in one's control across the generations, rather than to alienate them.[42]

The bonds of kitomu with the body are also suggested in another way. Gawans view kitomu rights as prototypically derived from a person's own work in manufacturing the product. Gawans do not make kula shells, but they assume that the man who made a shell is its first owner, and his kitomu rights over the shell derive from this work (see Damon, 1978). Speaking of locations where, in his view, armshells are still made, one Gawan kula man conceived of this derivation as follows:

Armshells are ground at [the southern island of] Ware. They make them and give them names; they think "my kitomu" because they work hard (*i-payisiyo-s*). The Ware people's kitomu. When they get necklaces for them [which then become their kitomu], they put them on their throats and wear them: their kitomu.

The speaker viewed hard work as being converted into an artifact that the worker appropriates as his kitomu – the objectification of vital bodily activity; moreover, when armshells are transacted for necklaces they are then reappropriated as body decor. What has been objectified by bodily work and has become separated from the person in transaction (entering, it may be noted, into the transactive work, *wotet*, of kula) is now returned to the body as its beautifying enhancement: the display of the body's value as maker of an artifact with the capacity to go beyond the body.

This conceptualization of kitomu shell manufacture resonates with the relation between canoes and their Gawan builders, since the canoes are similarly products of vital bodily work that objectify the body in iconic, beautified form, exhibiting both in object form and in their capacity to make a path or passage, the body's own capacity to transcend itself by means of vital activity. Transacted outward, the canoe then returns to the body its ornament of kitomu shell decor.

In this respect, it is significant that Gawans tend to think of the canoe as the only true or original source of kitomu other than the making of the shell itself, although they are well aware that kitomu can be received from various sources.[43] (This tendency is, of course, consistent with their view that canoes are appropriate marriage partners or kakaloula of armshells; and with the fact that canoes provide the main means by which Gawans can tap into inter-island shell circulation to obtain kitomu.) From this perspective, when the final kitomu payment is made to the Gawan building dala for their canoe work, the latter are converting work that they perform (canoe manufacture) into work that they do not perform (kula shell manufacture) and claiming kitomu as an aspect of the body, as the generic sign of product ownership based on vital bodily work. A separation from the material work products of one's own body that yields the work product of another foreign source transcending the (matrilineal) self results in reattachment to the self of a dialectically transformed potency.

But it would seem that this transformed potency is precisely the reconstitution of the interior matrilineal mode of reproductive continuity in terms of the exterior spacetime of kula circulation. This is most clearly conveyed in Gawan concepts by the fact that kitomu may be metaphorically described as "stones," a description that connects them with the reproductive storage potencies of the dala land and of gardens (Chapter 4). We have seen that the heaviness of the immobilized, bounding or centering, matrilineal stones in the gardens assures the perpetuity of the reproductive capacities of the soil across the transient (or mortal) gardens. Stabilizing the crops inside the soil, they provide the internal heaviness and containment that is necessary for the sprouting, upward growth (lightweightness) and plentifulness of the crop.

Similarly, a kitomu is *dakula* because it is a concentrate of reproductive and expansive potency in a man's kula: On the one hand, as we have seen, it has an intrinsic capacity to create new transactions out of old ones (since it is always vaga, or potential vaga for a man, even when it is returned to him as the gulugwalu for a previous kitomu transacted); on the other hand, linked to this capacity is its potentiality for attracting other partners and shells to a man's paths – in this sense its potentiality for multiplying a man's kula. As dala-based personal possessions and heirlooms, kitomu are like heavy stones in the matrilineal land; it is as if they are drawn back toward the owner or draw additional shells back toward him (in this respect, one is reminded of the Maussian, 1968:158ff., paradigm of the Maori *hau*; see also, Weiner's 1985 argument concerning the *hau*). In short, kitomu are as near as one can get to an intrinsic, stabilized aspect of the self in a mobile medium that can be separated from the self in circulation.

Although Gawans do not, to my knowledge, draw an explicit parallel (for example, in metaphors) between the means of creating continuity in the garden and the way in which kitomu reproduce themselves in circulation, such a parallel is not without interest. Since each new return shell that substitutes for a previous kitomu shell is a new instantiation of the same kitomu and has the potentiality for producing further shells from itself, it has certain similarities to the substantive mode of garden reproduction in which new plants are produced from cuttings or seed yams of a previous harvest (see Chapter 4). Similar parallels are suggested with the bodily reproduction of the matriline in which each new member has an intrinsic substantive connection with the mother, and with previous generations so that each is an instantiation of the one dala that is ideally reproduced down the generations.[44]

Returning to the consideration of kitomu in terms of the affinal canoe cycle, we see emerging from a process by which a Gawan artifact is permanently transacted away from Gawa and the matrilineal self of its builder-owners, an artifact that reinstantiates the matrilineal bond in another spatiotemporal mode: that is, in a form that can be both transacted away from Gawa and yet continually return to Gawa and its owner, and that can be matrilineally inherited down the generations as the canoe itself cannot be. Thus kitomu reconstitute the value level of the interior Gawan order in terms of the maximally extended spatiotemporal value of kula.

THE RECURSIVE LOGIC OF THE
CANOE EXCHANGE CYCLE

Before turning to the question of symmetry and asymmetry in the affinal cycle involving kula shells, we should consider the recursive logic reflected in the canoe cycle. As we have seen, the transformational development of the cycle is toward increasing masculinization and spatiotemporal extension as the object conversions shift from the relatively feminized base of edible garden resources through the mediating internal-external artifactual level of the wooden canoe to the culminating level of the durable shell and pottery artifacts from the external inter-island world. The transformational cycle of spacetime reflected in these conversions incorporates Gawa into the encompassing (relatively masculinized) inter-island order.

In each level of the exchange cycle the pattern of relationships between the key value products is recursively generated by the same basic formula: Thus the relationship between objects of the more expansive spatiotemporal levels in later phases of the cycle reflects that between objects of the less expansive levels in the earlier phases. We may consider this from different angles. On the one hand, the pattern of the relationship between garden food and canoes is reflected in that between pots and kitomu. Stated in terms of a ratio: *garden food* (the relatively feminine and interior comestible) is to *canoes* (the masculinized, relatively durable and exterior artifact) as *pots* (the relatively feminine artifacts for cooking that are assimilated back into the intra-island order) are to *kitomu armshells* (the relatively masculinized artifacts with their potential for inter-island circulation). Relative to food, canoes are beautified, body-related artifacts that exhibit the positive qualisigns of motion and brilliance, that is, the value signs of spatiotemporal extension of self; relative to the black cooking pots, kitomu armshells are beautified body decor with decorative, mobile attachments parallel to those of the canoe (see Chapter 5). That is to say, the basic food–body or body decor nexus is repeated in the two sets of media.

But the recursions in this reading of the relationships reflect only one form of the parallelism. Another, perhaps more significant one, can be expressed in the ratio garden food:canoe :: canoe:armshell-kitomu (the finalizing equivalent of the canoe). In this case, the canoe, which is the relatively masculinized inter-island term vis à vis garden food, becomes the relatively feminine, interior term vis à vis kitomu shells. (As we have seen, the canoe is Gawan made; its origin narrative identifies its materials with female reproductive capacities; it carries food in its hold, and women's cooking is a basic precondition of its production.) Indeed, as I shall discuss shortly, the canoe moves in the direction of what Gawans characterize as the *feminine* kula shell, the necklace, which they contrast with the maleness of the armshell; and this may perhaps be significant in considering the relative femininity of the canoe. Both kitomu and canoe exhibit the beautifying qualisigns of value, but the kitomu armshells as items of body decor mark a return to the body, in contrast to the canoe as a vehicle of travel. On the other hand, relative to the food produce of the interior value level, it is the canoe that is the body-related, decorative form. Just as the canoe exhibits the value of separating food from the self (in effect, the transcendence of self), so at the more expansive level of spacetime the kitomu armshells exhibit the value of separating the *canoe* from the self (a further transcendence creating the most comprehensive value of the inter-island order that condenses the transformed potencies of the lesser levels).

In this second recursive pattern, the relative asymmetry of the elements in the primary conversion (the more radical differentiation of comestibles and artifact) is replaced in the next conversion by a relatively more homogeneous relation (the kakaloula couple of the canoe and armshells finalizing the exchange). As the asymmetric differentiation closes down, an equation is reached that closes the cycle; but at the same time, the more differentiated primary phase is reflected in the closing, more homogeneous one. The same pattern will also be seen in the kula shell cycle examined below.

GENDER, EQUIVALENCE, AND HIERARCHY IN KULA SHELLS

The asymmetry of necklaces and armshells in kula exchange goes beyond the more overt features of artifactual and directional polarization. As briefly suggested earlier, shells are gender linked; they are also differentially weighted with respect to the qualisigns of value. Necklaces, always described as female, are regarded as being slow and tight – more difficult to obtain – because, as men explain, it is difficult to persuade women to accede to masculine wishes (as for instance, in sexual matters, the example usually drawn on in this context). Conversely, armshells are male because they are more readily moved; since they travel fast, they are like men, the more mobile sex in contrast to the more sedentary women.

One man explained these differences historically. Like some others, he regarded necklaces as being prior to pig tusks and armshells in kula. When tusks began to be exchanged for necklaces, the tusk "went to meet its wife." The necklace was therefore the stable, initially unmoved article that had, in effect, to be moved by the visiting tusk, the male article (Munn,

1983:306). In this sense, the necklace that did *not* move first, controlled space because it *engendered* motion. Furthermore, when a person goes to visit another in his hamlet, as for example, a kula partner, he is showing respect to the person visited, and this visit is necessary in order for the visitor to obtain what he wishes from the host. So, for instance, a sign that a man is a guyaw is that many people visit him. The notion that the necklace was the unmoving shell that engendered motion thus suggests its guyaw-like status compared to the armshell.[45]

Similarly, I have heard the view expressed in present-day kula politics that armshells should "go to meet" necklaces because armshells are male and necklaces female. This rhetorical point was made in the context of a conflict over the timing of a kula expedition regarding whether a trip to Muyuw for armshells should take precedence over a trip northward for necklaces (or vice versa). The man heading the proposed uvelaku for armshells asserted that armshells should go to meet the necklaces, that is, that Gawans should go to Muyuw first. Underlying this assertion was the argument that, given the immediate presence of both armshells in the southeast and necklaces in the northern sector, Gawans needed to obtain armshells first to aid them in acquiring necklaces that are the female shell and harder to obtain.

In both the historical notion, and the use of the idea exemplified from present-day kula, the female shell is represented as the one that moves last and that must therefore be persuaded to move by armshells that act as "bait" (to adopt a metaphor Gawans sometimes use in discussing kula procedures in other contexts). Indeed, Gawans maintain the stereotype (not necessarily carried out in practice) that one must pokala more frequently for necklaces than for armshells, and that formal kula magic should be performed on major northern trips for necklaces, but not on similar armshell journeys. The explanation for these measures is always that necklaces are more difficult to obtain than armshells, and that one may have to sail more than once for a desired shell.

What comes to the fore in the gender definition of the kula shells is the model of the political relation between men and women, namely, that men must influence women in order to gain their agreement to masculine ends. The female element is thus envisioned as the independent locus of control that has to be influenced. In this context, the implicit superordination of the female element becomes overt.

This apparent superordination of necklaces is conveyed in the Gawan view of the two directions and segments of the inter-island world that compose the totality of kula space time. Gawans identify the northwestern area with what they call Kura Dobu, the "hard," difficult form of kula in which it is felt that the agreement of partners to release shells is harder to obtain. In Kura Dobu, the emphasis is on creating long-term debt and building enduring path partnerships through the transaction of multiple vaga shells linked to an initial vaga transaction, rather than through gaining a single, relatively immediate equivalent for the first shell (see Chapter 3). As a style of kula operation, Kura Dobu has the highest prestige.

By contrast, Kura Masim has associations with the southerly area and represents the less prestigious easy kula exchanges with immediate or quick closure as the dominant exchange style (see Munn, 1983:306). Just as male (fast-moving, easy) armshells come into Gawa from the southeasterly area and the slow, hard necklaces come in from the northwest, so also the two styles of kula are associated, according to Gawan concepts, with these segments of the inter-island order. In this sense, each part of kula spacetime is opposed in a hierarchical, stereotypic model entailing different spatiotemporal levels: female-linked, tight-slow but temporally reproducible spacetime versus male-linked, easy-fast, temporally discontinuous spacetime.

In this binary, political model of kula spacetime, the gender principles are phrased in the idiom of persuasion and consent; what is difficult to move has, by virtue of this fact, control over motion. In this context, women epitomize recalcitrance, hence the fact that motion (consent to release something from the self) must be created by *men* through acts of persuasion. This emphasis is crystallized in some of the imagery of Gawan kula spells and narrative.

The two Rama Dobu women flew to Dobu from Kweawata, north of Gawa. The older sister is an evil witch (*bwagaw*) who insisted on deserting their brother in Kweawata.[46] She now sits on Dobu "looking away from" Gawa (and Kweawata), that is, away from the eastern sector of the kula region. The younger sister, however, who was more sympathetic to the brother (and who flew back temporarily to Kweawata to show him how to build a canoe), sits looking toward this region of their old home. The older sister is Kura Dobu, while the younger sister is said to be Kura Masim.

In performing magic addressed to these women, a Gawan attempts to make the older sister turn toward him (*i-katouvira nano-ra*, he turns her mind) and be sympathetic (*-karin nuwa-ra*) like the younger sister – in effect, to turn the "slow-hard" into the "fast-easy." Thus the aim is to influence partners who are "hard in kula" (Malinowski, 1922:360) to release their shells easily. He is also attempting to obtain a necklace from the older sister who represents the northwesterly direction from which the necklaces come. The difficult sister is equated with the wife of a man's kula partner, whose mind must be moved to change her rejection of the Gawan into consent to his receipt of a kula shell (see Munn, 1983:285).

Several features of this telling imagery require comment. The Rama Dobu embodiment of female recalcitrance is a condensed, formulaic version not only of the political role of women vis à vis men, but more specifically of the considerable importance Gawan men place on the role of women in kula. Like Gawan women, women on other islands are seen as influencing their husbands and own dala kinsmen with regard to kula decisions that the latter must make.[47] The hopeful kula recipient must therefore influence them with gifts, notably skirts and mats, objects made by Gawan women on whom men are therefore dependent for these articles of exchange. Seen from this perspective, moving the woman's mind is equated with moving the partner's mind, and so moving the kula shell. Here we see a further ramification of the same formulation as that discussed in previous contexts: At the base of the male power for controlling and transforming spacetime is the female control level, which forms the dynamic grounds and precondition of the masculine level of the process. The Rama Dobu not only encapsulate this female level of potency, but they display it as the encompassing one: The two sides of kula spacetime are encompassed within this Janus-like image of the two women looking in different directions. The positively oriented younger sister (Kura Masima) is like the armshell, the male article from the eastern region toward which she looks. She represents, in effect, the way the Gawan would like the older sister, Kura Dobu, to be, and provides an image of this desire. Looking back across the region from Dobu to her lost home – *remembering* her brother – she depicts an expanded spatiotemporal potential (the release of the necklace), which can, however, be realized only by moving the *older* sister. But the latter, like the desired necklace, epitomizes female recalcitrance; looking away from the region of her past home, she creates a contracted spacetime without potentiality, one that must be, as it were, expanded through releasing the shell (turning her mind around, or as it were, making her remember). Both a contracted spacetime (not remembering the other and refusing to give) and its expansion in movement (remembering and releasing) are formulated in the model of the two women.

It would seem that the Rama Dobu also depict the ambiguous face women present to Gawan men with respect to masculine endeavors. On the one hand, women give supportive aid to men, in kula and in other activities, and their help is both crucial and appreciated, as we have seen. On the other hand, women must be actively persuaded to agree to a man's wishes, and in this respect they may be viewed as recalcitrant, or as the epitome of the recalcitrance that can characterize intersubjective relations in general – grounded as they are in the autonomous kareiwaga of the individual. But note that the positive "face" is encompassed within the negative one in this image, for the evil older sister is the controlling force: It is she who caused the younger to leave the brother and fly away to Dobu. This connection between women and the political model of rejection and consent (with rejection as the encompassing dimension) will come into focus when we consider the subversive world of negative value production constituted by witchcraft. We may compare the image of female encompassment in the Rama Dobu women with the image of women provided in the Gawan canoe origin account (a comparison that has some additional weight, since the Rama Dobu are connected with canoe origins on Kweawata, see note 46). In each case, the female principle is depicted as the source of concentrated power. In the case of the Gawan canoe, this superordinating encompassment refers to the primacy of the female principle in the constitution of appropriate raw materials and bodily media of reproduction; in the kula context, the Rama Dobu refer to women as politically primary in the sense that they epitomize the control exerted in intersubjective relations by the refusal and consent of the other.

In kula it would appear that Gawan men are exchanging male and female elements in which the slow-moving, female article is implicitly superordinate to the fast-moving male article. It is the female necklace that encompasses both male mobility and female tightness and recalcitrance. Considered in terms of spatiotemporal transformative powers, the necklace as icon of what is hard to move encodes the necessity of creating motion through persuasive action, and in this sense constitutes a model of the totality (motion and stasis, the south-southeast sector and north-northeast sector). The necklace connotes the superordination of the power of consent – the agreement to release something from the self – over the element released, or the motion created by the persuasive process. The armshell, conversely, is the icon of the motion generated by release: It embodies the swift transformation of stasis that men desire.

We must nevertheless keep in mind that the hierarchical reversal expressed in the relation of necklaces to armshells is encompassed within the essentially male-controlled or masculinized inter-island value level of the transformational system. As we have seen, kula shells are essentially masculine articles for Gawans, and in this respect, the gender polarization of male and female is encompassed by the more comprehensive order. In sum, it appears that the same sort of asymmetries and complementarities occur within kula shell exchange as within the primary, internal segment of the affinal exchange cycle, but with a reversal of superordination in the asymmetric relation between the media.

Let us return to the affinal exchange cycle. In making return for the female harvest gift with a kula shell, the husband's kin need not necessarily give a male armshell to the women's kinsmen, with the latter returning a female necklace to close the exchange (or vice versa). As we have seen, it is simply the kula medium in general that constitutes the appropriate male gift. But the exchange of kula shells that then finalizes the transaction constitutes a model of the primary value level of the transaction: When affines transact a necklace and armshell (in whatever order), they are transacting objects marked for the same polarized qualisigns of value (with the concomitant gender association) as the kula shells (motion, male) and garden produce (heaviness, stasis) in the primary spatiotemporal transformation. In other words, the necklace is to the armshell as the harvest gift is to the kula shell (necklace or armshell).[48]

On the kula level, the equivalence or symmetry that replaces the primary level asymmetry in order to effect closure is created by two elements of body decor (*bubura*). As body decor, the two types of shell exhibit the basic beautifying qualisigns of positive value. As they circulate *fully* only against each other in the contemporary kula system, the value of the transaction of each type is exclusively exhibited in the capacities and properties of the other. Thus the spatiotemporal value of the female principle is exhibited in the male shell, and vice versa. Since in Gawan kula exchange generally, a necklace should eventually be converted into an equivalent armshell and an armshell into an equivalent necklace, each object "produces" the other, containing its opposite as a potentiality of itself. There is thus no directionality in the sense of sequential-temporal priority. Through their mutual potentializing of each other in ongoing circulation, the shells create a self-perpetuating totality. What appears to be shown in this process is precisely the *equality* of the male and female principles (and of the coordinate differential directions or segments of inter-island kula spacetime) whose asymmetries are resolved in terms of their mutual necessity and ongoing potentialization of each other in a reversible circular process.

7

Mortuary exchanges and the deconstitution of self

Le corps est dans le monde social mais le monde social est dans le corps.
        Pierre Bourdieu, *Leçon inaugurale, Collège de France*, 1982:24

In the present chapter, we shall see that the same underlying generative schema of value production and signification governs the transformations of Gawan mortuary exchanges as was shown to operate in the marriage exchanges discussed in Chapter 6, but in a variant form. The more obvious differences between the two practices are those appearing in such overt features as for example, the elements carrying the qualisigns of value (which in the mortuary rites are items of body decor directly attached to the bodies of participants, and in certain contexts interchanged between them); more critical differences, however, are those relating to the structure of the value transformations. Whereas the transformative acts occurring in marriage exchanges are essentially positive, yielding increasing expansions of intersubjective spacetime, mortuary exchanges have, as it were, a double motion: on the one hand, they entail a negative transformation in which intersubjective spacetime is contracted and a fragmenting process occurs; on the other hand, this negative process is simultaneously the means of a positive, expansive transformation.

THE ORGANIZATION OF THE MORTUARY EXCHANGES

When a Gawan woman or man dies, the focal social categories engaged in the mortuary transactions are aligned differently than in the marriage exchanges. Marriage exchanges are aimed at forming a connectivity built upon a marital couple; the interrelations of the parts forming the marital totality are specified, as we have seen, in terms of the internal–external gender asymmetry that defines the couple. The bodily being of each member of the couple, in turn, is an amalgam of such connectivities formed in the previous generation (i.e., through his or her parents). These connectivities are mapped within the body in terms of internal matri-substance (the bodily connection with the other who is the self) and surface definitions of male patri-bonds involving relations between self and relatively external other. The new marital relationship entails a further spatiotemporal extension of bodily being for both the man and the woman in the close marriage bond with its physical intimacy of sexuality, and potential for bodily reproduction of the next generation (see Chatpers 2 and 6). As I pointed out in Chapter 2, the opposition between the marital relationship and that of cross-sex siblings epitomizes the distinction between the internal, blood bond linking persons who form a given, homogeneous whole, and the marital bonds of exteriority that create a differentiated whole or totality.

In contrast to marriage exchanges, which are concerned with the spatiotemporal extension developed in the formation of the marital whole, Gawan mortuary exchanges are concerned with factoring out the marital, paternal, and matrilineal components, which have been amalgamated to form the deceased's holistic being, and with returning this being to a partial, detotalized state – its unamalgamated matrilineal source. That is to say, a negative transformation or decomposition of intersubjective space-time must be effected. Death itself initiates only a *physical* dissolution of the body. Although the balouma or life element leaves the body when a person dies,[1] death dissolves neither the intersubjective amalgam that constitutes the *bodily person* and forms the ground of each self,[2] nor the intersubjective connections between others built on and condensed within the deceased's person.

Accordingly, the focal social categories engaged in mortuary transac-tions are pivoted on an opposition between the dala of the deceased and the two key extrinsic dala through whom the deceased's personal being has been formed in life: the spouse and his or her dala (and less focally, the ex-spouse's dala if a previous marriage was involved); and the deceased's father and the latter's dala.[3] The deceased's dala is called umata (-mata, die; roughly, the ones of the dead); the marital dala is distinguished as ta-karuvay (-vay, marry; those of the marriage); and the paternal dala, as ta-koupoy (the fathers, those who nurtured).[4] The two affinal dala (the kakawa) take parallel roles in the rite, thus setting them off from the Umata.[5] The asymmetry of the exchange is not centered therefore on the opposition of the woman's kinspeople and those of the man's, as in marital exchanges. Rather, asymmetry is based on the opposition of the male *or* female deceased's dala as the locus of the deceased's internal blood relations and the two basic types of affinal dala (those who are not the ones of the dead) as the loci of exterior relational bonds.

In line with this different basis for asymmetry in the transaction, we find, for example, that gender-linked exchange items such as fish (which are a gift from the husband and his kin made in return for cooked vegetables from the woman and her kin in routine marriage exchanges; see Chapter 6, note 3) and cooked vegetable food are not transacted strictly uni-directionally throughout the mortuary rites. For instance, fish (*in*) and vegetable food (i.e., *karu*) are transacted together in a symmetric exchange between Umata and affines marking the last time the chief mourners (the affinal side) may eat fish before mourning prohibitions are imposed. In this exchange, men fish for the respective contributions of their sides, while women of each side prepare and cook the vegetable food in the hamlets. Similarly, the key mortuary transaction of raw produce that I discuss in some detail later in the chapter should have a topping of cooked vegetable food and fish. In both examples, the gift from each side combines male- and female-associated products (although the female predominates), thus suggesting the dual potencies operating on both Umata and affinal sides. Although fish and vegetable food are asymmetrically transacted *against* each other in certain mortuary transactions,[6] the lack of *exclusive* unidirectionality and the combination of male and female gender opposi-tions in a unified gift from each side point to the shift of organizational principles demarcating the oppositions constituting transactions in the mortuary exchanges as against the marriage exchanges.

The Umata and affinal dala groups form the core of the mortuary organization, but they are joined by other individuals and other dala groups who align themselves with one or the other of these key groups. These additional persons include husbands and wives (the *sinavarama*) of members of each of the key dala, who will typically help their spouses to carry out mourning duties; and other dala of the same kumila as the affines and Umata respectively – most notably those who have special kinship bonds with the dala concerned (see Chapter 2). Other helpers (usually not of the Umata's kumila) may align themselves with the affines on an individual basis.[7]

The result is that a large part of the Gawan community is likely to be involved in the mortuary rites for a married man or woman, although rites vary in size, of course. As some Gawans said, people more generous in life are likely to have many more mourners. For the present argument, however, what is significant is that the structure in terms of which these alignments take place and the wider community is engaged involves minimally three dala, organized dyadically and asymmetrically, so that relative to the deceased's dala, the affinal polarity constitutes "the other."

It is the affinal side, and not the Umata, whose members take on the bodily qualities of mourning.[8] The mortuary process involves a superposi-tion of the deceased's negative state of being upon the external other. By this means, the dala of the dead is able to reclaim in concrete transaction the dimensions of the social person that have been matrixed in these external bonds by birth and marriage, and coordinately to transform the mortuary state of the community imposed by the death of the dala's member back to a positive revivified level of value potential. The responsibility for effecting these transformations rests upon the deceased's dala – as people say, it is "their dead person" (si-toumata).

As I have suggested, the separative aspect of the procedure engages a negative spatiotemporal transformation (a contraction of spacetime). But the revivification entails a positive transformation: an expansion of the spatiotemporal level of the living (as conveyed in the positive conversion of the bodies of the mourners) and thus a positive transformation of the spatiotemporal level or value of the community, which has been drained by the loss of one of its members. Once the negative value state produced by death has been signified on the bodies of the affines in specific mourning qualities, these directionally polarized transformations – on the one hand, reclamation of the dead back to the self of the stricken dala, on the other hand, release of the deathlike state caused by the death of one of this dala's members, from the affines and the wider community – are conjoined within the subsequent transformational acts. In this transformative cycle, the memory of the dead as a bodily being is to be both materialized in an objective form that defines the conjunction of the dead with the other (that is, the dala affines) and then through a long-term process, erased piece by piece in the withdrawal or deletion of different aspects of this objectivation in the other (see Coppet, 1981; Weiner, 1976:80ff.). Mortuary rites thus involve the creation of a temporary memorialization so that, paradoxically, forgetting can be generated.

In connection with this transformative process, it will be recalled that all deaths except those of the very old – for whom it is felt that his or her time (kara-tuta) has come – are attributed to witchcraft, although the degree to which this attribution surfaces in any given death varies, as Gawans do not attempt to diagnose a possible killer during the mortuary rites. Nevertheless, most deaths are viewed as the result of subversive acts of witchery that threaten the potency of both the dala and the wider Gawan community in destroying or consuming (as the witch consumes the bodies of the dead) its value products. As one woman of the deceased's dala said, referring to the community at large at the formal blackening of mourners for a death in 1974 (a period when there had been a few deaths in succession): "You think about bwagaw (witchcraft), now you will paint black."

In the following discussion I do not attempt to analyze the entire complex sequence of the mortuary rites, but merely to consider certain aspects relevant to the present argument. The account of the rite is therefore not intended to be complete, and my description is necessarily simplified.[9]

THE BODY AND THE NEGATIVE TRANSFORMATION OF SPACETIME

As I have just indicated, it is the affines who take on their bodies the overt qualities of death. Full mourning attire consists of a blackened body and a fully shaved head. Women also wear mourning skirts (*sileileiw*), which are longer than the dress skirts for ceremonial beautification and youthful attire, and thus extend further below the sexually charged areas of the upper thighs. These skirts are made with a rough stripping of coconut fronds rather than the fine shredding of the dressy skirt. Men generally wear old cloth shorts or laplaps in addition to blackened bodies and shaved heads. Most of the key mourners in full mourning attire and many of the other, less focal participants are women, but men also take on mourning attire. The chief female mourner (the spouse of a male deceased, if living) wears an unusually long skirt (*dabalutu*)[10] that is supposed to sweep the ground when she walks. Varying degrees of mourning may be marked on the body by variations in the treatment of hair and in degrees of blackening (for example, minor mourning may involve simply trimming the hair and going unwashed).

The substance used in blackening (*koura*) is charred coconut husks that are mixed into a paste with water and smeared over the shaved heads and bodies of the chief mourners. Each key affinal dala must be represented by one or more chief mourners. The latter are shaved and blackened in a formal rite outside the house of mourning where they have been living since the burial, usually about a week earlier. After this formal rite, various other individuals across the community will decide to darken their bodies and shave or trim their hair. These individuals make their own decisions (or an adult may decide to paint a child), but all decisions involving the chief mourners who will live in the mourning house are made by the Umata. The latter regulate the formal qualities of the bodies of those who visibly represent their own (i.e., the Umata's) state of being.

Thus the mourning affines become the means by which the deceased's dala observe their own grief and loss (their own dead person) objectified outside them in the other. They are, as it were, the witnesses of their own deathlike state. Conversely, the mourning affines objectify their identification with the other (a dead spouse, child, brother's child, etc. of another dala) in their own bodies. For them, the other becomes identified as an aspect of the self, just as for the Umata, an aspect of the self becomes temporarily separated as the other.

Plate 9. The blackening and hair shaving of the chief mourners in a mortuary rite. The woman who is standing wears a mwaagula band and a long mourning skirt.

The Umata can refuse to permit the affines in general to paint black – that is, to be publicly perceived in terms of their identification with the Umata's dead. If they do so, they signify not only their displeasure with their affines, but they may also be implying the latter's complicity (as witches) in the death.[11] The fact that the affines are painted black signifies that the deceased's dala recognizes the formers' identification with the dead: It sees them as having taken care of the deceased – as having their identities embedded in the deceased's being, and the deceased as having been partially identified with them. It is the Umata who allow the affines to express their grief in visible mourning.

The affines' bodily identification with the dead is not confined, however, to the phase of blackening. The blackening rite is rather the moment of formal recognition, through the total resurfacing of the body, of identifications that have been emerging in the preburial context. Thus, the affines physically attend the dead before burial. When the body lies in state inside the house of mourning the night before burial, the living spouse must lie down all night with the dead embracing him or her for the last time.[12] Close affinal kin (especially the spouse, but also the children of a male deceased, etc.) may also rub the spittle or mucous of the dying or recently dead person on their bodies: In this way, they physically identify themselves with the dying person. According to one Gawan, if they fail to do this it may appear that they have rejected the deceased and are treating him or her like a stranger (*toubwaga*). As in the case of bloodletting noted earlier (Chapter 6), body fluids that traverse the bodily boundaries of one person are smeared on the skin of another person outside his or her dala and kumila. These substances then become the media of identification with the other.

During the night-long mourning,[13] the body is tended by various kin of the affinal type (including not only members of the key affinal dala groups, but also sinavarama of the deceased's dala and others outside the dala and kumila of the deceased). These people crowd into the house and sit all night singing songs of wailing and tending the dead. Although the Umata initiate the singing and the night of mourning, they cannot stay in the house; however, they enter at intervals with the other members of the community to wail during the night.

At this time, women in the house may compose songs about the dead that frequently recall the buwaa exchanges in which the latter was involved, or remember other aspects of the deceased such as his or her beauty when young. The songs about buwaa exchanges are particularly significant for these exchanges are formally finished when one of the marriage partners dies. One woman explained to me that mourners compose songs about buwaa for this reason.[14] Similarly, one woman weeping for her husband as she embraced his body during the night wailed, "O my husband, you gave me so much buwaa; I, my path [was] like a *kousiray* [the red wood of the canoe hull used as a synechdoche to refer to the canoe]." In this moving expression of grief, we see not only the importance of the buwaa in the value it bestows on the recipient spouse (and her or his kin), but also, more generally, how the memory of the donor is embedded in the things given, for, as we saw earlier, these things are themselves a sign that this person has remembered the recipient. Thus confined through the night in the crowded space of the house, the spouse and affines not only physically identify themselves with the dead before burial, but they also create the memorial songs recalling the deceased's now finished life. The intersubjective spacetime formed in this phase of the rites combines bodily identifications between affines and the dead body with the affines' common focus on the "pastness" of the past that prefigures later mourning phases.

When the body is rushed out of the house in the late morning to be buried, the living spouse is carried with it (or sometimes helped separately) to the grave where frequently he or she must be pulled from the body by the Umata; the latter comfort the spouse, helping him or her away from the grave. Other close affines may also rush into the grave sobbing, and have to be drawn away by the Umata before the body is buried.

Finally, it is important to note that close affinal kin will wear amulets of nails or hair taken from the dead.[15] Some years later these amulets are reclaimed by the Umata with a gift of pork, but the Umata themselves are forbidden to wear the amulets (cf. Weiner, 1976:198). Affines are like material reliquaries of the dead who take onto their body surfaces physical substances from the deceased.

After the burial, the blackening (-kum koura, smear with charred coconut husks) of the affines' bodies reconstitutes the dead person, as, in effect, the generalized form of death itself within the visible world of the living. Just as this reconstitution provides a transient living memorial of the dead, so also the blackened mourners (especially the chief mourners) are regarded as being in a state of emotional heaviness, for their minds are weighed down (i-mwaw nanei-s) as they remember the dead. As some Gawans told me, when the mourning is over, the chief mourners will return to the activities of daily life and forget (i-lum-leve-sa) the dead.

This kind of remembering begins, as we have seen, in the house of mourning, before burial. Like the affinal physical identification with the body of the deceased, it is translated into visible form in the bodily qualisign of blackness on the mourners' bodies in the postburial physical embodiment of death. It is also emphasized in the selective food taboos that mourners choose to take on in memory of the deceased. Obviously, this kind of remembering contains no intimations of the future, but involves looking backward to something now finished and without potential – as when one grieves for a person who has gone away as "hands that [once] gave" (Chapter 3).

Much as past buwaa transactions involving the deceased may be sung about before burial, so also memory of these gifts is a not uncommon reason given by less immediate mourners for painting black. These people may have received food from the deceased's buwaa to eat; or they may have been among the recipients of canoes that were part of the deceased's buwaa, or that the deceased had given for another couple's buwaa. Blackening is then regarded as being in return (mapu-ra) for the buwaa.

In 1974, one woman blackened for the death of an elderly woman whose husband (who had predeceased her by some years) had once been the source of a canoe given along a canoe path to the current mourner's husband. The canoe was the elderly woman's buwaa gift, and the mourner showed that she and her husband (for whom she was "standing in") were remembering this canoe transaction completed long ago.

Thus, buwaa recipients objectify their memories of the deceased's past transactions from which they have benefited (in this way honoring the deceased as a giver) by darkening their bodies at a buwaa donor's death. This objectification of memories is in turn dissolved in the later washing away of the darkness.

Darkening also connotes an element of bodily self-sacrifice: the blackness of koura is explicitly intended to make the body appear dirty (*bikibiki*) and ugly (*gagera magi-ra*) in contrast to the cleansed, attractive appearance, which, as we have seen, gains admiration and conveys vitality. In fact, charcoal blackening is an intensification of ordinary dirt. When people who have taken on the lesser grades of mourning by not washing their bodies are being paid by the Umata, the payment is "for their bikibiki," whereas payments for blackening proper are referred to in terms of *koura* (see below). Much as the blackened coconut husks create qualities directly opposed to the sweet-scented, glowing coconut oil rubbed on the body for beautification, so koura is the polar opposite of cleansed and glowing beauty.

Similarly, blackened mourners should not handle or transact kula shells. The latter are beautiful objects whose transaction is directly identified with happiness (*mwaasaw*), bodily beautification, and a concern with transactive activities and their value-producing potential. As one woman pointed out: The mourners' "minds are heavy" and they should neither throw kula shells nor discuss canoe exchanges; later when their bodies are *murakata* (cleansed and bright), the prohibition of the koura is finished, and they may do these things again.

In sum, the qualisign of koura involves a contraction of bodily spacetime into dark unattractiveness, mental heaviness, and a remembrance of things finished. Thus the body exhibits a depletion of positive value, the negative transformational state of the mourners, the bereaved dala, and the wider community at a death.

As we might expect, this contraction is further shown in the limitations of movement imposed on the chief mourners, which articulate their bodies with the appropriate domain of island space. The chief mourners live inside the house of mourning where, before burial, the body lay in state. Ideally, this house should be in a hamlet of the deceased's dala, although this is not always the case.[16] The deceased's dala members have primary responsibility for feeding and caring for the mourners during their travail, although the latters' own kin also help. Until the close of the main mortuary rites about one and a half months later, varying limitations are imposed on the movements of these mourners beyond the house.[17] A surviving spouse is the most heavily confined, for this person cannot move out of the hamlet (except for the performance of bodily functions when he or she may go to the bush at the edge of the hamlet). Initially, the spouse does not sit outside the house at all.

The house interior, where those subject to the most stringent prohibitions spend their time, is also dark. Thus, not only is the body itself dark, but it is also, in effect, contained within darkness. In this warm, dark and delimited space, mourners and their visitors speak in sotto voce while the former pursue sedentary tasks usually related to the mortuary process, such as shredding mourning skirts or stringing and blackening berries to wear as mourning beads. Moreover, while they are living in the house, the mourners should not be referred to by their personal names but by the term for mourner (na/ta-kakaw), a feature that further marks their interiorization within the cover of darkness.

During the mourning phase, the mourning house and its occupants signify the contracted spacetime or negative value level of the community. The negative qualisigns of darkness, immobility (slowing of tempo) and interiorization within a minimal, controlled space, as well as the focus on the memory of a past without future potential are concentrated in the bodies of the chief mourners and their residential location.

FOOD TRANSACTIONS AND VALUE TRANSFORMATION

Once the formal blackening rite has created this negative intersubjective spacetime, the Umata immediately initiate the procedure whereby the attributes of value depletion are reclaimed through payment to the mourners, and the negative state of the society slowly transformed.

The fundamental transformative procedure consists of the transmission of wooden dishes (kaboma) piled with raw produce from the Umata and their helpers to all those who have assumed any of the various degrees of mourning. The transaction is called by the familiar Massim term sagali[18] and these dishes are considered replacements or payments (i.e., the mapura) for the mourning. A kaboma is made up of raw taro (the primary comestible used), yams, and bananas (if available) decoratively arranged in a conical pile on the large flat wooden dish that gives its name to the whole construct. To complete the structure, a few pieces of cooked food with a cooked fish should be placed on top of the pile (kuludabala, the head of the dish) so that, according to some people, the recipient side would have something to eat that night. It seems significant that the essentially male component of fish makes up the head of the dish, and the female-associated garden produce, the essential core of the gift, although Gawans did not make a point of this feature.

Produce piles of this kind (but lacking the cooked food-fish topping, and arranged on different foundations) also serve as gifts in other formalized contexts of Gawan exchange. One type (mentioned earlier, see Chapter 6, note 1) is given to mark a stage in a special sequence of gifts made from the woman's side in marriage exchanges between affines (and paid for by the appropriate nonedible goods from the husband's kin). Another type appears in the finales (and at some other stages) of Gawan community entertainments (see Chapter 8) where much of the vegetable produce and

Plate 10. Two women pile taro, yams, and bananas (at the bottom of the pile) for a mortuary exchange. The women's protective head coverings indicate that they have given birth within the last few months (see Chapter 2).

preparation of the pile of an adult male donor generally comes from his wife and her kinspeople. Thus, like ordinary, repetitive harvest gifts, these specialized food prestations are part of or have connections with the female-side gift in marriage relations. However, unlike the ordinary harvest gift, they are artifacts made for special occasions. In the mortuary rites, the produce piles are the basic transformative gift coming from the matrilineal dala of the deceased; but the gift is not strictly asymmetric – a point of some significance, which I discuss later.

Considerable care is given to the piling of the kaboma, so that the layers taper evenly to the top to give it an attractive appearance. (The emphasis on the even edges is reminiscent of the more general Gawan esthetic of clearing and smoothing discussed earlier in connection with hamlet space, paths, and the body.) The pile should be at least five layers in height. A long vine, which is later used by recipients to measure the size, is wrapped around it to hold the layers in place. Size or spatial extension as well as refinement of form (beautification) are thus significant features of these artifacts. The addition of cooked food and fish at the top also has decorative import.[19]

Piles of this sort differ from the ordinary harvest gifts of raw produce in that they are shaped to create an aesthetic display that can be actually sized up by height and width, and that demonstrates by its carefully piled layers the concern of the workers with their artifact. However, Gawans are not competitive about the size or excellence of each dish. Rather, the main aim of the Umata is to collect sufficient dishes of respectable size to meet their obligations to the mourners. Donors simply attempt to make as attractive, appropriate a contribution as is within their means. These beautified food prestations repay the mourners for the darkened, ugly state of their bodies.

Each dish is typically contributed by a marital couple, one of whom (the husband or wife) is a member of the Umata, or is one of the Umata's helpers; an unmarried person (for example, a widow of an Umata man, or a widowed kinswoman) may also pile a dish. Dishes are piled in the hamlet of the donor and then assembled at dusk through the efforts of both men and women in the hamlet of the mourning house (or of the male head of the sagali, if he lives in a different hamlet), where the Umata men decide on their distribution, arranging them into groups for each affinal category.

One dish must be given for each person who has assumed mourning, and usually more than one for each of the chief mourners in the house. In the distribution process, dishes are categorically distinguished by labels referring to *the state of the body (or action affecting the state of the body) that they are aimed at achieving in the mourner.* Dishes are called "washing" or "their washing" (*kasi-vakaakay*) if they are given for an individual to wash and so divest her or him of the mourning. A person receiving one of these dishes should go and wash in the sea. Other dishes are called *lawalala koura* if given so that the recipients will maintain their koura until they later receive a dish for washing. The chief mourners are the last to receive vakaakay dishes, after which a formal washing and skirt exchange between Umata and affinal mourners takes place.

The food dishes are not simply payment for the assumption of mourning, but their transmission is also the means of releasing the mourning. Thus they regulate the length of the mourning phase for any given person and bring about the final conversion of bodily qualisigns from darkness to light (washing). The verbal identification between the food dishes and the bodily state they are intended to create marks the causal nexus between the bodily qualities of the mourners (or the changes in these qualities) and the act of food transmission.[20]

The sense in which these transactions are also a separation of the deceased from his or her identification with the paternal and spouse's dala can be clarified by examining an additional feature of the chief mourners' attire. Those who have undertaken the most stringent mourning wear one or more special necklets made of braided, blackened pandanus thread (similar bands are worn in Trobriand mourning, Weiner, 1976:212). These bands, called by the general term *mwaagula* (with distinctive terms for different bands) are made by men of the affinal side; the affines also determine those of their own dala groups living in the house of mourning who are to wear them. Except in the case of a bereaved husband, the wearers of mwaagula are generally women (see Plate 9).

Gawans describe these bands as *guyaw*; thus they constitute a superordinate control over the body of the wearer. Wearers must not go beyond the immediate hamlet area while the control of the mwaagula is imposed on them; wearers also maintain the most stringent food taboos. For instance, in addition to those food prohibitions that they and all other mourners in the house voluntarily assume in memory of the dead, those wearing the mwaagula are forbidden to eat boiled food. Since vegetables cooked in water are slippery, they are swiftly consumed (i.e., the person eats a lot), and regulation of food consumption epitomizes bodily control, as we have seen previously (Chapter 4).

The mwaagula itself must be taken off when the wearer is *eating* and *sleeping* because it is *guyaw*. The point of these prohibitions should be clear in the light of the significance of eating and sleeping examined earlier (Chapter 3). As guyaw, the mwaagula must be kept apart from those acts and bodily states that typify value negation. Should any prohibitions linked with the mwaagula be ignored, it is said that the wearer may lose her (or his) mind; according to one Gawan, a dark cloud might climb (*b-ei-mwen bwaw*) over the body when the taboo-breaker finally goes to wash and be beautified by the Umata, so that instead of being cleansed and brightened, the body would be shrouded in darkness.[21]

Once a food dish has been given as *lawalala koura* for a mourner wearing mwaagula bands, one of the Umata women may take a band from the mourner and wear it herself (or give it to another Umata woman to wear). As the sagali proceeds, the bands will slowly be removed until at the time of the final washing, only the most important mourner (the spouse if living) will still be wearing a band. This last band, called *yabalouma* (*balouma* apparently referring here to a generalized notion of the dead as ancestral spirits)[22] is the one that most typifies guyaw control over the wearer's mobility and food consumption; it is removed only at the washing, and like the other bands will then be worn by an Umata woman.

The right to take the mwaagula bands is created by the transaction of food dishes. By this means a part of the insignia of death can be released from the external other and taken onto the self of the deceased's dala by means of a direct transfer that connects and separates the bodies of each. Worn by the deceased's dala, the bands no longer constrain the wearer. The transfer marks a partial or token dissolution of the memorialization of the dead embodied in the other, and of the affines' definition of the dead as a bodily aspect of themselves.

But we have not yet considered the completion of the food transaction. Given the Gawan view that food dishes from the Umata are a return for the mourning state of the affines, one might expect that no further return would come from the affinal side. But this is not the case. On the day following the Umata's transmission of the dishes, the affinal side returns the *same* wooden dishes, now piled by recipient couples (or individuals)[23] with their helpers, and containing an ideally equal number of layers of produce from their own resources. Each pile is tied with the vine used by the Umata donor on the previous day; it is said that if the vine appears to have been cut, the latter may be annoyed, for the vine measures the equality of the return. In practice, Gawans appear easygoing about the actual equality of the return, but the principle is important.

The food transmission from the affinal side is called by a term that may be glossed "its return or replacement" (*karamapu*). The first gift is always made by the Umata, whereas karamapu comes from the affinal side. Members of the dala of the deceased (but not people of other dala helping them) are forbidden to eat these returns; this regulation does not apply to any of the original affinal recipients, and points to the fact that the Umata rather than the affines are the primary food donors. Furthermore, the affinal return always closes the transaction.

Two such transactions are made in sequence, and if necessary a less formal third transaction is made to be sure that all persons, whatever their grade of mourning, have received a dish in payment.[24] After this initial set of transactions, all persons have been given dishes for washing except for those in the house. The final washing and formal beautification of the chief mourners occurs only after another month or so (in order to provide time for collecting betel nut and making skirts for the finale), but it, too, is preceded by an exchange of piled dishes between the Umata and the affines. All these dishes are now *vakaakay*.

Since the Umata food is supposed to pay for the affinal mourning, one may ask why the affines should have to make a return for the dishes. Gawans themselves were, in fact, somewhat puzzled about the reason. Some people whom I questioned suggested they thought it a little odd, and that the tradition seemed somewhat unfair when one thought about it. But one senior man said simply that the return "squared" the Umata's gift: That is, food is equivalent to food (cf. the notion of kakaloula discussed in Chapter 6).

Structurally, it is apparent that these mortuary transactions conform to the basic template in which the actor's body is the medium of qualisigns that exhibit the transformative value of operations on food. In the initial part of the mortuary transaction, food transmission yields a return that encodes bodily qualisigns of transformation to a relatively more expansive level of spatiotemporal control. Transmission of the beautified food dishes produces the slow dissolution of darkness and release of the interiorization and immobilization of the mourners, a process that transforms the negative state of the community brought on by the bodily immobilization of death.

A revealing parallel occurs in the pattern of the Gawan community entertainments discussed in detail later. In both mortuary and entertainment contexts, elements of body decor are regarded as returns for transactions of conical piles of food, but in each case, the exchange can only be finished by a reversal of food donors and recipients. In the case of the entertainments, this requires the performance of two entertainments owned by dala groups of different kumila, and is constructed as a long-term debt rather than an immediate return. In the context of the entertainments, Gawans make it very explicit that the reversal of food donors and food recipients is necessary to create equivalence between the opposed categories of actors, and thus to effect a closure of the debt. It would seem that similarly, the equality of the affinal and Umata dala groups is reiterated in the reversal of food donors and recipients in the dish exchange of the mortuary rites,[25] but that the bodies of the mourners exhibit the qualisigns of value effected by the initial food transmission from the Umata.

Since the dish exchanges are the core of the mortuary rites, it seems significant that they should reiterate, through an equal exchange of comestibles, not only the equality of the two sets of participants, but also by this means, a closure, or finishing of relationship. But although the ritual is a stage in the dissolution of the extra-dala relationships embodied by the deceased, of which he or she is a linchpin, it should be kept in mind that the rite for any married person with living children does not in fact totally sever the external relationships built through the deceased. Although buwaa exchanges lapse at the death of one spouse, informal exchanges may still be maintained on a more optional basis, and if there is a living spouse, he or she may still maintain sinavarama aid relationships with the deceased's kinspeople. Furthermore, the two dala that are in the spouse relation to each other in mortuary rites for a husband and wife will also participate together in the mortuary rites for each of the children of the marriage, when the husband's dala will become the paternal takoupoy mourners. Nevertheless, as soon as one spouse dies, the severance process begins, and the buwaa relationships stop; and when the mortuary rites for the last child are performed, the two dala will no longer exchange food (as either Umata and Takoupoy, or Umata and Takaruvay in-laws) in virtue of that particular marital relationship at further mortuary rites. Thus it would seem that the equal exchange of food dishes in any given death may be seen as depicting closure or "ending" as a process engaged by the death of each person who figures in a given social nexus. This ending, however, is what makes possible the kind of value *potential* signified in the *positive* body conversions of the rites.

THE WASHING AND SKIRT EXCHANGES

The conclusion of the mortuary exchange sequences is centered in an exchange of skirts between Umata and affines. This exchange must be preceded, as I have noted, by the food transaction that enables the washing and beautification of the chief mourners to take place.

On the morning of the day called "the washing," the Umata conduct the chief mourners out of the house, taking them down the cliffs to the sea.[26] The emergence of the mourners from the closed space of their confinement, and their movement along the path to the sea is subsequently marked on their bodies by the washing and by their later beautification upon return to the hamlet. These activities form the by now familiar processes of positive spatiotemporal transformation.

Prior to these rites, women of both the Umata and affinal sides have been preparing skirts for the event. The Umata and their helpers prepare short, finely stripped decorative skirts (*doba*) to be given to the female mourners to wear.[27] Additional skirts are also prepared for more general distribution to the affinal side. The affines, on the other hand, prepare roughly stripped, longer skirts of the relatively dark, mourning type (*sileileiw*) to be given to the deceased's dala and their helpers. In each case, all those women involved in preparing food dishes, as well as those wearing koura, should receive a skirt. There are also cases in which individuals arrange to give their food dishes to particular persons on the affinal side, and these same individuals then also exchange skirts in the transactions of the finale. In such cases, the integral relation between the dish and the skirt transactions becomes especially prominent.

After the mourners and the Umata have returned to the hamlet of the mourning house on the day of the washing, the Umata dress and decorate the chief mourners, putting on and trimming the skirts they (the Umata) have prepared, as well as painting the faces of the mourners with decorative black and white designs, and reddening their mouths with betel. Thus the mourners regain their personal identities, which reemerge, as it were, from the undifferentiated darkness that has covered their faces and bodies (cf. Plates 9 and 11).

The rough skirts that the mourners have been wearing are put on by the Umata women, who wear them casually as the remains of mourning but not as a sign of the prohibitive mourning state. This interchange of bodily qualisigns withdraws identification with the deceased from the bodies of the affines back into the dala group of those whose "dead person it is."[28]

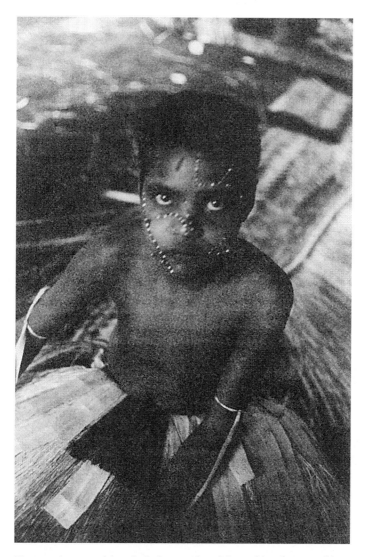

Plate 11. A young girl washed, decorated, and dressed in a fine new skirt at the end of the mourning period.

Thus, the Umata release their mourning decree, and the bodily state of the affines is fully reconstituted with the qualisigns of positive value; these signs convey the spatiotemporal transformation entailed in the conversion from death (immobility and darkness) and grievous memory of the dead, to life (expansive motion and light) and the assuaged mental state that makes it possible to take up one's daily productive work again.

Whereas the withdrawal of the negative value signs back to the deceased's dala involves a detotalization of the person – from this perspective, a contraction of bodily and intersubjective spacetime back into the interiority of matriliny – the transmission of beautifying qualities to the affines entails a transcendence of this internal level. This expansion of bodily spacetime exhibits the final reconstitution of the community (including the dala of the deceased, who perform the cleansing procedures) with positive value potential. However, the positive transformation is *conditional upon the fragmenting (negative) process.*

The key exchange items in this transformative process are the essentially female-produced and transacted skirts.[29] The cycle that begins with the food dishes (connotative of the female-side gift in marriage exchanges, but in this context ideally marked also with fish, a male gift) prepared by women and men, and technically transacted by men, yields an exchange of body-decor elements produced and transacted largely by women. These latter elements directly exhibit the negative *and* positive qualisigns of value.

The skirt transaction condenses the overall transformation that has occurred in the ritual. It is both the *outcome* produced by the gifts of food dishes that have preceded it, and the *value signifier* of the transformation effected by the Umata's food giving. Like the food exchange, it creates both closure and potential. Thus, as I have suggested, the food exchange both detotalizes the amalgam concentrated in the person of the deceased (separating the deceased from his or her affinal or external identifications, and depicting closure in the relationship), and at the same time it enables the expansion of bodily being in the slow renewal of vitalizing qualities or positive potentiality. The same dialectic appears in the final skirt transaction: The rough mourning skirts exhibit the contraction of bodily spacetime in death, and the fine skirts, its expansion in youthful vitality, sexuality, and life potential.

Since the mortuary rite transforms the intersubjective spacetime constituted in the bodily being of the deceased back into the prior, internal matrilineal order, it is clearly fitting that women and their goods should be the focal agents in the concluding exchange (see Weiner, 1976, on the female principle in Trobriand mortuary rites). Buwaa marriage exchanges, in contrast, involve a masculinization process of incremental expansion in the exchange cycle: As we have seen, they entail transformation to a more comprehensive intersubjective spacetime, and the amalgamation of components of social being rather than their dissolution.[30]

8

The Drum dance and the Comb

Today we are having the exciting thing (*kaymwan*); we don't die . . . we are happy;
there is no witchery. . . . The dancing makes their [the dancers' and the
community's] bodies buoyant.

Gawan woman talking about the Drum dance, 1975

The two major community entertainments (*kayasa*) currently performed
by Gawans, which I referred to in Chapter 2 as the Drum dance (*kupi* and
other Gawan names) and the Comb (*sinatu*) are also formulated in terms
of the basic template of Gawan value transformation that we have seen
developed in the marriage and mortuary exchanges. But here, as shall be
seen, the process is activated in practices that constitute a Gawa-wide
community mode of spacetime and are directly concerned with the
demonstration and mediation of hierarchy.

Gawans explicitly oppose these joyful community entertainments
(especially the Drum dance, which appears to be the more traditional of
the two)[1] to the sorrowful mortuary rites and the destructive acts of
witchery and death. During mortuary rites it is forbidden to beat the drum;
and there is a Gawan notion that when there has been a death and people
mourn in the hamlets, the witches perform a Drum dance in the bush.
However, despite this categorical opposition between the two contexts, the
subversive tensions of witchcraft are in no sense excluded from the positive
value transformations uppermost in the entertainments, a feature that will
be suggested briefly in the present discussion.

THE SPATIOTEMPORAL CYCLE OF
THE ENTERTAINMENTS

I have already pointed out that the Drum dance and the Comb each belong
(*tarawagara*) to a single dala of different kumila: the Drum dance to a
Nukubay dala and the Comb to a Nukwasisi dala, and that they appear to

be a contemporary fraction of a previous pattern in which all four kumila
were represented by at least one major community entertainment whose
performances were more or less alternately performed (Chapter 2). In the
contemporary pattern the two entertainments form a reciprocal cycle. This
cycle creates a moiety-like totality involving the community at large, but
centered in established partnerships between men of the two kumila, which
now represent the whole community.

Both the entertainments extend over more than one Gawan bwalima
(southeast wind year), although their ideal length and the standard number
of major feast types involved in each are substantially different. Thus the
Drum dance has a seven-year feast sequence, but it would appear that the
amount of time involved is subject to variables such as the state of the food
supply, interruptive deaths, and other factors. The Comb has a much
shorter two-year feast sequence, but similarly, the amount of time involved
need not coincide with this pattern.[2] As in other major community
ventures such as the kula uvelaku, periodicity is partly contingent on
current states of affairs, rather than defined by a determinate schedule.
The scheduling of the two entertainments and of the special feast days
involved is the kareiwaga of the guyaw of the owning dala and the senior
men of that kumila. Where major exchanges of raw yams are involved, as
in the finales of the entertainments, the performances must be planned
ahead of time (at the previous planting season) so that the festivities may
take place just after the harvest in the coming year. The importance of
relatively senior men in controlling the calendrics for major community
ventures (here, the entertainments) is exemplified in this process.[3]

The two entertainments[4] are treated as vaga and gulugwalu[4] to each
other. In theory, either may be the starting or the finishing transaction, but
in the reciprocal cycle I observed, the Drum dance began the cycle and the
Comb squared the Drum dance, while the cycle subsequent to this one
switched back again to the Drum as the starter.[5] The exchange of
entertainments between the Nukubay and Nukwasisi creates a long-term
debt carried over a number of years, which involves individuals of all
kumila throughout the island community. The duality of this long-term
temporal cycle also penetrates the internal performance structure of each
entertainment, since each is defined on the model of an immediate,
asymmetric exchange between the Nukubay and the Nukwasisi, which goes
on *within* the particular entertainment. This exchange involves gifts of
comestibles from the current entertainment owners in return for certain
bodily elements (including body decor and performance) from the
recipients. Since each entertainment reverses the roles of food giver and
performer, this ongoing, asymmetric exchange is repeated within the more
comprehensive long-term alternation of the entertainments, which creates
the equivalence that finishes a given cycle.

Once a given cycle is finished, the basic structure of the exchange does not in itself provide the means for beginning a new cycle, but certain informal ways of pressing for a renewal may occur. For instance, the owners of the finishing entertainment may attempt to give more food at the finale than the owners of the starting entertainment; or individual recipients may distribute some of their returns to kin and affines as starting gifts to obligate the latter to help them when the current recipients must later act as entertainment owners and food donors.

Performances of an entertainment are held in the hamlet of the leading man of the owning dala. During performances, this hamlet becomes a community center. As Gawans stress, the kayasa are held for the people at large – for everyone to enjoy. Currently, complex politico-historical factors have resulted in both the Drum dance and the Comb being held in one hamlet in Utaru neighborhood where members of owning dala of both entertainments, and the leading man of the owning dala of the Drum dance, reside. The reasons for this situation (which has been a point of some contention in the recent past) cannot be dealt with here, but we may note simply that the result appears to be the formation, at least for the present, of a single center for the major entertainments, rather than a spatial alternation of centers coordinate with the temporal performance cycle and the egalitarian alternation of ownership.[6]

Gawan entertainments do not merely involve internal exchanges. Gawans hope that overseas visitors will attend the major feasts and they look forward especially to hosting visitors at the grand finales. A lavish entertainment contributes to the fame of Gawa in the inter-island world, and gifts of pork and raw produce to individual visitors further ensure that Gawans will be welcome at the latters' memorial feasts (the *sagali soy* performed on Yanaba, Yeguma and Muyuw but not on Gawa and northward)[7] or kayasa entertainments on their own islands. Vaga gifts made to individual overseas visitors at Gawan entertainments may then be reciprocated, and Gawans may be given vaga in these feasts, which they in turn reciprocate with finishing gifts and further vaga at performances of their own kayasa. Thus Gawan entertainments do not merely form intra-island reciprocities of communal spacetime that engage Gawans in planning for internal returns (a forward projection of concerns that, as we shall see, Gawans stress within the entertainments themselves); but they also engage inter-island connectivities, and contribute to the formation of a common spacetime between Gawans and their consociates to the north and south, articulating with the community feasts and entertainments of these islands. In this respect, the Gawan entertainments have affinities with the community-organized kula uvelaku (see Chapter 3).[8]

The distinction that Gawans draw between their own mortuary rites and the entertainments is instructive in this respect. They note that in contrast to their neighbors to the south who perform the sagali soy memorials in which overseas visitors are an integral part of the organization of the exchanges, Gawans do not *formally* invite visitors to any part of their mortuary exchanges; Gawan mortuary rites are essentially internal matters.[9] As we have seen, the rites are centered in the dala of the deceased, whose kareiwaga over the mourning is explicitly linked with a segmentary locus rather than a community center. The hamlet of the house of mourning itself (like the bodies of mourners who reside there) conveys the contraction of intersubjective spacetime in darkness and heaviness, and the internalizing effect of death. When deaths interrupt the performance of Gawan entertainments (whether for longer or shorter periods of time), a temporary contraction or fractioning of the community spacetime formed by the entertainment occurs, as the house of mourning representing the dissolution of relations becomes the focus of activity rather than the community center. We have seen an example of how death can interfere with community ventures and both the intra- and inter-island connectivities they entail in the case cited in Chapter 3, in which the disruption of plans for an uvelaku led to the untimely consumption of part of the uvelaku feast food.

THE DRUM DANCE

The Drum dance is supposed to be held nightly during the years of its performance at Siwayedi, except when interrupted by a death. One of its main functions is to provide a licensed, collective meeting place for the island's young people to make sexual assignations; the theme of youthful sexuality pervades the entertainment. The dance itself consists of a line of men and women circling anticlockwise around the trunk of a special tree (the *dabedeba*[10] tree), which has been set up in the center of the hamlet. Each dancer carries a pandanus streamer[11] (*bisila*), held with the right hand at one end and balanced by the left at the other end, which is moved rhythmically during the dance.

Male drummers and singers (drummers also sing, but not all singers have drums) stand at the dabedeba during the dance. At the top of the tree is a sprouting coconut placed there at the opening of the dance, which ages with the performance cycle.[12] The dabedeba is the concentrating locus of the dance vitality: Leaves buried beneath it, as well as a pandanus streamer initially tied at the top, have been bespelled to make the dancers dance all night. This tree is also the place where betel nut and certain comestibles are hung by the Nukubay owners for the dancers to enjoy. Any condiments or comestibles actually or figuratively located at the dabedeba are forbidden to all Nukubay, since they are defined as the donors of these items; although they dance like people of other kumila, they alone must not chew or consume the gifts. Thus Gawans may use the expression "at

Plate 12. With drums prepared, Tarakubay and other men and boys gather at the dabedeba tree before a major performance. Betel nut for the dancers is tied to the fork of the tree.

the dabedeba" to refer metonymically to what comes under the aegis of the entertainment. In such usages the Drum dance is named by reference to its center. Just as the hamlet understood as the locus of the dance shifts its reference point from the segmentary dala to the more encompassing island community, so also the internal space of the hamlet becomes focused in its open central space (*baku*) as embodied in the dabedeba, the fixed emblem of the drumming and dancing by which the community is concentrated in vital, synchronized form.

Although the drum is supposed to be beaten each night at Siwayedi, there are some nights when for one reason or another no one arrives; many others when primarily young unmarrieds come to dance and children to play; and still others when because of the availability of a pig to be distributed by the Nukubay, or the fact that there are overseas visitors, or the moon is full, and so on, many people – both unmarried youths and more senior marrieds – arrive and may stay until early morning. During this time, young, unmarried dancers may also make assignations and slip away together. The Drum dance creates a night world of waking activity (lit by the moon rather than the sun) apart from the ordinary daily world of dispersed work activity.

These ongoing nightly, and relatively casual, performances are punctuated by major feasts held during the daytime. Nukubay men decide on the timing of these feasts and their organization. At much more formal daytime performances, dancers decorate elaborately, wearing coconut frond ceremonial skirts and painting black and white designs on their faces; many men don elaborate feather headdresses. Although some head decor may be worn at night, full regalia, including facial painting is restricted to the daytime performances. Cooked and in some instances raw food as well as condiments are always distributed formally by the Nukubay as part of the daytime performances. The latter are also the arena for public speaking related to affairs of the Drum dance and other intra- and inter-island matters, although in special cases, public speaking may take place at night. The elaborate finale discussed below[13] involves a sequence of day performances (as well as night dancing) and a major distribution of garden produce, cooked food, and pig.

These daytime performances typify the organizational control and participation of the senior, married members of the community who remain for the most part behind the scenes at the night performances when the unmarried youths are the main participants. It will be recalled (see Chapter 2) that these youths constitute a peer group cutting across the segmentary order of hamlets and forming a collectivity apart from marital units. As explained in Chapter 2, this differentiation is also represented in the special youth sleeping houses of a hamlet where youths from different hamlets may gather for nightly entertainment. Each marriage then separates the couple from their youthful friendships to form a distinct marital unit apart from the premarital collectivity.

The nightly Drum dance brings this parallel, nonsegmentary world of youthful sexuality and exuberance into a single community arena, organized and scheduled by the seniors of the community (as represented especially by the leading Nukubay men). This center contrasts with the dispersed hamlets of married couples, where sleep rather than dance is the ordinary activity of the night. Furthermore, the contrast between unmarried youths and more senior married couples is also integrated into the "ongoing-nocturnal (youths) versus periodic-diurnal (seniors)" phasing of the Drum dance. As we shall see later, the internal structuring of exchange within the entertainment center refracts this formation as a reciprocal one between *dancing*, which typifies the sexual vitality of youth (even though all people may take part), and *major produce transactions*, which typify the potencies of married men and couples (even though unmarried male youths may in some instances act as transactors).

FOOD TRANSMISSION AND DANCING

The Drum dance is cast in the form of an exchange of comestibles and condiments provided by the dala owners and the Nukubay as a whole, for dancing that is the return payment provided by the community, as represented by the Nukwasisi. The Nukubay are also defined as those who beat the drum (although it is important for Nukwasisi to contribute to the drumming as well).[14] In the leliyu of the origin of the Drum dance, it is said that the dala of the Tarakwasisi that owns the opposing entertainment first put the drum in their own canoe when they came from Muyuw, but a Tarakubay man said: "Give me this drum, I will carry it. You come here and carry our food." This exchange was made, and the Tarakubay man said: "I will beat the drum; you Tarakwasisi will dance." The drumming defines both the time of the dance and its timing: The drum is always beaten before the dance begins, in order to call in the dancers, as well as during the dance itself. As drummers and drum owners, the Nukubay establish the "rhythms of the scene" (Chernoff, 1979:113)

In fact, members of all kumila, including the Nukubay themselves, may dance. Similarly, as I have pointed out, men of different kumila, including especially the Tarakwasisi men, are among the drummers[15] at the dabedeba. It is important, nevertheless, that some Nukubay men should drum just as Nukwasisi in particular should dance. The point is that the Nukwasisi are those whose specific role it is to be the dancers and food recipients. In this respect, they represent the community at large relative to the Nukubay who give the food and decree the beating of the drum that establishes the affair.

Whereas the Nukubay owners who kareiwaga the entertainment are called *guyaw*, the Nukwasisi are called the *ramugway*. The latter eat the food given by men of the Guyaw (capitalized when referring to the entertainment status) category. But Ramugway men also act in some of the daytime contexts to distribute the Guyaw's food to the community at large. Although, in a general sense, all kumila except the Nukubay are regarded as Ramugway, the Nukwasisi men and women epitomize the status, and only their men have the right to distribute the Guyaw's food gifts.

As I have remarked, the Guyaw are prohibited from eating any of the entertainment foods. As in other cases where explicit prohibitions on consumption in the context of transaction appear (such as the nodal couple in the buwaa transaction discussed earlier), this marks them as embodiments of the transmissive principle and thus of the transactional process as potentiality for the creation of positive value. The food donor's Guyaw status brings into the foreground this transformative role. In the entertainment context it epitomizes to Gawans the generous food giving by means of which influence is achieved, the generative base, as we have seen, of the positive transformative process.

The Ramugway, in contrast, are explicitly regarded as inferior to the Guyaw because they are consumers. As one woman explained, the names of the food donors climb whereas those of the recipient consumers decline, but, she went on to point out, this reverses in the next entertainment where the Drum dance Ramugway become Guyaw.[16] However, as noted above, the role of the Ramugway is more complex than this concept suggests: It is typified not only in food consumption, but also in food distribution and especially in dancing. These multiple dimensions suggest a contradictory liminality condensed in the Ramugway category in the context of entertainments, which has fundamental importance for understanding the exchange process.

The relationship of Guyaw and Ramugway is formalized in sets of dyadic partnerships between individual Tarakubay and Tarakwasisi men. These partnerships, once established, are expected to continue until the death of one of the partners, when the designated replacement from the deceased's dala will take over his obligations.[17] Partners call each other *nube*, the label for same-sex personal friends and cross-cousins of different kumila, as well as lovers and sexually available cross-cousins of the opposite sex (see Chapter 2).[18] The young, unmarried Nukwasisi and Nukubay men and women are supposed to have sexual relationships with each other, and are called reciprocally each other's "food for eating" (*kasi-karoug*), a notion that formalizes the sexual emphasis of the Drum dance in terms of the dualistic organization.

The male nube relationships come to the fore especially in the entertainment finale when each Tarakubay partner must give his nube a several-tiered conical pile of raw yams (*noukay*). The largest of these piles may stand some six feet tall, and a large part of the resources for them derive from the donor's *wife and wife's kinspeople*.[19] These affines also do much of the preparatory work in constructing the yam pile and setting it up in the dance center. Moreover, when the Tarakwasisi partner distributes the yams and other comestibles he has received, he usually gives a considerable part of it to his wife's people; the latter (and any other men who have received some of the noukay) are then obligated to help him make returns to his Tarakubay partner at the Comb entertainment some years later, when he becomes a donor.

We see then that the affinal food transmission from the woman's side has been incorporated into the mode of spacetime formed in the community entertainment cycle, which involves intra-island exchanges *between men*. Instead of the recipient of the female-side food being a kinsperson of the husband's, as in the buwaa exchanges, the recipient is an arranged, personal male friend whose relationship to the husband is defined simply by reference to his kumila. Each individual nube partnership and the affinal relationships it incorporates is, moreover, not simply a separate unit, but a component parallel to other component partnerships that make up the moiety-like totality representing the community whole.[20] This construction of the community whole is given a condensed spatial localization at the community center during a crucial phase of the entertainment finales.

In sum, the entertainment partnerships establish a special relationship between a man and another man outside his own dala and affinal kin. This relation also forms a synapse between two affinal segments (that of *each partner* to the exchange). Each such segment, with its nodal couple is encompassed in a more comprehensive structure in which the male–male links of nube (rather than those of a marital couple) form the pivot of the relationship. We may note certain similarities between this feature and what occurs when affinal units are integrated into the more comprehensive inter-island order in the context of kula shell or canoe transmissions. As we saw in Chapter 6, at the point of inter-island transmission, the canoe or shell is typically transacted directly between *men* rather than indirectly, through the mediation of women and of marital couples as linking nodes. Similarly, the opening out of space from the segmentary, individual affinal connection to the kumila-defined community order entails the introduction of symmetric, male–male relationships that form the linking nodes of the community spacetime of entertainment exchange.

I add one further remark regarding the nube relationships. We have seen that these relations carry connotations of youthful sexuality and personal friendship rather than any reference to marital bonds. One may marry one's cross-sex nube, but the marriage relationship is not itself a nube relationship. Just as the youthful nube relationships are at once personalized and connected with a community or islandwide category of youths, so the nube bonds between men in the entertainments free the compartmentalized, segmenting order of affinal kinship units redefining them in community terms. Thus they take on some of the connotations of this youthful ordering of relations in a mediated form.

DANCING AND THE RAMUGWAY ROLE

I have suggested that as consumers, food distributors, and dancers, the Ramugway hold a complex position. As helpers in the distribution of some of the food gifts, the male Ramugway perform a function similar to a man's sinavarama affines, one of whose responsibilities is to help a man in the distribution of comestibles at feasts. As helpers, the Ramugway are not simply consumers, the polar opposite of the Guyaw food donors, but also themselves food-distributing representatives of the Guyaw.

Male Ramugway also have the right to snatch comestibles or condiments from the dabedeba tree (*-kirisi karu*, a form of *kwaya*) and run around giving it to the assembled audience during a daytime performance. This act, which contains an element of aggressive license, seems to indicate that the Ramugway, as rightful consumers, can claim such resources on demand and give them at their own behest to others. The behavior is also consistent with the *opposition* between Ramugway and Guyaw, for the former are defined as brash or aggressive (*ta-gagasisi*) in contrast to the Guyaw who should be quiet and controlled (*ta-manumanum*) in their style. According to one man, the Ramugway can snatch food, whereas a person who is a Guyaw should wait to have food given to him. If a Tarakubay man should take and distribute food in this fashion, others would reprimand him saying, "This is not your *leliyu*." This notion of appropriate guyaw behavior is not confined to the entertainments, but refers to a style felt to be appropriate for the guyaw in general.

These notions increase the ambiguities in the polarization of the two roles. Whereas the Ramugway's food distribution mediates the Guyaw role as donors, the brash style of snatching food is antithetical to the latter's appropriate behavior. The snatching suggests not merely the Ramugway role as distributors, but also their role as the rightful recipients or consumers. Nevertheless, in this type of act, as in their ordinary aid to the Guyaw in some parts of the food distribution, the Tarakwasisi subordination as consumers appears ambiguous because they distribute food on behalf of the Guyaw food donors. While typifying the other relative to the Guyaw, the Ramugway represent the Guyaw relative to the wider community. This double role of polar opposition and substitutive representation is even more clearly developed in the reciprocal Comb entertainment, as will become apparent later, although there are also additional, more central aspects of the Drum dance that reinforce this point. However, we have already seen a similar mediation in the mortuary rites where the deceased of the Umata dala is identified with the affinal other. In both contexts (although with different significance) the identity of the food donor is in certain respects relocated in the other. Although clearly specified as the polar opposite, the other is also an aspect of the food donor's self.

In the entertainments this mediation is developed most notably in the dancing role of the Ramugway. Gawans stress that the latter should not merely dance at the night performances, but that they should "dance until daylight" (*i-kaywousi b-ei-yam*). Posed in this ideal, rhetorical form (one that, although infrequently carried out, does take place in some performances), this return is exactly the opposite of sleep. This opposition is clearly made in a spell intended to spoil the Drum dance, which could be used by a person who for one personal reason or another is angry and wishes to keep the joyful dance from being successful. In this spell the dancer is to become heavy so that he crawls slowly, becomes tired, and goes to sleep. Part of the spell goes as follows:

> Heavy heavy Tudava
> He gets up and falls down [back to sleep] in the north
> You crawl very slowly to the south
> The body is tired
> Its speech is tired

> Its blood is tired . . .
> Food he consumes . . .
> It is not his drum, Ramugway,
> His drum is his wife's buttocks
> You lie down you lie down [i.e., lie down and sleep].

The Ramugway protagonist of the spell is first identified with the stones of the garden in the ancestral personage of Tudava (see Chapter 4): His human bodily vitality is thus converted into heaviness and he falls down toward the ground and crawls, rather than engaging in the buoyant upward motion of the dance. In contrast, songs for the Drum dance are called *wousi-tota* (songs–stand up) because one should get up and dance at the entertainment. The food motif implicit in the reference to Tudava (and which is followed by images of the body's total tiredness and heaviness) then emerges explicitly in the assertions of eating and sleeping. Eating and sleeping are given an amusing sexual connotation in the image of the wife's buttocks, which is substituted for the dancing drum, since the husband sleeps with her instead of dancing all night. Marital sexuality and the Ramugway man's local hamlet substitute for the vital mobility of the Drum dance (with its premarital sexual connotations) and the community center. The spell attempts to negate the spatiotemporal level of the Drum dance by reducing the night dancer to the consumer-sleeper who stays at home.

In contrast to this spell are those intended for use at the opening of the Drum dance when dancers are scratched in order to let blood as they walk around the dabedeba tree. The bloodletting makes the body buoyant and light; as one man explained, it is intended to make the dancer's "heaviness descend" (*b-ei-busi kara-mwaw*) – an aim contrasting with the "tired blood" inside the Ramugway's body that a speaker of the negative spell wishes to produce. As mentioned earlier, a bespelled streamer is also tied to the top of the dabedeba tree; this streamer is also supposed, according to one of my informants, to scratch the body so that blood flows and keeps the dancers from lying down and sleeping.

> . . . I break open-cleanse [i.e., the face] . . .
> Not his/her face, his/her face dawn
> Not his/her chest, his/her chest pure and shining,
> I shine, I am happy the morning, I am happy the evening;
> Not their eyes, their eyes the morning star
> Not their bodies, their bodies bisila streamers
> Not east, not west they dance-tremble . . .

In this spell, the bloodletting, in effect, makes the dancers' faces and bodies into the dawn; their eyes become the morning star – that is, as my informant explained, the dancers dance until daylight. Indeed, it is as if

they are the night turning into dawn as they dance. The final phrase above
was said to mean that the dancers do not stop at all, but they dance,
east-west and west-east:[21] They do not refuse or reject (-*pek*) the dancing.
The totality of spatiotemporal movement – that is, circling in the dance
without stopping through the night – thus suggests the dancers' total
willingness or agreement. We have already seen some of the significance of
consent and the destructive effect of disagreement or individual unwillingness on collective projects (Chapter 3). Participation in a collective activity
signifies an individual's consent and support of the aims of an activity.

The identification of the body with pandanus streamers in this spell
suggests that it is to become so light that it trembles like the streamers
(*bisila*) that men and women carry during the dance (and that are handled
in different movement styles). Still another spell associates the alternating
diagonal motion of the streamers as they are moved up and down in dance
time, with a standard dance step; and this step in turn with the inner
excitement of the dancer who is enjoying himself so greatly. This latter
spell is called *Ulibutu* (-*butu*, fame), and begins with a phrase that refers to
the fact that the speaker is seen by others as he dances:

> Ulibutu, he/she sees me
> Streamers shaken, he "scrapes foot up and down
> against the other leg" (*i-dudu*) . . . .
> My inside (*nuwa-gu*) "scrapes foot up and down" (*i-dudu*) . . . .

Pandanus streamers occur in various contexts where, as I have pointed
out elsewhere (Munn, 1977), they are identified with beautification and
energetic motion. For instance, spells for decorative canoe streamers may
aim both at making the canoe speedy and at exciting the kula partner to
give shells quickly so that the canoe returns laden with shells. In one such
spell, the streamers "call" the kula partner, "turning his mind" to the
Gawan. As a result the Gawan's fame "climbs" like blowing pandanus
(Munn, 1977:50). In its identification with the dance, the light streamer
conveys the body's expanded level of spatiotemporal control. Dancing thus
appears as the embodiment of persuasiveness and the movement of fame.
The dancers concentrate into themselves the qualisigns of positive
transformative value, displaying this value in their dancing.

Yet those who typify the role of dancer are also the type consumers of
the feast. The nonproductive, subordinated role of the Ramugway as those
who eat the feast is, in fact, mediated by their role as dancers who are
paying for their food by creating and displaying the qualisigns of positive
value transformation. Conversely, failure to participate in the dance is
marked by the negative bodily qualities of somnolence and heaviness
associated with food consumption, and suggests a rejection of the dance.
This negative contraction of bodily spacetime is not simply conveyed in

spells aimed at spoiling the dance, but, as we shall see, it is a key notion in the teasing insults of the Guyaw that may accompany the transmission of yam piles to the Ramugway partners at the finale.

THE DANCE FINALE

In May 1975, I observed the six days of festivities that closed the Drum dance running at that time. This finale is called *kavesa*, the "honor" or "praising." I shall concentrate here on the last three days, when the final gift of yam piles is constructed and transacted, and the final daytime dance is performed.

On the first of these last three days, the yams are piled. This procedure begins in the local hamlets of the different Tarakubay men who have partners among the Tarakwasisi. Much of the work is done by a man's wife's kinspeople (including for instance, wife's father, and brother, etc., and the couple's sons). As I have pointed out, much of the produce comes from the gardens of these people, as well as from a man's own gardens; men of his own dala and others variously obligated to him may also make more minor contributions. All the help either creates or closes debts in yams between the latter and the contributors. Gawans emphasized that it is men who do the construction work, but one may observe women helping as well (although they are less in evidence, in the preparatory stages at least, than they are in the preparation of the mortuary dishes where they clearly predominate). In contrast to the piling at mortuary exchanges, however, the noukay piling is viewed as essentially the product of masculine work.

The piles are built up on a circular rope base (*noukay*, also the name of the whole construction) with diameters varying between about two and four feet. Yams are carefully layered around the peripheries (with a central yam infill) so that the artifact tapers in regular fashion as it rises to the top, creating a conical form. Noukay I observed had as many as fourteen tiers. A vine tied around the noukay measures (*-sikoreke*) its size: Recipients may either remember the length of this vine in making returns at the reciprocal entertainment or they may keep the vine; alternatively, they may count the number of layers. The aim is to approximate the original in the return or, occasionally, if they so wish, to give a slightly larger return, thus putting the recipient in debt. As in the case of the mortuary dishes, great care is given to the form and evenness of the layering so as to create a fine gift.

Once the noukay have been set up in the individual hamlets to try them out for size and form, they are taken apart and carried to the dance center where they are again carefully reassembled in their final form. If a particular array appears uneven or crooked, it will be taken down and reconstructed until the builders are satisfied with its appearance. When the

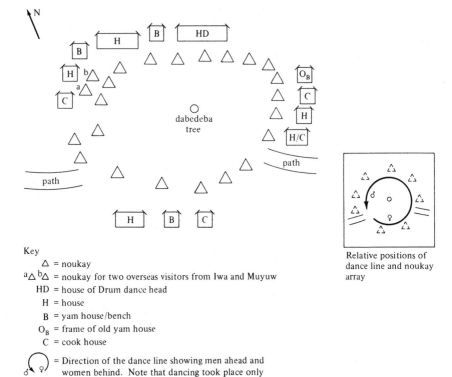

Key

△ = noukay

a△ b△ = noukay for two overseas visitors from Iwa and Muyuw

HD = house of Drum dance head

H = house

B = yam house/bench

O_B = frame of old yam house

C = cook house

⟲ = Direction of the dance line showing men ahead and
women behind. Note that dancing took place only
once with noukay present (see text).

Relative positions of
dance line and noukay
array

Figure 5. Noukay array at the Drum dance finale, 1975 (not to scale).

piling is completed, the tall, beautiful noukay are supported by poles bound together at the top. They are not finished, however, until the following day, when their final decoration is attached.

Each pile is destined for a Tarakubay man's partner, or in one or two cases for an important visitor, and is assigned a place on the periphery of the dancing ground (see Figure 5). In the case I observed, the organization was based upon the residential location of the recipient's hamlet. This is probably the usual way of organizing the arrangement, although there were some alterations of this plan in the reciprocal finale of the Comb in 1980. In any case, the noukay always form a circle around the periphery of the dance ground. In this respect, they concentrate the spatially dispersed hamlets of individual male partners (and their affinal segments) in a unitary spatial array (the circle of noukay). Each noukay is itself created through a collection from the gardens and garden work of different individuals (of various hamlets and dala) so that the artifact must also be seen as concentrating dispersed spatial elements into a single vertical form, which,

Plate 13. Noukay yam piles placed around the edge of the dance ground. Men at the center are preparing to cut up the pig.

as one man put it to me, should "climb to the sky." From this perspective, the total array (each noukay and the collection of noukay of which it is a part) can be seen as the unitary outcome of a concentrating process. The noukay piles in temporary collective array in the dance center are poised, as it were, betwixt and between individual donors and recipients. When the latter receive their gifts, they will again dismantle them and distribute the produce to their own kin and affines.

The dance held the night of the yam piling was the only time the huge, immobile noukay framed the dancers who circled around the dabedeba tree. On the following day, the yam piles were completed and transacted, and by the time of the final daytime dance, they had disappeared from the dance ground. However, to consider the concentration that is occurring at the entertainment center, we must examine the noukay as a formative process in relation to that occurring in the dancing for which they are exchanged. Thus it is useful to depict the dance and noukay positions relative to each other, as I do in the inset to Figure 5, even though all the daytime dances and all except one of the night dances at the finale take place without the presence of the noukay.

Figure 5 (inset) shows the dancers circling between the noukay and the dabedeba tree where the drummers and singers stand. As I have pointed out, the dabedeba is itself bespelled with the desired mobility of the dance, and the drummers and singers who stand here actually provide the dance's rhythmic aural form. The organization of the dance is of some importance. In the line-up, men always dance ahead of women; the latter must follow the male dance steps[22] and streamer movement. Children may occasionally tag behind,[23] after the women, but there does not appear to be any firm tendency for older men or women to dance ahead of (or behind) younger people. In the major performances however, the dance leader is not infrequently a man of some seniority who determines the movements of the pandanus streamers that define a particular dance. The Gawan audience sitting at the edge around the houses and on the yam house sitting platforms shout approval for particular displays of virtuosity.

Most apparent in the daytime dancing is the differentiation of male and female body decor. The coconut frond skirts must be donned by both men and women for dancing: They define the common apparel, the visible uniformity of all who dance.[24] These skirts are made by women for both sexes to wear, just as shell decor derived from masculine inter-island exchange activities may be worn by both men and women. However, men tie their skirts (called *kanaagway* in explicit contrast with women's *doba*) in the front, whereas women tie them on the side. Men's kanaagway are always made with decorative flat pandanus strips and bunches of a coconut-blackened vine stripping bound along the top of the skirt; women may wear this or sometimes other decorative styles.

Although both men and women put sweet-smelling leaves in their armlets, paint their faces for the daytime dances, and as I have pointed out, may wear kula and other shell decor, masculine decor tends to be the more flamboyant. For instance, only men wear a shell imitation of a pig's tusk (*diginaakum*) as a necklace pendant. Most significant is the difference in head gear. Although on occasion, a woman may wear a feather in her hair, only men wear the full decorative headdresses (*dagula*) of white cockatoo feathers. In their most elaborate form, these headdresses create an auriole around the head. Some young men may grow a large bush of hair so that their headdresses create an unusually wide frame around their heads that is especially admired.

Thus the essentially female-associated skirts covering the lower genital area of the body[25] provide the uniform emblem of the dance worn in differing arrangements by both men and women, whereas the masculine headdresses (as well as the tusk necklace) create a marked differentiation between the sexes in the dance attire. The positioning of these different components conveys again the spatiotemporal extension of masculine powers in comparison with feminine potency. Whereas bird feathers suggesting the speedy mobility of flight extend around the head, the skirts made of the leaves of trees are worn on the lower bodily area. The female element is the homogeneous element without which a person is not permitted to dance, and the male element conveys the increment of speed and upward motion beyond this common female ground defining the dancers as a whole.

The dance decor and the relative position of men and women in the dance line embody the different levels of masculine and feminine transformational capacities within the dance context: As those who are ahead in the dance line, and who have the most elaborate, extended head decor and brilliance, men have, in effect, greater bodily extension in space than women. The ordering of the dance visually forms the relatively internal spatial associations of women, as against the externalizing, leading role of men. Moreover, the virtuosity of the movement is centered in masculine action that women dancers follow. In this sense, dancing as the zenith of bodily buoyancy focuses in men rather than women while at the same time forming motion as a bodily synchronization in which women coordinate their own bodies with the movements led or determined by men. (It will be remembered that women are figured as those who must be persuaded to agree to masculine projects.) This view of the intersubjective spacetime formed in the dance is reinforced when one considers that the drumming that defines the rhythmic pattern is a masculine activity.

All of these features are consistent with the hierarchical model of spatiotemporal extension discussed in Chapter 6. The basic, gender hierarchy of the community is thus brought into unitary form and displayed in the dance. Recalling that any member of the community may actually dance irrespective of his or her kumila category, we can see the dance as a concentration of the community in the form of a moving continuum (a circling, linear formation) that presents the people in energetic, vital, and youthful form as the essence of potent persuasiveness – that is, with bodily value qualities of self-transcendence. In this continuum, the community is, on the one hand, totalized in hierarchical form; on the other hand, the dance constitutes the hierarchizing process of positive spatiotemporal transformation as an attribute of the community as a whole.

This totalization may be compared with that created more peripherally by the immobile food piles. As I have indicated, each of these piles is the result of a man's ability to garner resources in large part from his *wife's* kinspeople. The dance, on the other hand, configures the male–female relationship abstracted from the segmental kinship and affinal bonds, and in the generalized form of the gender hierarchy.[26] In the center, women follow men, whereas on the periphery the food piles exhibit the affinal produce support men gain *through* women. It is also apparent that the noukay, which are unusually large variants of conical food constructions such as those given by the female-side kin in certain marriage exchanges (see Chapter 6, note 1) and initiated by the matrilineal dala of the deceased in mortuary exchanges, are comparable to a female-side gift; whereas the dancing, as the zenith of bodily buoyancy with the control of its motion based in men, is a masculinized form.

Additional features emerge when we compare the dance and the noukay

Plate 14. Decorated men and women dance in linear formation around the dabedeba tree (at the right). As the men who are leading the dance swing forward on the left, they pass the women at the end of the line. More frequently, dancers spread out to form a circle (generally with some space between the beginning and the end) rather than a spiral.

from the perspective of hierarchy and equality. Although some noukay are noticeably higher than others, and some partnerships involve senior men and are of longer standing than others, no *formal* hierarchy is displayed in the collective arrangement. Furthermore, although a great deal of pride is clearly taken by each group in its display, and each individual attempts to provide some special element to deck its noukay and make it attractive, there is no *overt* competition between those displaying their resources and aesthetic work. Rather, the arrangement represents each food donor (and recipient – i.e., each pair of partners) as equal to any other, and none is formally given specific focus or preference. On this view, the noukay constitute and display the formal equality of each partnership (and the affinal segments concentrated in each noukay) in a collective formation.

In contrast, as I have pointed out, the dancing explicitly defines the community in terms of a gender hierarchy in which segmental localization and distinctions built along the lines of dala and affinal connections are not represented. If the buoyant motion of the dancing condenses the hierarchizing process, concentrating the expansive control of spacetime in its vital form, the huge food piles on the dance ground periphery convey the qualities of heaviness and immobility necessary to generate this mobility.

Yet this view, which seems to place the image of hierarchic potency where one might expect – nearer the center (see Lévi-Strauss, 1967:131ff.) – clearly has certain complications. For the food collection embodies the Guyaw superordinating role of food transmission, whereas the more centralized dancing embodies the subordinating Ramugway role – even though it is that role in its mediating form of a payment for the food. Moreover, the noukay, which are the largest and most elaborate food artifacts Gawans construct, carry qualisigns of height (-size) and beautification. The noukay convey the strength and influential status of each donor as a member of the Guyaw category in the dance entertainment, and his potential influence upon his recipient partner. Each of the Tarakubay donors is thus displayed *as guyaw* (i.e., as superordinate); it is in this sense that they are all equal to each other.

Nevertheless, the dance creates the bodily image of transcendence: the spatiotemporal extension of the self in motion and decorative beauty that epitomizes the potency of the person. Its relation to the food gifts of the Guyaw appears to have fundamental parallels to the buwaa marriage exchanges in which the husband's gifts of mobile artifacts are returns for the harvest produce from the woman's kinspeople and exhibit, as I have argued, the hierarchic value increment generated by the latter's kin through their acts of food transmission.

But in the entertainments (in contrast to the marriage exchanges) the hierarchic significance of food transmission emerges in the definition of the food givers as Guyaw. Exchanged for dancing, the food is converted into positive qualisigns of spatiotemporal transformation in the body. Thus the Ramugway dancers can be understood as returning to the Guyaw a bodily icon or *value form* of the spatiotemporal transformation, which the Guyaw generate through their transmission of food.[27] Indeed, at the finale, the noukay are transmitted to the Ramugway the day before the final dance when, as I discuss later, the Guyaw take certain pieces of decor from the Ramugway dancers' bodies.

In effect, then, the Guyaw are getting back the icons of their own value – the enhanced form that the self takes when reconstituted in transmissive processes to the other. *It is as if the Ramugway dancers were the embodied fame of the Guyaw mirroring back to them their own self-enhancement and energetic potency from the bodies of the external other.* These signs are also icons of the community's positive value state, the level of intersubjective relation carried in its experience of happiness and vitality, which has been generated by the Guyaw feast. Thus in the quotation cited at the beginning of this chapter, my informant is remarking on the community's feelings of excited buoyancy that are both expressed and created in the dancers' motion. In similar fashion (but with the reverse, negative implications), the affines in the mortuary rites mirror the loss and grief of the deceased's dala back to them from the other, and signify the negative value state of the community at large.

On the day after the noukay are piled, they are completed by added decorative attachments (*deimu*), which, like decorative attachments on kula shells and canoes, are necessary in the Gawan view to complete the beauty of the noukay. Different deimu may also give each noukay a somewhat individualized appearance apart from differences of height. The standard decor consists of bright green or orange betel nut, coconuts, or sugarcane attached to the top or leaning against the noukay; but additional deimu range from a live pig trussed up at the side of a noukay, to an unusually long yam (which Gawans distinguish as "male" in contrast to more rounded or shorter "female" yams) decorated with tassles, or a bright cloth pennant. We may note that, like the female skirt in the dance decor, the relatively female component defines the basic uniformity of the ensemble, whereas the added, more distinctive deimu elements have a stronger masculine component (e.g., tree produce gathered by men, long yams, etc.).

Before its transmission, each noukay is thus displayed for all to enjoy. The height, fine form and additional decor are matters of pride to the donors and to Gawans as a whole for they exhibit the community wealth in food *in the process of being transacted*; the strength of the community is being shown in its capacity to concentrate and transmit raw comestibles.[28]

The sense in which such displays are clearly demonstrations of strength is conveyed in metaphoric uses Gawans sometimes make of the images of strong trees in connection with transactional capacities. For instance, a person of whom major gifts (e.g., pigs, banana stalks, kula shells, etc.) have been demanded in certain rites[29] may shout in response: "If I were a *kalala* tree, I would fall; today, however, I sit in the crotch of a *meiku* tree." A kalala is a weak tree whose leaves also fall easily so that it is soon bare; such a person would be weak (-*gweya*) and worthless (-*gwaageyo*). The meiku tree, however, is strong and its wood is used for house posts; a person sitting high up in that tree would be capable of making rich gifts.

The huge noukay at the Drum dance finale similarly display the strength of the donors, and the communal strength of Gawa concentrated at the dance center. The height of the noukay in particular is a sign of this potency, as is illustrated in the following case.

Several months before the Drum dance finale, G., one of the key Gawan garden specialists, had died under grievous circumstances. The Drum dance leader, speaking to the people at the finale, said that the yam piles had only two layers (*kasetara*) – i.e., they were too short – and that the cooked food was also inadequate. In fact, I was told, this was a figurative allusion (*karaabay*) to the death of G. for which Gawans, as the presumed source of the witchery, were being chastised.

Short noukay signify the negative, weakened state of the community, and the concept was used in this instance to convey the destructive effect of witchcraft upon the community's transactional ability. This allusion was only one part of more extensive references to the death of the garden specialist in the speeches at the Drum dance finale (see Chapter 9). In the midst of the high noukay, Gawans were reminded of their value-negating acts, and the resultant loss of the garden specialist, by the assertion that the noukay were not tall enough, and that there was not enough food.

THE "THROWING" (*KOULOVA*) OF THE NOUKAY AND THE PIG OF THE FEAST

At dusk on the day the noukay are completed, their formal transmission takes place as part of a wider cooked pig and vegetable food distribution. At this time, the "pig of the dabedeba," called *yedeba*, is killed, singed, and laid out at the base of the dabedeba tree on a fine white mat where the cuts are marked out on its body. This mat should be supplied by a woman who has been involved in raising the pig. According to one man, the pig is placed on the mat because the person who raised it "is pained" (*i-neka nuwa-ra*) by its death.[30] The mat is then snatched out from under the pig by one of the Ramugway (who is expected to make an equivalent mat return at the reciprocal feast) before it is cut up. This pig belongs to the leading man of the dala that owns the entertainment, and it has been raised at the Drum dance center during the current cycle; it can be killed only in this hamlet for the climax of the entertainment.

At the finale I observed, the pig itself was named *Guyaw* and had been the subject of some concern in the preceding year when the Drum dance leader had feared that he might become ill (i.e., bewitched) because of the large size of this pig (see Chapter 9). A very large pig should be raised for the entertainments only. Anyone raising such an animal to meet personal or dala obligations would be frightened of witch attack. Thus, the owner had reminded the people that he was giving them the pig to eat at the finale of the entertainment. But if he himself got sick, then he would have to kill and distribute the pig beforehand, and then there would be no yedeba for the finale.

It can be seen from this case that the yedeba pig is invested with the identity of the Guyaw donor. Its size conveys a level of superordination permitted only in the context of a community-based activity in which everyone is supposed to receive pork and other comestibles to eat. Apart from the preparation of resources for the Drum dance, the owner of the entertainment does not have the right to raise an exceptionally large pig, and even in this context it is apparent that he does not regard himself as being excluded from possible witch attack. The pig's killing at the entertainment has sacrificial overtones that will emerge more sharply in the later discussion of witchcraft. For the moment, however, we may point to the identification of this pig with guyaw status and potency, and its formal laying out at the debedeba tree as the centerpiece of the feast, the emblem of the Guyaw transactional capacities at the entertainment.

Like all the comestibles transmitted in the Drum dance, the yedeba pig cannot be eaten by the Guyaw. Its cutting up and distribution for consumption by others appears as a token transaction and distribution of the Guyaw themselves – a release and dissolution of the superordination concentrated in the exceptionally large pig, through its parceling out to others. Although Gawans do not explicitly make such a point in this context, we may keep in mind the two features noted above: The Drum dance leader threatened to kill the pig for earlier distribution should he have become ill from witchcraft (to allay the witch, see Chapter 9); and a particular emphasis in connection with the Drum dance is that it does not operate as a dala function, but as a community function in which it is held that *everyone* will eat.[31] The pig appears to be the condensed token of the means by which the Guyaw create their own value, thus constituting themselves as truly guyaw: That is, *they do so in the process of parceling out their concentrated, hierarchic potency to the community at large.*

If we consider the sum of activities that take place at the dabedeba tree at different times, it is apparent that the tree condenses the oppositions or differentiated potencies of the entertainment. Here singers and drummers beat out the dance rhythms, and various comestibles prohibited to the Guyaw are brought in for distribution. It will be recalled that the base of the dabedeba is invested with the vital motion of the dancers, and the sprouting coconut at the top is supposed to express the temporal passage of the entertainment. The tree condenses the spacetime of the entertainment: on the one hand, it defines the spatial centering of the community at the dance hamlet for the period of the performance; on the other, it contains the motion of the dance and dance rhythms; finally, it brings together the type Guyaw and Ramugway acts involving, respectively, the distribution of comestibles and the display of the value of this distribution in the hierarchic signification carried in the bodies of dancers.

After the yedeba pig has been laid out, other pigs that have been killed and partially cooked and cut up in the dispersed hamlets of their contributors are brought to the dabedeba for distribution along with the yedeba. These pigs are presented by different Tarakubay men, and may be contributed by various individuals (including Nukubay, their female side or other affines, and other individuals of any kumila, including the Nukwasisi) to the feast. A person who has no immediate relation to the Nukubay may also "make a path" *via* some kinsperson and contribute in this way. The collection of pork, like that of the noukay, also concentrates the dispersed, relatively autonomous or segmented space of the community (but in contrast to the noukay, pork pieces are initially brought together at the dabedeba and dispersed from there).

As the dusk deepens, the actual distribution of food by the Tarakubay (and their affinal aids) begins. This distribution is called *koulova*, which means "the release" or "throwing" (cf. *-lev*), and involves shouting the recipient's name as his gift is made. The first cut of pork and cooked vegetable food should be called out for Tamudurera, an invisible being who represents witchcraft, and to whom the comestibles are given as an offering so that he will not make people ill or cause rain and spoil the entertainment.[32] Cuts of pig along with cooked vegetable food that are to be given to the Tarakwasis partners and visitors receiving noukay are rushed over to the noukay and given to representatives of the recipients when the latters' names are called. Thus comestibles intended for the Tarakwasisi are distributed at their respective noukay. The meat collected at the center starts to move toward the periphery in release to the representative Ramugway of the feast.

The Ramugway partners are not, however, the only recipients represented on the entertainment ground. The separate hamlets of the community will all receive a portion of cooked food and pig once the noukay have been formally transmitted.[33] Each dish of cooked food comes from a single hamlet (or household within a hamlet), which in turn will receive a different dish of food supplied by another hamlet, and some pork from the central collection. Hamlet dishes are laid out on the ground in a swath from roughly southeast to northwest according to the actual, relative position of each receiving hamlet; they are then called out by hamlet name (or sometimes by the name of the hamlet or household head) starting at the southern end. People from each hamlet take their food and carry it off home to be eaten as the gathering breaks up. Thus, the dispersed hamlets are represented in the model of a relational, directionally sequenced and linear whole within the community center, and Gawans ensure that each receives food and pig from the feast. The equivalence of each hamlet vis à vis each other is represented, just as in the circular array of noukay each pair of partners is given essentially equivalent standing.[34]

Let us return now to the formal noukay transmission that occurs after the distribution of pig to each partner. The leading man of the dala owning the Drum dance and a few other Tarakubay men go to each noukay and shout out the recipient's name, usually along with a teasing joke that chastises (-*kane*) the recipient if it is felt that he has been lax in attendance at the dances during the performance cycle.[35] As pointed out in Chapter 3, the aim of this chastisement is to "spark the insides" (-*yik nuwa-ra*) of the recipient so that he will be reminded to make returns for the noukay at the finale of the reciprocal Comb entertainment and encouraged to plan his gardens ahead (*wunikougwa*) in preparation for the Comb. Reciprocation may then start swiftly and it is hoped that a long time will not elapse between the closing of the Drum dance and the opening of the Comb. Thus the entertainment in the process of closing is infused with the future that is directly brought into the participants' focus in the present.

The jibes shouted out by the Tarakubay are partially standardized; the following examples used at the 1975 finale illustrate their crucial features:

1. Oh D.! Your food! You eat, you bury it under the house post [forget]; you think you will repay. You have no axe, you have no knife [so that] you may repay [i.e., you have no gardening tools; you do no garden work].

2. M.! You don't make repayment you don't come, you don't *kalibomu* [the label for the night phase of the Drum dance]. [If] you come, you lie down/sleep, you go back to your hamlet.

3. T.! ... You have no knife, you have no axe to make repayment. You eat, the repayment will disappear [i.e., as eating destroys the food, so the return will disappear].

4. R.! In the evening ... [you would say] "I am going to the dance," [but] you stay here [i.e., sitting outside your own house]. When the youths come back [from the dance] you go into your house and lie down.

It will be seen that the jibes refer either to the recipient's failure to come to the night dancing during the years of the Drum dance or his inability to repay later the garden produce he is currently receiving. In examples 2 and 4, the partner lies down and sleeps, staying in his own hamlet or returning to it without dancing. Thus he negates the spacetime of the dance. In examples 1 and 3, the recipients' gardening abilities are impugned in a stereotypic phrase; the jibe asserts that the partner will be unable to repay the Drum dance food. The first describes this failure figuratively as a process of burying one's memory under the house post, an image that depicts retention rather than the release of food to others and depicts the recipient as one who forgets debts (see Chapter 3). Again, a contraction of intersubjective spacetime is represented. Number 3 asserts that the payment disappears – a process that my informants explained as being "like eating."[36]

In all these depictions, the recipient is envisioned as a consumer who eats without repaying. At the moment of food transmission, the Ramugway's role as prototypic consumer is made manifest rather than his mediating role as dancer or his potential role of Guyaw food donor in the reciprocal entertainment. As one man explained to me, these jibes make the Ramugway "ashamed" (*mwasira*) because they did not stay up to dance. "They ate the food without reason (*sabwamu*)" (see Chapter 3). Such a person is "like a pig" because he lies around and does not work, but goes to the garden and "eats without reason." Clearly, "not dancing" and "not working in the gardens" are different sides of the image of a lazy man, a person lacking in vitality who sleeps rather than dancing or working, and who therefore does not remember his debts and make repayments.

It is just at this moment of release that the Guyaw rhetorically assert the recipients' subordination, for now they are entrusting the potential of their gifts to the uncertain ministrations of the other. Moreover, the very process by which the Guyaw demonstrate their strength and create influence for themselves with the recipients consists of releasing to the latter the Guyaw's amassed potency. This release is visibly conveyed in the disassembling of the noukay the following morning when the recipients come to take their gifts, but it is formally effected at the koulova. The capacity to control the final outcome now depends upon the kareiwaga of the Ramugway who must make the decisions determining when the reciprocating entertainment will be performed, as well as plan for the gardening and collection of largesse for the return. The future is, so to speak, in their hands.

The recipient who has been chastised by the Guyaw frequently responds with a repartee defending himself. Some repartees refer to the magnificent return the recipient will make at the reciprocal entertainment. In one instance a man also asserted that he would give most of his current largesse to his wife's kinspeople so that they would then be obligated to help him at the time of reciprocation. In contrast to the donors, the recipients point to their capacities to be Guyaw: to give rather than to receive food and to organize and collect the largesse necessary for an entertainment that may even exceed the present one in the size of its gifts. The donors' negative construction of their partners prods the latter into asserting their own positive capacities and strengths: At the moment at which they become consumers they redefine themselves as Guyaw, thus embedding the present with potentiality; in effect, they assert that rather than disappear or be consumed, the present entertainment will be reconstituted in its reciprocal form at a later time. In this dialectical process of joking chastisement and repartee, the contradictions in transaction emerge: Those who are superordinate demonstrate their superordination by *giving up* their superordinating potency, and at the same time asserting the subordination of the recipient; those who are subordinate consumers may, if they wish, respond by asserting their superordinative capacities as those who will later amass and release potency.

THE FINAL DANCE AND THE TAKING (*KWAYA*) OF THE DECOR

The climax of the Drum dance is a daylight performance of the dance in which the Guyaw partners or their male or female representatives claim the dance skirts and other special decor from the bodies of the Ramugway dancers. The Tarakwasisi partners (or *their* male or female representatives) put on dance skirts especially prepared for this transaction by their kinswomen or wives (or the latters' helping kinswomen). Other standard decor to be taken includes a wreath of green betel nuts, with additional optional elements such as money attached to a headdress, a shirt, or a kula shell. The dancer is divested of this festive decor during the dance performance.[37]

After individual preparations have been made in the various hamlets throughout the morning, the dancers in full regalia file in formal dance formation into the dance hamlet in the early afternoon. After a period of dancing, the dancers stop and the Nukubay step in and cut off the betel nut wreaths and other decor such as money or kula shells. The dancing continues again, and at the next pause, the skirts are taken from the Ramugway (who are wearing the gift skirts over other apparel). Some of these skirts may be directly put on over their own apparel by those who take them. A young Tarakubay man then climbs the dabedeba tree and ties a pandanus streamer to it marking the end of the Drum dance. Audience and dancers then sit around, chat and listen to any final speeches and commentaries.

In this finale, the Guyaw actually take their due from the dancers, divesting the latter of their decor and the emblematic clothing of the dance as payment for the food (*meyisara karu*). The dancers yield up aspects of their beautification or vital form to the food donors who appropriate the bodily qualisigns of their own transformative "guyaw" value: the beautifying media that exhibit the value they have generated in food giving. In this way they temporarily replace the amassed potency they have given away with bodily signs that are icons of the value produced. Put another way, those who give food have the capacity to create motion.

THE COMB

The Comb entertainment consists of feasts held at the hamlet of the Nukwasisi dala owners (currently, as I have indicated, the same hamlet as the one where the Drum dance is held) during the day. At this time, green bananas are cooked and eaten, and cooked food and pork when available are distributed at the end of the day. I shall describe the Comb more briefly than the Drum dance in order to focus on a limited set of points relevant to the argument. In this account I draw on my observation of the entertainment during 1980–1.

The thematic element of the entertainment is an article of head decor made and worn by the Nukubay, who are now the food-recipient Ramugway. This consists of a long specialty comb made ideally of a wood called *sinata* (comb), which comes from Muyuw. The beginning of the entertainment (which I have not observed) requires a trip to Muyuw to obtain the wood. The comb is strung with a bead, nut, and shell decor of the sort used on kula shells; indeed, at the close of the entertainment, the decor is taken off the combs by the Tarakwasisi recipients and may be recycled into the decoration of kitomu kula shells, a use that points to associations between the comb decor and kula shells. Further, the term for this decor, *loubu* is also used to refer to human and canoe shell decoration, and to the shell and bead decor on kula shells.

Combs are of three lengths. The longest and most elaborately decorated are those displayed on the houses of hamlet heads of different Nukubay dala. These may also be worn by dala men, like other combs, but for Comb feasts only. The next size is worn by individual men and boys; the shortest combs, of which there appear to be fewer, are worn by women and girls. The latter two comb categories may be worn on a daily basis (more frequently by men than by women in my experience, as the men's combs are most important), as well as for the feasts.[38] The relative spatial extension and elaborateness of the individual combs are thus a qualisign of the relative transformational potencies of men and women, whereas the most elaborate dala comb conveys the guyaw standing of each of the Nukubay dala.

Although combs are made and worn by the Nukubay, they are regarded as the possessions (*vavaga*) of the Nukwasisi, particularly the partners of the wearers. The bodily connection of the comb wearers and the actual owners is made explicit in certain prohibitions. For instance, the comb wearers should not cut their hair (at least during the last year of the entertainment) before the finale, since to do so is to (figuratively) "cut off the neck" (-*kapitoni kayo*-) of the Guyaw owners. At the finale of the entertainment, the owners or their representatives will claim the combs from the heads of the Nukubay and put them in their own hair in the same fashion that the dance skirts and other body decor items are taken from the wearers at the finale of the Drum dance.

Wearing the comb is payment for the food gifts of the Guyaw. The comb should be worn as frequently as possible during the years of the entertainment (especially in the closing year) so that the Nukwasisi, especially a man's partner, will see the wearer and will likely be more generous with their closing gifts.[39] When sailing to other islands, the sailors take off their combs to protect them, but they may then attach the combs to the canoe to advertise to the islanders they are visiting that Gawans are performing a Comb entertainment. Again the canoe appears as a decorated person, as well as a decorative extension of the person.

By wearing and displaying the comb, a Gawan wearer both makes himself persuasive to his partners and indicates that he (or she) is thinking ahead (*i-nanams wunikougwa*) – looking forward (-*kougwa*) to potential returns that may be achieved through actions in the present. Yet, as in the Drum dance, those who assume these beautifying, persuasive qualities are also prototypic consumers. The contradiction is made explicit in the responsibilities surrounding the comb and rules about wearing it.

The Nukubay are responsible for keeping the combs finely decorated and oiled with coconut scrapings so that they do not darken (grow dirty, dry, and cracked). Although this is to be done by each wearer on a day-to-day basis, certain community feast days (called *vaaged*, scraping down or grinding) are arranged by the Nukwasisi for the collective cleansing of the combs. On these days, the Nukubay bring their combs to the hamlet of the entertainment to wash them in a single wooden bowl, rub them in the oil of fresh coconut scrapings provided by the Nukwasisi owners, and hang them out to dry on a cord strung across the hamlet. During the day, people sit around chatting and eating roasted green bananas supplied by the Guyaw, who as in the case of the Drum dance, are forbidden to eat from their own gifts. In the early evening, there are speeches and a distribution of cooked vegetable food and pork (if available). The community as a whole is entertained at the feast, not just those with combs.

But although eating is the central activity of the Comb entertainment, it is forbidden to wear one's comb while eating, whether at one of the feasts or otherwise; combs should always be removed at this time. Failure to observe this prohibition will result in the comb losing its luster: as one man put it, it will become "rubbish." As a result, the partner whose property is being tarnished is angered (*kavikura*). Thus failure to remove the comb while eating functions like breaking food prohibitions in other contexts where, as we have seen, the brilliant effect desired in beautification may be converted into darkness (Chapter 4). In the context of the Comb, we see especially clearly that this negative transformation of bodily spacetime iconically signifies the negation or dissolution of positive intersubjective relations – in this case, relations that form a community mode of spacetime. Each partner is, in effect, adorned by the comb: The Ramugway wearer is adorned in an immediate sense, the owner with respect to future appropriation and bodily adornment. The comb is not only the "arena" of their transaction, but also the sign of the value of each. Failure to maintain the appropriate qualisigns destroys the sign of the owner's value as food donor and proprietor of the entertainment, as well as the value of the wearer as the one who is physically adorned. In effect, it negates the intersubjective community partnership set up by the entertainment.

On the other hand, by observing the prohibition that separates adornment and eating, those defined as consumers of the feast are marked as nonconsumers in a number of senses. They present themselves as at once persuasive persons and as those who make a return for the Guyaw food gifts. In addition, they represent the Guyaw in their role as food-givers who generate positive transformative value rather than destroy it through consumption. Thus the wearer presents and maintains the donor's value as an aspect of himself, or as *his* value, and in this process both acquires food and makes return for it.

We can now look back at the Drum dance and suggest that there, as well as in the context of the Comb, the stated hierarchy in the relation of the Guyaw and the Ramugway is constituted in a mediating form that *dissembles* the explicit hierarchic definition of their relation. This dissemblance itself contains the figuration or *semblance* of hierarchy (i.e., the bodily qualisigns of transcendence or guyaw standing), and is formed in the identification of the bodily signs of superordination (which actually belong to the Guyaw donors) with the subordinate Ramugway. It is then this "dissembling semblance" that mediates the hierarchically defined relationship of Guyaw donor and Ramugway consumer.

The food transmission at the finale of the Comb is similar to that of the Drum dance and a description need not be repeated in detail here. In the finale I observed, however, the comb transfer took place just before that of the noukay, and both transfers occurred on the same day. In addition to the combs, other items are worn at this time to be appropriated by the Guyaw. For example, money may be attached to the comb or worn in a

Plate 15. A young man puts on a decorated comb at the kwaya of the combs. One of the yam noukay may be seen in the background. The tree at the right with the head carved on the trunk (see note 10 to this chapter) is the dabedeba.

separate headdress; betel nut wreaths, men's shirts, a kula shell, and so forth may be added to the items given to the Tarakwasisi partners. These items of body decor are the returns for equivalent gifts made by the Nukwasisi to their partners in the Drum dance. For instance, if money was given at that time, the partner attempts to repay an equivalent amount of money in the Comb. As the leading owner of the Drum dance exhorted the Nukubay at the finale of the Comb, the latter should "remember" the Drum dance when the *Nukwasisi* put money in their hair and decorated themselves. Today, he said, money should be put on the combs in return. The Nukubay must not "forget," letting it "disappear."[40]

WITCHCRAFT AND THE ENTERTAINMENTS: A CONCLUDING NOTE

In the present chapter I have concentrated primarily on the basic symbolic formations of positive value transformation in the Drum dance and the Comb, pointing to the way in which Gawans assert that these can be undercut by negative acts (e.g., sleeping and not attending the dance; forgetting rather than remembering debts). However, as I remarked earlier, the subversive potential of witchcraft is not excluded from the entertainments; indeed, this potential may be conveyed within them directly, a feature that appears to be especially marked in the finales. Because of the concentrated, elaborate display and distribution of comestibles involved at the finales of the entertainments (but also at other transactions throughout the performance cycles), Gawans may be concerned that some people will complain (-sugwa) about not receiving enough from the transactions, and that witch attacks could ensue. Thus at the end of the Drum dance in 1975, a senior man of each kumila stood up and told members of his own kumila not to bewitch others because of the food. Such warnings are composed in a standardized rhetoric and are an expected part of the proceedings. Furthermore, public speeches in certain sections of the finales, like Gawan public speeches in various other contexts, may warn people in general not to bewitch others, or as we saw in the case of the garden specialist referred to earlier, may admonish the people for bewitching others and so draining value from the entertainments.

In the next part of this study, which concerns the negative transformations of witchcraft, we will have reason to consider this aspect of the entertainments more carefully. For the present, we may note that speeches and exhortations like those referred to above confront Gawans with the tension between positive transformations and the possibility or actuality of loss from witchcraft. Moreover, the use of warnings about witchcraft as a discourse for dealing with fundamental contradictions of their social order is a basic feature of Gawan public speaking.

PART IV

Witchcraft: the subversion of value

9

The identity of the witch

Un monde sans mal ne saurait être bon.

Louis Dumont, 1979:243

In previous chapters I have been concerned with value production largely from the perspective of the system of positive value transformations. Concurrently, I have discussed the dialectical tension of negative transformations and pointed to various ways in which the Gawan capacity to generate positive value is underlaid with the intentional subversion of witchcraft. In this and the next chapter, I shift my perspective to examine the production of destructive, subversive value that takes place through witch activity, and Gawan attempts to transform this negative state of the Gawan world back into conditions within which positive value can be created.

Bwagaw (witch, or witchery,[1] used as a noun or a verb) may be understood as a hidden construction of the Gawan self latent in the overt world of Gawan everyday life: the source of a covert reality and spacetime that subverts Gawan value production. Although witchcraft forms, from one point of view, a "world" of its own – with a specific construction of self brought into operation through the witch persona, and particular kinds of action, value production, and spatiotemporal modalities – it is nevertheless lived as an integral part of the Gawan social world. Witchcraft is held, as it were, like an open secret within that world.

As we have seen, the final outcomes of the activity of witchcraft are long-term illness and death. Although other disturbances such as the depletion of the gardens, theft, weather disorders, and so on can be perceived as witch caused, the ultimate aim of witches is to cause death so that they can appropriate and consume the corpse. When there is sickness and death on Gawa, people may say, "We have found our heaviness." Both the bodily state of the ill person and the experience of the general populace or of relevant kinspeople of the patient thus are embedded with

215

the qualities of negative value. In this and the following chapter, I shall examine these negative kinds of production processes, the modes of intersubjective spacetime they entail, and the means by which Gawans attempt to work on and positively transform their negative value outcomes. I begin by considering the witch persona and its relation to the self of the individual Gawan.

THE IDENTITY OF THE WITCH

Gawans regard witchcraft as being caused primarily by other Gawans who thus destroy Gawa from within.[2] As one man remarked in a public meeting: These witches are not people of other islands, but "we ourselves" (*totorei-des*). For any given individual, affines, his or her own clanspeople, as well as other nonkin could be the source of witch attack. Bwagaw are typified as women, but men as well as women may be thought to act as witches. Furthermore, although women as a gender category typify the witch, this notion also has important ambiguities. In theory, a woman does not act without the instigation of a male member of her dala.[3] It is the man whose *kareiwaga* is supposed to lie behind the woman's action. These ambiguities reflect the fundamental stereotype of the political relationship between men and women (i.e., men kareiwaga, whereas women give consent or have the right of refusal; see Chapter 6) as well as pointing to the notion that men and women together are responsible for acts of witchcraft. I shall come back to this pattern of witch responsibility in the next chapter.

Whereas women form the focal category identified with acts of witchcraft, only men function to defend the people against witches. As noted earlier (Chapter 2), these men have specific magic for curing as well as for killing and identifying (finding, -*ban*) witches. The general label for this category is also *bwagaw*, but the more precise and polite term (although less commonly used in my experience) is *kayuwawsi* or *ta-kaymouva*, one who makes alive. (For brevity, I shall refer to these men as *defenders*.)[4]

The two sides of the notion of bwagaw again convey the political dialectic of male and female action: In this context women are identified with interiority as they are thought of as performing hidden acts of bwagaw power (and possess spells empowering these acts); men, on the other hand, publicly identify themselves as having bwagaw (defending) powers, thus making use of their power for benevolent purposes. The defender also possesses spells that focus (among other things) on revealing the hidden identity of the witch, bringing it out into the open, that is, *ou-murakata*. Similarly, senior men of influence are identified with the ideal of bringing falsities out into the open or revealing the truth (see Chapter 10). We can see here a gender framework similar to that discussed previously: Masculine political potency is identified with exteriorizing processes; feminine potency is essentially interior and hidden.

Nevertheless, in individual cases, defenders can also be suspected of witchery, as can senior men of guyaw standing. In the case of the former, (who may also be guyaw) this possibility is implied in the use of the term *bwagaw* to refer to the defender category: The power to control witchcraft suggests a potential for use of its negative power. However, defenders (especially the most important of them, the community functionary) are regarded as essentially men who "take care of" (*-yamata*) the people as, in general, senior men of influence are expected to do. Since women by contrast typify the witch, in what follows I shall use the feminine pronoun to refer to the witch except where the context requires otherwise.

All Gawan assumptions about the typical identities of witches have to be understood in the context of a political process that opposes the public identification of any individual as a witch. As I pointed out earlier, although Gawan leaders or men of influence try to persuade witches through public speeches not to bewitch others, they do not publicly name and try them, for no one can accuse another without fear of retaliation by the accused person and his or her dala.[5] In effect, the witch's individual identity remains hidden from the public at large.

In community-wide meetings[6] held for various purposes (not only those held specifically to dissuade witches from pursuing their destructive activities), exhortations against witches are frequent, their extent and intensity depending upon the general state of the community. In some contexts, as we have seen briefly in the case of the Drum dance entertainment, they are standardized parts of the presentation.

When people are concerned about specific illnesses, defenders and other men may hint through figurative speech (*karaabay*) – that is, "veiled speech," as Strathern (1975) has characterized it for the Melpa – that they know the identity of the witch in a given case. Although suspected social categories may be mentioned (for example, "the women of two neighborhoods" or "a senior man"), individual names are not mentioned lest (as I have pointed out) the speaker seriously anger the accused and his or her dala.[7] Even though no name has been publicly stated, a person may sometimes take umbrage at an allusion felt to point directly to him or her. In one instance with which I am familiar, this anger caused a rift between affines who were in exchange relations with each other so that the person who felt offended refused the offender's buwaa food gifts.

Gawans also hold special meetings (*kawrawora*) called by men of a patient's dala in case of a long-term illness or the fear of impending death. In these meetings, individuals who have been the subject of gossip, or who are possible suspects because of diagnosis by a defender regarding the reason for an illness, speak to deny (-yaakara) rather than confess (-kaamata) their complicity.[8] Although some Gawans admitted to me that such disclaimers could perhaps be untrue, the statements are accepted.

On Gawa, therefore, there are no viable mechanisms for publicly exposing a witch's identity and demanding punishment or confession. Unlike societies where temporary cleansing of suspected witchery may occur through the public trial and punishment of individual suspects, or where, as Ruel (1970:345) has pointed out for the African Banyang, "'Confession' rectifies the deceit of ... a double existence [and] harmonizes the submerged with the public identity," on Gawa, this believed deceit cannot be rectified. Rather, witches continually remain under the surface of the overt world of public identities to which they are never with any certainty fixed – a feature that significantly contradicts the Gawan emphasis on bringing the hidden out into the open. Thus the subordinating redefinition of a person's identity, which as Sansom (1972:197ff.) has suggested occurs in witchcraft accusation – the moral "degradation" of the accused that superordinates the accuser – is not supportable on Gawa. Rather, the community at large remains the diffuse locus of witchery.

It may be noted in this connection that the emphasis on not mentioning the name of any witch suspect in public (although remarks may, of course, be whispered in private conversation and build up to a suspicion) is the reverse of the emphasis on the circulation of the name of the guyaw. The witch's name is not to be publicly circulated: Being known as a witch maligns and defames the individual involved. Should Gawa itself gain the reputation of being infested with witchery, the community as a whole is defamed (i-busi butu-ra, its fame goes down). In the context of witchcraft, then, an inverse value is given to the circulation of one's name.

In a society where public naming of witches is not permissible, and no one ever admits to being a witch, the witch is always the other, never the self.[9] On Gawa, no one ever says, "I am a witch" either publicly or privately. The primary public mode of dealing with witchcraft is by means of didactic exhortation (gweiguya) and denial rather than confession. Nevertheless, since it is essentially "we Gawans" who are recognized as the witches, such acts are projected as attributes of the collective Gawan self (the possible acts of any Gawan or members of any Gawan dala), even while each particular Gawan treats them as detached from his or her own identity and identified with someone else.

Although people think that the main source of witchery against Gawans is other Gawans, the inter-island world may also enter into the transaction. So, for instance, when serious illness and death preoccupy Gawans, talk of the "witch canoe" (bwagaw si-waga)[10] may surface in conversation or public speaking. The witch canoe is thought to be manned by men and women from other islands who travel from island to island loading the dead, taking them off to be eaten. The canoe may be seen in the form of mist rising from the sea, or in other similar signs. It can enter Gawa by sailing right up into the bushland, thus intruding directly within the island space to take its dread cargo. Gawans (particularly women) may be cautioned in public meetings not to agree to the entry of this canoe, but to send it away. The canoe is a mystic image of death and bodily dissolution (consumption by witches) figured as an intruder into Gawan space from the sea and other islands; control over this space is, however, in Gawan hands.

Protection from this canoe, and from inter-island sources of illness in general, may also be provided by defenders who may bound Gawa with a bespelled protective barrier (*gamu*). The term *gamu* also denotes mats tied around betel trees to taboo them and prevent theft from these trees. Similarly, in the present context, a gamu is intended to prevent intrusions into Gawan space that result in the "thieving" of people. It is thus aimed at keeping out sickness in general as well as the witch canoe. This bounding functions for a period of time, but when people feel it has been breached because of illness or deaths on Gawa, or when a period of time has past and it is felt to have weakened, the barrier must be renewed (see Chapter 4).

Still another set of notions relates Gawan witchery to the inter-island world. It is thought that Gawan women (in the guise of witches) may fly[11] to the Dobuan side of the Massim to have intercourse with an evil source of disease, a man called Tawuvaw (see Malinowski, 1954:130); returning to Gawa they may infect the community with disease. In a meeting held in 1974 during the Drum dance cycle, women were exhorted to stay home and enjoy themselves at the Gawan entertainment rather than fly to Dobu.

The western Massim, which was cannibalistic in the past, has special associations with illness and evil. The travel of the Gawan women in witch form to this distant area is seen as yielding an intrusion of disease and bodily destruction from the outside. The locus of responsibility is again Gawan: The women bring the diseases in from the outside and are cautioned to stay home instead. Staying home is equivalent to rejecting these outside influences.

These bounding procedures attempt to reestablish an appropriate spatial distancing, controlling the witches' radical powers to break down or violate the differentiated ordering of this space (as, for instance, in the case of the witch canoe that sails up into the land), as well as to violate ordinary bodily spacetime in flying, a capacity that conveys a radical expansion of spatiotemporal control. The witch has the power to appropriate this control within herself, as we shall see in more detail later. Positive value, or the potentiality for this value, can therefore only be reestablished by reconstituting boundaries (rejection of the witches, bounding procedures, staying home, etc.) that reappropriate this control from the bwagaw. When the notion of bwagaw is uppermost in Gawan thinking, it is as if the positive potentialities of inter-island relations have been subverted into negatives; witchery is experienced as encroaching from the wider island world. Acts of bounding off, keeping to oneself, and rejecting – the creation of a protective separation rather than an expansion of connectivities – must then be put into effect in order to regain control by counterposing oneself to the destructive other. This control reconstitutes both the person (through rejection of the witches' violation of space), and the island community (through bounding the island as a whole, the protective action of official witch defenders). A case example of this process is discussed in Chapter 10.

WITCHES, CONSUMPTION, AND THEFT

It will be recalled that Gawans describe a greedy, selfish person as "one who eats." This label also applies to witches, whose greedy aggrandizement is figured as their continual desire to eat (cf. Mair, 1969:37; Wilson, 1951:92ff.). The identification of witches with this desire is one of the reasons Gawan men sometimes give for the tendency to regard women as the prime suspect category in witch attack. It is said that, in contrast to men, women are "consumers,"[12] a description for which there is a special label, *vila-kamkwamu* (female-eat). According to one man's explanation, women sit, cook, and eat food all day; men's work, on the other hand, takes them to the beaches for fishing and canoe building and thus involves mobility. Women, he said, might even refuse food to their husbands who have been on the beach all day: "Women are tight," he said, "they bewitch; they refuse food."

In fact, as we know, women as well as men work in the gardens, and either may on occasion attend to tasks in the hamlet during the day; but my Gawan informant was reasoning here in terms of the characteristic gender stereotyping and role complementarity that has become familiar in previous chapters. In the phrasing of this account, we can also see an example of the connection made between tightness (as unwillingness to accede to another's demands) and eating, the two being closely allied in this instance as acts of retentiveness. Thus the comment emphasizes masculine dependence on women for cooked food that the latter could refuse if they wished. These characteristic associations suggest some of the grounds on which women as a category are felt to provide more appropriate embodiments of the witch persona than men as a category.

As we have seen, however, the self-focused concerns epitomized in eating and retentiveness are regarded as fundamental to the Gawan self, not just to women. Gawans may simply ascribe this greedy desire to eat to

Gawans in general (the implication being that some Gawans may have acted in terms of this desire in a given case).

Just before the end of the dance entertainment in 1975, the disturbing illnesses of a woman and her son belonging to a dala closely allied with that of the dance entertainment's owner were attributed to the fact that the latter had given two pigs to visitors from other islands. One person told me that the Gawan people (*mira Gaw*) might be angry (*kavikura*) because they wanted the pigs to eat themselves (i.e., possibly for the Drum dance).

This case is particularly telling because it involves the assumption that a gift made to overseas visitors was the cause of witchery on Gawa. As we have seen, it is just such a transaction that is expected to generate positive value for Gawans from the inter-island world. But here it is taken as the possible cause of witch attack: The retentiveness of Gawans who want to eat the pig themselves is taken as the hidden dimension of the Gawan view, which surfaces as signs of illness in those who may have violated this covert view by giving to others. The anger of the excluded takes form in secret acts that in effect subvert the outcome of the pig transaction to other islands into Gawan illness, rather than converting it into the positive value expected from overseas gift giving. In effect, instead of positive spatiotemporal transformations, a negative transformational process takes place that involves the fracturing of intersubjective relations within Gawa (some people do not agree to the pig transaction). This divisiveness is demonstrated by the negative qualisigns of bodily disturbance.

As indicated in Chapter 8, the entertainments themselves provide a field for the emergence of these negativities because it is felt that, in the context of such an extensive display and transmission of food, some people might be dissatisfied and might complain (*-sugwa*) that they had not received enough of the largesse. To *sugwa* implies that one is angered by the inadequacy of one's own portion. Gawans say that when witches see that another person has something the witches themselves lack, they hate (*-kamiriwey*) that person and desire these things for themselves. The witch is jealous (*-pogi*); the stomach becomes angry (*-kapasala nuwa-ra*); the mind is made bad (*-yageiga nano-ra*), or the forehead made heavy (*-mwaw daba-ra*) from seeing that others have more than oneself. We can gloss these ideas as conveying the view (similar to that well known as the emotional currency of witchery in many societies) that the witch develops a jealous anger. Simmel's (1955:50) definition of jealousy fits the Gawan concepts rather well: In Gawan jealousy the individual's desire for another's possessions entails the assumption of a "rightful claim."

At major feasts, as some men told me, Gawans try to give everyone enough so they won't complain, but will be happy instead. Happiness, as we have seen, is the state of mind that transactions of this kind are supposed to yield. Yet the positive value it implies can always be subverted by the possibility that some people feel they have not received enough or have gotten less than other people. As one man remarked in a public speech: If there is insufficient food, "one woman will eat, one woman won't"; that is, there may be witchery.

In these examples we can see that the witch is a third party other who enters into a transaction as one who does not receive, or who receives a share perceived as unequal (too small). The importance of a third party in a transaction between a donor and recipient has previously been discussed in different terms. In examining fame, I suggested that it is the third party, the "virtual observer" who "favors" a transaction with his notice, giving it a known identity beyond the spacetime location of the transaction and the participant actors (Chapter 5). But in the present context, the third party other is negatively inclined as the one who does not receive, or who perceives himself or herself as inadequately supplied in comparison with some other recipient (see Leroy, 1979:185). This kind of observer is implicit in all transactions, standing ready, as it were, to subvert the transaction. Witchcraft is always a possibility: If donor or recipient falls ill, the anger of others whose share has been stinted can be inferred. The outcome of food transmission then becomes witch attack rather than the positive valuation of the donor(s) typified in fame. Overtly positive acts can thus yield negative transformations of value. In the Gawan perception of the situation, such acts can then amount to the same thing as a refusal to give, a selfish retentiveness on the part of the apparent donor; indeed, from the perspective of an offended party, a refusal has, in fact, occurred.

The fine line between refusing to give to the other (keeping for oneself) and giving to another in the context of a presumed third party claim is seen in the following case:

In 1974, it was suspected that the lingering illness of an Imukubay woman had been caused by witchcraft due in part to her Tarakwasisi husband's choice of the recipients for three of his pigs. One of these had been given in payment for a canoe and so had gone to the dala owners of the canoe. Speaking at the kawrawora meeting held by the woman's dala kinsmen to aid her, one of the husband's clansmen took the view that the pig should have been given to the Drum dance rather than used to fulfill the personal obligation for the canoe. The pig was a large one, and the speaker felt that since the Nukwasisi were Ramugway (and not Guyaw) in the entertainment (see Chapter 8), they should not have held a large pig; rather, the husband should have arranged for it to be donated to the Drum dance.[13] (The reasoning here, as one woman explained to me, was that whereas only *some* people will eat pig from a canoe payment, the Drum dance is a community entertainment in which *everyone* eats; the Nukubay may therefore hold large pigs; see Chapter 8.)

The husband's dala brothers also preferred another recipient for a second pig. They thought it should have been given to a mortuary rite[14] for a woman of their dala (whose husband was Tarakubay), but the husband of the currently ill woman had refused at the time, because he wanted to hold the pig for his own children.

A third pig also entered into the case. This pig had been given to the Nukubay dala of the sick woman in payment for a canoe they had built, and they had cooked and distributed it, as was appropriate, to their kinspeople and workers for the canoe. Some of the women of this dala, and other recipients, spoke denying their complicity in the woman's illness, pointing out that they had eaten from this pig; since they had eaten plenty of pig, they would not bewitch the ill woman.

Several features are notable in this case. The woman's husband is felt to be *at fault*, but is not himself implicated in the witchcraft. Rather, his acts may have contributed to the witch's anger; he is thus closely identified with the suffering of his wife. The man's dala brothers, by asserting that they had tried to convince him to give the pigs differently, or to release the pig rather than to keep it for those close to himself, attempt to exonerate themselves from the fault, and simultaneously to deny complicity in any witchcraft against the ill woman.[15] In this way, they also express their concern for the woman and her husband, their kinsman.

In this case, giving in one direction rather than another and keeping for oneself or for a potential gift to close kin are treated as similar acts, since they are perceived as rejections of a transaction deemed more appropriate. Through this review process (i.e., in hindsight), transactions are designated as faults with a significance that is the inverse of that ascribed to separating food from the self. This evaluation derives, as it were, from the perspective of the disgruntled third party observer, the person(s) who might otherwise have received, but didn't. Thus any transaction has a negative potentiality that derives from the claim of the excluded other. Any act of keeping for oneself, giving, or receiving (as for instance obtaining something not made available to others) contains this negative potentiality – a potentiality that may or may not be actualized – actualization only occurring, of course, by a process of reading backward from the negative value signs of later disturbing events.

The witch's anger at a given transaction may last a long time so that illnesses or deaths occurring at a given time could be the result of transactions well in the past, in addition to more recent acts. Just as acts of giving may be remembered by a recipient, moving him or her to make positive returns to the donor in the future (see Chapter 3), so it is assumed that acts that a person feels place him or her in an unequal position vis à vis another, or by which someone feels deprived relative to what another has, may also be remembered, and a negative outcome produced years later. For instance, it is possible for an illness or death to be the result of anger over the transaction of a pig held long ago, rather than one more recently held. The excluded other is the hidden "fixed center of the turning world": acts of transmission like acts of keeping become a mode of refusal when formulated in terms of this latent perspective.

The typical relationships between witch and victim make it clear that the witch is in some respects a reciprocal image of the victim's imputed retentiveness. So, for example, one Gawan told me that witches decide to load on the witch canoe, those who refuse (-kayus) food; who don't give when people beg (-nigada), or who have a large pig and don't give it. These selfish people are the focus of the witches' hatred (kasi-meriyu).

Gawans often suppose that they are being bewitched because of a pig currently in their possession. When an individual's illness has been diagnosed in this way, the pig may be killed, cooked, and distributed to the neighborhood or beyond, in an attempt to allay the witch's desire to eat the pig. If distribution is just within the neighborhood and people of a more distant neighborhood hear of it, the original donors may feel it necessary to find another pig to distribute to the latter.

In such cases, the long illness of the patient (kara-mwaw, his or her heaviness) has been taken as a sign of retentiveness. The witch's greed to acquire and consume the pig is an intensive form of this retentiveness: The witch personifies this state in its dynamic form of acquisitive greed, which attempts to appropriate what is desired through force. Since what the witch does is to make the victim's body heavy with illness, it is as if the latter's own retentiveness were acting back upon him or her from outside through the agency of the witch, its intensive, active form. The witch and the victim taken together can be seen as a model of the appropriative or retentive dimension of the self projected in the dialectical form of a self–other relation. This intersubjective relation defines the dominion of greed – in the form of the excluded other – over the self of the victim, and the latter's ultimate death unless this dominion is itself dominated. The inequality created initially by the victim's possession of something denied to the other (his or her superordination relative to the other), yields an icon of itself with the superordination and subordination reversed and exaggerated.

To transform the negative value created by this imbalanced relation, the victim must sacrifice the pig, giving it to others to eat, and so, hopefully, assuaging the witch's hunger. In effect, the pig is a substitute for the person, for if the witch does not receive it to eat, she may eventually kill and consume the patient. Pigs are not the only possession that cause witch attack, but there is a specific equation of pigs and people relative to witches. As one young man put it: "The pigs (bulukwa) of the bwagaw are we humans (gamag)." His point was that witches consume the bodies of the dead, just as humans consume those of pigs. Similarly, a speaker at one gathering, attempting to deflect witches from attacking others, addressed the witches rhetorically, saying: "Let me be your pig" – that is, "Don't eat them, eat me!" At the same time, the flesh of pigs is itself particularly attractive to witches.[16]

The killing and distribution of the pig attempts to persuade the witch to desist, soothing her anger by detaching from the victim that aspect of self or personal increment that makes him or her superordinate to the other. By means of a single act the socially unregenerate, unregulated aspects of the will of each (victim and victimizer) are reformed. The result should be a change in the bodily state of the patient from illness to health, heaviness to vital mobility.

Such conversions signal the successful persuasiveness of the pig transmission. But this is unlike other such transactions in that the donor cannot expect any future return for the pig. Gawans tend to view such a transaction as a loss in the sense that it drains resources usually saved to meet some other obligation or to achieve some desired end. In this respect, as in others, witches take possessions without giving any equivalent return.

Actually, witches are also regarded as being thieves who steal (-*veiraw*) their victims' possessions. This theft may be referred to as "bewitching" the particular wealth item, an act also implying the possible or potential illness of the owner.

In late 1973, the head of the dala owning the Drum dance told the people that he had recently dreamed of a bwagaw coming to steal his large pig – the one being held as the yedeba centerpiece for the finale of the Drum dance being projected for 1975 (see commentary on the yedeba pig, Chapter 8). He had had the same dream for two nights, and a third dream would cause him to catch and kill the pig for immediate distribution.[17]

The witch's desire to steal the pig (equivalent to the desire to cause the illness of the owner) would make it impossible to hold the animal any longer for the community entertainment. The speaker thereby warned the people that the community would lose; in such a case, the pig would, indeed, have been stolen from the entertainment.

Just as witches steal pigs (a theft that connotes human illness), so also witches steal people; that is, they kill them. As one man put it when referring in a speech to witch-caused deaths: Witches "steal their [the dala's or, more generally, the community's] plantings." We have seen (Chapter 4) that planting creates reproductive continuity through retention (keeping resources in the ground). Theft is thus the negation of this process. "Plantings" here is a metaphor for the dala reproduction that witches threaten. In the end the witches' thievery leads to the loss of human beings and the threat to reproductive continuity this implies.

The witch's "negative reciprocity" (Sahlins, 1972:191, after Gouldner) has its parallel in the witch's gift. When the witch gives rather than takes food, it is the "gift that kills" (see Bailey, 1971; Mauss, 1968:255). As mentioned in Chapter 3, a witch may put a piece of vegetable food or pig inside a victim's body in retaliation for the latter's insufficient food gifts. This insertion is called *po-sugwa*; the root *sugwa*, as we have seen, means to complain of inadequate gifts, especially of food. The posugwa can be released from the body only through the ministrations of a curer who attempts to abstract it by spells and related means.[18] Obviously the posugwa represents the retentiveness or tightness attributed to the patient by the witch – the patient's own excessive eating or failure to give – just as it represents the witch's complaint regarding the insufficient gifts of the patient. In effect, all of these relations (those of the patient and the witch to food and of the patient and witch to each other) are condensed in the posugwa and must be transformed in order to cure the patient.

The concept of posugwa has a parallel in a more general notion about long-term illness conveyed in the metaphor of "knots." A witch may be said to tie or put knots (*sipu*) in a victim's body that a curer's spell releases or unties (*-liku*). When a kawrawora is held for a sick person, coconut, sugarcane, or betel nut distributed at the meeting are part of the request being made by the dala kin of the patient that the witch stop killing their kinsperson. These gifts may also be described (as they were to me at one meeting) as the "untying of the knots."

This distribution, like that of pieces of cooked pig, attempts a positive conversion of the state of the body by releasing or untying the elements of witchcraft identified with the patient's possession or consumption of comestibles (the knot in the body). In distribution a division or piecemealing of an undivided or collected whole results in a dispersal into many hands of what has been held by one (see also the processes of collection and dispersal at the Drum dance, Chapter 8). We have seen examples of such distributions in formal contexts, but it should be stressed that on an informal basis it is a standard operation on Gawa. For instance, when a person receives a small collection of raw or cooked food from a larger distribution, he will lay it out in little portions for distribution to others. The piecemeal distribution of the pig in very small morsels of pork is a prototypic example of this procedure because when alive, the pig is a single entity belonging to one person that undergoes dissolution (cooking, killing, and cutting up) of its bodily wholeness in the process of being given to others. This sacrificial partition and disaggregation is a fundamental icon of equalization on Gawa.

The immediate object of a witch's jealousy is not always food. For instance, it may be the acquisition of a major kula shell, a woman's pregnancy (which indicates the reproductive viabilty of a particular dala), an unusually large house, superior gardens, or any apparent imbalance that can be interpreted as concentrating in a particular individual or group something exceeding what others possess. Although any such perceived incremental imbalance may be the cause of witch attack, the witch's desire to consume is still relevant since, as we have seen, Gawan witches are necrophagous, and their desire to eat the dead serves as a general rationale for all their death-dealing, thieving activities.

The witch's necrophagy epitomizes the nature of the witch as consumer: Bwagaw consume the community's capacity to exist, by eating not merely resources external to the body, but the human body itself. Rather than giving food to others to eat, the witch converts others into food, thus destroying the self–other relation. Appropriating the other inside herself, the witch consumes the preconditions of any intersubjective spacetime: namely, the bodily being (or bodily spacetime) of the person. The form of self-construction and value creation that characterizes the witch is thus one of absolute dominion and autonomy. In contrast to the attempt to coopt the specific choice made through the persuasiveness of food giving, the witch attempts to coopt the general capacity to make a choice; she destroys relationality (and its embedded potentials) as such.

Even though the witch's victim may be guilty of a moral fault, the witch is clearly regarded by Gawans as not simply wrong but evil. Cannibalism is a "shameful" act[19] and the secret killing or destruction of others is reprehensible even if provoked. But the evil lies deeper. The cause of witch attack is not *simply* the witch's desire to eat: In a more fundamental sense, it is the assertion of one's own desires or greed over and against the desires of *all* others. We have seen that whether the victim is defined in the context of illness as having kept something for himself or herself, as keeping it to give to someone else, or as having given to others, he or she may always become the focus of witch attack by someone angry at not receiving, or at not receiving enough. The witch's aggression is focused on the limiting other per se.

In short, the witch constitutes the self as autonomous to the exclusion of the autonomy of other selves. In this sense, the witch is autonomy itself, the unregenerate will of *each* person, personified as the other. Like the Dinka night witch described by Lienhardt (1951:317), the Gawan witch "is an outlaw because he embodies those appetites and passions ... which, if ungoverned, would destroy any moral law. The ... witch may be seen to correspond to the concealed intention, the amorality and hence the opposition to those ... moral values which make community possible, of the ... individual self existing and acting as such." Since the witch's jealousy constitutes that point at which the claim of the excluded other destroys the person on whom it is made, the claim destroys itself, dissolving the very possibility of social relation on which it is predicated. For as Simmel (1955:55) has pointed out in his examination of jealousy: "The jealous individual destroys the relation just as much as that relation invites him to destroy his partner."

The relation between the patient's perceived transgression and the witch's greedy aggression cannot, therefore, be conceived of simply as punishment for an individual's failure to observe the ethic of generosity through which positive value is created. As appears to be characteristic of witch activity in most places,[20] the punishing acts are themselves transgressions; I have argued that they violate the preconditions of Gawan society. I suggest therefore that the witch's action converts the victim's presumed fault into a generalized model of the fault's *intrinsic significance* – its essentially negative or radically destructive *value*.

If we recall the positive value construction processes discussed in previous chapters, we can see that the present schema is comparable to them, although in a negative register. The witch as jealous aggressor exhibits the *value* of the victim's act. Like other value forms, the witch is not identical with the referent whose value is exhibited, but is rather an iconic objectification of its value. The witch as personified value form of the victim's own acts inscribes on the victim the qualisigns of that value: the heaviness of illness or death. Conversely, as I discuss in the next section, the witch herself possesses the dialectically opposed qualities of light-weightness. It is to these qualities that we must now turn to fill out the wider picture of the witch's dominion, and the sense in which the subversive witch persona can be seen as a value form of negative spatiotemporal transformation.

THE WITCH'S CONTROL OF SPACETIME

Like night witches in many places, Gawan witches fly (*youwa*). But the significance of this capacity for Gawans is not simply due to the fact that flying transcends or distorts normal human capacities. As we have seen, being lightweight is the attribute that defines human bodily vitality, and its emergence in other contexts signifies positive value transformations. Yet, as one Gawan pointed out to me, "buoyancy is the special possession of the witch" (*gagaabala si-vavaga bwagaw*). Interestingly enough, this statement was intended to explain to me a speaker's exhortation to Gawans at the Drum dance that they should not "go *gagaabala* along the paths at night." As we have seen, however, dancers are supposed to dance buoyantly all night. The statement puzzled me and my informant explained that the audience was being exhorted not to engage in witchery.

In theory, witches acquire their bodily powers in babyhood through bespelling by the mother (or, less appropriately, by the father with spells from his dala). One view is that the mother's balouma goes inside the child's body to instruct it and give it bwagaw magic to be held within its own body (in the stomach, where all spells are stored). According to the comments of one person, only one or two individuals of each dala would be bespelled in this way in babyhood, or possibly receive the magic as youths. However, as we might expect, given the generalized concept of witch identities discussed earlier, there is no fixed notion as to who these individuals might be, and suspicions in a particular instance are framed in terms of the immediate exigencies of the case rather than in terms of concepts about a prior set of bespelled persons.[21] Nevertheless, the broad association between wtiches and dala units is a significant aspect of Gawan ideas about witches (see also Chapter 10), and there is standard magic available for the childhood bespelling of a witch.

Spells that Gawans told me might be used to give a child bwagaw powers of flying are much the same in content as those for making an ordinary child walk early and fast (see Chapter 5), although distinguished categorically from them. Furthermore, witch magic may involve washing the face or slapping the body with bespelled leaves to make the body lightweight. Both of these latter techniques are used in other contexts for procedures connected with health and beautification (see Chapter 4). The witch's capacity to fly is not simply a distortion, but an intensification or expansion of desired bodily capacities beyond those available to anyone else. Speed as a concentrated potency is maximized in flying. In magic the speed and upward direction may be captured in such images as the witch's propulsion on fire up through a chimney hole as she takes off into the sky; similarly, the witch may use a bespelled vine to climb a tall tree on the cliffs and leap off from its branches to fly across the sea.

The significance of the witch's speed can also be exemplified by its special association with canoes. Canoe magic aimed at making a canoe exceptionally fast so that it will win races with other canoes may use the image of flying and invoke the witch (see also Malinowski, 1922:131f.; Munn, 1977; Tambiah, 1983). The swift canoe, gaining an edge over another canoe, is an image of superordination. Conversely, in order to ensure equality (e.g., on a kula uvelaku or major sailing trip), Gawans emphasize that the canoes should travel together, all leaving as one. This synchronization is not only an important sign of consensus (whereas failure to travel together signifies disagreement, see Chapter 10), but like consensus it also entails the equality of each canoe. The effect of starting before others is similar to that involved in being faster; the canoe that starts ahead has a competitive edge – one that could affect the other canoes in kula, if the first canoe arrives well before them.[22] Thus the leading canoe could be bewitched, or witch attack could afflict the fleet.

Being ahead (or faster) is given its radical form in flying, which "goes beyond" vertically as well as horizontally. To climb, as we have seen, is the standard phrasing of relative superiority. Thus flying signifies an excessive or radical superiority entailing both vertical and horizontal spatial transcendence of others and minimal time taken for passage. I suggest that flying is the condensed sign of ego's ability to surpass all others. Indeed, since it conveys absolute freedom of bodily movement unconstrained by ordinary spatiotemporal limits on the motion of the human body, it conveys bodily dominion over space and time as such. We shall see that this dominion characterizes the personal mode of being of the witch.

The witch's capacity to fly connects her especially, as we might expect, with the sea, making her a threat to inter-island travel. As in the case of the Trobriand flying witch (*mulukwawsi*), Gawan witches are particularly prone to flying over the sea or from island to island, causing shipwreck and eating the drowning sailors. A serious canoe accident about 1970, for example, was the subject of gossip on Gawa in 1974 when the island was afflicted with a number of illnesses and deaths (see Chapter 10). The accident had resulted in the deaths of a number of the crew, and whispered gossip focused on the supposed witchery of a particular Gawan woman to whom some women attributed the bewitching of the canoe and the consumption of the dead.

The witch's association with killing at sea is comparable to her travels to the Dobuan region that result in the introduction of disease *into* Gawa. A parallel may also be drawn with the notion mentioned earlier that the witch canoe can sail right up onto the Gawan land, thus intruding on Gawan soil. These notions of unorthodox mobility, identifying witchcraft with the inter-island sphere, convey the radical capacity of the witch to, as it were, overrun, or expand control of spacetime. This capacity yields disease and death for others. The absolute dominion of the witch results in a negative transformation of the bodies of others. The capacity to fly thus signifies the transformational level of the body's spacetime in which the actor's ends are achieved through the destructive appropriation of the other within her own body.

Other characteristics of the witch persona illuminate more features of this destructive spacetime. I have already remarked that the witch is hidden or invisible (*gamag gera i-kin-es*, people cannot see [the witch]) to all except the witch defender who can search her out with magical powers comparable to hers that are used, however, in the service of the community. Sometimes the witch is said to take off her skin (*-valili kalevi-ra*), or the balouma spirit that represents life within the body may be said to leave the body in sleep and travel around invisibly, stealing pigs and killing people by entering their bodies, spearing or piercing them, or using other destructive means. In either image, an otherwise internal or covered element – the bones inside the skin or the spirit inside the body – is externalized and becomes an invisible, lethal actor whereas the disengaged overt dimension remains visible but inanimate, its spatiotemporal level radically contracted (see Chapter 4).

Others might see a person sleeping who is in fact roaming around in the darkness (night being the time particularly associated with witch activities). One defender explained that people may also deliberately deceive (-*katudew*) others saying they are going to the bush to work, when in fact they go to sleep and their balouma flies out over the sea to perform witchery (for instance, to attack canoes), hiding itself in dark rain clouds. Ego's person has thus been divided into the socially visible (the aspect that connects self with other) and the invisible acting part (an autonomous inner dimension). This disintegrative level of bodily conversion frees one part of the body to merge with the external spatial order and act invisibly on the visible world. The disintegration of the body constitutes a coordinate disintegration of self–other relations, creating the model of an autonomous self that operates at a level that destroys all possibility of social relation. The division of ego's identity as a bodily being thus mirrors the division of intersubjective spacetime created.

When the witch's balouma is thought of as hiding in dark rain clouds, a new visible covering hides its presence and identity, yet reveals it through a threatening sign. The choice of covering clearly derives from the association between darkness and the destructive violence of rain storms, especially storms at sea, and witch activity. Witches may also change shape, assuming various nonhuman forms. A defender is said to be able to perform magic to make the witch come out (*sakapu*) into the daylight (*ou-murakata*), so that he (the defender) may himself see and learn its human identity. Similarly, a witch could "carry off the face" (*i-kouw magi-ra*) of another and hide within the latter's identity, making an ill person believe falsely that this innocent person is the true witch. This image of trickery and theft focuses on the duplicity that characterizes the witch who creates a world divided between surface appearance and actual intention or reality. Similarly, in this mode of being and the world it forms, the self is split in its own immediate being and this division entails (and is entailed in) the division of the relation between self and other. The structure of this witch-formed world is marked out along a fault line: Deception systematically creates a dual order. As will become clear later, this contradictory, divided mode of being can emerge in still other ways in public oratory aimed at transforming the state of the Gawan community when it is felt to be undermined by witchery.

All these familiar features of witch phenomena – shape changing, identity masking, and invisibility – mark a spatiotemporal level of the body that in the Gawan system is the inverse of beautification or self-enhancement. The latter, as we have seen, makes the individual more visible (*ou-murakata*) – clear (*migerew*), or brilliant with light. Clarity is, moreover, a quality that Gawans use to characterize excellence of character (a person who works hard is generous, does not steal, and is not jealous of his or her fellows), in contrast to the inverse state of being in which the person is characterized as being in darkness and shadow (*ou-daduba*).

These points recall from a slightly different perspective my previous remarks regarding witchcraft and fame. It would seem that the witch's mode of spatiotemporal extension of the person is the inversion of the model developed through fame: Whereas the latter is created by a circulation of the identity beyond the physical body via transacted objects that carry with them one's name and the embedment of the self in the reconnaissance of others, the former is constituted through the autonomous circulation of the inner, noncognizable and unrecognizable component of the person.

But although others cannot see the witch, the latter's own vision exceeds the ordinary. The witch can see through the opaque forms of houses and other persons. In one folktale, a witch's visionary capacity is depicted as an actual extension of the body: an old woman sent her eyes out each day to roam in the four directions across the seas to other islands to eat. This spatial extension of seeing is the reverse of the body's capacity to be seen by others. The witch's extension of her own vision is the reciprocal of her capacity to consume that of others, and conveys her dominion over the definition of the object world and its ordinary spatial relationships. The level of bodily integration represented by the witch thus destroys the morphology of space – the ordinary constraints governing relations between the body and external space – and negates the spatial control of other persons, who become, therefore, totally vulnerable.

In summary, it may be useful to recall in this context the Gawan emphasis on the inability of any actor to know another's mind. From one perspective, the witch appears not only as an expansion of individual potency through the detachment of this invisible intentional dimension of the person from the overt dimension (the skin, the visible bodily form) but also, it would seem, as the hidden construction of the subject in his or her desire for autonomy (see Chapter 10). The witch crystallizes a mode of being in which self-aggrandizement is expanded to the level where the actor transcends the spatiotemporal structures limiting ordinary human transactions and becomes the active controlling principle of spacetime. Just as the witch's body magnifies capacities for controlling spacetime, so the bodily spacetime of others is negated. Both the body's health and the person's capacity to produce positive value through transactions or the possession of goods for transaction are nullified.

THE WITCH, DOMINION, AND EQUALITY

It is now possible to draw together some aspects of the previous discussion in the light of the egalitarianism that characterizes Gawan polity. We have seen that the witch condenses a contradiction: On the one hand, the witch is a personification of dominion and radical superordination that negate equalization and balance in intersubjective relations. On the other hand, the witch emerges punitively in contexts where an element of increment or imbalance appears to violate the egalitarian ethos:[23] The witch then operates to enforce the principle that any increment accruing to one or more persons over and above what others have is subject to another's claim. For any sense in which ego has climbed contains the implication that someone else has, relatively speaking, been made lower.

How shall we reconcile the apparent contradiction? I suggest that Gawans experience the individualistic egalitarianism of their society *as domination*, in the shape of the witch. Creating, as I have shown, an intersubjective spacetime of radical dominion, the witch gives specific iconic form to the domination of the Gawan community by its inseparable controlling principles of the autonomous kareiwaga and equality of each individual (or dala). The witch thus embodies the hegemony[24] of these principles over the community, and each person's subjection to their control. Although Gawans "live" the control of this ego-centered or segmentary autonomy in the diffuse process of everyday life (in Raymond Williams's, 1977:110 words, as "a saturation of the whole process of living"), the bwagaw concept, with the mode of intersubjective spacetime it activates, crystallizes this experience directly in consciousness. Put another way, the emergence of the witch as the secret actor in a given context represents the surfacing of the domination of these principles in consciousness. When they assume their subjugating form as the witch, the principles of autonomy and equality alienate positive value from the actor and the community (in effect, the witch consumes this value within herself), forming the Gawan world in terms of a radical *inequality* in which the autonomy of one person subverts that of all others.

10

Didactic speech, consensus, and the control of witchcraft

> The Yes-or-No of *shall not* gets its quasi-positive in the idea of the "will," the hypothetical watershed that slopes off into obedience or disobedience.
>
> Kenneth Burke, 1961:284

I have pointed out that, on Gawa, chastening public speech is a central collective means of positively transforming the subversive intersubjective world and destructive value of witchcraft. In this chapter I shall examine how public speaking aims at reconstituting this world by considering certain meetings and speeches involving particular events that occurred on Gawa primarily between December 1973 and April 1974.

Speakers at meetings are ordinarily adult men (especially elders, *tamumoya*),[1] although there are special cases in which women or youths speak. Although we have seen that women as well as men may speak up at kawrawora meetings denying complicity, it is men whose role is to persuade people against witchery. In major community-wide gatherings, and in particular, those most directly concerned with such exhortations, it is most important that elders who are notable guyaw of community standing speak to the people. Indeed, a central function of guyaw is to exhort Gawans not to bewitch their fellows.

These exhortations are part of a more general type of speech called *gweiguya* (cf. *guyaw*): didactic, chastening, and persuasive speech.[2] The speakers attempt to persuade the witches to listen to them: that is, to agree to stop their evil acts or desist from any future evil.[3] In this sense, the attempt is to persuade witches to conform to a will beyond that of the individual – namely to the combined wills of the adult men, especially the leading elders. In such contexts these speakers represent the efforts of the community as a whole to transform the subverted value state of the society, or to ensure that the ever-present possibility of subversion is not actualized. Through this verbal process guyaw strive to make possible the production of the positive value that the witch's activity threatens and ultimately destroys. The process of transformation is thus one in which the autonomous self in its hegemonic form as bwagaw (released from all constraint by the other) is to be subordinated to the will of the other to come under the influence of the collective will of the community or in Mead's (1956:231) terms, the "generalized other." It is significant that this intersubjective process turns on gaining the agreement of the bwagaw, for as we have seen, the use of persuasion (verbal or nonverbal) to obtain consent is fundamental to positive transformation and value creation in Gawan society.

Guyaw care for (-yamata) Gawans most notably in their efforts to ward off witchcraft and to plan and carry out various community ventures. The two functions are closely intertwined, for if witchcraft is operative in the community, collective projects cannot be carried out. So, for instance, as one man put it, if anyone should die, "work will stop for weeping." Moreover, the successful production of projects, like the negation of witchcraft, depends on the influence these men concentrate into themselves through their successful engagement in positive transformational acts of influencing (e.g., acts of food giving and speaking rather than consumption). Both in their negation of the destructive potency of the witch and their organization of community projects they condense a "potentializing" capacity to bring about events that will yield positive value for the community. The guyaw's mode of spatiotemporal control thus contrasts with that exerted by the witch and condensed in her bodily qualities: If the former embodies influence (signified by the circulation of the name), the latter embodies the alienating force of dominion (signified by the circulation of the inner, invisible being apart from the body). As types of social role, "guyaw" and "bwagaw" form a dialectic of reverse modes of action and signs of spatiotemporal power in the creation of value.[4] Thus, in their exhortations, guyaw attempt to transform the unmediated intersubjective spacetime of domination created by witchcraft back into the moderated, ideally equalizing order of spacetime formed by relations of influence. But in doing this, they must strive to create a more comprehensive "oneness" that is both built on and transcends equalization. The handling of this basic problem of egalitarian polity will be considered later.

A key feature of the rhetoric speakers use in their exhortations involves pointing to the destruction of positive value potential entailed in continuous acts of witchery: Speakers may warn the people of the crucial losses to the community as a whole and its inability to carry out current projects of the moment should any of its members continue to bwagaw others. They may remind the people of community projects current or planned, such as kula sailings, entertainments, or relevant work projects that return positive value to the community as long as there is no witch-caused illness and death. Speakers may also inform people of the scheduling of activities aimed at dealing with any disorders.[5]

In early January 1974, Gawans were faced with spreading illness and general malaise; of particular concern was the illness of G., one of the two leading garden specialists, the last of his dala. Although this was the preferred period for northward kula sailings, Gawans were not yet prepared for the trip (for example, canoes needed for the trip were not finished). Community leaders called a meeting at a night performance of the Drum dance in which they told the people that in the near future they would perform Bibira rites for cleansing Gawa and bounding it off from illness (see Chapter 4); the schedule for this operation was communicated to the people.

The first speaker (the leading guyaw of the clan that owns the Drum dance) told the people that the garden specialist who was ill had informed him that he was leaving Gawa for Iwa, saying that if he remained on Gawa he might die. The speaker had asked G. not to go. Discussing the illness on Gawa, he warned the people not to gather around bewitching others (gera ku-vaakwari-s). (If a number of people on the island are ill, Gawans fear that bwagaws will gather and come in to kill them. The term -vaakwari-s denotes this activity.) Should the bewitching continue, the Gawan people will get nothing when they sail (for kula): "not a single 'mat'[6] will we find. The people of Kweawata [who are in competition with Gawans for kula] are sailing 'today'. It was like this in the past: We 'sat' [didn't sail]; they finished the armshells [i.e., they got everything]."[7]

The speaker further warned the people (particularly by implication, the women) not to approach the bwagaw canoe. Telling of a time when the canoe was sighted on a Muyuwan beach by a woman of Dekwoyas village, he pointed out that this woman had rejected the canoe, and told Gawans that they should do the same.

A second speaker, the leading witch defender, asserted that the witch canoe is the traditional responsibility (-pakura) of other islands, not of Gawa. The Gawan pakura is kay-mariya, the provision of food plenty for the Drum dance, for which the food has been taboo'd (i.e., put aside exclusively). Gawans should not go and meet that canoe: "Let us listen to the people's [men's] speech. Let us obey/agree (kabikawra). . . . The kareiwaga is inside the meeting." The point being made here is that Gawans should remember these speeches and not go to meet the witch canoe.

Referring to the garden specialist who was supposed to have gone to Iwa to escape the witch malaise, the defender warned Gawan bwagaws not to fly to Iwa. He (the garden specialist) should get well: He should "wash his body and be healthy and buoyant (gagaabula)." His magic "goes beyond anything we have." That is to say, no one can match this man's garden magic, and his loss could mean famine for Gawa.

Still a third speaker, V., the most important man on Gawa at that time and one of the leading garden specialists, deeply concerned about the illness of his colleague, continued the warnings about the witch canoe saying for instance: "[Should] you women bring in the canoe, it will load us [i.e., we men]." (His emphasis on the notion that women would in this way be attacking the men, appears to be related to his special concern for G., the garden specialist.) V.

chastised the people for the illness of G. and emphasized the importance of provisioning the dabedeba (the Drum dance) to whose current performance cycle all had agreed. Therefore they should "close off" whatever sickness comes. Commenting on the history of the planning for the present Drum dance, he pointed out that when the plans were first projected he had told the people to "throw away deceit (*katudew*)." As he asserted at different points: The people have "one mind, another 'tongue' (speech)" – i.e., they agree to do one thing (the Drum dance) but they also engage in witchery that contradicts it (this concept is discussed later in connection with V.'s speech in the conflict over the school).

These are, of course, only brief abstracts and summaries of complex speeches (nor have I commented on all who spoke up at this particular meeting), but they illustrate some key features of this meeting, as well as certain broad characteristics of these transformational procedures in general. In a number of the speeches, the bwagaw canoe was set up as a protagonist in terms of which correct action, namely, the rejection of witchery, could be constructed. The reference to the apparently legendary historical incident involving this canoe on Muyuw, and some of the other subsequent references to the canoe, treated current signs of its present travels near Gawa as part of a historically grounded inter-island world, while also providing a parable-like model for right as against wrong Gawan action (especially by Gawan women who should follow the correct behavior of the Muyuwan woman who refused entry to the canoe). In this context, the witch canoe condenses "possibilities of both obedience and disobedience" (Burke, 1961:194). Gawans might choose, contrary to the exhortations of the speakers, to identify with the canoe, or in obedience to their wishes, to separate themselves from it. The canoe becomes an arena of possible positive or negative acts and their alternative results, the medium of a "rite of separation" grounded in the kareiwaga or decision-making powers of Gawans themselves.

Rejection of the canoe has its reciprocal in the acceptance of the words of speakers, the senior men, and of the community events that they organize: namely, the Drum dance at which the meeting was held, and the curing rite that is being publicly scheduled within this meeting. The meeting at the Drum dance itself becomes posed against acts of witchery and the undesirable acceptance of the canoe. What the speeches are about is only completed indexically by incorporation of the meeting process and the speakers themselves into the project as positive protagonists with whom, in effect, a "rite of identification" is being formed (see the "school speech" discussed later in the chapter).[8] For instance, a dialectical transaction is set up between the speakers, the witch canoe (witchcraft projected outside the Gawan collective self), and the Gawan people (especially Gawan women as representing possible identification with or separation of witchcraft from the Gawan self).

The proximity of the witch canoe is not the only element of negativity in inter-island relations as construed in this meeting. Of special importance is the fact that G., the ill garden specialist, was supposed to have fled to Iwa in order to escape the witches of Gawa. One speaker (not referred to above) also pointed to the previous departure to Muyuw of the leading man of his own dala for similar reasons; as a result, he said the protective bespelled *gamu* (see Chapter 9) bounding Gawa had been breached. His remarks implied that this gamu needed renewal, one of the aims of the projected Bibira rite.

To understand the significance of these negative, inter-island travels, we have to consider that this meeting occurred at a time when Gawans were concerned about their lack of preparation for a northern kula trip. Early January is about the latest the Gawans can expect to find adequate winds for sailing north, and January is a time in which Gawan men may be either out on kula, ready to go, or may even have returned from the north. But instead of this positive value-producing travel, the travel going on is that of witches, or is the effect of illness and consequent fears of witchcraft. What is projected in this travel is the dissolution of positive value: the possibility of its deadly consumption by witches, or the dissolution of the community in the loss of important men who flee its shores for fear of witch attack. Illness keeps Gawans themselves from sailing on the legitimate journeys that yield the positive value embedded in kula shells and other items.

Thus it seems to be no accident that the imagery of the witch canoe and its concomitants emerge so dominantly at this time. The spacetime of the inter-island world is inverted: Gawans are kept home, and cannot engage in activities that yield the positive potentials of inter-island resources; instead it is felt that witches are traveling and might invade Gawan shores. Gawans must prepare to bound themselves off from destructive intrusions and illness in general (the disturbed state of the community that signifies their imminence), planning the collective action that secures this so that they themselves can travel. It will be recalled that the Bibira rite itself involves an outwardly mobile process culminating in overseas travel: The illness chased down the paths of Gawa to the sea is finally loaded on a model canoe and sent away northward to disappear from the immediate island world. Thus different kinds of sea travel and mobility are drawn into dialectical relation to form a meaningful process in the effort to create a positive transformation of Gawan spacetime, and to develop the enabling conditions for travel that yields desired value from overseas.

As I have pointed out, the Drum dance is drawn into the project being constituted in the speeches. The dance itself forms a community level of connectivity and the appropriate constitution of the relation between senior men and people. According to V., the leading garden specialist, the people *agreed* to the current performance cycle, which (as he indicated in a historical commentary) had been established originally by the arrangements of senior men. In effect, Gawans are enjoined to focus on the food provisioning that is central to the Drum dance – and which enables them to enjoy themselves, dance, and eat – rather than on provisioning the witch canoe with the dead and so consuming others, as it were, with their secret aggrandizement.

On the other hand, if the Drum dance does not reflect agreement, but is undermined by an unspoken disagreement, ("the people speak one thing while their minds are opposed," as V. puts it) then this community activity itself becomes a model of the deceptiveness that characterizes the intersubjective spacetime of witchcraft. In short, if Gawans bewitch their fellows, senior men cannot organize entertainments such as the Drum dance, and resources needed for them are drained off in mortuary rites, just as the body itself is destroyed; as a result, all planning, all positive potentiality is negated.

THE CASE OF G., THE GARDEN SPECIALIST

The particular concern with the illness of the garden specialist is a central part of these speeches, and constituted a theme that surfaced in later meetings as well. G.'s illness and his desire to leave Gawa to escape witch attack signified the possible loss of value in a particularly poignant way. It condensed in his person the loss of senior men through death with the loss of food, since G.'s death was taken to mean the loss of his garden magic. As we have seen, the strength of Gawa as a polity is epitomized for Gawans in its men of influence. Thus when V. said that women who acceded to the entry of the witch canoe would be killing "we men," he was pointing to the draining of this potency in general through witchery, and by implication to the possible loss of G., whom he had advised to leave Gawa in order to escape further Gawan attack. The former's journey represented travel that generates a draining of masculine, externalizing value from Gawa rather than the production of the condensed media of this value brought back into Gawa in the form of kula shells: It entailed a reduction of control over intersubjective spacetime rather than its expansion.

Although G. recovered from his immediate sickness, he died before the finale of the Drum dance in 1975.[9] As I have already noted (Chapter 8), his loss was a theme of chastisement at the finale, especially in the speech of V., who lamented the death of his colleague, chastening Gawans for "doing him in" (*ku-vage-s mtowen*), and saying that "men and women bwagaw, so there is not enough food." Again he lambasted the deceit of Gawans who, he said, say one thing outside (*ou-murakata*), but then do another (i.e., bwagaw). For G. had helped his colleague prepare the dabedeba tree for the Drum dance by bespelling the dance hamlet so that food would be plentiful. Although they had bespelled the hamlet, making it "straight," people then engaged in witchery. As a result, they had begun with plenty of food, but now, V. asserted, there was not enough. G.'s death was thus intimately tied up with the Drum dance: Just as witchcraft in general is in dialectical tension with the entertainment – its antithesis entailed within the dance as its negative potentiality – so G.'s sad death personalized this dialectic, bringing together in a particular person and his fate, both the creation of food plenty for the entertainment, and its loss through witchcraft.

THE SCHOOL CONFLICT

During the building of a school house on Gawa in March 1974,[10] Gawans feared that the new school teacher was being bewitched because of the large size of the school; since the school building was bigger than any building on the island except for the church (also built by Gawans themselves with indigenous materials), it was felt that this feature could have made it the focus of jealousy on the part of some individual(s). Furthermore, underlying these witch fears was a conflict between the work groups building the school. The conflict, its crystallization in witch fears, and the resultant attempts to transform the negative intersubjective state of Gawa that was threatening the capacity of Gawans to build the school is discussed here to exemplify dialectical processes in value production as they emerged in a particular case involving the introduction of a nonindigenous institution on Gawa. In this analysis, I shall begin by examining certain aspects of a single major speech by V., the senior community garden specialist, and at that time the most influential man on Gawa in kula. This speech was given at a community meeting held in the partly built school when the sense of threat from witch activity and the group work conflict was cresting. The land for the school was donated by V.'s dala, and his speech attempting to quell the disturbance was of special importance in the meeting.[11] A translation of the speech precedes the discussion. I conclude discussion of the speech by considering the fractioning process in the work group and suggesting the relation between the spatiotemporal fragmentation occurring there and the subsequent emergence of the divided intersubjective spacetime of witchcraft as formulated in particular in V.'s speech.

V.'s school speech[12]

1. The senior man chastises (*i-gweiguya*), kula's, "acts as guyaw" (*i-gwiyaw*). . . . You all agreed, let us hear speech, please speak [you said] for [the children's] schooling, our work and whatever else; you agreed. . . . It becomes me and my fellows to stand up [and speak]; our [excl.] bodies are like a stone, like a stone [i.e., V. is deeply upset].

2. [The people are] two tongued: one lying, one truthful. Now they go along, now

they go along. We [incl.] lie. He [the school teacher] is staying here. You wanted [him]. He came, stayed, we think we will "raise it" (*bi-ta-rupe-s*) [i.e., build the school].... It's certainly true, I think it's certainly true isn't it? We all want it. Kareiwaga, women, men. What do we want within Gawa? I want us to hold on to (*ta-yousi-s*) his [the teacher's] kareiwaga.

3. This house, this land, is the kareiwaga, if they would only tell the tradition (*leliyu*), of Guyoraba who came out within Gawa. We came here, he gave it out piecemeal – this one his land, that one his land. He gave it to us. His kareiwaga came, I got my land long ago (*a-bogwa*). I, I agreed [to give] this, my land. I agreed [to give the land] they gave me, the men of old, I came and stayed on his [Guyoraba's?] land; I agreed, I gave [the land]. You bewitch this house, I think it is I; I would kareiwaga. Why would it be I who would kareiwaga? Because of the land. I a guyaw, my head would be heavy, I might "do in" (*ba-vaga*) this house; it is my possession; [I might do it in] because of the land.

4. Eh! Eh! I will recount the history, our history. Because we called the missionary P. [to come to Gawa]; we built, we thought to raise the church up high (*ira wa-nakayouwa*). You did him in like this, he died. [Another, who replaced him died similarly, within Gawa].... We built the house, this church – we built and built, eh. "Two-tongues" emerged, this deceit, "two-tongues": one true, one false.

5. Another tradition of ours has the name – what's its name? – Guyoraba. You speak, we listen. And why do you speak of Guyoraba? Eh! Guyoraba, why [him]? Tradition (*leliyu*). Guyoraba! Guyoraba rules (*kareiwog*) Gawa. We came here and stayed [on] his land.... Kirivila[a] [their kareiwaga is] Tabalu. It is fitting, it befits them ... [If the Tabalu go to another village and see] a kadiguway [house decoration, an identifying emblem of the Tabalu]; they tear it away entirely [from the house it is on]. [They say]: you can't hold onto it, let go. [But] we, our leliyu, its name is Guyoraba. Each one his own kareiwaga. No one's head is higher than anyone else's. He [Guyoraba] made this kareiwaga. No Tabalu made this kareiwaga, [but] I, Guyoreb. You "put one over the other": Labaya [where the Tabalu came out on Kiriwina], Tabaya [where the original Gawan dala emerged on Gawa].[b]

6. We are [like] the Japanese[c]: the guyaw in the forehead, everyone his own kareiwaga. We can't command each other, no. [Not] like it befitted Mutakata [a previous head of the Tabalu dala]: Whatever he found, a pig, a betel branch, [whatever] his eye saw [i.e., he could go into another village and take a pig, or betel].... [That's the way it is] in the north. We of Gawa, our tradition is this one, called Guyoraba. Everyone his own kareiwaga. And now this new man [the school teacher] has come, we all have our land, our fields, which he [Guyoraba] gave us. And I agreed, I agreed [to give] that land.... [Should I want to bwagaw] I would tell my *gamagali* [the women of V.'s dala to whom he gives food]: "let us bewitch

[a] The main island of the Trobriands; here the reference is to the northern region in particular.

[b] Gawans do not have any standard explanation for the parallel in the names of the two origin places. I was told the dala of Guyoraba came out at Tabay.

[c] During World War II, individual Japanese were shot down in the Solomon Sea and one or two found their way by boat to Gawa. It is possibly owing in part to the nature of these experiences that V. conceives of the Japanese as having a kareiwaga similar to Gawa's rather than that of the Trobriands.

this house" – should my head be heavy. O why? Because of the land. It is
appropriate for me [to do this]. But we [excl.] said "Don't do it." How ashamed we
all are. How ashamed we all are. Oh Gawa is like this [i.e., crooked]. We are like
this. From the times of the ancestors (*tamumoya*). Today you agree [to build the
school]. How will you make things straight? Your minds, I wonder how are they,
eh? And that's it. We [i.e., the old men] will die soon; we are finished "tomorrow."
. . .

7. Does this possession [the school] befit you? what will you choose? Will you
choose the white man's (*dimdim*) kareiwaga, or will you choose us [the Papuan
kareiwaga]? I don't think so.[d] Because how many months we all speak, we all speak
about this possession [the school]. You all come [and say] "thank you so much" [for
the speech; the expression *kama-touki*, "we (excl.) thank you" is always used by
the audience at the end of a speech]. A deception. A lie, a deception. Inside [the
"thank you"] a deception. You are not truthful, no. You only deceive. Lies, truth.
We shouldn't lie, we should listen, we should make the thing – no! [i.e., we
shouldn't lie]. Listen: lies, truth.

8. Women, men, we are all greatly ashamed. How are we all ashamed? Time after
time we just lose it. No matter what is said, no matter what is said – we come
together, bwagaw; we come together, bwagaw. And it is only we ourselves [who
bwagaw]. Today this house does not [yet] stand. . . . [V. then asks how many the
senior men add up to; his point is apparently that there are only a few, and that they
speak and speak, to no avail].

9. Woman [or] man, where are you? [V. rhetorically addresses whoever is causing
the witchery]. This work is not hard. Decide! Do you want [a house like this]?
Speak up! You make it like this. They will make it. It's not hard, not at all. You see
this wood, the wood of Gawa [i.e., it's not difficult, the wood is your familiar
Gawan wood]. Whoever you are, you whose head is "made heavy" by this house,
you just speak up; it will be made, it won't be refused you, because you might make
trouble.

10. This house, let's go and build it – [now] he [the teacher] has come to stay – let's
raise it up high (*bi-ta-rupe-s beira wa-nakayouwa*). The "one who turns things
around" [i.e., the witch], what for? Our minds, how are they? How are your
minds?[e] . . . Don't deny (*yaakara*) [what you are doing?], no. This kareiwaga you

[d] My commentators interpreted this to mean that V. is saying he thinks the people will take
    up a white man's kareiwaga and not a Papuan kareiwaga. However, the phrasing and
    context also suggest to me that he may be chiding the people, saying (rhetorically) that he
    doesn't think that they will achieve the white man's kareiwaga (the school and its
    productive potential) because of the lying, witching, and so on.

[e] V. says "*Ba-na-ta-ninisi, amakaawara* (how)? *Ku-ninisi amakaawara?*" My commentator
    explained that this passage referred to the Gawan attitude toward "the white man's good
    kareiwaga, such as food, housing, and so forth." It is not entirely clear to me whether V.'s
    subsequent reference to the "kareiwaga you are making" is intended to denote the
    kareiwaga to build the school, or the kareiwaga of witchcraft. If the former is intended, the
    sense of *sina peyola* (see text) is that the schoolhouse is a very productive, strong project.
    However, context inclines me toward the latter interpretation (i.e., that the reference is to
    witchcraft). Accordingly, I have translated these remarks somewhat ambiguously, but
    more on the presumption that V. is referring to the witch kareiwaga.

are making is too much, too much (*sina peyola*).... And now the new arrival [the school teacher] has come; you haven't seen his country. He certainly doesn't know our customs (*bunera*). Gawa is very "tight" [i.e., difficult; takes a long time to complete something, etc.].

11. Today you prepare food for a [taro pudding] feast; I told you do this so that we would make it "straight." [V. goes on to refer to the division made between the two work groups so that each is now working on one part of the school].[f] ... One group, one part, one group another part, no. We should all make it together [as one group]. You stood up, you made this division in a meeting. I reject it.

12. You give us a taro pudding feast and today we are in famine.[g] ... [The people are then chastised as being "like children," for when there is only a limited amount of food and someone gets less than someone else, "the one to whom we gave less cries" because he or she has not gotten enough. V. continues, telling people to prepare for other jobs necessary inside the school once the initial construction is done, thus implying extensive work still remains and is taking time from other Gawan responsibilities].

13. Our songfest [the Drum dance] is still waiting. When, I ask you, will we make the final feast [if] you bwagaw it, you bwagaw this songfest, you bwagaw U. [the owner of the Drum dance].[h] Two tongues.

14. I with my people are certainly ashamed. I, my body is like a stone, a biribiri stone. I rise to give my strong speech, or I might not rise [to speak].... You speak of witchery, for what reason? The reason, for what reason? And he [the school teacher] will go away to Kitava. They will take away the [bad] news. We raise this house, and then afterward we "do it in" (*ta-vage-s*).... We all agreed, we will make it. We agreed. We agreed [to give] the land, we agreed to build this; no one should say, no, [that it is] his house, [just] for himself. We ourselves, our name, our fame (*yakaa-dayesa, yaga-desa butu-deisa*). So [other people] will see our fine work, one house, another, we [our work]. And listen! he said it's for us alone.[i] Not

---

[f] This division would also have involved a division in any feast planned, and this problem, which had been a recent issue is also, apparently, part of the implications. Three of the most important men (including V.) had arranged for a single feast in an effort to bring the conflicting groups together. My commentator pointed out that for people to be of "one mind" is "straight," and that V. is angry because of the division of the work (see my discussion of the work conflict below).

[g] One commentator explained that the taro pudding cooking would use up food, thus creating a food shortage. Then, he said, the bwagaw wouldn't be able to see any food and would stop attacking. However, there had also been some concern about a drain on the gardens, both because of recent deaths (requiring mortuary exchanges) and the extensive work on the school, and this seems to have been on V.'s mind in this context.

[h] The importance of 12 and 13 is that they point to the fact that Gawans should be preparing for the school's opening feast when government officials and teachers are supposed to come from other islands; further, they should be looking to other major projects of their own (notably the Drum dance finale), instead of having to channel food supplies to the present feast arranged because of the destructive disturbances.

[i] The school teacher himself had spoken before V., emphasizing that the school was not his, but belonged to the community. He did not, however, refer to the fame of Gawa, an emphasis developed by V.

for him, no; for *us*. We agreed (*ta-kabikawre-s*); [it is] our kareiwaga. We raise it [the house], they come. [They say]: "Like leliyu, ha! Oh, your place (*mi-veru*)."
15. We built the church, they stood up [and] jealously bewitched it (*i-pogi-s*). . . . And now this new man [the school teacher], the very same thing. We raise it, those others will come, later they will see it. They will see our work within Gawa. . . . We agreed [to give] the land, we raise this thing. And now later, "two tongues", one lying, one true. You make us ashamed. Ashamed indeed. . . .

You know, listen! You came [to the school teacher's home], you put holes in it, and he found you out. That's it! I know you. . . . Women, men, we have found you men. We are all very ashamed. . . . You all trick/deceive. What do you do this for?
16. Only one of the sailors of a canoe steals. He gives our [whole] canoe the name of "thief" (*I-seika ma-waga "kay-veiraw"*). And women and men, we "carry" shame today. Only kula, you see, ha!*ʲ* Gawa's custom is like this, ha! No it isn't like this [i.e., this isn't the right way?] [V. continues asking what they went to the school teacher's house for: "what do you want?"]
17. Our bodies are shamed [by witchery]. As when we go on the sea, we [are ashamed when] we meet [sailors from other islands], certainly, our leliyu, our leliyu [i.e., this witchery]. You eat canoes on the sea, whatever things (*youdarera*) we people make [in the hamlets] you "do in." That's our leliyu, we Gawans. Today we are ashamed. There is no senior man, no guyaw, his custom thieving, so that what he sees may "bite his brow" [make his brow heavy].*ᵏ* No, I said our leliyu is Guyoreba.*ˡ* Guyoraba. His name is Guyoraba. We cannot go and command (*ta-kuyori*) each other. Each one his own kareiwaga. Our kareiwaga is "little" – in our hamlets only [it extends no further than the hamlet]. It's name is Guyoreba. Those Tabalu, they control the kadaguwayi [house decoration]. Those people, it's fitting like this for them. For us it is not suitable, no it isn't.

And whoever you are, you want [a house like this one], we will make it; oh just speak up; [you think] no they won't give it, we will all refuse. No, we will not refuse. You want it, we will make it. We won't refuse, no we won't.
18. What do we listen to their speech for, [concerning] bwagaw? [i.e., the men's speech relating to bwagaws, intended to stop them]. O that bwagaw, how many "yam years" (*teitu*) have we spoken their speech, the bwagaws? How many "yam years," how many moons [*tubukon*]? And now you all listen. We are all so ashamed. He [the school teacher] didn't chastise (*kane*) you [i.e., whoever was haunting the teacher's house]; he might have found you out. He recognized your faces, [but] he didn't mention names; he didn't mention names. Oh it is us [Gawans]. No other thieves come, no. It is simply us. And today we heard that you

ʲ My commentator interpreted this to mean that just the fame from kula is desirable, but the news that circulates from witchcraft will make Gawan fame disappear (*b-i-tamwaw*). This interpretation points to the subversion of spacetime that emerges in witchcraft. Becoming known for witchcraft (the circulation of Gawa's name) destroys rather than increases the spatiotemporal control of the community.

ᵏ The point of this statement, as my commentator explained, is that there is no guyaw on Gawa who climbs over others: Men are afraid to have an unusually large pig or food supply because they fear witchery. Thus there is no one who has the right to go in and claim the large schoolhouse.

ˡ *Guyoreba* is an alternative form of *Guyoraba*.

came in the evening – I thought you were "doing in" the Yanaba [visitors]. Stop it! Certainly don't do that again. The Yanaba people have come and spoken. And today he [a Yanaba visitor] has revealed it."[m]

[A passage follows again asking the people what they are up to; and referring to plans for the taro feast to be held next day because of the conflict over the school work and the witch fears. A shortage of food is implied.]

19. And he [the teacher] has spoken [and] revealed this bwagaw ... your voices are "tight" [i.e., you don't agree easily]; that's enough from us [incl.]. We [incl.] are so ashamed. The men speak [and when] it is finished [people say] "thank you"; a lie. "Thank you" is a lie: it is not true, no it isn't.

[V. refers again to the fact that the school teacher didn't mention the names of the troublemakers haunting his house at night that is, the bwagaws. The point is, the teacher does not yet know peoples' names.]

20. We all are so ashamed, you make this kareiwaga. We senior men, you know us, we make speeches. . . . We want happiness, the name of Gawa to be "carried." Let [Gawa's] name in Kula stand up high; let the white man's kareiwaga stand up high; we [excl.] want us to get hold of (*ta-kayousi*) [these things]. We ponder in this way. [But] you make the [kareiwaga of the senior men] go down. You oppose the meetings, and you don't speak up in front of the group. It is we senior men who speak. We [excl.] speak the truth (*ka-monida*), it will be straight (*b-i-dumwalu*) . . . Listen! You are crooked (ku-dadogu). Such lying. You agree to hearing the gweiguya speech. . . . We are all so ashamed. And that's it, I have told you, that's it.

DISCUSSION OF THE SPEECH

V. begins (1) by distinguishing the category of senior men as speakers from the populace as a whole – who he says, "agreed" that there should be speakers and a school meeting – and locating himself within the speaker category. This deictic frame or "self-declaration of status" (Goldmann, 1983:69) constructs a tensional social field in which the senior men are defined as upstanding men of influence (they are kula men, those who guyaw and engage in didactic speech) in contrast to the populace who are (or some of whom are) two tongued (*kayu m'era*, a contraction of *mayera*, tongue). He ends the speech in a similar deictic frame (20), which sums up this formulation and the transformational process at which it is aimed, by the description of "we senior men" as those who attempt to produce for Gawa the positive values that are destroyed through witchcraft. The characterization is phrased in terms that bring into play qualisigns of positive value and corresponding subjective states: "We want happiness, that the name of Gawa be carried. Let Gawa's name in kula stand high; let the white man's kareiwaga [referring here to the school building as the present embodiment of this kareiwaga] stand up high." Moreover, these

---

[m] My commentator said the Yanaba visitors have come and seen what is going on and "brought out into the open" the name of Gawa as "bwagaw."

aims are embedded in the senior men's "straight," "truthful" speech, which attempts to engage Gawans in a genuine agreement to work on value-producing undertakings such as the school. The people, however, through their contradictory false agreement, give "crookedness" to this speech so that the kareiwaga of the senior men "goes down," and it becomes impossible to complete the project and generate the desired potentialities.

The significance of the opposition between straightness and crookedness deserves further comment. As we saw earlier, V. similarly stressed his and his colleague's straight action in bespelling the dance hamlet to create food plenty for the entertainment at the 1975 finale of the Drum dance, and the subversive effect of witchcraft on this productive act. As one Gawan put it to me in another context, when people agree to work together on a collective project this "makes the place straight" (*i-yudumwalu veru*); but when even one person refuses, this "makes the place crooked" (*i-yadadoga veru*). Moreover, straightness connotes "oneness": the people agree and work together, creating a unified Gawan spacetime. Similarly, in V.'s talk, the notion of two tongues is identified in one context (2) with dispersal: The people agree in a common meeting (true speech), but then they go off (*i-rora-s*) to their different hamlets and say something else (a fragmentation of the unitary agreement that is part of the spatial dispersion). This connotation is also made quite explicit in the emphasis Gawans place on one speech and one kareiwaga as straight (*dumwalu*). When there is truly one kareiwaga, people work as one; "one speech" is implicit in collective work, just as the unity of collective work is implicit in "one speech." We might say that unitary work signifies that a single kareiwaga governs the will of the individual, just as a single kareiwaga defines a unitary work project.

In 1980 Gawans were having some problems in preparing the finale of the Comb entertainment. One Gawan commented to me that there were "too many kareiwaga": the church, and the government, for instance, had certain projects that Gawans were working on and that required food; the kareiwaga for the Comb finale was thus only one among others. In the past, he claimed, each senior man organized an entertainment in turn, so that Gawans all went to work *first* for one kareiwaga and *then* another. This was "straight": "there was one speech." But now, he said, the "many kareiwaga" are indicative of "untruthful" (*soup*)[13] speech, and as a result "we find bwagaw" and related disorders (i.e., because there is not sufficient food).

We can see then that V.'s formulation in the 1974 school speech is part of a basic Gawan formulation connecting straight, unified speech, the model of truth,[14] and the capacity to carry out collective projects; and that when there is a division of the community into "too many kareiwaga" (whether due to too many different projects making claims on both people and resources, or to divisiveness within a single project), the possibility of subversive acts of witchery, representing this disordered intersubjective spacetime, may surface in experience.

In V.'s speech, the structure of contradiction is repeatedly epitomized in the expression "two tongued, one false and one true." Gawans explained to me that this was like being of two minds, so that one set of actions contradicts the other. One agrees to do something (true) but then one acts against it (falsification). It also conveys a deception (*katudew*): For example, people pretend everything is all right, but then they go and bwagaw the school teacher, haunting his house at night and threatening him. The phrase "two tongued" was used, in my experience, most often by V. in his antiwitchcraft speeches, but was generally known as a standard image. In it, deceit is formed as an aspect of speech and of the mind. Although the deception is applicable to each person, it also reflects the intersubjective state of the collectivity for it means that one or more people who appeared on the surface to agree to the building of the school behaved falsely, and actually do not agree; thus there is divisiveness within the collectivity.

Another related contradiction was frequently formulated by Gawan preachers in church. But there it typically occurred in parables based on biblical sources about good and bad people or modes of life (for example, two men, or two kariewaga, a good, productive, and generous one, and a bad, lying, or thieving one – the latter, the way of the bwagaw). In these contexts the model of contradiction is formed as a polarity between separate types, one true and one false (e.g., types of person or ways of life). As Burke (1961:23) has pointed out, such "polar terms (with their strong sense of choice)" are "the center of a moralistic ('Dramatistic') vocabulary (the vocabulary of action)."

Similarly, in V.'s school speech, the contradiction is posed rhetorically not only in terms of a division within the subject (being of two minds or two tongued), but also in the polarity of the straight senior men or guyaw and those defined as crooked, the populace or addressees. In this respect, the speech embeds the divided self (which both agrees to build the school and refuses to build the school) in the opposition between the speakers (who provide a unitary, straight speech, and represent, in effect, the truthful agreement to build the school) and the listeners (the two tongued who represent the hidden disagreement, and those who perform acts of witchery – itself the epitome of the divided self). This creates the moral rhetoric of choice and transformative possibility. Defining the self as "divided" and coordinately mapping it into a tensional social field formed by the speech process creates an external other, the senior men or speakers, who attempt to act positively upon this self and reunify its contradictory desires by divesting it of the deceit personified in the witch (i.e., by attempting to create an identification with the truthful other).

In short, the lying felt to be embedded in the kareiwaga to build the school, and in the building activity itself, is iconically mapped into the verbal dialectic of speaking and listening – the immediate action that joins the speaker and the listeners. Moreover, deictic usages referring to public speaking itself also occur in other parts of the speech. For example, a point that is repeated (7, 19) is that the audience says, "thank you" at the end of a speech (the standard response) but that this "thank you" is false; in effect, they are not "listening." Thus the threatened project of building the school is layered directly into the speech project of the meeting in the attempt to transform its negative state.[15]

The particular position of the speaker himself in the current disturbed state of affairs also plays an important part in the speech. V.'s assertion, that his "body is like a stone" (1, 14) conveys not simply his general feeling of shame (*mwasira*) due to the apparent witch attack on the teacher and the problems in building the school, but his specific aggravation because of the fact that he and his dala own the land on which the school is being built, and it was he who agreed that the school be built there. Thus blame for the witch attack could, in theory, be placed on V., (see 3, 6). The assumption here is that the owner of the land is the one who might bwagaw the large building being built on that land by others. If this were the case, V. would appear to have both given the land for the school ("agreed") and to be angrily bewitching the school teacher. In effect, it might seem as if V. himself were "two tongued": Thus he himself embodies the contradiction. Just as V.'s speech exhorts the people to divest themselves of their witchery, so also it involves a denial (*yaakara*) of his own complicity, a distancing of himself from the witch activity, and a suggestion that by *their* acts the people are implicating him and his dala. We shall see that both arguments (exhortation and denial) are intertwined in part of the speech.

Thus a number of dialectical tensions are being formed in the speech. As I have said, the speaker himself, in this instance, embodies the contradiction. This internal tension in turn is encompassed in the contradiction between it and V.'s position as a guyaw speaker, a senior man who establishes a truthful unifying kareiwaga relative to the people who create contradiction. Finally, these contradictions are themselves encompassed in the one that is "fractioning" the entire event: Namely, the building of the large schoolhouse and the coming of the teacher, in connection with which agreements were made by the community as a whole that are now being violated by witch attack and the conflict underlying it. All these contradictions are formulated in the speech, and are "spoken at once" in a transformative mode that attempts to overcome them or negate the negation and create a unity by divesting the community of witchcraft.

Although V. begins and ends his talk in a polarization of senior speakers (identifying himself with the senior men) and audience, he does not, of course, always speak in these polarized terms. For instance, in much of the speech, he also uses the first person plural in its inclusive form to convey "we Gawans" as in the statement (2) "we all want it. Kareiwaga, women, men. What do we want within Gawa?" And at different points (8, 15, 17) he expresses collective shame (*kada-mwasira*, our-inclusive shame). The "amplification" of the plural here brings into play the diffuse, categorical "we" (see Benveniste, 1966:235). In fact, an important rhetorical strategy of V.'s speech involves a focus on the identity of the Gawan community as a whole and a relocation of identity and experience of self onto the community plane.

This process of self-definition involves V. in drawing attention to certain fundamental features of Gawan polity that are condensed in the historical figure of Guyoraba (3, 6 and other passages). The introduction of Guyoraba has a complex significance. On the one hand, it anchors the argument in traditional land claims and transmission: V. does not merely say that he and his dala own the land that he agreed to give for the school, but he validates the claim by reference to the origins of his land (3). On the other hand, Guyoraba is an ancestor whose name is identified with the egalitarian kareiwaga of Gawa as a whole (see Chapter 3).[16] Part of the argument through which the bwagaw is divested of any "right" to anger is built on the nature of this kareiwaga as V. presents it. In the speech, "Guyoraba" forms a dynamic field of connections (a kind of "conceptual tool" or "operator" in Lévi-Strauss's 1966:149 terms) between segmentary land ownership – connected with the particular position of V. in the current situation and with the distribution of Gawan land (see 3, 5) – and the general political kareiwaga adhered to by the community as a whole.

Moreover, it is the kind of political kareiwaga that Guyoraba represents that forms the general presumptive grounds for V.'s assertion that should anyone bwagaw the school, it would be he (i.e., the speaker) who could make the kareiwaga and not anyone else. This point emerges in 5 where the contrast is first drawn between Gawa and the northern Trobriands, whose kareiwaga is represented by the Tabalu, the chiefly dala of Omarakana village (see Malinowski, 1935). The segmentary hamlet autonomy and egalitarianism of Gawa are differentiated from the hierarchic order of the Trobriands by contrasting the kareiwaga of the Tabalu with that of Guyoraba. According to Gawan commentators, the implicit point being made here is that the school hamlet is not the hamlet of the bwagaw, it is not on his or her land; therefore, he has no right (*gera i-bod*, it is not fitting or rightful) under the Gawan kareiwaga of Guyoraba, to go in and angrily claim it as the Tabalu can go into another dala's village and claim a Tabalu emblem, should the latter wrongfully display it. This emblem represents, according to my informants, the hierarchical authority of the Tabalu, and the increment of their power over that of any other dala. Similarly, the leading guyaw of the Tabalu could go into another dala's place and take a pig, for example (6). To draw out the comparison further: The Tabalu may have the right to go into another place that displays some object violating their own superiority (as, for instance, a very large house such as the Gawan schoolhouse), but no Gawan dala has that right.

The contrast is reiterated in 15, where V. points out that the Gawan kareiwaga is "little," for it comprehends only the segmentary hamlet (ou-da-veru-s). According to this view, the right to violate segmentary space characterizes the kareiwaga of the Tabalu but not that of Guyoraba. V. says that on Gawa, however, everyone has his own kareiwaga: "No one's head is above anyone else's" (5). One Gawan commentator bunched all his fingers together at one level to illustrate this phrase in V.'s speech.

In sum, should anyone bwagaw the school, he is behaving as if he were superior to others, and could violate the space of another hamlet, and someone else's land. V. himself, a Gawan guyaw, is subject to and identified with the kareiwaga of Guyoraba and not that of the Tabalu; by implication, then, he would not act in this way. Yet, at the same time, V. is the only person (and his only dala) for whom, according to this kareiwaga, it is "fitting" to bwagaw the school because the land is theirs. Indeed, if he had been angered by the size of the schoolhouse, V. might have told his *gamagali* (women of his dala to whom he gives food) to do so (6). But it was V. who agreed to give the land to the school, and he is deeply shamed by the witchery that makes it look as if he were implicated.

It will be noted that just as in the previous examples of speeches, where we have the movement to a wider inter-island order in the process of constructing redefinitions of the Gawan self, here as well such a move is made to establish collective identity by contrast with the Trobriands. (Similarly, a brief comparison is drawn with the Japanese who are depicted as being like Gawans rather than Trobrianders – see explanatory note c – and whose introduction brings in the modern external order of the post–World War II era.)[17] The figure of Guyoraba operates as a conduit along which the argument moves from the segmentary individual self to the Gawan collective identity or self defined by reference to the external, inter-island other: Ego's identity as a Gawan is defined with reference to the kinds of rights she or he has relative to other individuals and dala, and this pattern is applied to Gawa as a community in contrast to another island community as the speech shifts to a form of "we–they dialogue" (see Singer, 1984:92). Furthermore, the term *Guyoraba* names the political mode-of-being applicable to all Gawans and in terms of which each Gawan may describe his or her own identity. Through this process the person may experience him- or herself as part of a totality that is not just Gawa, but Gawa as a component of an encompassing inter-island order.

It is apparent that Guyoraba is not simply a spatial conduit, but also a temporal, historical one. Like any such originating figure, he both draws the contemporary situation and ordering of Gawan space back into the past (defined by V. as the indigenous past since, according to the speech, Guyoraba "came out" on Gawa) and forward from the past into the present. In 3, for instance, Guyoraba is the conduit that shifts the listener from the contemporary project of "this [newly introduced] schoolhouse" into the indigenous "leliyu" of the Gawan past, and then back again in terms of the reference to land distribution and segmentation to the immediate problem of the community.

Thus Guyoraba serves as a key means used by V. to relocate experience in terms of the spatiotemporal unity of Gawa. Interestingly, it is precisely an emphasis on the fractioning, segmentary character of Gawa, and the autonomy of the self that this entails, that becomes the means of drawing the *unified* identity of Gawa into experience: Guyoraba represents the structure of this autonomous equality *as the structure of the whole*. It is because *each* hamlet, dala, and person is relatively autonomous and equal that the witch does not have the right to assert his or her personal autonomy and violate the autonomy of others, for in doing so he or she acts as if superordinate (see Chapter 9). The witch has to be brought back, as it were, into an intersubjective world where, to put it in Rousseau's terms, the "particular will" is subordinated to the "general will," and hence the constraints of the other operate upon the self.

Guyoraba is not the only reference V. makes to Gawan history. The initial comments on the leliyu of Guyoraba (3) lead into another historical reference (4) where he comments on the building of the Gawan church some years previously, which he relates to the building of the school. Both buildings represent different Dimdim (white man) kareiwaga, and until the school construction, the Gawan community church was the largest building on Gawa. V. defines this earlier event in a way that draws a parallel between the deceit and apparent witchery involved in the building of the school and similar problems in the building of the church (see also 15).[18] In the past, Gawans themselves asked for missionaries to come to Gawa, just as currently they had asked for the school teacher, but when they attempted to raise up (-*rupa*) the church, the people (according to this account) bewitched the missionaries and they died.

V.'s point is that the same double-dealing characterized the building of the church as in the current building of the school. Thus history is perceived as repeating itself, and the loss experienced in relation to the church could happen again in the current context of the school. Indeed, later in the talk (12) V. points out that the school teacher might leave Gawa and go elsewhere, a possibility that had been voiced by the school teacher himself. (We have seen departures connected with witch fears and their implication of value loss in the case of G., the ill garden specialist, discussed earlier; the school teacher's threat of departure falls into this pattern.) In short, the present and past could both constitute the same negative kind of intersubjective spacetime in which the hoped for potentials entailed in the action cannot be realized because of the lack of true agreement, the hidden anger it implies with respect to the large building, and accordingly, the emergence of the principle governing this spacetime that is embodied in witchery.

The nature of this loss has to be understood in terms of what Gawans at that time hoped would be the productive value generated by the school (see 10). Gawans were concerned at this time that their children learn to read, write, and speak English; later they could help Gawans deal with English speakers coming to the island, and some could go to high school in Alotau, the mainland capital of the Milne Bay province; obtaining jobs in the nonindigenous economy, they could then send money and trade goods back to Gawa. The contradiction at the heart of the Gawan production effort would thus deprive Gawans of the potentialities embedded in this kareiwaga.

Although it is not possible to discuss the historical issues more fully here, it will be noted that this concern formulates, in terms of the cash economy and the wider, nationalized social context of Papua New Guinea, basic modes of Gawan value transformation discussed earlier. Gawan work would produce the school within Gawa that contains the new level of potency and potentialities that (via the learning of the children) could generate a long-term connective process between Gawans and the wider Papua New Guinea world and white people with whom the flow of trade goods and cash is identified. English, and the education it entailed, was conceived of as particularly important in providing the medium of influence necessary for tapping into that world and bringing its externally derived resources into Gawa. The Gawan school building thus contained potentials for spatiotemporal extension of Gawan control in the wider world beyond the islands or with persons who came from that world and mediated its resources.

Furthermore, in keeping with the basic value process, V. emphasizes that the school building itself redounds to Gawan fame. In this context (14, 15), V. stresses that Gawa as a community consented to give the land and build the school ("we ourselves consented, our kareiwaga"). In the passage (14), "no one should say ... [that it is] his house, for [the school teacher] himself. We ourselves, our name, our fame! So [other people] will see our fine work ...," he emphasizes that the building does not belong to one individual, the school teacher, to the exclusion of everyone else, but to *all* Gawans. Coordinately, he introduces the witness, the outside other, who confers positive value on the collectivity for its group effort, the schoolhouse, which is itself an aspect of the community. Since the school belongs to *all* Gawans and does not superordinate any single individual, the witch not only has no basis for his or her jealousy, but the assertion of autonomous self-interest represented by the witch actually negates self-interest by destroying the value that is returned to all Gawans through the school. The rhetoric attempts to transpose self-reference to a more inclusive collective frame in terms of which the bwagaw experiences his or her actions as harming him or herself (i.e., *as a Gawan*) rather than simply as harming others.

The direction of subjective movement is thus again outward from the less to the more encompassing intersubjective order of Gawa and the wider island world represented by a value-bestowing external other. In the present case, these others were, most immediately, not only other islanders (whom Gawans hoped to impress) but also school officials and teachers from other schools in the region who were expected at a feast for the conclusion of the school construction. Thus Gawan work was supposed to be seen and admired as well by those outsiders who represented the wider Papua New Guinea world.

But, by the same token, the other may bestow upon Gawa the identity of thief or witch. V. continues (16): "Only one of the sailors of a canoe steals. He gives our [whole] canoe the name 'thief.'" As my Gawan commentator pointed out, this analogy suggests that people will say all Gawans bwagaw, not simply one Gawan. Emphasizing the shame (*mwasira*) associated with this negative characterization, V. develops the canoe imagery further (17) by pointing out that Gawans encountering travelers from other islands on the sea are then shamed by being known for witchery: "You eat canoes on the sea, whatever things we people make [on land, in the hamlets] you 'do in.'" Instead of the fame of Gawa climbing, it declines or disappears: All productive potentiality is "done in" and Gawans are ashamed in front of others. When Gawans behave like this, their leliyu becomes that of witchcraft, a negative version of Gawan tradition that V. counters just below with the assertion: "I said our leliyu is Guyoraba." This latter remark draws attention again to the lack of justification in Gawan polity for the overweening power being asserted by the aggrandizement of witches.

In this witchcraft, therefore, we see again that the positive value entailed in spatiotemporal circulation of one's name is subverted: Instead of constituting a positive transformation of self, this circulation degrades and produces shame.[19] The people become known as witches – they get a bad name. On the other hand, the fine schoolhouse – the product of Gawan collective work, which they themselves have "raised"[20] – creates renown (the climbing of one's name) as an aspect of the self rather than the stone-like heaviness of shame in front of others that results from the value-consuming actions of witch attack. Thus Gawa "recognizes" itself through its appearance to the other (see Sartre, 1966:302).

This concern with the relation between witchcraft and loss of fame is not confined to this particular speech. I shall digress briefly here to exemplify other rhetorical forms in which this concern was conveyed in speeches at the finale of the Drum dance in 1975 when the 1974 period of illnesses and a number of deaths were still very much on people's minds.

At the finale of the drum entertainment, Gawans were told by one speaker that Kweawatans (who, it may be recalled, are in competition with the Gawans for Kula shells) had told some Muyuw men that the latter should not give Gawans any armshells because Gawans were having a "witch *kayasa* (entertainment)." This comment refers to the notion that witches dance in the bush when Gawans are having mortuary ceremonies in the hamlets (see Chapter 8). The supposed Kweawatan insult meant that the Gawans would not be engaging in kula because they were preoccupied with mortuary rites instead. According to the speaker, Gawa's witchery had been "noised abroad" to many islands. Some of the talks expressed concern about what was felt to be the small number of visitors from other islands at the finale.

One senior man referred to a leliyu involving the origin of different dala from a single hole (*Kabat*) on Muyuw. Frightened by a snake at this place, each group fled, setting sail to various islands, although, as the speaker explained to me later, they had originated from a single hole. In the same way, he explained, visitors coming to Gawa would leave the place immediately because of fears of being bewitched – dispersing, presumably, back to their widely distributed home islands. The capacity of Gawa to draw together peoples from different islands (and so enhance the fame of Gawa) would be destroyed by witchery. Similarly, some Gawans told me after the talks that this evil reputation would make visitors frightened to come and visit Gawa for kula. Here again, the reputation of witchery is shown as yielding a subverted inter-island spacetime, one in which the spatiotemporal expansion of motion entails a dissolution and dispersal rather than a construction of connectivities and potentiality for further positive value. Such visitors, instead of taking back with them the fame of Gawa (see Chapter 3) would "noise abroad" its endangering state.

Still another speaker pointed out that continued witch attacks would empty the island of people: "The fame of Gawa is not like this (*gera makaawara butu-ra Gaw*'); the fame of Gawa Ooo! [spreads oh so far]." But should the attacks continue, the elders would all die, and then only the young men would be left to kareiwaga. Gawa is then without protection against other islanders who could kill them.[21] The expression used here is *ge'sam vatu* (without a rock). A vatu is a coral rock in the sea where fish hide to escape predators. The vatu of Gawa is the senior men who turn away fighting and whose straight kareiwaga and strength protect Gawa. If the Gawans have no vatu, then the Kweawatans, for instance, who traditionally were meek in comparison with Gawans, would not listen to the Gawans, If, furthermore, all the men died, no visitors would come to Gawa, there would be no "happiness" (i.e., collective entertainments and kula feasts) because, as an informant later explained, men kareiwaga all these things; Gawans would then be weak. As a northern Muyuwan visitor at the Drum dance said: "If you Gawan women bewitch the men until they are finished and there are none left, what will you do? The speaker went on to point out that the northern Muyuw communities, for example, do not kareiwaga the Drum dance, but their kareiwaga is instead, the sagali soy memorial rites (see Chapter 8); Gawans alone speak for the Drum dance (i.e., if Gawans are not able to perform it, it will lapse).

These comments illustrate the way in which the negative reputation of witchcraft makes it impossible to gather visitors within Gawa; Gawans cannot then display the generosity and distribute the gifts with which the former take back the fame of Gawa overseas (see Chapter 3). Instead, the speakers say, visitors disperse in fear.

The essential capacity for creating fame is embedded in the influential senior men (and, more generally, in the adult men) with their capacity to organize such community ventures as the Drum dance where visitors from other islands congregate; it is the strength of such men that protects Gawa, ensuring viable inter-island relationships, for other islanders will "listen" to these men. The rhetoric of the speeches warns Gawans of the loss of these generative capacities: Without famous men, Gawa will be perceived as vulnerable by other islanders who are the very ones whose favorable attitudes bestow positive value on them. The Muyuwan visitor's warning is itself an outsider evaluation that points to the Drum dance as a Gawan specialty that cannot be run by the other islanders, and for which Gawa is favorably known abroad. The witch who destroys Gawa from within is seen not only as destroying the people themselves, but in particular the essential strength or influence (embodied in senior men) that enables Gawa to maintain itself as a community, and to recognize itself as having worth, through the positive evaluations of outsiders who come to enjoy the island's hospitality as its admiring visitors.

THE CONFLICT BETWEEN THE WORK GROUPS

Let us return now to V.'s speech at the school to consider the relation between the witch's subversion of the kareiwaga to build the school that V. defines in terms of the model of self-divisiveness discussed above, and divisive conflict within the community that developed in the process of building the school. The alleged witch attack on the school teacher emerged in the context of a conflict that involved the organization of the work groups; the length of time it was taking to build the school; and the ongoing pattern of the work that kept people[22] from their gardens and other subsistence activities (raising anxiety about the food situation), as well as from canoe building and kula sailing.

The size of the schoolhouse raised problems for Gawans not simply because (as in the thrust of V.'s speech) it could become a source of a witch's jealousy, but also because it was requiring an exceptional amount of community work. V.'s rhetorical offer (9; 17, para. 2) to build a house of similar size for anyone who wishes (since, as he emphasized, it is really not hard work at all!), must be seen in the light of this second difficulty as well as the first. In fact, the school's size was viewed as the cause of very heavy (*mwaw*) work and had been requiring community-wide, collective labor on a more or less daily basis for several weeks. This kind of operation cut into the more typical family or individual-based and varied daily organization of Gawan work (see Chapter 2) in which community-wide group labor is an occasional, or at the most a weekly rather than a daily concern.[23] Furthermore, the newly arrived teacher, who expected the type of organization of labor-time closer to that involved in a cash economy, rather than the "irregular work-rhythms" (Thompson, 1967:75) of the Gawan economy, was pressing for faster work in order to finish the school.

But Gawans regard anger over excessively heavy work, like that over a perceived inequality, as a possible source of witchery. The large schoolhouse could thus become the focus of different kinds of disturbed feelings: anger at the heavy, long-term work, as well as jealousy over the size of the schoolhouse. In each case, something excessive is involved – in the one case, an excessive external demand upon individual effort that may be felt to intrude upon a person's own work plans or kareiwaga; on the other, an excess over what any other individual possesses. The schoolhouse objectifies these different excesses, each of which violates the egalitarian autonomy of the self. The witch persona, in turn, personifies this anger, representing the self in its aggressive state.

Moreover, a specific argument emerged that crystallized the underlying diffuse disturbance posed by this situation. The division between the work groups to which V. alludes in his speech (11) involved the decision to split the work on the roofing so that one grouping of neighborhoods would work on one part of the roof and one on another part. This decision derived from a quarrel between workers from the different Gawan neighborhoods. The latter (or sometimes a set of contiguous neighborhoods) frequently form separate subgroupings of workers on a community project and constitute "fault lines" of potential cleavage and conflict.[24]

This quarrel concerned decisions about the work job to be accomplished on a given day, and the view that one group of two contiguous neighborhoods was not working as hard as the other three. It was said that members of the delinquent neighborhood group (which I shall call group *A*) were going hunting for flying fox, or fishing, or doing other jobs when they were supposed to be working for the school. Group *A* wanted to climb for coconuts (for refreshment during the work) one day, while the other neighborhoods (which I shall call group *B*) wanted to gather and prepare materials for the roofing instead.[25] Since the two groups couldn't agree, each then went its own way. As a result, group *B* finished preparation for thatching before group *A*. When the former wanted to arrange the

Plate 16. Men work on the thatching of the schoolhouse. The coconuts in the foreground have been collected for midday refreshment.

thatching for the next day, the latter said (as one of my narrators put it): "Good, you thatch; tommorow we [i.e., group *A*] will go to gather thatching materials, and we will thatch on Friday." The result was that the spatial (for example, cooperation of the different neighborhoods, working on the same job for the house, etc.) and temporal (same day) coordination of work jobs was skewed. Thus we could say in the Gawan idiom that "the place was made crooked" (*i-ya-dadogu veru*).

We have seen in other contexts that the "synchronization" (using the term to cover spatial coordination as well) of collective activity constitutes the processual form of agreeing or consensus, and its converse, in the case of a group project, is the form of a disagreement that can cause the breakdown of the project altogether.[26] It should be kept in mind that the work activity is not simply the "sign" of an agreement or disagreement, but also entails (as, of course, any action in which people engage) the experience of these intersubjective processes. An individual must agree to do this work, so his or her spatiotemporal coordination with others in work is a positive intersubjective process in which the self of the actor is being formed as one who listens and agrees. Conversely, the lack of agreement constitutes the actor in the relatively autonomous state of rejection, or disagreement with others, and the project in a state of divisiveness or fragmentation.

The progressive schismogenic process in the building of the schoolhouse came to be mapped into the house structure itself through the decision made by one of the senior men of group *B* who felt that group A men were

not working hard enough; annoyed by their apparent laxity, he decided that each group should work on different sides of the house. I was told that another man (of *A*) who keenly supported the school, later went and saw some group *A* men working for the church (on the day usually devoted to that work) instead of the school, and said to them angrily, that now they had "divided the work" (*i-katuvi-sa wotet*).

The spatial organization of work directly on the house frame now reflected the schismogenesis in the work groups. Although a single day was finally arranged for the thatching (largely, it seems, through the intervention of other senior men),[27] each group worked on a single end of the roof. The house, at this point, took on the divisiveness of its creators. These disagreements extended to the decision of the school committee (which did not comprise the senior men, but consisted of younger married men in the community)[28] to have a feast (*paka*) at the close of the thatching because of the heaviness of the work. Group A, however, refused to fish for the thatching feast on the day wanted by Group B, in retaliation I was told, for the refusal of the latter to climb for coconuts when group-*A* wanted to do so.

Without going fully into the complexities of this affair, I shall merely say that, although no feast was held at the end of the thatching, it was arranged (initially at the suggestion of V., see 18, para. 2 in the speech) that a special feast of taro pudding be held about a week after the thatching when the walls of the school had been finished.

In the meantime, the affair had developed in another related direction: The teacher had been frightened at night by strange sounds around his house, and by what he told me was a stick coming up through the slats in the floor. It was these events that were interpreted by the people, and by the teacher as well,[29] as signs that he was being threatened by witches. Now the wider disturbance became crystallized in this threat. The meeting from which V.'s speech is drawn was held on the afternoon of the day on which the siding for the schoolhouse had been put up. The taro pudding feast, to the scheduling of which he refers in the speech (18, para. 2), was held the next day. The aim of this feast was to stop the witch attack and the anger that underlay it; and so to create a coherent work group out of the divided one. As one important older woman put it after the food had been distributed: "Let's go. The witchery is finished. No longer are there to be two work groups (*koy bod*)."

If the taro cooking was aimed at healing schism – at creating consensus out of disagreement – the nature of this healing process has to be considered in terms of the processes engaged by such feasts. Each hamlet or family contributes: In this case, either a pot of taro pudding, or a sweet potato pudding, or baskets of cooked vegetables were appropriate. As in the building project itself, the feast constructs the self in a particular form of social being. The divisiveness pertaining to the communal work project is to be reversed through procedures that are by now familiar (Chapters 3 and 8): Each hamlet or family makes a contribution of food; a unifying collection is made and redistributed so that people both give and eat, but they do not eat their own food.

In the ideal feast, Gawans attempt to arrange the food distribution so that with some adjustments, everyone shares more or less equally. It is important, as we have seen (Chapters 8 and 9), that no one complain (-sugwa) of inadequate food, for this in itself suggests the possibility of potential witch attack. In the present case Gawans felt that certain inadequacies in what was available made the distribution less than ideal. Moreover, without the social conflict, this particular feast would not have been held. Rather, there would have been a single major feast at the grand finale of the school building when (as it was believed at the time) school officials, teachers from other islands, and other visitors would come to Gawa to celebrate the formal opening of the school. (In fact, this second feast never took place, although the school itself, a beautiful building, was finished to everyone's satisfaction.) Therefore, at the present intermediary feast, a number of speakers pointed to the fact that it was being held at the wrong time because of the recalcitrant witchery in the community. The appropriate feast, they pointed out, would have been supplied in part with Dimdim food (rice, flour, and so forth). By implication, the current feast was a draining one, taxing already strained food resources,[30] yet not redounding to the fame of Gawa.

Thus the wages of witchcraft are shown by the speakers to be loss, for the very attempt to transform the disordering process that was imperiling the project, itself contains a destructive component. The time and space are still, in effect, slightly out of joint: The feast is being held at the wrong time, for the visitors from other places have not congregated on Gawa yet (as they would, it was presumed, at the later time).

In sum, we have seen that in building the school problems emerged that were crystallized as forms of disagreement. The underlying potential for a loss of consensus emerged in the perception of the work as heavy: The house was very large, and it was taking too long. This was translated into the view that people weren't working hard enough. As one man said to me, the people "agreed" to the building of the school, but now they won't work for it. This diffuse spatiotemporal disorder was crystallized in the argument about timing: One group was perceived as taking longer than the other, and as not working hard enough. This mapped the slowness onto one segment of the community, creating a divisive polarity. The affair then moved to the point where it was brought under the notion of bwagaw.

It is at this stage that V.'s school speech stresses disagreement as a contradiction of intention in which the bwagaw is the negation of a positive agreement to build the school – that is, *the witch defines the locus of refusal.* Argumentation has been shifted to a public discourse about the self and its intentions, and, coordinately, about the lack of consensus, or the experience of disagreement. The witch provides a "language" for talking about particular disagreements in which particular people are implicated at a level at which no one in particular is publicly implicated. V. stresses, rather, that it is "we Gawans" who are doing this, and whose minds are divided. Everyone (and no one) is implicated.[31] The positive transformation of value-negating conflict and serious disturbance thus entails a movement to a level of discourse where particularities can be released and talked about through a bwagaw who, not being publicly fixed to any individual identity (at the most, as has been indicated, a broad category of persons may be publicly implicated), is therefore the responsibility of "all of us." This paradox is as central to the transformational process as is accusation or confession in a system that works through particularization.

This creation of public responsibility as a community is part of the process of attempting to create agreement out of disagreement: an agreement between the intentions of the mind so that they no longer contradict each other, and between persons so that they no longer disagree with each other. If this process is successful, a unified intersubjective spacetime is created that is visibly constituted in the coordinated work process that brings together workers from the island as a whole, and is embodied in the house that is the product of the work. This house like a self-decoration to be admired by other islanders and it was hoped, by government and similar visitors, contains a new level of Gawan potentiality for further positive value transformations: the education of Gawan children that would extend Gawan ability to tap into the external cash economy and the encompassing westernized world beyond the island and the immediate inter-island world, bringing back into Gawa the external returns from their work.

THE GENDER DESIGNATION OF THE WITCH

If listening or agreeing to persuasion can be understood as representing the willingness of the individual to coordinate his or her own interests with those of another – in this sense, to *limit* the operation of his or her own will or individual kareiwaga – it can be suggested that the *autonomy* of the will is epitomized by the power of refusal (*-pek*). From this perspective, withholding consent is the epitome of the socially unlimited, unregenerate will.

It is significant that in referring to the didactic speeches of the senior men, Gawans say that witches are "tight" (*kasay*), for it is difficult to get them to "agree" to stop their witchery. V., for instance, asks how many years they have had to speak against witchery (18); but witches are "tight" (19) and after the men speak, people simply lie, saying "thank you," while continuing in their wrongdoing. In their exhortations, speakers attempt to control this "willfulness" through persuasion. Successful persuasion is a process in which the speakers' *own* wills as guyaw "taking care of" the people, and thus as community representatives, are superordinated to those of the witch's; by creating consent, they reform the recalcitrant will, encompassing it within the regulation of the wider community (cf. M. Strathern, 1981b:183).

This perspective helps us to throw light on the role of women as the social type of the witch in Gawan concepts of witchery. As I have pointed out, women rarely give public speeches in the meetings, although they may speak up briefly on occasion. The occasions on which women do speak up are frequently those requiring the denial of an implied witch charge against women. Male speakers, on the other hand, may sometimes directly address their exhortations to women since the latter are the primary social category linked on a general basis with acts of witchcraft. We have seen an example of this in the January 1974 meetings where the witch canoe became a theme in men's speeches, and in the Drum dance warnings to women not to bewitch the senior men. To the extent that women become the focus of speakers' warnings, it is women who then represent the willfulness of the people (the autonomous will of *each individual, male or female*) in the transaction between speakers and audience.

Why it should be women who tend to function as the typical representative category may now perhaps be clear. We have seen in earlier chapters that women as a category are not only in certain respects the type of consumer as against donor, but they also typify the consensual role of refusing or accepting, and as such may be considered tight. In contrast, men typify those who initiate requests, make decisions, and construct collective projects.[32]

This complementary stereotyping of political roles is also related to the emphasis Gawans put on the complementarity of women in important masculine activities carried on apart from women, especially collective male projects. For example, women may be asked to give their consent when men go on a major hunt for wild pigs. When men planned a wild pig hunt for the projected final feast of the school building, women were exhorted not to engage in witchcraft that would enable the pig to escape. Three senior women spoke at the end of the meeting telling the women not to engage in trickery (*katudew*) and hide (-*katubwein*) the pig. As one man told me, if the bwagaw consents, then men will catch a pig, but if not, then they are likely to fail.

Similarly, in 1980 when men diving for shells for commercial sale failed to find them in sufficient quantity, one of the senior women at the work feast held at the end of the fishing day denied the women's complicity in this failure, saying that since women also ate food at the feast, why should they keep men from finding these shells?

A similar separation of men and women occurs when men go on a major kula venture. The women's role back on Gawa then ideally includes their agreement not to bewitch men on the sea. To ensure that women enjoy themselves in equal measure as do men on the kula trip, the latter may decide to arrange that women run their own exchange entertainment (*bisila*) before the men depart; in addition, they make available to the women the resources of the island for the latters' enjoyment in group activities when the men are away.[33]

In activities where men are concerned in this way that women's agreement be obtained, they are operating collectively quite apart from women, in areas of space outside the hamlets and the gardens, or beyond Gawa itself; but the success of their projects is linked in part to the action of the women (the latter's consent, in effect, to the men's kareiwaga and its enactment in a particular project). The interior space relative to male activity is the domain of this positive feminine participation, a feature that is part of the wider complex of associations I have discussed linking women to relatively interior domains of island space.

Since women typify the power to give and withhold agreement, they can come to stand for what lies outside *any* person's direct control, namely, the consent of *another* person to do one's bidding. For although the person who desires to obtain consent can attempt to persuade another, ultimately, the latter's agreement depends on his or her *own* kareiwaga or decision-making powers; in this respect, it is ineluctably *outside* the control of the would-be persuader. It is the will of the other, over which ultimate control is always external to the self of any individual, that appears to be hypostatized in the power of refusal or consent. This experience of the other, I suggest, conveys the autonomy of the will and the autonomy of each person relative to the other, *via* the experience of the other's autonomy relative to the self.

This point may help to explain why women, who are associated with stability rather than motion and with relatively interior spatial domains and intra-island resources, should be identified with the inter-island mobility and radically extended spatiotemporal control of witches. Obviously it begs the question to say merely that the identification reverses their ordinary spatiotemporal capacities, or typical associations. Indeed, as I have suggested in Chapter 6, reversal may be a rhetorical formulation that marks a shift to explicitness of a state that lies implicit in a more basic or unmarked context. In this sense, reversal need not be a reversal. A similar explanation may be suggested here.

I have argued that the dominion of the will is embodied in the radical autonomy of the witch. To the extent that women come to typify this mode of control – the ineluctable power of the individual will – they are icons of the essential power of the autonomous individual as such, which is personified in the spatiotemporal dominion of the bwagaw.

It is important to keep in mind here, however, the wider picture of the Gawan paradigm of responsibility for witchcraft. It will be recalled that this paradigm specifies that men are the motive force behind a woman's witch attack since they kareiwaga the acts of the female witch. This concept is referred to by V. when he says (6) that it is he who would have the right to tell the women of his dala to perform witchcraft against the school, since his dala owns the land. The assumption of male responsibility is not always treated as relevant nor is it made explicit in every case, but sometimes people may be reminded of it as a fundamental part of Gawan assumptions. For instance, in one meeting a speaker said: "We tell and tell the women [not to bwagaw]. ... You think the women do it. No. These women don't have the kareiwaga. ... It is we [men] who kareiwaga." Here, as in the comment by V. in his school speech, the reference was explicitly to the *gamagali* of a man, by which was meant women of the man's dala to whom he gives food.

This view requires some further examination. The notion is that a man gives a woman of his dala special gifts of food so that she will perform the desired witchery. The direction of food gifts parallels that of ordinary buwaa or related food gifts to a kinswoman (but here made for perverse, destructive purposes). The concept locates responsibility for witchcraft at the dala level, rather than simply at the level of the individual. But relative to the social whole, the individual and the dala have a certain parallelism, since each represents the focus of the demand for equality and is a center of autonomy, a domain of possible recalcitrance refusing to be regulated by an outsider in its demand for equality, or by the more comprehensive community of which it is a part. Furthermore, the notion of the witch's body as an interior bodily component (sometimes, as we have seen, thought of as the matrilineal balouma) operating apart from the external, surface aspect of the person, is an apt model in bodily terms of both the individual and the dala as autonomous isolates detached from their external nexus of relations.

We should not, however, emphasize the dala implications of this concept for locating witch responsibility apart from its more general gender implications. According to this paradigm, both men and women operate as a complementary whole in witchcraft, the man performing in the typical male political role as the one who makes the kareiwaga and provides the persuasive food payment; the woman as the one who listens and agrees to carry out the decision. Between them they represent the two aspects of the will of *any* actor (decision making and consent or in indigenous terms, *kareiwaga* and *tagwara*), and of the polity as a whole (as female consenter and male decision maker), as well as of the dala unit.

Thus the speaker in the last example was drawing attention not so much to dala responsibility for witchery as he was to the responsibility of men as a gender category who tell women to bwagaw. In this sense, both men and women are responsible, not simply one representative category of Gawans alone. Although women may represent the recalcitrance of the individual will conveyed in witchery, Gawans may "penetrate" (see Willis, 1977: 119ff.) under this surface representation to a view that lays bare a deeper, felt truth that men and women are *equally* to blame – that blame cannot be laid on one general subcategory as against another. For at the base of the activity is the nature of the individual will that is felt to characterize all Gawans, men and women alike.

CONSENSUS AND TRANSFORMATION

Following the arguments set out in the previous sections, we can see that in an effort to make the witch desist, speakers must attempt to create a new transformational level of spatiotemporal order consisting of a community consensus, a unity of wills unmarred by the hidden refusal of one or more individuals who put themselves above all others.

The importance of obtaining consensus is stressed by Gawans in connection with all significant group activities including canoe building, the entertainments, and other collective work. Of those I have discussed, a paradigmatic example is that of group sailing. I have already commented on the importance Gawans give to the principle that canoes should sail at the same time on major kula ventures, especially when an uvelaku competition is involved. On such ventures, the fleet should sail together, for this spatial coherence and synchronization is the visible sign of a consensus regarding the organization of the project. If they do not do so, any serious difficulties on the trip may be attributed to lack of agreement or ascribed to witchery.

On the one hand, major collective activities should not be performed without a sense of common agreement; on the other hand, the successful carrying out of the activity is itself a consensual process and a sign of agreement to perform the activity. In such activities one is continually involved in a coordination of wills. But when there is disagreement, this coordination has broken down. If there is serious illness or any threat of real injury to someone in the community during such activity, this disturbance may then be taken as a sign of anger and disagreement.

Group or community consensus constitutes an intersubjective spacetime that is the reverse of the witch's destructive bodily incorporation of the other. Rather than forming the radical superordination and dominion of one actor over another, it creates a likeness of intention, or in Durkheim's (1947) terms, a "mechanical unity," in which each person and dala maintains an independent kareiwaga and position of equality.

This consensual reform of intersubjective relations also implies the formation of unity *within* the person. We have seen that in different ways the domination of the witch encodes a division in the self as well as in the community. This division is conveyed in such notions of contradictory intention or deceit as that expressed in the idea of two tongues, (a lack of likeness between the overt and covert attitudes of the person, or a contradiction between two attitudes). But divisiveness of this kind is also figured in the images of the witch's body, since it is the fragmentation of ordinary bodily being (a separation of inner and outer, visible components) that makes possible the emergence of the radical expansion of spatiotemporal control and dominion of the aggressive, autonomous witch. This fracturing of connectivities within the person as witch constitutes the body in deceitful form (Chapter 9), and in turn appears to model in bodily terms (or to contain the bodily qualisigns of) the intersubjective relations between persons that characterize the community's experience of itself when witches are felt to be active: namely a state of deceit, dissolution, and dominion by the recalcitrant angry demands and aggressive will of one or more of its members. In short, fragmentation in the nexus of intersubjective relations and fragmentation of the person in deceitful contradictory actions (or modes of being) mutually imply each other. Similarly, the creation of collective "oneness" uniting persons in agreement is also a oneness of mind uniting the intentions of the individual so that the visible social surface or apparent intention of the person and the interior intention are at one with each other.

Posed against the destructive hierarchization of the witch, whose dominion is characterized by a fracturing of relations, is the hierarchic type represented by the guyaw leader. The latter's potency should construct social relations of agreement or unity and truth (instead of deceit). As guyaw, or elder statesman, a man ideally operates through persuasion rather than aggressive destruction of the body of the other, attempting to overcome the hidden aggression of any individual – more fundamentally, the aggressive domination of the autonomous will – and divest the community, for the time being at least, of this destructive dominion. The guyaw represents that kind of hierarchical mediator through whom a model of egalitarian governance may be created in experience in the epitomizing form of a consensual agreement (which I take here to include "agreement" within the individual's self). If consensus is not that reduction of "all wills into one will" of which Hobbes speaks, it would appear to be its equivalent in an egalitarian, acephalous society where the individual will remains irreducible and cannot be concentrated in any singular power. The consensual model of order constitutes the essential paradigm of egalitarian governance where, as Colson (1974:93) has put it: "The reform of all is demanded, since the burden of order is assumed to rest on all."

The transformation to be achieved in meetings thus involves the construction of an intersubjective spacetime that incorporates the will of the witch in changed form as an agreement to stop bewitching others. In contrast with the fragmented spacetime of disagreement that lacks positive value potentials, this consensual order contains potentials for the acquisition of desired value products through collective projects, and hence for the generation of positive value transformations.

Of course, the success of the transformative effort is by no means assured. Success is signified, however, by the lack of any witch-caused deaths or illnesses, misfortunes or disagreements (which could entail violence or potential violence) overtaking a current project – that is, by the community's ability to maintain the health and bodily vitality of its members that Gawans typify as "lightweightness" or "buoyancy" and that is epitomized, for instance, in the dance entertainment. But the witch could refuse; the disturbances or illness then continue, or death overtakes a victim, thus leading to the mortuary rites in which the heavy bodily qualities of sorrow mark the state of the community. Other projects that contribute to the fame of Gawa may then have to be put aside, and hoped-for positive value temporarily lost.

Conclusion

In this study I have explored certain symbolic processes of value transformation and their generative structures in Gawan society. My concern has been not only with particular issues of analysis, but also with general problems of anthropological discourse that are more or less implicit in the argument. By way of conclusion, I should like to point briefly to some of these general concerns, while also remarking on certain more specific strands of the argument. I do not attempt, however, to draw together many of the particular points developed in the course of the book.

One result of the present approach has been that certain anthropological topics have been reformulated in terms of a model of value transformation. Exchange structures and witchcraft, for example, are topics that anthropologists usually deal with as separate categories designating self-evident domains of the social world.[1] Such categories artificially segment interrelations internal to the social process, and the social process itself then takes on, in the anthropological models, the form imposed by these segmentations. The approach advanced in this book, on the other hand, attempts to avoid this kind of segmentation by developing a model of a more general transformative process entailed in different sociocultural practices or actions, of which transmitting or exchanging and bewitching may be instances, in a given case. Acts of "exchange" and "witchcraft" (and the characteristic structuring of the relevant practices) are then related within the terms of the model as parts of a unitary dialectical symbolism of self and societal construction.

My treatment of kula exchange exemplifies this formulation. Classical anthropological approaches have tended to see kula as an exchange or trading system sealed off from other exchanges (e.g., as a "ceremonial" exchange set apart from or only functionally connected with "utilitarian" exchanges; see Fortune, 1963:206–7; Malinowski, 1922; Uberoi, 1971:148). Recent studies (e.g., Damon, 1978; Macintyre, 1983; Munn, 1977; Weiner, 1983) have developed more process-oriented, unifying frameworks that take kula to be integral to wider exchange cycles, and this approach has been related to a trend toward symbolic and temporally oriented approaches to exchange (e.g., Barraud, Coppet, et al., 1979; Iteanu, 1983; Schwimmer, 1973; Weiner, 1978, 1980). However, the present study, rather than approaching kula specifically as a problem in exchange, attempts to relocate it (and other exchanges) within a more inclusive model of practice. Thus I have viewed Gawan kula as a process of constructing an intersubjective spacetime, one that engages a particular (spatiotemporal) value level, and is part of a wider symbolism of Gawan value transformations entailed in different kinds of acts and practices (yielding both positive and negative value in Gawan terms). This level of redefinition shifts the framework of our understanding so that such apparently diverse practices as witch attack and its control and kula may be brought into relation with each other as components of a single symbolic system.

As in any theoretical framework, certain premises underlie the choice of analytic concepts. I have already pointed to my assumption that symbolic process should be conceptualized in terms that, rather than ignoring its existential form, attempt to take account of this form in the model. For instance, since the basic form of social (or sociocultural) being is intrinsically spatiotemporal, it follows that spacetime should not be abstracted from the analytical concept of the sociocultural: That is, some attempt to conceptualize the latter *as spatiotemporal* must appear in our analytical models (cf. Bourdieu, 1977). My notion of intersubjective spacetime was developed for this purpose. For instance, certain problems that might otherwise relate to aspects of social structure in the more usual anthropological framework (e.g., the structures of marriage exchanges or kula, certain features of matri- and patri-kin relationships, etc.) are recast here in terms of intersubjective spacetime.

This emphasis on taking account of the existential form of sociocultural phenomena in anthropological models is clearly essential, as well, to my view of symbolic anthropology. In general, symbolic anthropology is predicated upon the importance of examining the distinctive meaning relations internal to a given sociocultural order. However, analyses that assume these relations form systems of concepts (sometimes contrasted with "action" in such well-entrenched dualisms as "belief and action") deprive the approach of part of its intrinsic power: namely, its thrust toward an understanding of different lived worlds; for such worlds clearly do not take the form simply of ideational orders or logics of conceptual relations. If symbolic analysis attempts to explore specific cultural meanings – the particularities of the ways in which a given sociocultural world is constituted – so, also, an effort to take account of the more general, phenomenal forms in terms of which these *specific* forms present themselves would seem to be implied in its aims. In other words, as I see it, developing analytic models that take account of the basic phenomenal form of social being is integral to the core method and aims of symbolic anthropology.

By this I do not mean, however, to exclude the problem of the logical structures entailed in symbolic processes. On the contrary, in the present study this emphasis on the lived form of the social world has been combined with an analysis of a logic of symbolic structures. In these respects, the study joins phenomenological and certain kinds of structuralist emphases frequently regarded as mutually exclusive. Thus I have attempted to analyze a sociocultural logic in symbolic processes without substituting "an ensemble of comparable and transposable signs for the world of subjects mutually constituting themselves as objects-subjects" (Lefort, 1951:1409, my translation).

In line with these premises, I have argued, for instance, that the basic generative schema or template of Gawan value transformation and signification is not simply a logic of binary oppositions, but a generative or causal-sequential and iconic nexus of relations between a type of action involving the separation or identification of food with the actor's self, and certain qualitative (essentially bodily or body-related) signs of positive or negative value that are outcomes of this act (Chapters 4, 6–8). Since this schema refers to certain meaning relations regularly formed in the structuring of different kinds of actions and practices, it necessarily includes more than just a representation of binary opposition that "abstracts away" the actor and the generative relations intrinsic in the dynamic character of action. Rather, the meaning relations involved are stated in terms of categories of actor, type of action, and possible positive or negative outcomes; whereas the relevant abstract ordering functions or formal semantic principles entailed in these relations involve causality, sequence, iconicity, and binary opposition (see Chapter 6). Further, we may note that the binary relations of positive versus negative value do not simply involve logical oppositions of transformational potency; rather, these oppositions are intrinsically moralistic. The moral dimension, central to the broad concerns of this study with self–other relationships, may also be seen therefore as one of the ordering functions or formal semantic principles that cohere in the basic schema of value transformation. I return to this point later.

The particular form taken by this schema derives initially from my focus on action (i.e., culturally defined types of act and practice) as providing the elementary framing notion of the analysis. As the creative, "potentializing" mode of social being, action implicitly provides a dynamic perspective on modes of meaning relation or order. In the analysis of Chapter 3, for example, these relations begin to emerge in the form of negative or positive productive possibilities or potentialities implicated in particular types of Gawan acts and the different practices of which they are a part. Thus I examined certain potentialities that in the Gawan view are implied in acts of giving food as opposed to eating (as they appear in various specific Gawan contexts), and discussed specific entailments of these and other acts (for example, kula speech) that Gawans emphasize – especially those relating to their relative capacities to yield outcomes that engage spatiotemporal continuities going beyond the actor and the immediate action. In connection with this analysis, I also examined what I called subjective conversions or outcomes implicated in these actions, thus bringing the intersubjective dimension into the analysis from this action-oriented perspective: For instance, I discussed the way in which Gawans may attempt to influence others to remember them over time so that a given type of act performed by one actor may project the possibility of future hoped-for acts by another into the immediate present, and eventually yield a desired objective outcome.

This approach to symbolic analysis via the paradigm of action (and acts as media of value transformation) affects the way in which particular features of Gawan symbolism such as that of gender, are construed in this study. Rather than being framed simply in terms of static binary polarities, masculine and feminine capacities appear as "moments" in transformative processes. For instance, the female dimension appears as the dynamic base (the wouwura, in Gawan terms) of the capacities to generate a more expansive intersubjective spacetime of positive value. As such, it is, in certain respects, subordinate (less expansive, engaging less spatiotemporal control) to the superordinate male elements; yet as the enabling power of the expansive male capacities, it has primacy over them. In this formulation, the ambiguity in the relation of subordination and superordination comes to the fore: Although what is primary and generative may appear from one point of view to be subordinate to the more expansive levels of spatiotemporal potency, from another viewpoint, the overtly superordinate potency appears grounded in and produced by the female potency and in this sense, subordinate to it. These ambiguities are expressed in different Gawan formulations of the value process (for example, in the reversals of the canoe origin narrative and female vs. male kula shells). Similarly, they emerge in the problematic hierarchy of relations between acts of persuasion and decision making, typified as masculine action, and acts of consent or rejection typified as feminine action (Chapters 6, 10).

In examining action as a medium of transformation, I have stressed not only potentialities and outcomes (involving causal-sequential ordering functions) but also the iconicity that may inhere in the relation between acts and particular outcomes through the reconstitution of relevant characteristics of the former by means of certain properties of the latter.

Not simply a matter of likeness, iconicity may be defined more explicitly as a compounding of relations of likeness and difference. Whereas likeness conveys the connection between distinctive elements, the differentiation entailed in iconicity may mark a semantic shift in which one element serves to make explicit a *more general* significance implicit in another; the actor may then come to experience this more general significance through its objectification in the icon. In this sense, iconicity can be seen as an ordering function within practices that makes it possible for actors to move between different orders of meaning.

This point can be illustrated by any of the practices that embody the Gawan schema of value transformation and signification referred to above, but I shall use a simplified version of the value transformation involving the witch discussed in Chapter 9. The witch's act of cannibalistic greed can be seen as an icon of the greedy acts of the victim, since it reconstitutes the latter's action in a form exhibiting its negative value. Whereas the likeness between the two acts exhibits the connection of the witch's action to the victim's, the difference between the witch's act (for example, its cannibalistic focus that involves an extreme vision of greed) and that of the victim's is crucial to rendering the latter's act in a "new" form. Rather than merely replicating the first act, the second abstracts and objectifies its general significance. Thus through the persona of the witch and the heavy illness with which she afflicts the victim, the negative intersubjective value of the victim's action is given its specific currency and made experientially available to him or her and others.

I turn now to the moral dimension. The part that it plays as a formative-semantic principle or ordering function of symbolic processes is developed most clearly in the present argument with reference to the dialectic between positive and negative value. The difference between logical or epistemological polarity and moral polarity is illustrated by Burke's (1961:20ff.) characterization in terms of the kind of negativity they entail: One he suggests, refers to a "propositional negative" (the "is not") and the other to a "negative of command," the hortatory negative ("shall not"), or "moralistic no" (see also Chapter 4). The infusion of logical polarities with the moralistic opposition creates a tension between elements that derives from the formative effect of command or imperative and thus relates symbolic form to the will, that is, to the principle of the active social being. Embedded in particular symbolic acts, the moralistic opposition can "organize" (to adopt Durkheim's, 1915:209, expression) the will in terms of the conditions of viability of a given social order. As a critical link between symbolic ordering functions and volition, the moralistic requires special attention in any model of the dynamic structuring of sociocultural meaning processes (cf. Beidelman, 1980:34).

I wish to close by drawing attention to certain features pertaining to this moral aspect. In analyzing value transformation as a mode of self-construction, I have suggested how value production and evaluation (a rendering of the self in terms of the favorable or unfavorable attitude of a significant other) may be synthesized within symbolic processes. I have dealt with these evaluative renderings in various ways: for example, in considering the donor's ability to persuade the recipient to remember him or her or to consent to his (the donor's) own desires (Chapter 3).

In particular, the evaluation of the significant other is generalized and objectified in the key value forms of fame, on the one hand, and the witch (or acts of witchcraft), on the other. Whereas fame represents the positive evaluative attitude deriving from the perspective of the distant other external to Gawa and acquired as a positive attribute of the self, the witch embodies a negative evaluation of an actor (or actors) from the perspective of the primarily Gawan excluded other (Chapter 9). The witch defines the negativity of the Gawan self in a complex form. On the one hand, the person who is the focus of witch attack is negatively evaluated relative to fundamental egalitarian premises of the society, especially as these premises are embedded in acts of giving as opposed to keeping or consuming for oneself. On the other hand, the witch is a negative persona who specifically embodies, as I have argued, the construction of the principles of autonomy and egalitarianism basic to Gawan polity in a hegemonic, subjugating form that makes the polity nonviable. Hence the activities of the witch can themselves be felt to yield the negative evaluations of distant others (producing shame, a negative construction of self in which the body is heavy; Chapter 10). This evaluative dialectic – the formulation, in effect, of positive and negative evaluative discourses about the Gawan self – is intrinsic to the transformational process of value production. Indeed, without these evaluative discourses Gawa cannot produce value for itself, inasmuch as it is through their operation that Gawans define and bring into consciousness their own value state or the general state of viability of the community.

These possible negative and positive evaluations can in turn be played upon by guyaw in their own moral criticism of a given negative state of affairs in order to transform that state back into one with positive potential, that is, a state in which the possibility of producing positive evaluations by distant others asserts that all is well in the body politic. As one who concentrates within his person the positive evaluations of distant others, and thus condenses the essential viability of Gawan society, the guyaw, as Burridge (1975:87) has aptly put it, "reveals to others the kinds of moral conflict in which they are involved."

This brings me to my final point. If I have stressed the importance of the dialectical form of the system of value creation, I have also tried to show how this dialectic is posed in certain immediate procedures of social activity. As we have seen, Gawans are regularly reminded of negativities as part of the activity of striving toward positive value production. For example, the joking insults of food recipients being paid for their vital dancing at the Drum dance finale describe them in negative terms as consumers who forget debts in order to remind them to pay their debts; the chastising and exhorting speech against witchery and the warnings about its destructive effects, which occur in various public meetings where projects are being planned, point to the possibility of failure if Gawans do not listen to the senior men (Chapters 8, 10, passim). In this way, experience is being formulated in terms of a model of choice, for the actor is regularly confronted with negative and positive possibilities whose realizations (i.e., in one direction or the other) are being grounded by this procedure in determinations of the personal will. Not only the dialectical construction of the system and its premises, but also the dialectic of choosing, regularly posed within Gawan projects and activities, locates the capacity to produce value directly within the actor's will.

Returning to the problem of communal viability as considered in Chapter 1, we may conclude that in order for the Gawan community to create the value essential to this viability, and so act to define itself "as an agent of its own self-production" (Touraine, 1977:4), it must constitute this acting as part of the form of the process. That is to say, the persistent formulation of value production as a process created through choices that Gawans themselves make is intrinsic to the creation of the experience of a viable intersubjective world – one within which some measure of control is felt to be maintained over the negative possibilities deriving from its own internal contradictions.

Notes

Chapter 1. The conceptual framework

1 An ethnographic introduction to Gawan society is reserved for Chapter 2. Some readers may prefer to turn to that account in order to obtain an ethnographic backdrop for their reading of the present theoretical statement.

2 With the exception of *butu*, I do not cite indigenous terms in this chapter. My intent here is to set out the general framework in relatively abstract form; citation and discussion of relevant Gawan terms is reserved for later chapters.

3 The field of anthropological studies concerned with meaning incorporates diverse theoretical perspectives. Among other recent general statements and collections, see, for example, Basso and Selby (1976), Boon (1982), Crick (1976), Dolgin et al. (1977), Cunningham, Dougherty, Fernandez, et al. (1981), Geertz, (1983), Hanson (1975), Parkin, (1982), Sahlins (1976), Schwimmer (1973), Sperber (1974), V. Turner (1975), Wagner (1986), Willis (1975). This is not the place to consider the various positions and methods of analysis represented in these and numerous other studies. My own approach is demonstrated in the course of this book, and in the theoretical framework explained in this chapter.

4 The term *sign* is used here in a more restricted sense that I explain later in the chapter.

5 The concept of value has been approached from many different viewpoints in modern social theory (for one review see Dumont, 1983, and for a recent attempt to develop an anthropological model of value that draws on Marxist and Saussurian theories, see T. Turner, 1984, 1979b). My own thinking has been informed by studies involving diverse approaches and concepts, but my theorefical framework has been developed specifically from the perspective of an analysis of sociocultural symbolism. Among those studies that have been suggestive for various aspects of my analysis are Barraud, Coppet, et al. (1979), Baudrillard (1981), Bohannon (1955), Marx (1906), Saussure (1966), Simmel (1978), Turner (1984). Of less interest to the present study have been the psychological and concept-oriented models of values as "preferences" (for example, the classic study by Kluckhohn in Parsons and Shils, 1951).

6 The necessity of treating space and time together as a unitary analytic concept (*spacetime*) is also assumed by Hugh-Jones (1979). See, in addition, Devisch (1982,

1983) on "bodily spacetime." A similar synthesis is made in the context of a discussion of narrative by Bakhtin (1981:84) whose notion of the "chronotype" emphasizes "the inseparability of space and time." My use of the term *intersubjective* is explained later in the chapter.

The study of sociocultural time and space has a long history in the anthropological literature, going back to Durkheim and Mauss (1963, first published 1901–2/ 1903) and Hubert's (1909) seminal study. Among the numerous and varied modern ethnographic analyses, see, for example, Ardener (1981), Barnes (1974), Bourdieu (1970, 1977, 1979), Burman (1981), Coppet (1970), Devisch (1983), Evans-Pritchard (1940), Fernandez (1982), Hallowell (1955), Howe, (1981), Hugh-Jones (1979), Kaplan (1977), Leach (1961), Middleton (1967), Moore (1986), Pocock (1966), Thornton (1980).

Some of the recent literature on exchange has been particularly concerned with incorporating temporality into exchange theory (see Bourdieu, 1977:5ff.; Coppet, 1981; Weiner, 1980).

7   One could also consider the spacetime of the visits themselves (e.g., movements between the host's home and the shore). Although in the particular case of inter-island hospitality, I do not deal with micro-spatiotemporal dimensions like these, they are examined in other contexts in this book.

8   Although I have stressed the production of spacetime in human action, I do not mean to ignore the fact that this production presupposes certain spatiotemporal coordinates that are also intrinsic to the spacetime produced. Some of these presuppositions become relevant in considering the difference between witchcraft, where the actor may be invisible to others and flying is possible, and the spacetime of ordinary human practice.

9   As Sahlins (1965:215) has put it, "Food dealings are a delicate barometer, a ritual statement of social relations, and food is thus employed instrumentally as a starting, a sustaining or a destroying mechanism of sociability." On various aspects of the symbolism of food transmission and consumption in New Guinea see, for example, Ernst (1978), Iteanu (1983), Kahn (1980), Rubel and Rosman (1978), A. Strathern (1982), Weiner (1978), Young (1971).

10   For a short overview of the concept of the intersubjective as developed in the phenomenological tradition see Schutz (1962, especially pp. 156–97).

11   In anthropology the view is integral especially to studies of ritual process (see, e.g., Comaroff, 1985; Gell, 1975; Poole, 1982; V. Turner, 1967; and many others). See also, in the Marxist idiom, the focus on action constituting the *bodily being* of the actor conveyed in the statement of Berthelot (1983:126): "All social work of the body is able to be conceived simultaneously as social work upon the body."

Different approaches to the construction of self in social action or interaction (i.e., in the dynamic of self–other relations) are familiar from the well-known social psychology of Mead, 1956 (recently applied by Kapferer, 1983, to a symbolic analysis of Sri Lankan curing ritual); the social phenomenology of Schutz (1962); and the phenomenological sociology of writers such as Berger and Luckmann (1967:72ff.).

12   Heidegger is actually referring here to the understanding of one's being via *objects* (e.g., "the shoemaker ... understands *himself* from his things [i.e., the shoes he makes]," 1982:160), and this view is also applicable here, in the sense that objects are aspects of practices. See especially the examination of certain features of canoes and canoe production in the context of Gawan marriage exchanges, Chapter 6.

13 Various anthropological studies have drawn attention to this aspect of exchange (e.g., Crocker, 1973, 1979; Leroy, 1979; Lévi-Strauss, 1949; Marriott, 1976; Mauss, 1968, [1926]; Schwimmer, 1973). For emphasis on this aspect in witchcraft, see especially Favret-Saada (1977).

14 Peirce's "qualisign" is a quality (for him, an "essence," or "mere logical possibility" such as "redness") that operates as a sign. Since, in his view, qualities can only signify through likeness to their referents, qualisigns are necessarily "iconic" when considered in terms of the relation between sign and referent (Peirce, 1955:115ff.). Peirce would distinguish between qualisigns and what he calls "*sinsigns*," which are actualities or "existents" (as against pure "possibilities") that signify by virtue of certain of their qualities. Thus my "embodied qualities" would presumably be "sinsigns" in his formulation. I am not concerned, however, with his categories or philosophical premises, but merely with using his expressive terms *qualisign* and *icon* to convey similar but not precisely the same notions to handle a specific set of problems. The term *iconic* has at any rate been widely used in current anthropology and linguistics.

15 I use the label *conversion* rather than *transformation* to refer to changes of specific qualities and other particular value products that occur as part of the general process of spatiotemporal (value) transformation. Although I use the former term to refer to changes occurring via acts of exchange (i.e., the receipt of one category of goods as an outcome of a previous transmission of another), its use is not confined to exchange. Since *conversion* has been widely used in economic anthropology (and as a technical term by Bohannon, 1955, and Bohannon and Dalton, 1962:5f., to distinguish exchanges that they regard as translating goods across "transactional spheres" from those operating within one "sphere"), I note the difference in my usage.

16 I refer here simply to broad principles defining the different symbolic orders of positive and negative-subversive value transformations. However, we shall see that in the contexts of specific events, apparently positive types of act can also be interpreted after the fact as possible causes of witch attack. Indeed, this is one of the reasons it is apt to refer to witchcraft as a subversive mode of value transformation, since it may actually subvert the positive value capacities of particular acts.

17 For the positive transformative value of certain kinds of speech, as well as the contrast in this respect between speech and consumption, see especially Chapters 3, 5, and 10.

Chapter 2. Gawa in the 1970s

1 In this chapter, I have not made specific comparative references in the text to the many points of comparison and difference between Gawan society and other societies of the Massim (most notably the Trobriands, well known from Malinowski's early studies), reserving comparative references for the main argument. Because there is no other systematic account of Gawan society (the only other anthropological source outside of my own work being that of Seligmann, 1910) I have included a fairly detailed ethnographic introduction. My account is keyed to a number of emphases and types of content relevant to the argument of the study, as well as being an attempt to give the reader a broad picture of Gawan life, social organization, and the situation of the community in the inter-island order during the general period of my field research (i.e., the early and late 1970s). I have not attempted, however, to build up a historical picture of Gawa out of the extremely sparse written documentation available and my own information from Gawan informants. Where historical factors or changes are relevant to the argument, I have made reference to them here or in later chapters. In addition, Chapter 10 brings the theoretical argument to bear upon current events relating to changes on Gawa in 1974.

2   The number is based on my census figures. The government census of 1980 showed 546 people. My 1973 figure is lower (see Munn, 1983:305).

3   Hamlet numbers change as groupings may occasionally divide or combine.

4   Sweet potatoes, a European introduction, are planted in gardens further afield from the hamlets. Now a significant subsistence staple, they are not used in major exchanges of raw produce. Some other nonindigenous crops such as squash may also be planted in the gardens.

5   The emphasis on the main thoroughfare and keeping it clear is undoubtedly a postpacification feature, an outcome of the characteristic concern of the Australian patrols. See Chapter 4, notes 8, 21.

6   According to the Gawans' own views, these interactions have increased considerably since pacification, a change also in accord with current information about the elaboration and democratization of kula exchange in the postpacification era (see Young, 1983a:8f.).

7   Boagis and Nasikwabu people who speak the Misima language are conversant with Muyuw (see also Lithgow, 1973:107).

8   One Gawan suggested to me that there may be some unowned land on the distant cliffs, but for all intents and purposes, Gawans generally regard the island as entirely owned by dala groups, or more rarely, by subdivisions of dala. Thus two of the current dala are internally segmented into two subgroups, and each subgroup holds dala lands in different neighborhoods or separate areas.

9   This term is discussed in Chapter 3. In the present chapter, I use it to refer to "sphere of authority," one of its basic meanings.

10   One of these dala is partially fused with another larger dala. Of course, the number of groups is subject to change over time.

11   I counted as adults, men and women who had passed through the youthful courting phase discussed later in this chapter.

12   In addition, dala have different food and fish taboos. These taboos also point to the bodily nature of dala bonds.

13   Gawans contrast this kind of affiliative process with that called -ka-nubere, which refers to making close friends of a marriageable kind outside your own dala and kumila category. Whereas kaveyora relations are modeled on the matri-kin bonds of veyo and convey nonmarriageability, kanubere relations are modeled on the nube relation, which connotes the possibility of sexual relations (i.e., between

nube of opposite sex), and may refer to cross-cousins. See further comments on *nube-* in the text that follows and in note 28.

14 The term *dala* can be used in a broad sense to refer to the kumila, in which case, the phrase "small dala" (*dala kwakita*) serves to distinguish the ancestral unit. Malinowski's well-known gloss of "subclan" for the Trobriand *dala*, and "clan" for *kumila*, is misleading for Gawa (as well as the Trobriands, see Weiner, 1976:51f.), since the Gawan kumila has no common ancestor.

In referring to the kumila names in the text, I use their plural forms (roughly equivalent to the Kulabutu, Kubay, etc., people). In Gawan usage, each kumila is also prefixed by male (*tara-*) or female (*imu-*) prefixes, as relevant.

15 The term *veyo-* can also be used for the father and close bilateral kin, although its focal referent is to people of one's own dala and kumila.

16 In fact, in some contexts Gawans recognize that in the relatively recent past, there were five named kumila, one of which has now been assimilated as one dala of another kumila. Nevertheless, they insist on the fixity of the number of kumila and its correlation with the four winds; and this was one of the first points stressed to me about the kumila. Unlike the dala, the kumila belongs to that order of social categories for which the number itself is significant, and is therefore treated at any given time as "fixed" (Nadel, 1957:17).

The situation with regard to bird identification is more complex because in the relatively recent past at least (and vaguely, in a few cases at the present time) birds appear to have been associated with different dala. I don't try to deal with these issues here (which are among a number involving the kumila). The general wind and current bird identifications for each kumila are as follows: *Kulabutu*, north, frigate bird (*Daweit*); *Kubay*, west, fish-hawk (*Buribwara*); *Kwasisi*, east, red parrot (*gagreyi*); *Malasi*, south, white pigeon (*bwabun*).

17 Gawans may also directly refer to the winds as coming from specific places, although this is more standard for a number of intermediate winds subsumed within the governing quadratic paradigm. The former are explicitly named after islands or other landmarks in the direction from which they come.

18 The term *teitu* (teitu yam) may also be used to refer to the year but appears less indigenous to Gawa (possibly adopted from the north) than the more common wind label. In terms of our months, the northwest winds tend to prevail roughly from late December or January into April, although they may start somewhat earlier. The southeast winds prevail from roughly May into November. Early December is likely to be a doldrum period. Between the most marked part of each phase of the year is an intermediate time when the winds of each phase alternate (*matarasay*). In general, however, the wind year is thought of as cycling between Iyavata and Bwalima.

19 Land use is very flexible and there are no regular land "rents" in yams or other produce at harvest comparable to the Trobriand system (Weiner, 1976:146ff.). People may use lands controlled by individuals of various dala with whose members they usually have ties so that they are likely to be in generalized food-giving relationships (*skwayobwa*, see Chapter 3) with them. Plots may also be planted in a large garden with people in various relationships to the gardener.

20 Gawans no longer have systematic familiarity with the lunar names and sequences of the traditional cycle, and they have only piecemeal knowledge of the

European names of the months, and their sequence. The traditional New Year was said by some to have been just after the yam harvest in the past, but now follows the western cycle beginning on January 1, and is marked in church-associated activities.

Gawans have a standard, general term for time, *tuta*, which is used in a manner similar to "time" in English. For example, one may express duration, as in *tuta papun*, "a short time"; used with a possessive prefix (as in *kara-tuta*), it carries the sense of "his/her/its time to . . . [come, die, etc.]."

21 Notably, the cooking of taro pudding (see Chapter 6), the smoking of fish, or its casual frying on the beach; and the initial cooking of pork. In addition, when men go to other islands, boys and unmarried youths do the cooking for the adult men of their own canoe.

22 Although such housing is usually built for a teenage boy, a girl (*kapugura*) may also occasionally have her own quarters.

23 When dala have close bonds, payment of this kind may not necessarily be made. Garden lands may also be temporarily transferred by the payment of a pig to the owning dala. The latter may then reclaim the land only by giving the payers a pig to replace the one that paid for the land.

24 For example, fathers can give trees and magic (except garden magic) to their sons, but not land (which is inherited within the dala).

25 A woman and her hushand do not return to her family for a second child, but the same protective prohibitions obtain.

26 Boys make gifts of betel and tobacco to girls to obtain sexual favors, and it is the girl's agreement that must be obtained for sexual relationship to take place; the significance of this feature will be seen later. Some of these gifts may be handed on to the girl's parents, whose acceptance indicates that they favor continuance of the sexual relationship with the boy, and a possible marriage. If parents want a youth to marry a particular person, they may instruct the youth to sleep with him or her. Thus parents exercise various kinds of pressure in controlling children's sexual and potential marriage partners.

Gawans prefer marriages with one's age-mates, or with persons who are approximately within the same metabouwen grouping. A man and wife are ideally proximal in age, moving through the life cycle together. This age equalization is a significant part of the marital structure, although it is not always actualized: Youthful marriages are brittle (divorces are common) and deaths in more long-term marriages may also skew the relative age of people in a subsequent marriage.

27 In addition, kula relationships themselves have metaphoric sexual connotations, and actual sexual liaisons with the unmarried host women are a part of kula visits (see Chapter 6).

28 The possessive is infixed (e.g., *nu-re-ta*, his/her cross-sex sibling). The Gawan kinship terminology is, with certain exceptions, the same (and with same or cognate terms) as the Crow-type Trobriand terminology reported by Malinowski, (1929:515–16) and Weiner, (1979:Figure 2). The following apparent differences may be noted: (1) Although the term *tabu-* may be used for all kin in the grandparental generation, the term *tama-* (father, father's brother, etc.) is also applied to the "fa's mo's br." The latter's children are then called by sibling/parallel cousin terms. Similarly, although "mo's mo's br." is called *tabu-* and not *kada-* (the mo's br. term), this man's children may be called *natu-* (child) by a man, like his *kada's* children (and they in turn call him *tama*). (2) In ego's parental generation, the terms *tabu* or *ina* may be used for "mo's br.wi." (3) In ego's generation, there is an important variation in the cross-cousin terms. Although the terms noted in the Trobriand terminology are also standard on Gawa, there is an alternate term *nube-* that can be used bilaterally for both sets of cross-cousins. I have already pointed out that this term is a friendship term and that it also carries connotations of sexual and marital availability when used to refer to a member of the opposite sex. Thus it is this term, and not the *tabu* term (used for "fa.sis.da." or "mo.br.ch.," wo.spkg.) that conveys sexuality and marriageability. (The term *tabu* should not be confused with *taabu*, a nonindigenous term for taboo.) As I have suggested, the attitude toward immediate cross-cousin marriage is complex on Gawa, and I do not go into it here.

29 The dala groups of foster parents will also be important where relevant, but they become classed as paternal and maternal dala.

30 If the surviving member is the woman's kinsman, he will continue to give food, which the woman and her husband then gain the right to eat. This gift is no longer called *buwaa*.

31 Cf. the term for "person": *gamag*. Gawans typify the category of a man's *gamagali* as women of his own dala for whom he gives food, but it can also include other women in this relationship to him.

32 The sister-in-law relationship, the key one here, is extremely important to a woman, quite apart from the buwaa relationship. It is interesting that the kin term for sister-in-law is the only one other than that for the cross-sex sibling in which the possessive pronoun is infixed: cf. *yeva–ta*, "sister-in-law," and *nu–ta*, "cross-sex sibling." The connection between the two relations seems even more marked in the light of the use of the term *gamagali* noted here.

33 There is evidence of a more hierarchical pattern on Gawa in the prepacification era, and some men of influence may have been the leaders of ranked dala (see Seligmann, 1910:674, 701). See also Chapter 10, note 16.

34 The possession of spells for these and many other purposes is not confined to a few men, but has a more general basis within the population. Women as well as men know spells; women may also hold spells and transmit them to men. Garden magic may not be legitimately transmitted across dala groups, a feature that emphasizes the close relation of dala and growth in the land (see Chapter 4). In the past, garden magic was more widely performed on an individual basis than it is today.

35 In 1973–4 there were three dala whose guyaw were looked to for community-wide rites assuring land fertility; one of these men was the most powerful kula man on Gawa (and one of the most influential in the kula ring as a whole); he dominated the group of agricultural experts. A second man, less influential in kula, was nevertheless deeply respected as the last representative of his dala and of their tradition of agricultural expertise. The third specialist had retired from kula, and also seemed to be somewhat less focal at that time than the other two, although still important. We shall see in Chapter 9 the way in which the illness of the second man entered into the symbolism of transformational processes on Gawa in 1974. By

1979 both these men were dead and their influence had not been fully replaced.

Between 1973 and 1981 one man, an outstanding kula figure, was recognized as predominant in curing and providing protection against witchcraft, and two other men of his dala were also well known, although these were not the only men with these powers. The leading man in this specialty did not receive his spells from within his dala.

36 When a cycle of the Comb closed in 1980, Gawan men discussed the scheduling of one of these entertainments next, but rejected it ostensibly because no one any longer knew the organizational details.

37 There has never been an Australian or non–New Guinean functionary living on Gawa. The Methodist Overseas Mission (now the United Church of Papua, New Guinea, and the Solomon Islands) bought land on Gawa for a school in 1920 (Kulumadau-Misima Station Journal, June 1920). The Methodist Overseas Mission Report for 1920 (1921:25) states that a Fijian teacher had been stationed on Gawa during the year; and my own information from a Gawan informant suggests the presence of a local Trobriand missionary on Gawa about 1924. However, the Australian patrol report for March 1924 states that the land purchased by the mission had not been "occupied" or "improved" by 1924. The school was established in 1974 (see Chapter 10) with a New Guinean school teacher.

38 Gawans do not refer to kula as a ring, but recognize that it -*parat* (comes around and closes).

39 Malinowski does not mention kitomu, but recent research indicates that kitomu are basic components of kula around the ring (see Leach and Leach, 1983). I discuss Gawan kitomu in Chapter 6.

40 According to Damon (1980:281), Muyuwans regard all kula shells as being someone's kitomu irrespective of whether or not the Muyuwan transactor knows who the owners are. Macintyre (1983:374) suggests a similar view for Tubetube. The Gawan view is more variable. Moreover, there are certain features in contemporary kula procedures in the north at least, and also in Gawan categories relating to rights over shells, which suggest a much more complex situation than the Muyuwan view that Damon emphasizes in his model of kula transaction. Nevertheless, kitomu are fundamental to the system.

Chapter 3. Food transmission and food consumption

1 The term -*kayus* may be used to refer to protecting another person from harm as, for instance, through the intervention of one's own body between the individual and an attacker in a fight, or simply by attempting to keep belligerents apart. In such contexts, the term's connotations of "bodily intervention," "obstruction," or "bounding off" are very clear, although in contrast to the present context, the connotations are favorable.

2 *Kamkwamu* appears to be a reduplicated form of -*kam*, "eat," and may be used instead of this term, or more variously to signify meanings such as "is eating" or "eats and eats."

3 *Vaakam* may also carry the more general sense of taking care of someone, but the center of this care is feeding.

4 The basic term for persuasive speech in kula is *kayuweila*. However, the general term for kula speech of all kinds is *livalela kura*.

5 I have not observed an uvelaku or the preparatory feast. My comments come from men's descriptions and the standard insults one man dictated to me. I have, however, observed this sort of ritual insult in other contexts (see, for example, Chapter 8).

6 I was impressed with the importance of this myself when I returned to Gawa with a respectable (although relatively small) shell. People in my hamlet were very pleased; my success clearly also affected them indirectly, and now it was felt that I had not sailed "emptily."

7 Women participate directly in kula on some of the other islands south and east of Gawa. My own shell was acquired from a female transactor on Mwadau island (northern Muyuw).

8 Damon (1978:226) states that on Muyuw, women are regarded as those who ideally "control the distribution" of food, although he does not make it clear whether he means that they necessarily perform the distribution in practice. The general question of New Guinea women as transactors has been the subject of some discussion in the literature (see M. Strathern, 1972, 1981a). M. Strathern (1981b) also discusses the identification of Mt. Hagen women with eating and consumption as against "investment" (p. 182), and its significance in Hagen society.

9 The term *karu* may be used for raw or cooked vegetable food, and sometimes as a general term for comestibles, but its specific meaning is root crops and vegetable food as opposed to fish (*in*), and pig meat or other animal flesh (*viniyon*).

10 The term *youd* can also be used figuratively for major community exchanges such as the uvelaku or entertainments.

11 Cf. Weiner's (1978:178) point referring to the Trobriands: "A full yam house constitutes a range of options for the recycling of yams in further transactions.... The most unproductive option is to eat those yams." In a more recent study Weiner (1982) has also been concerned with the relative durability of comestibles and other exchange media and their capacity to act as operators in what she calls processes of sociocultural "regeneration."

12 Arrival and departure gifts of skirts and mats are called *pari*. For example, on arrival, Gawans may give white mats (*gouwa*) to their northern partners for which they receive dark mats (*murigiyay*) on departure.

Pigs given in kerasi are differently transacted than other potentially edible gifts as they must eventually be returned in equal number and approximate size (whenever the initial donor needs a pig for his own public responsibilities). A Gawan should not kerasi for a pig from his partner simply for personal, internal purposes such as mortuary rites, but only for community-wide entertainments or uvelaku.

13 In these respects, *skwayobwa* has some of the characteristics Sahlens (1972:174) has ascribed to what he calls "generalised reciprocity" in which "the counter [return] is not stipulated by time, quality or quantity: the expectation of reciprocity is indefinite." However, in the Gawan case, in contrast to Sahlens's model, these relations may also be built up as I have suggested in distant, i.e., overseas, partnerships.

14 The term *mapu-ra* has, however, a general sense of temporal and causal connectivity and the substitution of one thing or person for another. Thus it is possible to use it loosely to refer to any items received that have some intrinsic connection with a previous gift or category of gift made to the recipient, irrespective of whether or not the item involved is regarded as being the return payment, or the equivalent *for* that gift. The term also may be used to refer to retribution, as well as to one person's replacement of another as his or her "heir" (on the cognate Trobriand term, see Malinowski, 1922:178f.; Weiner 1980). Thus it is possible to use the term loosely to refer to a shell received because, for instance, one has given hospitality in garden produce, and the like to one's partner. This usage, however, simply carries the sense of "something gotten for something given," which must be distinguished from mapura in the specific sense that the two items are exchanged for each other. The shell given, for instance, must then have its mapura in a shell of opposite category regarded as its equivalent. Similarly, a shell of opposite category received in connection with the transaction of a previous shell, and as part of the same nexus of path transactions, may be loosely called the mapura for the previous shell, even though the new shell is not the equivalent match and closing transaction for the former shell. Mapura in a specific sense, however, the "true" mapura, is the closing shell. It is important to distinguish these broad usages from the more specific one (as Gawans themselves do on questioning), and in this study I shall use the term in its narrow sense unless otherwise indicated.

15 This point suggests one immediate reason why a spheres-of-exchange model in Bohannon's (1955) sense is not adequate to formulate the relation between hospitality in food and kula exchange. The two are not simply separate "spheres" of goods transactions, but rather the former transactions enable the actor to transform his operations into kula without ever directly "converting" (in Bohannon's sense) food (for example) into kula shells. Other limitations of a spheres-of-exchange model are suggested by the analysis of marriage exchanges in Chapter 6. However, it is not my intention to examine this model and its general premises here.

16 This analysis contrasts with Damon's (1980) exclusion of *immediate* partnerships as units of dyadic exchange from his formulation of kula exchange structure.

17 Connections of other kinds may also occur. For instance, a man may have different partners in one island community who become the junctures of alternate routings (*kadalaalay*) on a common path of partners with ego. Thus B might have partners C and C′ on Kitava who are both on his path with A of northern Woodlark. If a shell on this path goes to C, he gives it on to D of Sinaketa, but if it goes to C′, the latter gives it to (for instance) E of Vakuta, and so forth.

18 "Endless" unidirectional movement is not a condition of circulation in the sense used here: A medium may circulate in a more limited way. For instance, Gawan canoes are named artifacts whose transactional paths are followed and remembered, but each canoe has a limited circulatory power since it is transacted only once (has only one path) and moves in a partial segment of the more comprehensive kula circuit.

19 Shells do not ordinarily return sequentially to the same person each time they return to the community, although there are special cases in which individuals attempt to keep a particular shell permanently on one of their paths (see Chapter 6, note 18). On Gawa, attempts at developing continuities of this latter kind generally involve a Gawan's kitomu (see Chapter 2) shells.

20 Men may also develop partnership paths that are not intended to close (*-parat*) in a circle, but that return instead to another person on their own island (-*sasa*, gaps, does not close); such paths make it possible for men on the same island to kula with each other by long distance, so to speak, and to tap into the shell resources of each other's partners.

21 This analytic model of food giving as having the potential for creating certain subjective conversions is to be kept distinct from the view that food is *exchanged for* certain subjective attitudes. The model differs in its treatment of the subjective dimension of transformation cycles from that developed, for instance, by Schwimmer (1973), who, drawing in part on exchange theorists such as Homans and Blau, treats sentiments or attitudes as among the possible objects of exchange, thus reifying the subjective dimension as an entity on the same ontological level as (and exchangeable for) any other entities (thus, for example, acts of service may be exchanged for influence, Schwimmer, 1973:5). Although Schwimmer is concerned with the forms of exchange cycles, one of the difficulties of his model is this reification, which tends to detach the subjective from existential processes, and by treating them as entities among other entities of the same order, to focus on the creation of binary oppositions (for example, "repentance" vs. "forgiveness" as "objects of exchange," and "acts of hostility" and "meat sharing" as opposed "mediating elements" in the same cycle, *ibid.*, p. 58). I do not mean by this brief comment to ignore the complexities of Schwimmer's argument, the details of which I cannot discuss here.

22 Another term used frequently to denote "agree" is -*kabikawra*, which carries the sense of "obey," "consent to do." For instance, to -*kabikawra livala* is to listen to instructive words and agree to do as the speaker asks. The term -*reg*, "listen," is also used as in English to convey "listening" in this sense of "obeying." The Muyan term -*tam* may also be heard as a synonym for -*tagwara*. *Tam* and *tagwara* are intransitive, whereas *kabikawra* and *reg* may function transitively. Additional terms refer to consensus: for example, when all relevant people agree, one may say *i-yuratote-s*.

23 The terms *magi-* and *yawu-* are noun forms suffixed with a possessive (as, for instance, *magi-gu*, my wanting, it is my desire). It seems significant that the suffix class for both terms is "intimate" (Lithgow, 1974:10) and of the type used for the mind, body, and names of body parts, many kinship terms, etc.

24 Moving the mind of another, or getting another to "think on you," is of course a widespread New Guinea emphasis. See, for instance, Lawrence, 1964:28.

25 It seems quite likely that the noun *vaga* (starting gift) is not merely homonymic with -*vaga*, "to make" or "do." Some of my informants regarded the terms as related. Furthermore, *vaga* is used to mean a starting or opening gift in a variety of transactional contexts not just in kula; thus the explicit sense of establishing rather than finishing a relationship or transaction does not appear to be very far from the notion of "making" or "doing something." Note also the term -*va-vaga* (causative-*vaga*, meaning "possession"), which may be used to describe a *gulugwalu* finishing gift, because the latter is something owed ego – as if it were his possession. For example, a gulugwalu is *gura-vavaga*, (my possession) and it is illicit for one's partner to give it to someone else. Both a parallel and contrast between *vaga* and *vavaga* are thus suggested.

26 Other such objectivations are the intermediary shells mentioned earlier, which do not match the opening transaction as its closing equivalent, but are linked to it as assurances that the transaction is still ongoing. However, until the closing shell is received, the initial shell still has a "book" and should be remembered.

27 The notion of sleeping and waking has other elaborations. For example, a shell that stays in the hands of a given recipient for a long time (*tuta vanon*) is said to lie down (*i-masisi*) or sleep (*i-sigagay*) there. See Chapter 4 on motionlessness and motion.

28 Because of difficulties with my tape recorder, I was unable to record this talk and the quotation derives from the speaker's dictation of his speech to me soon after the feast. However, I was present at the feast, and his emphasis on "not remembering" also accords with my understanding of the talk and my notes taken at the time.

29 The notion that the mind is in the throat (connecting it with speech) is the standard Trobriand concept (Malinowski, 1922:408). It is not clear to me whether the location of the mind in the forehead is a more recent Gawan concept. Note, however, that this latter location is connected with important standardized sayings relating to the political order, and thus, currently at any rate, it is a firmly entrenched view.

30 According to one informant, *-raba* or *-reb* means "younger brother" of a guyaw.

31 In some contexts (depending on the particularities of a transaction), a man's own kareiwaga about vaga shells may be limited by decisions made about the transaction of a given shell by those from whom the shell has been received, or by consultations between him and the donating partner. A man has the most freedom with his own kitomu shells (see Chapter 2) or with vaga shells that do not come on a long-term path; shells arriving on a long-term path should be transmitted along that path, although men sometimes shunt a shell elsewhere, giving it to a man (an old or new partner) who makes promises about desired shells, or has such a shell immediately in hand. This procedure is supposedly illicit, but it is quite frequent. A man may use different ploys to obtain desired or appropriate returns for a shell or to make decisions about to whom the shell will be given: e.g., by holding on to it (*-yousi*) for a long time and inviting men to give other shells that may or may not be sufficiently persuasive to release the shell. In all these procedures he exerts his own will, attempting to manipulate the shell in his possession to his best advantage.

32 Of course, I do not mean that food (to the exclusion of women and men as objects of sexual desire) is the only focus of these contradictory attitudes. My concern here, however, is with the critical importance of food in the Gawan system.

Chapter 4. Qualisigns of value

1 Although the most standard, well-known terms referring to the sun's daily position do not reflect human activity, one man suggested to me a set of terms for the latter part of the afternoon that connect the sun's descent with gardening. Thus he suggested that the time when the sun is just beginning to descend may be called "the lazy woman lights the fire for cooking" (*lakabuvakata na-bagumata*): The lazy woman comes out of the garden and starts to prepare to eat. When the sun is further down, this may be called "the woman who is a good gardener lights the fire for cooking" (*lakabuvakata na-kaibagula*). The term *-kaibagula* (with appropriate male or female prefixes) is the standard term for a hard-working gardener. Although the above expressions did not appear to be frequently used, they convey the synthesis of the sun's diurnal cycle with the activity of gardening and the latter's identification with moral vitality. The diurnal motion of the sun and vital bodily activity have other connections, as we shall see.

2 The balouma is the life entity sometimes said to be in the lungs (*nupouwu*), a term that can also be used, as Malinowski (1954:153) notes for the Trobriand cognate, to refer to "inside" in general (*wa-nupou-ra*). Although there are broad similarities between the Gawan balouma and the Trobriand balouma (see Malinowski, 1954; Weiner, 1976:39, 121), Gawans are little concerned with the way the balouma or its agent enters the body, and give it no specific role in conception. They are much more concerned with its departure from the body in states of bodily danger and death. Further, the notions of its existence in Tuma after death receive little emphasis as compared with the Trobriands. The matrilineal identification of the balouma is assumed, and balouma inside a person should be of his or her own dala. These ideas are not elaborated, however, and there is no notion of cycles of reincarnation. More explicit emphasis on matrilineal identifications of the balouma is found in contexts that are concerned with the location of ancestral balouma inside the stones of garden and hamlet lands (see the following text and note 8) rather than the body.

3 I have mentioned the spatial structure of the house in Chapter 2. Here I merely wish to make a point about the house in general as a spatial domain.

4 These differentiations between necklaces and armshells have gender associations that I discuss in Chapter 6.

5 This gender identification of canoes should not be taken as absolute, for as we shall see later (Chapter 6), the matter is much more complex. What is of general application, however, is the rationale uppermost in this context: namely, that women are identified with the stable land, rather than with the domain of inter-island travel represented by the sea.

6 These spells are known by women and men as are many types of Gawan spells (see note 13).

7 For an interesting account and analysis of a similar identification of stones as motionless weights connected with the retention of crops in Kalauna (Goodenough Island) myth, see Young (1983b:139f., 185f.). The connection of stone with the stabilization of food is also found in Trobriand garden and yam house spells (e.g, Malinowski, 1935, I:221ff., II:274).

8 Significant stones that are connected with dala ownership and land fertility and that are the residences of an ancestral (male or female) balouma are also found in some hamlets. It is not clear whether all hamlets contained a dala stone in the past or only some of them, but people say that many hamlet stones were left behind when people moved in from previously more scattered hamlet sites toward the main thoroughfare, a move that apparently has taken place within the last twenty-five years.

9 Like the balouma, the owner of a land plot is angered if he thinks that a user of the land (who, it will be recalled from Chapter 2, need not be a member of the land-owning dala) or of adjacent land, has moved the stone.

10 In the past, specific rites were performed to awaken the land, but these have lapsed on contemporary Gawa. I was told that each dala had one man who performed the awakening magic for the dala lands after the land had been cleared and burned off, and just before planting.

11 Certain parallels between the renewal of the garden and that of the person may be noted. The discussion of conception is reserved for Chapter 6 but brief comments on some of these parallels may be made here. If a garden is a temporary clearing and locus of growth that is fertile because of the dala stones that remain connecting each clearing to previous clearings, so also each dala member is connected to previous members through a continuity of blood (*buyay*), the basic reproductive medium, inside each person. There are some suggestions that blood is heavy (see Chapters 6 and 8); one of my informants also said that the balouma (like blood, a dala element in the body, although, in contrast to the Trobriands, not directly associated by Gawans with blood or, as I have indicated, conception) is "heavy" and "of the below."

In addition, since growth in the garden requires a substantive, physical continuity, one might say that new plantings grow out of old ones, much as the child is detached from the body of the mother. On Gawa, the bodily emblem of this linkage and separation is the navel (*pwaso-*) and the navel string (*pwaso-*); the latter has certain associations with the garden (see Chapter 6, note 40). Some other metaphoric and mythic connections also appear linking bodily reproduction and garden plants (see also Malinowski, 1935, II:263). Damon (1978:202f.) reports an identification of central garden stones on southern Muyuw with the navel, but Gawans do not seem to make an explicit equation, and the orientation and structure of their gardens differ from the Muyuw form (see note 14).

12 Magic is used at planting more rarely nowadays than in the past, and most people do not appear to perform it at all. In 1974 there were certainly some men performing it privately (I saw one such bespelling for a taro garden). In 1980, I did not see any such performances, but the excellent yam gardens of one man were ascribed by his helpers to the fact that he had performed spells over them. As mentioned in note 10, land reawakening rites and other rites performed by a dala specialist for personal gardening activities are no longer performed on Gawa. The reasons Gawans give for this lapse always refer to the opposition of the church. Despite these cultural losses, knowledge of garden spells, like that of spells for other purposes, is still widely held and treated as a source of power. We shall see that there are other contexts in which spell use, including garden spells, is still vital.

13 This magic may be used for garden or hamlet stones (see note 8). The spells discussed in this chapter were obtained in 1974 when many Gawan men and women made available to me a large number of spells used for varied purposes. I am grateful to them for their generosity in giving me these spells. To keep my promise to them about their use, I cite the spells in English only, rather than in the indigenous language. In addition, where marked, I have left out brief passages that do not affect the argument or distort the basic pattern of the spell. The deletion of some elements of a spell follows a Gawan custom: It is possible, I was told, that when Gawans perform spells in public or sometimes when they transmit a spell, they might leave out some spell component so that its full strength is not revealed freely. (Possibly some such elements were sometimes left out in transmitting spells to me as well!)

14 This orientation of the garden is the opposite of that required in southern Muyuw where the sun must travel parallel with the garden divisions rather than diagonally across them (see Damon, 1978:199ff.). An additional feature of the Gawan garden divisions (similar to those on Muyuw) is the use of descriptive terms that connect them with parts of the canoe. These connections appear to have had more immediate significance in the past when they were apparently associated with the orientation of the dala garden ritualist's performance. I do not attempt to deal with this problem here, but the linkage suggests the relation between canoe and garden as containers of crops (the canoe carries food in its hold) and may perhaps reinforce the sense of the containment of motion (i.e., in this case, the canoe) in the garden. (It should be added that the compartment dividers in the yam house have similar verbal connections to the canoe hold.)

15 It is outside the scope of this study to provide an analysis of Gawan magic as a form of action, and although this particular spell is a paradigmatic case of the construction of self in magic, my account is not intended to generalize from it about Gawan spell processes in general. Gawan magic is varied in form, and different forms must be analyzed in some detail before coming to more general conclusions. A theoretical approach to Gawan magic based on Munn (1976) is in preparation.

16 I stress again that this parallelism between the precise topology of the material medium and the topology of the spell is not to be taken as characteristic of all Gawan magic. However, variants of this sort of parallelism are characteristic in the sense that nonverbal media always carry attributes essential to the spell operations.

17 In particular contexts of famine, however, Gawans do not necessarily reason backward from the particular case, inferring that the famine has been caused by destructive spells or that stones have been drained out of the garden (although this and related notions are inferential possibilities that could be invoked). Whether these assumptions gain general currency or not seems to be contingent on the wider situational context. For instance, in 1980, a drought throughout the Massim area also affected Gawa; Gawans also knew that the whole area was afflicted. At the time, I heard some talk that someone on Gawa had been performing sun magic (see the magic discussed next in the text) to blight the gardens, but it did not appear to gain community-wide currency.

18 My informant explained that the ritualist did not go to the garden and abstract the stones, but that this procedure was performed only in or through the spell itself.

19 For instance, in 1974, a man who was suspected of having told Muyuwans whom he had recently visited that Gawa was in a state of moru (*i-yakara karu*, he denied [there was] food) was criticized in one of the speeches in a public meeting. Epstein (1984:11), discussing Hogbin's account of shame in Busama, points to a similar attitude there. According to Epstein, the reason Busama villagers were so ashamed that other villages should be aware of their current food shortage lay in the "whole complex of attitudes towards and about food, in particular the importance attached to giving it away." "A plentiful supply of food," he continues, "was a principal means of gaining the esteem of one's fellows, and ... of nourishing one's own self-esteem."

20 I give here only a short account, not including all the details.

21 The cleaning of the main path is also a community work job carried out under the kareiwaga of the Gawan government councillor when it is deemed necessary.

As elsewhere, the Australian administration placed considerable emphasis on keeping paths clear (see Chapter 2). The importance of the thoroughfare that runs across the island has undoubtedly been developed in the postpacification period. Similarly, the movement of Gawan hamlets toward this thoroughfare referred to in note 8 is part of the increasing postpacification emphasis on the community as a collective whole.

22 People did not explicitly talk to me about agreement in this context, but in various other cases the implication that consensus is being carried out and directly conveyed in the synchronization of collective action is made explicit (see especially the discussion in Chapter 10).

23 The stakes were paired as male (husband) and female (wife), with appropriate bespelled leaves put in each. For the use of the husband–wife pair as the model of a differentiated totality, see Chapter 6. In the present context, this created the power components needed to create control of the entryway. It is common in magic to use leaves with complementary male and female gender associations.

24 In fact, a number of deaths took place in the months after the performance of this rite. But the immediate efficacy of the rite lies in its construction of Gawan reality in a particular experiential form imbued with the desired positive potentials. In this it is not markedly different from other types of practice. If, as Gell (1975:275) points out, "What ritual does is to grasp actively the 'significant' aspect of the world so as to *create the sign-conditions* of the desired outcome," it is because what we call ritual is built on the basic structure and model of creative action to begin with. For instance, when people plant and tend a garden, they obviously attempt to "create the sign conditions of the desired outcome," whether or not magic is used; obviously, they can do this only if they direct their work in terms of what is considered significant in that context.

25 Gawans use food prohibitions in many contexts. I propose to deal illustratively here only with those most germane to my argument.

26 The point is that in kula each person must hand on what he receives to someone else, so that three persons form a structural minimum. Young (1983a:395, 1983b:140) points out that the terms *kula* and *kune* (the cognate term for kula in the Dobuan, Normanby, and Bwanabwana areas) are also cognate with Goodenough Island *niune*, which refers to a type of prestation that recipients must hand on to their exchange partners. "From ego's point of view, *niuneku* (i.e., 'my niune') means: 'a gift given to me which I cannot consume or use myself'" (Young, 1983c:395). Thune (1980:212) describes a similar structure for Normanby marriage feast exchanges.

27 Standard effects of breaking food taboos include skin disorders, a "hole" in the stomach, and losing one's mind. In some cases, there is a special kind of disturbance connected with a particular prohibition, but the stated effects always refer back to some aspect of the body (including the mind) of the taboo breaker.

28 The term *buwaa* is also used for premarital gifts of tobacco or betel nut made by the parents of a young man to the young woman with whom he is sleeping that are not for her own use, but are to be handed on to her parents. See Chapter 2, note 26.

29 A beautiful person is *na/ta-mnabweita* or *-mnabwein*. The term *bweina* is the most general term meaning morally or aesthetically "good," or "attractive." The term *mamaadaga*, "beautiful," "fine," is also widely used. Ugliness is expressed by the term *gagera*; an ugly or bad person is *ta/na-mgaga*. One may speak of an ugly or attractive face or appearance as *gagera magi-ra* or *bweina magi-ra*.

30 The paternal dala involved may be the woman's foster father's dala if the latter has been most important in her upbringing. The significance of the fact that it is the father's (*tama*) dala and the child's father's dala who perform the role of bespelling and decorating the woman will be clarified in Chapter 6.

31 The shaving of the eyebrows was a manicuring procedure I did not observe in decoration outside this context.

32 It is significant that breaking food prohibitions connected with magic makes the magic "blunt" – i.e., it loses its effectiveness ("sharpness"). There is a strong opposition made between spells internalized and stored within the belly through verbal transmission from others (a transmission achieved through the recipients' gifts and aid to the donor), and food consumption. To break food prohibitions integral to the magic is to "eat one's ancestor" (*tabu*) because the spell potency has been transmitted from the past, and key elements in the spells are identified with ancestors who originally named them; if edible, these items themselves are prohibited to the ritualist (see also Tambiah, 1968:198, who has rightly pointed out in connection with Trobriand magic that "identification [with elements of a spell] ... by physical ingestion is repudiated"). The positive intersubjective process that is entailed in the transmission of magic produces an internal potency of sharpness (a capacity for effective outward action upon the world) stored within the body, which is negated by consumption. Maintaining spell-related food prohibitions, on the other hand, retains the stored potency that enables the ritualist to extend spatiotemporal control and act outward upon the world. One may consider the interesting parallels between this power stored inside the body from the past, with its positive creative potential, and the storage of stones in the ground with their potential for the perennial insurance of rooted crop growth, and their association with ancestral balouma.

33 The most prominent usage is in folktales (*kwaneibu*).

34 The immediate pre-European past, characterized as a period of fighting (*naviyay*), is also said to be *ou-daduba*, "in the shade" or "darkness."

35 I have on occasion seen a married man painting the prowboards but for the most part the painters I have observed were youths, as is prescribed.

36 On curative bloodletting to make the body lightweight, see Chapters 6 and 8. There are, of course, different images in kula spells, of which the one remarked on here is only one kind.

37 Gawans may expect to have sexual affairs (with unmarried women) on kula journeys when they travel to areas where it is the custom, as is the case in the northern journeys, for example. There also appears to be an occasional reciprocal arrangement between long-standing partners and their wives in which each man's wife sleeps with the husband's partner on his visit to their community.

Chapter 5. Fame

1 It is worth noting that *butu-* takes what Lithgow (1974) describes as the "intimate" form of the classifier and thus belongs to the same noun class as body terms and most kin terms. The term for name, *yaga-*, closely associated with *butu-*, also belongs to this category.

2   A name given from the father that derives from his dala is returned at the father's death. A person and his or her matri-kin are forbidden to mention the name of a dead individual of the father's dala. If ego is named after such a person, then he or she is forbidden to mention this name, and ego's dala kin should call this individual by a name from their own dala (or by another name that is not prohibited). A person may be named after kula shells (as kula shells may also be named after persons), and land plots, but may not have the same names as pigs and dogs. A man sometimes likes to name his child after a well-known kula shell received about the time of the child's birth.

3   In this respect, kula is a special case of a more general principle that one can become well known through what one gives, or obtains and then gives on. In my own case, some people pointed out to me that visitors would come to see me on Gawa because they had heard of my gifts of tobacco, the news of which had been noised abroad! In kula, receiving a shell implies a potential for future transmission, the acquisition of a potency of interest to others that contains potentials for further extension of the self; thus the receipt of a shell is treated as the moment of ego's acquisition of fame (see the following discussion).

4   In discussing kula elsewhere (Munn, 1983), I have glossed *-busi*, in idiomatic English, as "falls"; "descends" is more literal. It may also be said, however, that a person has "fallen" (*-kapusi*). In such contexts, the notion of "falling" or "going down" expresses the contraction of potency (i.e., of ego's spatiotemporal control) involved in defamation or loss of fame, or the general condition of being lower in a particular hierarchical context. For example, when two unequal shells of opposite category are given as part of the same transaction, the lower-valued shell is said to "go down" and the higher one to "climb." Conversely, the higher-valued one can be referred to as *butubutura*. Nevertheless, the lowering of a person's fame may also be built on the traveling of news about the person (i.e., in this sense, like fame, the lowering of fame involves a spatiotemporal extension of self, in that news about ego – in this case, negative – is going around). Thus defamation *subverts* the positive value of spatiotemporal extension of the self. I reserve discussion of this subversion for the chapters on witchcraft (especially Chapter 10), where it is considered in connection with shame.

5   There are recognized exceptions to this. See note 8.

6   No lexemic distinction is made between these kinds of names. (The term *yaga-* is the only basic lexeme available for verbal sign units, including category words and proper names.) However, Gawans were very explicit about the difference between these generic names for shells and the personal names of higher-ranked shells.

7   Men sometimes point out that attempts are made to confuse transactors by calling a lower-ranked shell by the same name as the true, highly ranked one. In my experience, this sort of gamesmanship occurs most frequently in connection with shells of a middle range or in the lower part of the highest-ranked category. However, the handful of shells that are among the very highest in circulation are not duplicated in this way.

8   The exceptions are young men who have inherited paths from a senior man of importance and who, through their assiduous aid to that man over a long period,

have learned his paths and shell transactions and become known to his partners. In this case, these young men may be able to obtain the high-class shells ordinarily reserved for their seniors. When I was on Muyuw with Gawans during a small kula trip, one of the senior Gawans emphasized this feature to me by pointing to a young Muyuwan boy and saying that should a youngster like this obtain an important shell, his name could go around with the high-ranked shell just like a senior man's. This principle has an analogue among shells in the fact that a new shell of extraordinary quality can achieve the instant recognition of high rank. However, what I am concerned with here is the basic and most usual pattern of emphasized connections between high-ranked shells and seniority.

9 Turner (1980:121) points to a comparable emphasis on speaking and hearing as differentia of political hierarchy among the Brazilian Kayapo. He states: "[Speaking] is associated with the active expression and political construction of social order, while . . . [hearing] betoken[s] the receptiveness to such expressions as the attribute of all socialised persons. Speaking and 'hearing' (that is understanding and conforming) are the complementary and interdependent functions that constitute the Kayapo polity." We shall see that a rather similar centering of political process characterizes Gawan polity as well, although the cultural specifics are very different.

10 In the past, curved pig tusks circulated in kula, and were associated with the potency of influential men. Gawan men still wear the shell imitations as pendants to (what used to be kaloma shell, and are now usually plastic kaloma imitation) necklaces.

11 Necklaces may be cut into smaller sections and the various shell and nut attachments taken off when used for women's daily wear. They may then be resassembled for transmission onward.

12 Necklaces need not be worn around the neck: Men sometimes tie them around the upper arm for special ceremonial wear.

13 The expression this woman used referred to the father as the key kinsman involved, but on questioning she explained that various close male kin could give the woman a necklace to wear. The notion that the father should be the source of shell beautification for a child appears to be much stronger in the Trobriands (see Weiner, 1976:127), but it is also consistent with certain aspects of the Gawan system (see Chapter 6). I would add that an unmarried daughter may be the particular pride of her father, who may give her shells with which to decorate and let her sail on kula with him if there is sufficient room on the canoe. (Young women may occasionally sail with the men on kula expeditions.)

14 Greek *kleos*, as Redfield (1975:32) writes about it, has certain similarities to Gawan *butu*. "*Kleos* is 'what men say,' and a thing has a *kleos* if it is talked about." "The bard sings of events which have a *kleos*. . . . At the same time, the bard confers on his heroes a *kleos*, without which they would have no existence in the later world of the bardic audience."

15 A brief account of the details is given in Munn (1983:302f.).

16 Gawans seem to place more emphasis on these additional beautification procedures and on their seductive uses in kula than do, apparently, the Vakutans (see Campbell, 1983b).

17 I have not observed major kula visits to Gawa, but I have participated in nighttime transactions on smaller kula travels to northern Muyuw. Gawans similarly stress that the night is the time to attempt to obtain kula shells (although the actual transaction may also take place in the morning, after a hard night of talking). As in the Vakutan case, a man should not carry off his own shells.

18 Although the vaga typifies the fame-giving article, Gawans also attach importance to gulugwalu. For instance, a man may strive to obtain a particular shell of high standard as a closing return for a previous transaction. Others will also be interested in the movement of this shell and its acquisition redounds to his fame. Men who visit the recipient's island on kula may be interested in going to see the shell at his house. In addition, if the shell is to become the recipient's kitomu, its potentialities are those of vaga (see Chapters 2 and 6).

Chapter 6. Marriage exchanges as value transformations

1 This pattern of giving food in return for an immediate payment called takola is also continued in a limited sequence of exchanges of raw yam piles, which confirm the marriage relation and are supposed to be finished before the birth of the first child. These gifts involve carefully formed piles of raw yams that are reciprocated by takola on the following day. Similar piles of raw produce are discussed in other contexts (Chapters 7, 8). As pointed out in Chapter 2, there are also a variety of regular exchanges built up in the marriage relation, but I deal only with the key buwaa exchanges here.

2 According to one woman, the gifts from each side are returns (*mapu-* in its general sense) to the kin of the spouse for raising and feeding him or her from childhood. This view would suggest that buwaa is part of a life cycle process (cf. Weiner, 1978) in which the feeding, or contribution to the bodily person of another has the potential of yielding harvest gifts of raw garden produce or hard goods of canoes and kula shells. However, this was the only informant who suggested these connections to me. In addition, particular buwaa relationships are not specifically established in these terms, and a man can start such a relation with a woman by making harvest gifts after marriage.

It should be noted that although the marriage exchange gifts are asymmetric, there is no institutionalized superordination of one set of affinal donors to the other. Two of my male informants grumbled about the difference between the male and female gifts, pointing in one case to the durability of the male kula shell and canoe gifts in comparison to the female-side gift and in the other to the amount of work that goes into a canoe (which was seen as more than that involved in gardening). However, this sort of attitude appears as a complaint rather than as part of the formal exchange relationship. The matter of hierarchization is more complex, as we shall see.

3 This directional pattern is also reproduced in other kinds of affinal transactions in which both sides give edibles. Thus fish always come from the husband and his kinsmen, in exchange for cooked garden vegetables from the wife and her kinswomen.

4 Some of my informants felt that kula shells are given when the recipient has been more generous with taro buwaa, whereas canoes go to the individual more generous with yam buwaa. Others denied this.

5 Kula shells may also come directly from the husband (in addition to his kinsman) going to a man who is giving produce as buwaa for the shell donor's wife; such gifts occur especially as the husband matures and has more shells available to him. In strong buwaa relations (called *tabwaabwara*), a wife's kinsman is also likely to be making harvest gifts directly to the couple for *their own* consumption. These gifts are not buwaa because they are eaten by the recipients, but they go to build up the strength of the relationship between the couple and the woman's kinsman.

Ordinarily a shell does not make connections across more than one nodal couple for whom buwaa produce is being given. However, I recorded one case in which a second (and possibly a third) couple was involved. As a result, the shell had a longer internal path before it went overseas. Such paths are more common for canoes.

6 The probable reason for this is that the implication of two paths (those of the donor and the affinal recipient) in the arrangement weakens the control of the Gawans involved. The donor, in particular, becomes dependent for a return on the strength of his affine's paths (which need not necessarily be as strong as his own). Similarly, inter-island recipients may be less fastidious about making returns, since the shell will not go back to persons on their own paths of partners. Other factors can also intervene (e.g., it is not unknown for an affine to drain his sister's husband or the latter's kinsman). On the other hand, as I indicate later, important relations between affines (including a husband and his wife's brother, see note 5) can be built by judicious use of this form of internal kula.

7 The lashing has masculine sexual associations (and is made by men), whereas the skirts and mats are female products.

8 At times various agreements appear to take place between the immediate canoe donors and the new recipient as to who should be the next internal recipient, but people insist that the right to make the decision for onward movement belongs to each canoe recipient. My requests for information about who was going to get a particular canoe next generally elicited the response that we would have to wait and see whom the new recipient would choose. The influence of a man's wife in these matters is also of considerable importance, because whatever decision is made, it will depend on the buwaa and related harvest gifts of her kinsmen. She may thus want the canoe to go to a particular man who has been especially assiduous in harvest gifts and she may importune her husband to this effect.

9 Since any dala may build canoes, this does not in itself result in one dala amassing resources through canoe building. Such a procedure would undoubtedly be inimical to the emphasis on the equality of the dala groups.

10 In the cases I observed, most of the returns went to dala and kumila members and their spouses, who represent the core of the long-time workers on a canoe.

11 Unfortunately, I did not ask Gawans whether they had any views on the reason that a large part of these internal payments for canoes come from trees. As noted in Chapter 2, only men climb trees to obtain their produce, but to my knowledge Gawans do not make the explicit, extended connections between the male principle and the tops (*dabwara*) of trees that one finds on Vakuta (Campbell, 1984:160). Vakutans also explicitly identify the roots or base of trees (the wouwura) with the female principle, an exegetical emphasis that does not appear in quite this way in the Gawan process; interestingly enough, however, this Vakutan exegesis is consistent with the analysis I make of the Gawan exchange system and with various features of the system I discuss.

12   On the relation between technologies of food production and underlying structures of sociocultural significance see the important study by Hugh-Jones (1979).

13   There is a marked contrast in this respect between the Gawan method of transmitting the harvest gift and that of the Trobriands that is clearly connected with differences in the political systems of the two societies. On the Trobriand procedures, see Malinowski, 1935:176ff.

14   It is notable that, in the harvest gift, the produce donors do not markedly display their own persons as the donors: As we have seen, they do not themselves harvest the gift and take it to the recipients' hamlets.

15   For more details on the complexity of these buwaa relations, see Chapter 2, and note 5 in this chapter.

16   There are different return gifts of edibles from overseas recipients that I do not discuss here.

17   It is usually said that five armshells are the price of a canoe, but in fact this number can vary upward or downward, depending in part on the size of the shells returned. The number of pots is variable. I counted eighteen pots in the case of one canoe.

18   Some men attempt to continue to exchange the same two shells for each other in the case of a particular kitomu. Thus, rather than the particular shell instantiation changing from one transaction to the next, there are only two instantiations (one necklace and one armshell) of the kitomu, and the two shells involved are regarded as permanent possessions that should always travel along the same path and be exchanged for each other. Most men, however, engage only in the more usual pattern of transacting shells so that kitomu may have multiple instantiations over time. There is, in fact, a feeling among some that the former method is undesirable because one should not hold onto high-ranked shells and keep them from others who may wish to transact them.

19   Gawans will try to place kitomu with the safest partners they have. Thus some men told me that kitomu should be put on a path that involves men of one's own kumila (i.e., kinspeople) only, although transaction records I obtained do not necessarily reflect this ideal.

20   The term *tutu* (also *-tatu*) is the standard term used to refer to the hollowing or grooving of a log in canoe production. In addition, the groove into which the front, vertical prowboard slides on the ends of the canoe log is called *tatu-waga* (canoe groove).

21   This is only part of the narrative. The account continues with some additional mistakes on the part of the men once they set sail. Gawans find these mistakes, and the story in general, very humorous. The full narrative raises some other interesting points that I cannot deal with here.

22   It is worth noting that the knowledge is not stolen from the woman – as is so common a myth pattern in societies that, unlike Gawa, have male initiation – but that it is freely given in an effort to aid the men. (The narrative is told by men, and I originally heard parts of it from some young boys; but women are also familiar with it.)

23   Whereas the identification of the outrigger log (*kabalay*) as male and the canoe hull (*waga*) as female is always insisted upon in the context of a discussion of the canoe woods or origin narrative, in other contexts there is some variability. For

instance, when I asked about male and female identifications of parts of the completed canoe, there were some responses that identified the outrigger log as female and the hull as male. The rationale given in one instance was that the log balances or stabilizes the key part of the canoe, which is the hull. In this instance a different rationale – also as we have seen, fundamental to the system (i.e. that the female principle is the relatively subordinate "static" one) – was utilized to identify the male–female components.

24 Red paints on the canoe are not identified with blood (Munn 1977:49), and the same is true of red body decor.

25 The matrilineal balouma or balouma-related "spirit children" are given no specific role in conception (see Chapter 4, note 2).

26 The husband with his male kin and the male kinsmen of the woman carry water and cut firewood for the purifying heat necessary to protect the woman and child. A husband's claims to the child are built in part on his supportiveness in carrying out these jobs at childbirth. This is particularly important for the first child.

27 One of the later returns to which the father's kinswomen are entitled for this bodily aid is the right to take certain decor, especially betel wreaths, but also other gifts, directly from the child, thus detaching something directly from the bodily surface. This right may be exercised (with prearrangement) on certain festive occasions throughout life, although it is most frequently observable with respect to children. The act of ceremonially taking something directly from another's body (called -kwaya) cannot be performed by co-dala members. A child's father's immediate sister is also prohibited because of the physical taboos on touch connecting brother and sister, but other women may kwaya for her. We shall consider such transactions in other contexts later, but we may note here that they engage the body surface as a transactive arena for movement from self to other.

28 Weiner (1978:182) points out that in the Trobriands "the growth of a child (its external form) is shaped by a man from another *dala*." Thus she suggests that the "child embodies the balance between (1) *dala* identity, inner substance and women, and (2) external identity, external resources and men." See also Eyde (1983:67), who suggests that in the Trobriands, "substance comes from the mother, [and] its form from the father." Note, however, that Gawans do not develop the idea, prominent in the Trobriands (Austen, 1934:112; Malinowski, 1929:207; Weiner 1976:123) that a man's sexual intercourse with his wife moulds the child in the womb. We saw, however, that in the prebirth rites for a first child, the paternal role (mediated through a man's female kin) is to produce movement toward the outside – to induce the vital mobility of movement by applying substances of water and cosmetics on the body surface and giving bespelled water for internalization.

29 Some metaphors draw parallels between growth in the garden and bodily reproduction: For instance, one may say that the garden -kabinay, "congeals" or forms a mass, as the blood congeals to form the baby inside the mother; similarly, the garden may be said to -varura, "give birth." I have also heard the people of a dala referred to metaphorically as the dala's "plantings."

30 Bloodletting makes the body lightweight and dry inside, releasing "its heaviness." One informant compared the heating of canoe wood to dry it out (done as part of the canoe building) with the drying of blood involved in smoking a woman over the birth fire to cleanse or protect her after birth (whitening her skin), or in letting blood from the body.

31 Some of my informants assured me that in their view this was not simply a metaphor: The canoe truly (*mokita*) smells the land.

32 An analysis of the semantics of the canoe carvings is in preparation.

33 Gardens, canoes, and yam houses are all containers of crops. Certain verbal parallels are also made between them that focus on the internal divisions or compartmentalization of each artifact and connect both gardens and yam houses to canoes.

34 I have borrowed the expression "value form" from Marx's terminology in *Capital I* (1906:65ff.) to express the fact that one element (here an act and its medium) finds "the form of its own value" in the shape of another. Of course, I am adapting the notion to the concern of my own argument with a particular kind of symbolic transformation, as made clear in the text.

35 Furthermore, pots are most frequently employed nowadays in ceremonial taro cooking where men are the more immediate users. Note that on the Trobriands (in contrast to Gawa), pots are classed as male "valuables" (*veiguwa*) in exchange contexts (Weiner, 1976:179).

36 See Battaglia (1983) for an account of notions of complementarity on Sabarl in the southern Massim.

37 Gawans do not have a reciprocal term *marriage partner* apart from the asymmetric terms for husband and wife. However, they do use a reciprocal term *veivay*, which refers to one's affines or to affines as a category in contrast to *veyo*-kin. It is also notable that there is no single term for the two categories of kula shells apart from the broad term *kura*, which refers to the exchange system in general.

38 It should not be inferred from this particular usage of *gimwali* that the notion is never applied to the exchange of kula shells. In fact, Gawans may use the term *gimwali* in connection with the (devalued) immediate exchange of an armshell and a necklace, which turns the exchange into a kind of purchase. In the present case, the informant was pointing to the traditional, appropriate complementarity or "mateship" of the canoe and the kula shells in contrast to which the pots were being defined as more like a purchase in which the articles that are used to obtain another article may vary, and thus lack this traditional appropriateness.

39 Gawans sometimes say the kitomu "rigs" (*-ginola*) the path. The metaphor refers to rigging a canoe sail and conveys the infusion of tautness or hardness into something. In its metaphoric context, this conveys, according to informants, that it won't rot or disappear. It thus seems also to convey productiveness or fertility. The same metaphor may be used of garden or hamlet fertility magic that makes the land "tight" and "hard" and so maintains its fertile potentials (see Chapter 4).

40 As previously indicated (Chapter 4, note 11), the navel is the mark of both separation from and connection to, the mother. Gawans place considerable emphasis on the piece of navel string (*pwaso-*) that remains after birth; this must be manipulated by the child's father's female kinswomen in order to be removed some days later. When this remaining cord comes off, it is taken as a sign that the child is expected to live. The cord should then be taken out and put on a variety of taro or other plants in the garden of any one of its maternal or paternal kin. Maternal kin, I was told, would be prohibited from eating from this planting, but its produce may be eaten by paternal kin. Thus the *pwaso-* has two dimensions: The part that is separated from the body, thus marking the living child's successful separation from the mother is associated, as we might expect, with the activity of the paternal kin; the navel marking that remains as an intrinsic part of the child's body is a sign of the maternal bond and matrilineal identity and also encodes the creation at birth of the separate individual as a new member of the dala.

41 Gregory's (1982:197) dualistic treatment of kitomu in terms of two types of circulation – as a "commodity," when ego "alienates" the shell from himself, and as an "inalienable" (Maussian type) "gift" in kula exchange – obscures the fundamental unity of these operations of kitomu. Not only the "inalienability" of kitomu shells in kula circulation, but also their "alienability" are predicated on the fact that they are personal possessions, aspects of the self in the Maussian sense, and subject to one's own kareiwaga.

42 In a recent paper published after this discussion was completed, Weiner, (1985) has considered the integral relation of "keeping" to transactive processes. For an earlier account of Gawan kitomu relevant to this perspective, see Munn, 1977:46.

43 Gawans recognize that pigs, for example, are another major external source of kitomu, especially for the people to the south of them. However, in the view of some, pigs are a poor second to canoes, and some informants told me that in theory, at least, one should only get kitomu for pigs with curved tusks (a view that appears to reflect the past rather than the contemporary situation). Some Gawans pointed out to me that in their view northwestern peoples such as the Vakutans or Kitavans do not have any "real" source of kitomu and therefore they falsely label shells acquired within kula transactions of a certain type as their "kitomu."

44 Obviously, continuity is not a given in the case of the dala (which can die out, as some dala have in recent memory) any more than it is in kitomu transactions (which like other transactions can sometimes end in default). Gawans strive to create continuity and positive potentiality, a striving that is, of course, always subject to the possibility of failure.

45 See Young (1983b:200f., 262f.) on the formulation of hierarchy as stasis on Goodenough. As he points out, in Goodenough feasts, the "'chief of the feast,' as he sits immobile on his platform" (ibid., 263) conveys hierarchy. Significantly, on (patrilineal) Goodenough, the images of motion, flow, and mobility in general are feminine (ibid., 263). In contrast, Campbell (1984:227ff.) in discussing Vakutan kula journeys suggests that hosts (who are static and must be importuned by mobile visitors) are feminine in their connotations.

46 This version of the narrative derives from one informant, but reference to the Rama Dobu also recurs in kula spells, and some of my information comes from the comments of other men. The story is connected with the origin of canoes on Kweawata and has some similarities to the account of the flying canoe recorded by Malinowski (1922:311ff., especially 315–16), which refers to Kitava. In the Gawan version referred to here the two sisters lived with their brother on Kweawata. Both sisters were witches (*bwagaw*) but the older sister licked raw fish, which she then cooked and gave to her brother to eat. Although the two sisters, being witches, had no trouble in consuming the fish, the brother vomited it. When he pointed out that they had eaten well but he had become ill, the older sister became angered and taking her sister with her flew up through a hole in the house, taking off for Kitava. Passing from Kitava to Dobu they separated the island of Vakuta by splitting through the rock connecting it with the northern Trobriand island. But when they got to Dobu, the younger sister lied to the older one, saying she had left her mat behind. Going back, she taught her brother how to build a canoe and gave him the necessary canoe magic. This canoe was made on top of Kweawata, traveled down the cliff to the sea, and sailed off, but it didn't fly. The younger sister flew back to Dobu, but continued to miss and think sympathetically (*i-karin nuwa-ra*) about her brother.

In comparison with the Gawan myth of canoe origins, this one splits the power of women into favorable and unfavorable components, emphasizing not simply the free, benignly given gift of the woman to men, but a much more ambivalently coded transfer of knowledge. Furthermore, rather than focusing on gifts of substance and appropriate material, it directly stresses the gift of motion as a weakened but positive refraction of the flying powers of the witches. For further comments on aspects of this ambiguity relevant to the argument, see the discussion in the text.

47   One woman told me of a case in which she had actually tried to prevent her mother's brother from transacting a necklace he had given her to wear, by hiding in different hamlets. He eventually retrieved the necklace and transacted it as he had wished. My informant's objection to the transaction was due to the fact that the shell was a closing gift that her kinsman was wrongfully giving to another man (not the original donor).

48   It is of interest that the recursive form of the affinal cycle taken as a unitary whole accords well with a general theoretical model recently suggested by Turner (1985, 1979a:168ff.) for dealing with moieties and other polarized social forms that appear ambiguously symmetric and asymmetric, equal and hierarchical (see also Dumont, 1979; Lévi-Strauss, 1967; Tcherkézoff, 1983). According to Turner's model, such forms entail the reconstitution of a primary order of asymmetry within a higher-order binary structure that encompasses it; the higher structure in turn draws on the dominant hierarchic component of the lower order as the medium of its homogeneous form. Thus the encompassing order consists of two polarized units (as, for example, patrilineal moiety divisions) that are "replicated instances" (1985:368) of one term of the underlying asymmetric social form. For example, in a patrimoiety system, the male-patrilineal component is drawn from the lower-order relations (which also entail a female-matrilateral component) to create the principle of the encompassing order. Nevertheless, the latter's apparently symmetric and egalitarian units are themselves "symbolically associated with attributes which preserve ... the asymmetrical form of the underlying relationship" (ibid., 368). In this respect, the higher order dualism is a homology of the lower set of relations – a reconstitution of the latter in apparently egalitarian, symmetric terms.

If we apply this model to the Gawan case of the buwaa exchanges rather than to a moiety structure, kula exchange appears equivalent to the higher encompassing and homogeneous form that draws on the male dimension of the primary exchange to construct its terms. The female intermediary link in the internal affinal exchanges is not intrinsic to the higher order as such; although affinal bonds that contain this nexus still maintain the intervening female link in the *intra*-island segment when projected within kula, this female component is now matrixed in the primarily male–male links of the inter-island system. Moreover, kula draws on the male artifacts as the medium of the binary model of exchange equivalence and closure. The dominant term of the lower or primary segment thus becomes the replicated unit of the more encompassing order that involves men in each opposed direction exchanging appropriate (male) articles of shell decor. Conversely, the primary-phase subordinate term (food and the female link) is excluded.

The asymmetry of the internal exchange is nevertheless preserved in the opposition between female and male shell categories. Alternatively, the relatively homogeneous units are kula canoes and kitomu (both representative of the male kula dimension) that reconstitute the primary unequal exchange in terms of a closing equalization, and similarly preserve the female–male asymmetry (although in terms somewhat different from that of the kula shell exchange).

However, Turner's model (in contrast to Dumont's, 1979:811f.; see also Bourdieu, 1970) does not attempt to explain the possibility of reversal in the system (notably, in the higher order). The view I have suggested is that what appears as reversal is a movement to a contextual frame or perspective, within which some crucial meaning or principle of significance held implicit in another frame becomes manifest. The aspect manifested from this second perspective is the dimension along which the reversal takes place. For instance, the apparent reversal in the superordination of female to male goods makes explicit within the encompassing order of male-dominated kula exchange the particular power of women and the female principle implicit in the operation of the marriage exchange. The resulting structure conveys the dual potencies that regulate the Gawan system and create ambiguity in the apparent dominance of the masculine transformational powers.

Chapter 7. Mortuary exchanges and the deconstitution of self

1 The balouma is supposed to go away to Tuma at death or at the burial, although it may occasionally possess a kinsperson either during and just after the burial or even sometime after (as in one case where a person visiting from another island came to grieve at the house where the deceased had been mourned). Gawans do not treat the mortuary rites as a means of sending the balouma away, and the notions about its departure are vague.

2 Hertz's (1960:77) point that death "destroys the social being grafted onto the physical individual," and A. Strathern's (1981:222) that in Melanesia "death generates a separation of the paternal and maternal forces brought together at the time of birth," are not strictly accurate statements, as, in fact, Hertz's own work (despite the Durkheimian dualism of this statement) actually goes to show. On Gawa, it is the mortuary rites and not physical death that must, in Strathern's terms, separate "the paternal and maternal forces." Moreover, the bodily space-time that must be decomposed by the rites is not only that formed at birth, but also at marriage.

3 The children of males of the deceased's dala (i.e., those who are not the

deceased's children if the deceased is male) are also important mourners, although their participation need not be on a dala basis except in particular cases. If the deceased is male, his child belongs to his wife's dala, and the whole dala is therefore necessarily central to the procedure, the child of course, being a focal mourner in the rites.

4   It may be said of either a woman or a man that she or he -koupw a child. For a woman, this means that she gave birth to the child (which she feeds with her milk). For the father, it refers to his work in providing garden food, carrying water, and cutting firewood for the child.

5   This basic structure of the Gawan rites is not precisely the same as that of the Trobriand mortuary rites, although both share certain dualistic features: In both cases paternal and marital dala of the deceased form key categories of mourners or workers to whom major payments are made by the dala of the deceased (and their support networks), and whom the latter release from mourning (see Weiner, 1976:57, 63). However, in the Trobriand case, in contrast to Gawa, a distinctive position is occupied by the children of males of the deceased's dala who "play a dual role" by wearing mourning attire but contributing to the resources of the deceased's dala (Weiner, 1976:63). In this sense, the children of males are liminal between the categories of the workers and the deceased's dala or "owners." Although I cannot expand this comparison here, it would seem that the liminal people in the Gawan ceremonies are the spouses of dala members most directly involved in a given rite. For example, spouses of living members of the dala of the deceased both contribute resources with their spouses as part of a single co-operative unit and act as affines (sinavarama) who, unlike the deceased's dala kin, may, for example, stay with mourners all night in the house of mourning. These differences can be shown to be consistent with others in the Gawan as against the Trobriand system, but a comparison of Gawan and Trobriand mortuary organization lies outside the purview of this study. It should be noted, however, that despite these differences, the essentially dualistic structures of both Gawan and Trobriand mortuary rites contrast, for instance, with Muyuw (Damon, 1978) and the southern communities of Sabarl (Battaglia, 1981) and Paneati (Berde, 1974), where the three relationship categories of matri-kin, patri-kin, and spouse each play sharply distinguished roles. On Sabarl, for instance, patrikin (not matrilineal kin) of the deceased release the spouse from mourning.

6   The fact that whenever fish are transacted asymmetrically in the mortuary rites they come from the affinal side suggests the affines' external, male connotations. These asymmetric transactions also appear to occur at transitional points marking the lifting of a ban or the finalization of the entire mortuary ceremony, a feature that seems to be consistent with various qualities of fish: their slippery mobility, and their location in the external, buoyant world of the sea, as well as their colorful markings (called soba, the same term Gawans use for the ceremonial designs they paint on their faces for dances and other festive contexts).

7   As is usual in the organization of such ceremonies, the actual alignments may depend on weighting different sets of overlapping ties in order to determine with which side one may operate. Some people help both sides at once.

8   The only exception to this mourning pattern is the tawulakwabu: one token person of the Umata dala (usually a woman) who takes on mourning black in

immediate expression of the Umata's grief. However, her blackening is separate from the formal procedures, and she does not live in the house of mourning with the main mourners.

9   I observed some eleven funerals during the different periods I spent on Gawa. In addition to excluding some parts of the rites, the discussion does not attempt to consider variations in the individual rites, which may involve dala specializations.

10   See Weiner (1976:97ff.) for a discussion of the long sepwana skirt on the northern Trobriands that is a focus of competition, quite in contrast to the Gawan use of the skirt. The competitiveness of the Trobriand mortuary rites is absent in the Gawan equivalent.

11   In response to the church, an attempt has been made by some Gawans to introduce the wearing of black armbands instead of blackening the body. But body blackening is the focus of considerable import and emotional significance, as suggested in part by the points made here. Attempts to totally eliminate blackening were a source of conflict in at least three mortuary rites I observed, and Gawans have resisted such attempts.

12   When there is no spouse, usually the next closest person of the right category, for instance, a father or a man's son, might sit close to the body, or lie down with it part of the time.

13   Except for rare cases, Gawans always try to have the major mourning run through the night. In the morning, just at dawn, a representative of the Umata comes in and beautifies the dead. Thus the beautification should coincide with the rising of the light, just as in the ceremonial beautification processes described earlier. Burial is ordinarily in the later morning or by noon of this day. I do not deal here with the details of the preburial ceremonies, the burial, or the initial postburial rites. It should be noted, however, that these are very powerful and moving ceremonies that drain the populace emotionally and then set in motion (in the form of a collective singsong on the night of the burial day, meant to soothe the grief of all and especially of those inside the house of mourning after the burial) the initial process for healing the pain. The beautification at dawn of those who have sung all night marks the initial release of the wider community from prohibitions of the mourning night and burial.

14   Of course, if the deceased's spouse died earlier, then the formal buwaa will actually have stopped at that point.

15   Pieces of hair and sometimes the nails of *living* paternal or marital kin may also be worn in amulets, and the same principles of repayment and withdrawal hold.

16   In addition, at death a person should be buried in his or her own dala land. Otherwise, payment including a kitomu kula shell should be made to the owning dala.

17   For instance, some mourners are allowed to go to their gardens during the day, and these are called "those who can move around" (*kamaroray*). In the past, restrictions, especially on the spouse, were apparently much more severe, and the whole procedure was also lengthier.

18   Tall kaboma may also be made for an optional prestation called *uragayay*, which is made by the Umata to the affines before the blackening and directly after the singing that occurs through the night after the burial. This gift includes the presentation of pork. If an uragayay is made, the affines will make a large number

of skirts that go to the Umata in return. The connection of skirts and food dishes is discussed later in the chapter.

19 The significance of this topping as decor is less emphasized here than in the yam piles made for community entertainments where, as we shall see, additions are crucial, in Gawan thinking, to the beauty of the whole. The use of the device of addition to a core in creating beautification is characteristic of Gawan beautification procedures, as we have seen in the case of kula shells.

20 It is also felt that the most important mourners may be reluctant to be released from their grieving. There is some suggestion therefore that the food gift is required to persuade them to change their minds.

21 Dark clouds (*bwaw*) carry disturbing connotations since they may be a covering for evil balouma (e.g., of witches, or sometimes the dead in general) who may shroud themselves in the clouds and attack canoes on the sea (see Chapter 9). The implication of this statement is thus similar to others I heard in which women said the balouma spirits in the bush would "grab and hold" (-*yousi*) anyone who broke the rules of the *yabalouma* – the last mwaagula band to be removed (see note 22). The notion of being "grabbed and held" by a balouma, or by a balouma inside a stone occurs in certain other contexts of taboo breaking and is frequently said to cause the individual involved to lose his or her mind.

22 The prohibitions on the yabalouma wearer were explained by some informants as "taboo of the guyaw, balouma" (*boumiya-ra guyaw, balouma*). In order for a wearer to eat boiled food, fish, and taro pudding again after the band had been removed, a standard spell is performed over the legs of the ex-wearer by a member of the latter's dala. In this spell, the balouma is instructed to "come down" so that the individual can eat these foods safely again. This type of spell is used in other contexts where a taboo on eating that is associated with the authority of dala ancestors is lifted (cf. the pregnancy rite, Chapter 4). Since only the wearer's dala may make the yabalouma and lift the associated food taboo, the balouma removed in this way is also probably assumed to be the wearer's dala ancestor. Although I do not have explicit information regarding the balouma's dala identity in the present context, this is the assumption Gawans make in other similar contexts of release.

23 As in all such transactions, individual recipients on both sides will redistribute much of what they receive, keeping a small part for themselves.

24 This third transaction usually pays lesser grades of mourning, and recipients are not required to return a full food pile, although they will have received one from the Umata. According to one Gawan, Iwans and Kitavans to Gawa's north require only token food returns from all affines receiving kaboma in mortuary rites.

25 However, an implicit element of inequality remains, for the Umata are always those who initiate the food giving, and are in control of the sagali. The tokenism of the third return (see note 24) points also to this element of imbalance. If we consider the Gawan remark mentioned in note 24, that affines in some of the northern islands give only token returns for produce piles, the Gawan pattern suggests, on the one hand, an increased emphasis on the public assertion of equality, and, on the other, an attempt to constrain or deemphasize the element of inequality remaining. One might perhaps see this component as being balanced out at the death of the second spouse, but Gawans never conceptualized it in this way to me.

26 If any of the mourners are very old, or have difficulty in walking after the long confinement, they may be washed in the hamlet, but the basic principle of the rite is the movement to the sea.

27 If there are any male mourners in the house (e.g., a husband, or a father in the case of an unmarried child), they will receive a bright new or clean laplap from the Umata and will be decorated by men of the latter group.

28 Some fragments of the dead still remain as aspects of the affines and visible dimensions of the social world. On contemporary Gawa, these are most notably the packets of teeth or hair mentioned in note 15.

29 Men may roll the cord for the binding of these skirts (see Chapter 8, note 25).

30 Gawans do not articulate the mortuary process with the reconstitution of exchange networks, and unlike a number of other areas of the Massim and Melanesia (see e.g., Battaglia, 1983; Coppet, 1981; Damon 1983b; A. Strathern, 1981), they do not, through exchange procedures, create conversions of the mortal body into enduring goods that can be transacted. Although a kitomu shell may on occasion be given by affines at a death (engendering a return responsibility on the part of the Umata recipients at a funeral of the donor's dala), cycles of positive spatiotemporal transformation such as I examined for Gawan marriage exchanges do not emerge as part of Gawan mortuary exchanges. Thus the positive value of potentiality infused back into the society is the condition for the return of the more expansive activities (e.g., it now becomes appropriate for the deceased's dala members and mourning affines to engage in kula), but the mortuary procedures themselves do not entail this level of expansion.

Chapter 8. The Drum dance and the Comb

1 The Comb entertainment appears to have been introduced from the south within living memory, largely supplanting the Wild Pig kayasa of another branch of the same Nukwasisi dala. People are still conversant with the latter, however, and feel that it might be performed sometime in the future, although it has certain associations with overt aggression that appear to be a factor in making it less attractive than the Comb. I cannot examine the historical aspect more fully here, but it is notable that the Comb conforms well to the basic template that I have suggested is fundamental to Gawan value transformations.

2 For example, the Drum dance that I observed during 1973–4, and that was concluded in 1975, was apparently a renewal of a performance cycle begun in the 1960s that had been seriously interrupted by the deaths of important men and was then reopened in 1972. The Comb performance that I observed in 1979–80 was started, as far as I could tell from informants, about 1976, after I had left Gawa. It was concluded after the 1980 yam harvest, possibly interrupted by the death of a major kula man in 1978.

3 See Burman (1981) on control over community time schedules as basic to traditional Melanesian Big man leadership on Simbo (the Western Solomons).

4 Another more specialized term, *kalawoulu*, is frequently used in the context of community entertainments to refer to the closing gift.

5 It would seem that if the pattern limited to two major entertainments continues, the definition as to which is vaga and which gulugwalu could become relatively fixed, unless the Nukwasisi are willing to perform two Comb entertainments in sequence (one closing and one opening entertainment). Ideally, according to the egalitarian emphasis in the cycle, the sources of the closing or opening gift should not be fixed, but should alternate.

6 This may be part of the increasing community focus on Gawa but it also contradicts the emphasis on the segmentation of controls, and the equality of each dala, as well as that of the somewhat rivalrous neighborhoods, since the two entertainments are now combined in a hamlet of one neighborhood rather than alternating between two.

7 Malinowski (1922:490ff.) says that "So'i" were also performed on Kitava, but contemporary Gawans identify it with islands to their south.

8 Of course, kula shells may also be individually transacted when visitors come to Gawan entertainments.

9 This does not, of course, mean that any visitors who happen to be present are necessarily excluded. However, unless they are close kin or affines of the deceased, their formal participation is limited to the singsong held on the night of the burial day.

10 See Malinowski's (1929: plate facing 282) reference to the "*kaydebu* dance" in the Trobriands. The Gawan dabedeba that was set up for the dance was also carved with a lizard and a man wearing a diginaakum (imitation tusk) necklace of the kind worn in dancing. The lizard is a significant emblem because the head of the drum is made from a lizard skin. In connection with the regular anticlockwise dancing, one Gawan said that a reversal of this direction would put the right hand, which manipulates the pandanus streamer (that is balanced by the left hand), inappropriately on the inside.

11 I was told that the streamer used at night dances is another type of leaf, whereas the actual pandanus is usually used in the major daytime dances.

12 Malinowski (1922:492) refers to the use of a sprouting coconut in a different context as a device for signifying the passage of time.

13 My account simplifies the finale, as I discuss only the three final days of a six-day sequence. The first three days involved preliminary day- and nighttime dances and public speaking.

14 Members of one dala of the Nukubay closely identified with the drum and associated with the immediate owners of the entertainment are prohibited from eating after the drum has been beaten in the early evening to announce the dance. This is a dala prohibition that distinguishes them from other dala groups. It is said that a person breaking the prohibition would become deaf.

15 It is the Tarakwasisi men who are responsible for the preparation of the lizard skin timpanum on the drums that must initiate a new cycle of the Drum dance.

16 One Tarakubay man told me that the Nukubay never really became Ramugway when the entertainments reverse. In this man's view, Nukubay are essentially guyaw in the general sense of being of high standing, and cannot, in this sense, be Ramugway in the entertainments. His somewhat idiosyncratic remarks and certain other features about the Nukubay suggest something similar to what Young (1971:63) has called "submerged rank." There are indications that in the past the Nukubay or some Nukubay dala may have considered themselves dala of rank. Apart from the entertainments, *ramugway* is a status category that connotes an aggressive or subordinate role as against the superordinating guyaw category associated with peacemaking. The categories may have had wider significance historically than on contemporary Gawa, where, however, some components of this particular dualistic feature are reflected in the entertainments. The peace-making-aggressive opposition is reminiscent of a similar dualism in Kalauna, Goodenough Island (Young, 1971:228) where it also has a connection with the "festival" organization of the community.

17 Changes sometimes occur, but unlike kula partnerships, for instance, these internal partnerships on the community plane are not subject to the fragility of political negotiation.

18 Cf. the contrast between *nube-* and *veyo-* noted in Chapter 2, note 13.

19 The donor himself also contributes, as may other individuals of his own or other dala to whom he has given some produce from previous entertainment performances, or who are variously indebted to him for produce. These men will make contributions (e.g., a small basket of yams) in support. Men keep track of various small produce debts that they have incurred and will try to return them in an appropriate context.

20 Gawans make sure that the two nube partners are not *actual* in-laws. If the married couple is Nukwasisi-Nukubay, the dala of the man's entertainment partner must be different from that of his wife. Otherwise, at the entertainment in which the produce gift comes from the husband, it would be going to a man of his wife's dala, thus reversing the correct direction of food giving aid to the entertainment donor *from* his wife's immediate kin. In the Drum dance, for instance, a man of a dala of Nukwasisi may be giving produce to help an immediate Tarakubay affine and also be receiving produce from his Tarakubay partner, but these two Tarakubay men must be individuals of different dala.

21 This sort of motion – going from east to west and west to east, or from north to south and south to north as in the negative spell – appears to be a common figure for expressing encompassing movement in the spells. It also seems possible that in the present context, it may convey the circular motion of the dance.

22 There was one exception to this: In one sequence of the final dance, the women danced briefly up ahead of the men with a single man leading them. They then switched back behind the men again. However, even in this reversal, the women followed the man's dance leadership. Unfortunately, I do not have further information on the significance of this reversal.

23 Children are not expected to know how to dance – at least this was the case in 1974 when the school was first opened on Gawa. At that time, the teacher was interested in having the children perform the traditional dance, not at first realizing that it belonged to the activities of sexually active youths and adults and was not usually performed by children. Following the request of the teacher, Gawans began giving the children instruction in dancing.

24 Malinowski (1929:39) says that the only traditional Trobriand dance in which women may also dance is the one where men put on skirts. He remarks, however, that women rarely do in fact dance in these performances. There appears to me to be considerable evidence pointing to a greater specialization and demarcation of gender roles in both the Trobriands of Malinowski's era and of contemporary times than there is in contemporary Gawan society.

25 Women's skirts have strong sexual connotations, as they should cover not only the genitals, but also the thighs, a highly eroticized area of the female body. The ties for these skirts are made of a cord also used for men's fish nets. A little story told me quite spontaneously by a woman and her husband, while some of this cord was being prepared, points to the sexual implications involved. In this tale, a man comes home to find that his wife has used up the material for his fish net cord for the waistband of her skirt. He remarks, however, that it doesn't matter, because in either case, he will "eat" (i.e., eating stands here as a metaphor for sexual intercourse). The essentially female skirts thus contain a male component at the top (the waistband), and connote heterosexual relationships. Significantly, it would seem, the band at the top is sometimes made by men for women's skirts; in addition, it is this tie that binds together the separate bunches of coconut fronds out of which the skirt is made.

It is possible that the male headdresses that are also verbally identified with the long poles on canoes may be metaphorically equated with the penis. However, men never identified them or the poles in this way, although they were very explicit about the male sexual meanings given to elongated elements attached to fish nets.

There are other significant decor items: notably the facial designs (*soba*). I do not , attempt to discuss these here except to note that one woman described such designs as making the person youthful, "slippery" and "lightweight" as in dancing.

26 Cf. the connection of the Drum dance with the activities of unmarried youths, set apart, as we saw earlier, from the relatively fixed adult world of affinal bonds.

27 From one perspective, the food reciprocates the dancers for their performance, as Gawans reciprocate people who come to work for particular projects. It could be that the persuasiveness the dancers embody is itself supposed to release the food or move the Guyaw to give, for the dancers are creating the essence of persuasive qualities. Gawan ideas that support this view were made quite explicitly to me in connection with the Comb entertainment (but not the Drum dance), and will be noted later.

28 It may be useful to reiterate here that raw yams can be used by the recipient for seed yams or be given to others (who may also make choices about their use) as well as be consumed, whereas cooked food is subject to more or less immediate consumption or redistribution by the donor and immediate consumption by the second recipient.

29 I refer here in particular to collective activities called *bisila* (pandanus streamer), which involve a parade of either overseas male visitors to particular hamlets on Gawa demanding gifts and kula shells for their new canoe (cf. Malinowski, 1922:163ff.; Young, 1983c:398ff.); or of women from one Gawan neighborhood parading to another neighborhood to make similar demands of female partners (and their husbands and kinspeople) in the second neighborhood. The activity takes its name from the leafy branch – a substitute for the pandanus streamer – which is aggressively inserted in the side of the house to signify the demand. The verbal response I have quoted was told to me in the context of a bisila of the second type.

30 This was the only context in which the idea of sadness because of the death of a pig was ever mentioned to me by Gawans. Although the attitude is well known elsewhere in New Guinea, and in the Massim (see Macintyre, 1984:111), it has, in my experience, only a limited expression on Gawa.

31 For instance, the year before the finale when it seemed possible that the Drum dance leader might have to give the pig for use at a mortuary rite, there was considerable concern that he should refrain from doing so because the mortuary rite is a segmentary, dala matter. It was felt that distribution would not go widely enough, whereas the Drum dance is a community affair in which the pig (along with many other pigs) was being given to the community as a whole.

32 I observed this directly at the finale of the Comb entertainment, but missed it at the Drum dance distribution. However, Gawans told me that it had taken place at that time as well.

33 There is also a separate, large wooden platter of small pork pieces for children. Except for Nukubay children who, like the adults, are prohibited from eating what comes from the Drum dance center, the children are all called to rush in and take pieces after the pork has been cut up.

34 This method of hamlet distribution is used in all major festivities to make sure that everyone has received food. Variations in the portion of food given may reflect variables such as hamlet size and other factors. Larger hamlets may also be broken down into household units. A similar procedure is practiced in canoe feasts (see Chapter 3).

35 In the entertainment I observed, the only recipients excluded from this chastisement were one or two younger men who had been in regular attendance at the dance.

36 This is one more example of the identification of eating with loss or disappearance. In certain contexts, stealing can be referred to metaphorically as "eating." I have heard this usage particularly in the context of discussion of the theft of New Guinean money from the tradestore at Kulumadau in Muyuw, when people said that the thieves "ate" the money and so it disappeared.

37 Individuals of various kumila who do not have partners may also put on decor to be taken by an individual of another kumila. This person then becomes responsible for making an equivalent return at the reciprocal entertainment. As in the case of the dancing itself, participation is not confined to those with partners or to the two allied kumila. This sort of openness makes it possible for everyone to be included, irrespective of the formal organization of reciprocity.

38 With one or two special exceptions based on tradition, only Nukubay people have combs, but everyone participates in the feasts.

39 Since it is men who have the formal partners, it appears to be somewhat less important for women to wear the combs. Of course, women receive yams distributed by close kinsmen who have formal nube. A woman with a comb may also have a female nube who will be the one to contribute yams for her and to take her comb at the finale.

40 During the speeches, the Nukubay were chastised by their own senior men for not adequately decorating their combs with discs of red kaloma and other traditional shells in addition to the bead decor. However, at the distribution of the noukay, the joking chastisement of recipients did not take place. The reasons for this difference from the Drum entertainment I observed included the fact that the entertainment was a gulugwalu rather than a vaga; in addition, there appeared to be some feeling that there had been sufficient chastisement during the finale, so that further remarks were unnecessary.

Chapter 9. The identity of the witch

1 There are other categories of intentional death-dealing or disease-causing agents beside *bwagaw*, but the latter is the most central in the Gawan imagination and tends to be used as a covering category for intentional evildoing in a variety of disturbances. *Bwagaw* is a diffuse notion, a summary label for hidden acts of evil and wrongdoing, which also conveys the type for wrongdoing in the society (a similar broad use of the notion of witchcraft was noted among the Azande by Evans-Pritchard, 1937:107).

Of the other secretive disease-causing acts, the most prominent is *silami*, which involves the use of a variety of poisonous leaves. This category of death dealing could be glossed as "sorcery," but both bwagaw and silami are intentional acts. According to some Gawans, *silami* is an essentially masculine activity in contrast to *bwagaw* (a prototypically, but as we shall see, not entirely, female activity in the Gawan view). This contrast between silami and bwagaw suggests divisions between male and female modes of death dealing that have tended to become subordinated in Gawan thinking to the more ambiguous concept of bwagaw.

2 In individual kula cases, for instance, suspicion could fall on an external source, but kula-related cases may also involve suspicion directed at other men within Gawa who in a given instance may be perceived to be in competition with each other.

3 Apparently in the past a man who wanted a witch to act for him asked a woman of a dala of his kumila that had a special kind of affiliation with his own, but not a member of his own dala. Nadel (1954:169) also reports that among the Nupe a woman has a male partner, but the man is the passive partner, and the conditions of dual operation are quite different.

4 The term is borrowed from Wilson (1951). My impression is that one should not refer to a defender in his presence by the term *bwagaw* because of its negative connotations. In addition to defenders, there are also some curers who do not have magic for controlling witches.

5 See Baxter (1972) and Sansom (1972) for discussion of other cases in which "witches are not named." See Patterson (1974–5:136) for brief comments on the problem in a New Guinea context.

6 Gawans ordinarily use the English borrowing *miting* to refer to any gathering for the purpose of discussing community or other matters and in which public speaking is involved. The indigenous term for a general meeting is *liwola* or *lawawala*.

7 I heard of one case sometime before 1973 in which, according to the informant, the name of a suspect was mentioned, causing considerable anger, but the use of allusion through general categories is a common device aimed at frightening the witch. A defender's knowledge may be derived from diagnosis or the curer's ability to "see" the witch owing to his control of revelatory magic. The witch may be viewed in a dream, or a patient's dream may also serve as an indicator of identity for purposes of diagnosis. Gawans do not, however, diagnose the causes of a death before burial of the corpse, and, as we might expect, there are no elaborate diagnostic procedures.

8 The label given to all public hearings or moots involving conflicts of various kinds is *yaakara*, meaning "to deny." Gawans sometimes view the fact that bwagaw always deny their identity as a problem. For instance, in discussing earlier cargo cults that had come into the area after World War II, one man told me that as part of this brief movement it was held that "the place would turn around": i.e., the witches would all confess (*kaamata*) and thus the cargo could arrive. Gawans are aware that in nearby Muyuw witches confess and then become protectors of the people. In one instance, a public speaker suggested that (what was perceived at the time as) current Muyuwan good health, in contrast to Gawan illness, was due to the fact that Muyuwan witches confess.

9 In a well-known passage, Evans-Pritchard (1937:119f.) points to a similar problem concerning the Azande attitude toward responsibility for witchcraft, but, unlike Gawans, Azande make public accusations.

10 Another less emphasized version is that the witches now travel on western-styled ships. As one man told me in 1980, everything that people have in their daily life, witches also have. The witch canoe has a more complex narrative contextualization than I discuss here. I would add merely that it is thought to originate in the southern regions rather than those north of Gawa.

11 A related Gawan view is that Tawuvaw comes and sits on the outer cliffs of Gawa at times of extensive illness. It is up to the defender who protects the "back" of Gawa to make appropriate spells against this danger.

With respect to flying, one Gawan woman told me that Gawan male bwagaw (curers or witches) do not fly: Only women fly. This view suggests the Trobriand flying witches (*mulukwausi*, a label known on Gawa and appearing in some Gawan canoe magic) who are usually (although not always; see Weiner, 1976:118) women; indeed, Gawan bwagaw also engage in the mulukwausi specialty, which is killing and consuming sailors on the ocean, and this is primarily associated with women. However, as discussed later, there are generalized Gawan identifications between bwagaw as a category and "lightweightness." In addition, one defender told me that he had once caught a male bwagaw who had flown to Muyuw. In his view, male witches also fly. Nevertheless, when the concept of witches flying to other places emerges in discussion or public meetings, it is usually, in my experience, connected with female witchery.

12 For notions of women as consumers, see A. Strathern, 1982:115; M. Strathern, 1981b:175.

13 It will be recalled that anyone can contribute a pig to the Drum dance through appropriate kin; Ramugway also contribute pigs in this way, in addition to receiving pork (from other pigs) at the distribution.

14 The reference is to the optional urugayay mortuary gift mentioned in Chapter 7, note 18.

15 When a person is ill, the basic responsibility for his or her care rests with the spouse and the latter's kin, who could be blamed for inadequate care should the patient die. At the kawrawora, the kinspeople of the spouse in particular are expected to deny complicity in witchcraft, but others, including the patient's kin, may also make denials.

16 Unlike some of the peoples in the south and southwest regions of the Massim, Gawans have never practiced cannibalism, but they recognize its occurrence elsewhere in the region (especially the Dobuan area) in the past. Concomitantly, the associations between the flesh of pigs and persons appear to be (or to have been) more marked in the southwestern regions (note, for instance, the equation of the bodies of pigs and persons in Normanby narratives concerned with the origin of kula shells, recorded by Roheim, 1950:200ff.).

17 The reference to a dream may have simply been a *karaabay*, a metaphor or parable, meant to warn people against witchery that would cause this man to become ill. However, as indicated in note 6, Gawans also regard dreams as having predictive value.

18 This suggests the error in Douglas's (1971:xxvi–xxvii) hypothesis that notions about the projection of missiles *into* the body as a cause of witch-based illness are likely to be associated with distant witches – intruders from outside the community – and conversely, that where the witch is internal to the community, the victim's strength is likely to be "sucked out." To understand the significance of any procedure of this sort, one must examine the wider symbolic system entailed in witchcraft in a given community.

19 For example, one woman suggested to me that witches on Gawa don't confess because they would be ashamed (*kasi-mwasira*) to say they eat the dead.

20 On arguments in the literature about the legitimacy or illegitimacy of sorcery and witchcraft, see the recent brief review by Zelenietz (1981:3f.). On Normanby for example, the position of female witches is much more complex in this respect than on Gawa. According to Thune (1980:96ff.), Normanby witches operate to punish violations against the matrilineal susu, and also to protect susu members on the one hand; and as a collective group, to steal and cannibalize the dead, including their own susu members (thus operating as evil agents against society) on the other. As Crick (1976:109ff.) has pointed out, the "witch" is part of a wider "moral field" of identities and "persons" in a given cultural community and not interpretable apart from this field.

21 There was only one person (a man) of whom a number of people voluntarily said to me in privacy that he was a witch, but no specific remarks were made in this connection with bespelling in childhood. Other people were cited to me largely with reference to specific events in which the informant felt they had come under suspicion; one knowledgeable informant gave me a list of persons who had been "found" by a defender in the past. In these instances the notion of previous bespelling in childhood was not stated (although it is of course always possible for such views to be "read backward" into an identification should the speaker wish). In addition, I did not hear any allusion to childhood bespelling in the public speeches on witchcraft, although as I have indicated, other concepts connecting witches with the dala were in evidence (see Chapter 10).

22 Assumptions of this kind are also marked in Malinowski's (1922:313) account of the Kitavan myth of the Flying Canoe (see also the analysis in Munn, 1972).

23 This operation of "leveling" is, of course, a standard feature of witchcraft in many societies. See, for example, Wilson, 1970:253.

24 Although this application of the term *hegemony* is somewhat different from its more usual usage in the literature, it is not entirely out of keeping with the direction of thinking in Gramsci (1971) and Williams's (1977:108ff.) adaptation of Gramsci's ideas. It is also in line with Foucault's (1980:92ff.) concept of the pervasiveness of power relations as the pressures embedded in social interaction. I trust my point is clear in context, that the Gawan principles to which I refer have primacy in the constitution of the contemporary Gawan sociopolitical system, and that their very primacy embeds them in experience as a form of dominion and subjugation (hegemony). The witch concentrates this diffuse experience into personified, active being. See also Durkheim's (1915:206ff.) notion of the symbolic processes by which the "moral authority of society" is directly configured in experience.

Chapter 10. Didactic speech, consensus, and the control of witchcraft

1   The term *tamumoya* applies in general to men who are probably older than about forty-five. However, it can be used quite variably as its denotation is often relative to context, and younger adult men may sometimes be referred to in this way. It also may denote "men of old" – or "the old men of the past."

2   The term *-gweiguya* is distinguished from *-gouguya* (preaching in church), and may also be used to refer to "lecturing" children. (The more specific term for chastisement or verbal criticism is *-kane*.) Hutchins (1980:139) gives the Trobriand term *gumgweguya* as denoting "persons of intermediate rank *dala*, below [Trobriand] *guyau* but above *tokai* [commoners]." (The prefix *gum-* probably denotes "person.") On Gawa, of course, no such ranked categories are applicable, but as we have seen, speech is a superordinating potency contrasted in some contexts with eating (see Chapter 3). Gawan men whom I asked about how one becomes a guyaw frequently mentioned the importance of gweiguya. Emphasis on the connection between oratory and leadership is widely reported from New Guinea (see Goldman, 1983; A. Strathern, 1975; M, Strathern, 1981b).

3   Some people said witches are supposed to be "frightened" by the speakers (who may hint that they know the witch's identity) and so agree to stop their activities, but the general point is that witches should listen to the persuasive arguments of the speakers.

4   This does not mean that in particular contexts, senior men of influence cannot themselves fall under some suspicion of witchery, or of telling the women of their dala to bewitch others. See V.'s school speech analyzed in this chapter. Relevant senior men, like others, may deny their complicity at a kawrawora (as I have observed in one instance in an illness ascribed to a kula transaction).

5   The announcement of the scheduling of various events or work arrangements is a regular function of public meetings, and may occur within more general speeches.

6   The reference to mats is probably a figurative reference to kula shells, or may carry a general sense similar to the English use of "thing" in "There won't be a thing left."

7   Kweawata is the most immediate foreign competitor of Gawa. I have heard similar dramatic references to it made in public speaking when Gawan leaders are attempting to arouse Gawans to speed up Gawan preparations for kula. Although there is considerable intra-Gawan competition in kula, Gawans also consider themselves a collectivity in competition with other island communities, and may be mutually supportive of their own members as well as competitive. The focus of the

competition appears somewhat more ambiguous than that suggested by Uberoi (1971:147) for the Trobriands.

8   An adequate demonstration of this point would, of course, require a detailed analysis of the speeches. More evidence is given in the examination of a single speech later in the chapter.

9   His death was particularly sad because he died on a trip away from Gawa, having gone to Iwa on kula. On my return to Gawa in 1975, I was told that he had been carried home on a trawler; his kinspeople carried his body up the cliff at night to lay it out in the house of mourning before starting the wails that announce a death. The whole affair thus appears to have been unusually painful and traumatic.

10   Up to this time there had been no school on Gawa; the nearest government school for Gawan children was at Guasopa in southern Muyuw. Gawans were very anxious to have the school. In 1979, when I returned to Gawa, the fact that the school was temporarily inoperative owing to certain recent problems was of considerable concern to Gawan leadership, and every effort was made to have the school reopened (as it was after I left in 1981).

11   Obviously, the analysis of one speech can provide only a partial view of the more complex process of the meeting, and other speeches show variant structures and patterns of emphasis (although there is a tendency for speeches in a meeting of this type to cohere around a set of thematic images, as suggested earlier).

12   The following text is a fairly literal translation from my taping of the talk. Owing to technical difficulties, I began the recording after the speaker had just started, and a phrase or two is absent from the initial statement. I discussed the tape with a few informants, but one of them in particular, a young man of about twenty at the time, was willing to work with me more systematically on speeches of this kind. I reexamined this speech with him in 1975 on my brief return to Gawa. My translation and interpretations are based on these discussions, as well as my own knowledge of the language, of the cultural assumptions implicated in the speech, and of surrounding events.

I have used the following conventions in the translation:

(#) = Division of text for convenience of reference.

. . . = More than one or two words are left out in the text. If a general topic has been left out, this has been indicated by a summary in square brackets.

[ ] = My grammatical or explanatory interpolations in the text. I have indicated the distinction between the exclusive [Excl.] and inclusive [Incl.] forms of the first person plural pronoun where it is relevant to the argument and not apparent from the context or my translation.

a, b, c, etc. = Explanatory notes to the speech.

13   The longer form is *spasoupa*. The term is used to convey an untruth, whether intentional or not.

14   In a different context, Goldman (1983:220, 234) also points to important connections between "straightness," and the "unity" of truth as opposed to the "duality of lies" in Huli notions about speech.

15   On the contribution of "metapragmatic" language to the constitutive power of oratory, see Silverstein (1981).

16   According to one man, the rule of Guyoraba superseded an earlier order in which dala groups of two kumila were of high rank; this kareiwaga is now finished and its end is associated with the name of Guyoraba. A "chief" named "Gioraba" is mentioned in the Australian Patrol Report for 1928. Since names are recycled, this man need not, of course, have been the individual involved. However, as I have indicated (Chapter 2), there is additional evidence for a more hierarchical political structure on Gawa in the recent prepacification past.

17 The fact that the introduction of the Japanese (6) draws attention to modern contacts with non–New Guinean outsiders appears appropriate in the present context involving the incorporation of a nonindigenous institution into the Gawan community.

18 Gawans distinguish the kareiwaga of the government, the church, and the school. At the same time, there appears to be increasing emphasis on the relation and mutual supportiveness of the three kareiwaga.

19 For a comparative consideration of the importance of shame in other areas of New Guinea, see Epstein (1984).

20 The upward directionality of this verb for building (-rup, to raise up, or pick up) resonates in this context with the "climbing" of fame. The more general term for building a house (-yurisem) does not, to my knowledge, carry these connotations.

21 This sort of rhetorical figure appears to refer more directly to the realities of the prepacification era than to the present.

22 Both men and women worked on the school, but men organized the work, and men's jobs were more continuous. The women's work included the burning off of the land needed for the school hamlet, work on the plaiting of the coconut frond sides for the walls, etc. – i.e., their typical work tasks in construction processes.

23 Work such as the maintenance of the central path or any work for the medical aid post, both of which pertain to the government kareiwaga, was generally organized on Fridays. Wednesday, on the other hand, was at that time the weekday reserved for any collective work needed for the church.

24 In the past, the neighborhoods were frequently in direct conflict with each other. For example, it is said that the northwestern people of Kweata neighborhood would ally themselves with Kweawata Island to fight the more southerly Patulaway hamlets; the latter in turn are said to have allied themselves with Yanaba Island to the south.

25 The decision to climb for coconuts had apparently been made by the head of the school committee, a man from group A.

26 See Tuzin (1980:131ff.) on the importance of unanimity in work procedures among the Ilahita Arapesh. Tuzin's interesting account of the construction of a Tambaran house illuminates the way in which the construction process itself is a process forming the unity of the workers; however, disturbances during the building (for example, the snapping of vine supports in the critical procedure of hoisting the ridgepole) may be taken as a sign that "someone in the work force was . . . harboring ill will toward the operation." As a result the work lacks the "total unity of intention among the workers" that is required for the assistance of Nggwal, the religious power for whom the house is being built (ibid., p. 139). See also Huber, 1980, who discusses the Anggor pig hunt as a socially formative process pointing to the way these hunts "draw the dispersed daily lives of the villagers to a common point" (p. 49). A related perspective on work activities is developed by Feeley-Harnik (1982) in quite a different context.

27 An attempt was also made to effect reconciliation at the thatching by the gift of branches of betel nut from one of the senior men of community standing. Betel nut expresses the desire for peace. However, contrary to the wishes of these elders, the two groups continued to work separately.

28 The fact that the official school committee was made up entirely of young men was one of the factors contributing to the problems in organizing the work.

29 The teacher's interpretation of the events was undoubtedly fueled by his Gawan mentors. That this sort of night haunting constitutes threats by a bwagaw is a typical Gawan inference. Something similar happened to me after I had been on Gawa about a month in 1973. I was awakened at night by strange sounds around the house. The hamlet head decided I was being haunted by a bwagaw, and suggested that we have a distribution of tobacco the next day to make sure that no one was angry because they had not received tobacco from me. For reasons too complex to discuss here, some people felt that it was this man himself who had been doing the haunting! My own impression is that this use of the notion of the witch provides a means by which Gawans can come to terms with and also incorporate outsiders whose position in the egalitarian community is anomalous. This anomaly derives from the perception that the newcomers' control over resources and their requirements for living on the island entail (in one form or another) an ordinarily unacceptable concentration of goods, or demands on the people. What the process does is to construct events around these persons that subject them to the sanction of witch attack for the inequality they introduce into the island, and at the same time, provide the means for giving them an image of equality, thus making it possible for them to stay. In my case, this was done through a typical distribution of concentrated resources (the much wanted tobacco); in the more complex case of the teacher, it was done in part through the public meeting, with its emphasis on the community function the school was fulfilling (i.e., the focus on the fact that the school was not the teacher's, but the people's, and would be the source of value for Gawans as a whole).

30 The causes of these shortages were some recent funerals; in addition, as I have indicated, the building of the school was itself taxing Gawan resources, and temporarily curtailing work in the gardens.

31 A somewhat similar process is noted by Tuzin (1980:142–5) for the Ilahita Arapesh in the case of conflict occurring over a death during the preparation of a Tambaran "spirit house." Tuzin points out that "the case exemplifies the expansion of significance that typically occurs whenever the Tambaran is implicated: the individual tragedy first triggers social discord ... [after which] the invocation of the Tambaran [as a causal factor] accelerates the issue to the *total* community level ... diffusing blame throughout adult male society" (ibid., p. 145).

32 Attention should also be drawn to the opposed masculine and feminine relations to public speaking, and the connection between speech and the control of space. As previously noted (Chapter 5), public speaking is identified with a capacity to control and operate in an extended space. This speech creates talk that is not just casual, private conversation that, as one metaphor has it, "flutters down in the house," and is without a clear sense of positive outcome; rather, it can bring problems out into the open and publicly formulate unity in people's attitudes so as to enable the organization of projects. We have seen that the capacity for this latter kind of speaking is epitomized in the strength of senior men, and more generally in adult male externalizing powers. The fact that women, on the other hand, are identified with the relatively interior locales of private or casual speech suggests further their identification in public contexts with the role of the exhorted rather than those who exhort.

33 Women told me that when almost the whole male population has gone on a major kula journey, women may dress up as men and gather at the hamlet of the Drum dance for their own entertainments. Unfortunately, I have never been on Gawa during such a period to observe these affairs.

Conclusion

1 I do not mean, of course, that there have not been any attempts to revise this type of approach (see, for example, Crick, 1976:109ff.; Kelly, 1976). Crick in particular has been explicitly concerned with this problem in connection with the study of witchcraft. According to Crick (1976:112), "One of the reasons for the shortcomings of anthropological discussions of witchcraft is the idea that it is a phenomenon which should be treated as a [separate] topic at all."

References

Ardener, E. (1978) Some outstanding problems in the analysis of events. In E. Schwimmer (ed.), *Yearbook of Symbolic Anthropology*. London: C. Hurst.

Ardener, S., ed. (1981) *Women and Space: Ground Rules and Social Maps*. London: Croom Helm.

Austen, L. (1934) Procreation among the Trobriand Islanders. *Oceania* 5:102–13.

Australia Patrol (1924) Report 1923–24 (A 279, no. 496B), Misima Subdistrict, Southeast Division. Port Moresby: Papua New Guinea National Archives.

Australia Patrol (1928) Report no. 6-27/28 (file NT36), Misima Subdistrict, Southeast Division. Port Moresby: Papua New Guinea National Archives.

Australia Station Journal (1920) The Kulumadau-Misima Station Journal for June 1920 (GRS G91, no. 449N). Canberra: Commonwealth Archives.

Bailey, F. G. (1971) *Gifts and Poison*. Oxford: Basil Blackwell.

Bakhtin, M. M. (1981) *The Dialogic Imagination*. Austin: University of Texas Press.

Barnes, R. (1974) *Kédang: A Study of the Collective Thought of an Eastern Indonesian People*. Oxford: Clarendon Press.

Barraud, C., D. de Coppet, et al. (1979) Des relations et des morts. Quatre sociétés vues sous l'angle des échanges. In *Différences, valeurs, hiérarchie*. Paris: Editions de l'école des Hautes études en Sciences Sociales.

Basso, K. and H. Selby (1976) *Meaning in Anthropology*. Albuquerque: University of New Mexico Press.

Battaglia, D. (1981) Segaiya: Commemoration in a Massim society. Ph.D. diss., Cambridge University.

——— (1983) Projecting personhood in Melanesia: The dialectics of artifact symbolism on Sabarl Island. *Man* 8 (2):289–304.

Baudrillard, J. (1981) *For a Critique of the Political Economy of the Sign*. St. Louis: Telos Press.

Baxter, P. (1972) Absence makes the heart grow fonder: Some suggestions why witchcraft accusations are rare among East African pastoralists. In M. Gluckman (ed.), *The Allocation of Responsibility*. Manchester: Manchester University Press.

Beidelman, T. (1980) The moral imagination of the Kaguru: Some thoughts on tricksters, translations and comparative analysis. *American Ethnologist* 7 (1):27–42.

317

Benveniste, E. (1966) *Problèmes de linguistique generale*. Paris: Gallimard.

Berde, S. (1974) Melanesians as Methodists: Economy and marriage on a Papua New Guinea island. Ph.D. diss., University of Pennsylvania.

Berger, P. and T. Luckmann (1967) *The Social Construction of Reality*. New York: Doubleday.

Berthelot, J. (1983) Corps et société (Problémes méthodologiques posés par une approche sociologique du corps). *Cahiers internationaux de Sociologie* 74:119–31.

Bohannon, P. (1955) Some principles of exchange and investment among the Tiv. *American Anthropologist* 57:60–70.

Bohannon, P. and G. Dalton, eds. (1962) *Markets in Africa*. Evanston: Northwestern University Press.

Boon, J. A. (1982) *Other Tribes, Other Scribes. Symbolic Anthropology in the Comparative Study of Cultures, Histories, Religions, and Texts*. Cambridge: Cambridge University Press.

Bromilow, W. (1912) Dobuan (Papuan) beliefs and folklore. In *Report of the Thirteenth Meeting of the Australasian Association for the Advancement of Science, 1911*. Sydney: W. E. Smith.

Bourdieu, P. (1970) La maison ou le monde renversé. In *Esquisse d'une théorie de la pratique*. Paris: Librairie Droz.

(1977) *Outline of a Theory of Practice*. Cambridge: Cambridge University Press.

(1979) The disenchantment of the world. In *Algeria 1960*. Cambridge: Cambridge University Press.

(1982) Leçon inaugurale, Chaire de sociologie. Collège de France.

Burke, K. (1961) *The Rhetoric of Religion. Studies in Logology*. Boston: Beacon Press.

Burman, R. (1981) Time and socioeconomic change in Simbu. *Man* n.s. 16 (2):251–67.

Burridge, K. (1975) The Melanesian manager. In J. Beattie and R. Lienhardt (eds.), *Studies in Social Anthropology*. Oxford: Clarendon Press.

Campbell, S. (1983a) Kula in Vakuta: The mechanics of keda. In J. Leach and E. Leach (eds.), *The Kula: New Perspectives on Massim Exchange*. Cambridge: Cambridge University Press.

(1983b) Attaining rank: A classification of shell valuables. In J. Leach and E. Leach (eds.), *The Kula: New Perspectives on Massim Exchange*. Cambridge: Cambridge University Press.

(1984) The art of kula: An analysis of the Vakutan artistic system and the rituals of kula. Ph. D. diss., Australian National University.

Cassirer, E. (1953) *The Philosophy of Symbolic Forms*. Vol.1. New Haven: Yale University Press.

Chernoff, E. (1979) *African Rhythm and African Sensibility. Aesthetics and Social Action in African Musical Idiom*. Chicago: University of Chicago Press.

Colson, E. (1974) *Tradition and Contract. The Problem of Order*. Chicago: Aldine.

Comaroff, J. (1985) *Body of Power, Spirit of Resistance: The Culture and History of a South Africa People*. Chicago: University of Chicago Press.

Coppet, D. de (1970) 1, 4, 8:9, 7. La monnaie: Présence des morts et mesure du temps. *L'Homme* 10:17–39.

(1981) The life-giving death. In S. C. Humphreys and H. King (eds.), *Mortality and Immortality*. New York: Academic Press.

Crick, M. (1976) *Explorations in Language and Meaning. Towards a Semantic Anthropology.* New York: John Wiley.

Crocker, C. (1973) Ritual and the development of social structure (Appendix to article). In J. Shaughnessy (ed.), *The Roots of Ritual.* Grand Rapids: Erdmans.

—— (1979) Selves and alters among the Eastern Bororo. In D. Maybury-Lewis (ed.), *Dialectical Societies: The Gê and Bororo of Central Brazil.* Cambridge, Mass.: Harvard University Press.

Cunningham, C., J. Dougherty, J. Fernandez, et al., eds. (1981) Symbolism and cognition. Special Issue, *American Ethnologist* 8 (3).

Damon, F. (1978) Modes of production and the circulation of value on the other side of the kula ring. Woodlark Island, Muyuw. Ph.D. diss., Princeton University.

—— (1980) The kula and generalised exchange: Considering some unconsidered aspects of *The Elementary Structures of Kinship. Man* 15 (2):267–93.

—— (1983a) What moves the kula: Opening and closing gifts on Woodlark Island. In J. Leach and E. Leach (eds.), *The Kula: New Perspectives in Massim Exchange.* Cambridge: Cambridge University Press.

—— (1983b) Muyuw kinship and the metamorphosis of gender labour. *Man* 18 (2):305–26.

Derrida, J. (1972) *Marges de la philosophie.* Paris: Minuit.

Devisch, R. (1981) Spatial metaphors and bipolar individuation in the Yaka political function. Paper prepared for the African Studies Association Meetings, 1981.

—— (1982) Space-time and bodiliness: A semantic-praxiological approach. Unpublished manuscript. Centre for Social and Cultural Anthropology, Catholic University of Leuven.

—— (1983) Symbol and psycho-somatic symptom in bodily space-time: The case of the Yaka of Zaire. *The International Journal of Psychology* 18 (5).

Dolgin, J. L. et al. (1977) *Symbolic Anthropology. A Reader in the Study of Symbols and Meanings.* New York: Columbia University.

Douglas, M. (1971) Introduction. In M. Douglas (ed.), *Witchcraft Confessions and Accusations.* London: Tavistock.

Dumont, L. (1979) The anthropological community and ideology. *Social Science Information* 18 (6):785–817.

—— (1983) La valeur chez les modernes et chez les autres. In his *Essais sur l'individualisme. Une perspective anthropologique sur l'idéologie moderne.* Paris: Éditions du seuil.

Durkheim, E. (1915) *The Elementary Forms of the Religious Life.* London: Allen and Unwin.

—— (1947) *The Division of Labor in Society.* Glencoe: The Free Press.

Durkheim, E. and M. Mauss (1963) *Primitive Classification.* London: Cohen & West. First published 1901–2/1903.

Epstein, A. (1984) *The Experience of Shame in Melanesia.* RAI Occasional Paper no. 40. London: Royal Anthropological Institute.

Ernst, T. (1978) Aspects of meaning of exchanges and exchange items among the Onabasulu of the Great Papuan Plateau. *Mankind* 11 (3):187–97.

Evans-Pritchard, E. (1940) *The Nuer.* Oxford: Oxford University Press.

—— (1937) *Witchcraft, Oracles and Magic among the Azande.* Oxford: Clarendon Press.

Eyde, D. (1983) Sexuality and garden ritual in the Trobriands and Tikopia. Tudava meets the Atua I Kafika. *Mankind* 14(1):66–74.

Favret-Saada, I. (1977) *Deadly Words. Witchcraft in the Bocage*. Cambridge: Cambridge University Press.

Feeley-Harnik, G. (1982) The King's men in Madagascar. Slavery, citizenship and Sakalava monarchy. *Africa* 52(2):31–50.

Fernandez, J. (1982) *Bwiti. An Ethnography of the Religious Imagination in Africa*. Princeton: Princeton University Press.

Fortune, R. (1963) *Sorcerers of Dobu*. New York: E. P. Dutton.

Foucault, M. (1980) *The History of Sexuality*. Vol. 1. New York: Random House.

Fustel de Coulanges, N. D. (1956) *The Ancient City*. New York: Doubleday. First published 1864.

Geertz, C. (1973) *The Interpretation of Cultures*. New York: Basic Books.

(1983) *Local Knowledge*. New York: Basic Books.

Gell, A. (1975) *The Metamorphosis of the Cassowaries*. London: Athlone Press.

(1979) Reflections on a cut finger. In R. Hook (ed.), *Fantasy and Symbol: Essays in Anthropological Interpretations*. New York: Academic Press.

Giddens, A. (1979) *Central Problems in Social Theory. Action, Structure and Contradiction in Social Analysis*. Berkeley and Los Angeles: University of California Press.

(1981) *A Contemporary Critique of Historical Materialism*. Vol. 1. *Power, Property and the State*. Berkeley and Los Angeles: University of California Press.

Goldman, L. (1983) *Talk Never Dies*. London: Tavistock.

Gramsci, A. (1971) *Prison Notebooks*. New York: International Publications.

Gregory, C. A. (1982) *Gifts and Commodities*. London: Academic Press.

Guidieri, R. (1973) Il kula: Overro della truffa. Una reinterpretazione di pratiche simboliche delle isola Trobriand. *Rassegna italiana de sociologia* 14, no. 4.

Hallowell, A. I. (1955) *Culture and Experience*. Philadelphia: University of Pennsylvania Press.

Hanson, F. A. (1975) *Meaning in Culture*. London: Routledge and Kegan Paul.

Heidegger, M. (1982) *The Basic Problems of Phenomenology*. Bloomington: Indiana University Press.

Hegel, G. (1967) *The Phenomenology of Mind*. New York: Harper and Row.

Hertz, R. (1960) The collective representation of death (1907). In his *Death and the Right Hand*. Glencoe: The Free Press.

Holenstein, E. (1976) *Roman Jakobson's Approach to Language: Phenomenological Structuralism*. Bloomington: Indiana University Press.

Howe, E. (1981) The social determination of knowledge: Maurice Bloch and Balinese time. *Man* n.s. 16 (2):220–34.

Huber, P. (1980) The Anggor bowman: Ritual and society in Melanesia. *American Ethnologist* 7(1):43–57.

Hubert, H. (1909) Etude Sommaire de la représentation du Temps dans la religion et la magie. In H. Hubert and M. Mauss, *Mélanges d'histoire des religions*. Paris: Felix, Alcan and Guillamin.

Hugh-Jones, C. (1979) *From the Milk River: Spatial and Temporal Processes in Northwest Amazonia*. Cambridge: Cambridge University Press.

Hutchins, E. (1980) *Culture and Inference: A Trobriand Case Study*. Cambridge, Mass.: Harvard University Press.

Iteanu, A. (1983) *La ronde des échanges. De la circulation aux valeurs chez les Orokaiva*. Cambridge: Cambridge University Press.

Jakobson, R. (1939) Observations sur le classement phonologique des consonnes. In his *Selected Writings*, Vol. 1. The Hague: Mouton.

Kahn, M. (1980) Always in hunger: Food as metaphor for social identity in Wamira, Papua New Guinea. Ph.D. diss., Bryn Mawr College.

Kapferer, B. (1983) *A Celebration of Demons: Exorcism and the Aesthetics of Healing in Sri Lanka*. Bloomington: Indiana University Press.

Kaplan, J. O., ed. (1977) Social Time and Social Space in Lowland South American Societies. *Proceedings of the 42nd International Congress of Americanists, V. 2*. Paris: Société des Américanistes, Museé de l'Homme.

Kelly, R. (1976) Witchcraft and Sexual Relations: An exploration in the social and semantic implications of the structure of belief. In P. Brown and G. Buchbinder, (eds.), *Man and Woman in the New Guinea Highlands*. Washington, D.C.: The American Anthropological Association.

Lamphere, L. (1971) The Navajo cultural system: An analysis of concepts of cooperation and autonomy and their relation to gossip and witchcraft. In K. Basso and M. Opler (eds.), *Apachean Culture, History and Ethnology*. Tucson: University of Arizona Press.

Lawrence, P. (1964) *Road Belong Cargo*. Manchester: Manchester University Press.

Leach, E. (1961) Two essays concerning the symbolic representation of time. In his *Rethinking Anthropology*. London: Athlone Press.

Leach, J. and E. Leach (1983) *The Kula: New Perspectives on Massim Exchange*. Cambridge: Cambridge University Press.

Leenhardt, M. (1947) *Do Komo: Person and Myth in the Melanesian World*. Chicago: University of Chicago Press.

Lefort, C. (1951) L'échange et la lutte des hommes. *Les Temps Modernes* 64:1400–17.

Leroy, J. D. (1979) The ceremonial pig kill of the South Kewa. *Oceania* 49 (3):179–209.

Lévi-Strauss, C. (1949) *The Elementary Structures of Kinship*. London: Eyre and Spottiswoode.

(1966) *The Savage Mind*. Chicago: University of Chicago Press.

(1967) Do dual organizations exist? In his *Structural Anthropology*. Garden City: Doubleday.

Lienhardt, G. (1951) Some notions of witchcraft among the Dinka. *Africa* 31:303–18.

Lithgow, D. (1973) Language change on Woodlark Island. *Oceania* 44 (2):101–8.

(1974) *Muyuw Dictionary*. Ukarumpa (Papua New Guinea): Summer Institute of Linguistics.

(1976) Austronesian languages: Milne Bay and adjacent islands. In S. Wurm (ed.), *New Guinea Area Languages and Language Study*. Canberra: Australian National University.

Lyons, J. (1977) *Semantics*, Vol. 2. Cambridge: Cambridge University Press.

Macintyre, M. (1983) Changing paths. An historical ethnography of the traders of tubetube. Ph.D. diss., Australian National University.

(1984) The problem of the semi-alienable pig. *Canberra Anthropology* 7 (1 and 2):109–21.

Mair, L. (1969) *Witchcraft*. New York: McGraw Hill.

Malinowski, B. (1922) *Argonauts of the Western Pacific*. London: Routledge and Kegan Paul.

(1929) *The Sexual Life of Savages*. New York: Harcourt Brace and World.

(1935) *Coral Gardens and Their Magic*. 2 vols. New York: American Book Co.

(1954) *Magic, Science and Religion*. New York: Doubleday.

Marriott, M. (1976) Hindu transactions: Diversity without dualism. In B. Kapferer (ed.), *Transactions and Meaning*. Philadelphia: Ishi.

Marx, K. (1906) *Capital*. Vol. 1. New York: Charles Kerr (Random House edition).

Mauss, M. (1968) Essai sur le don. Forme et raison de l'échange dans les sociétés archaiques (1923–4). In his *Sociologie et anthropologie*. Paris: Presses Universitaires de France.

Mead, G. H. (1956) *The Social Psychology of George Herbert Mead*. Chicago: University of Chicago Press.

Merleau-Ponty, M. (1962) *The Phenomenology of Perception*. London: Routledge and Kegan Paul.

Methodist Missionary Society of Australasia (1921) *Reports for 1920, 1921*. Sydney: Epworth.

Middleton, J. (1967) Some social aspects of Lugbara myth. In J. Middleton (ed.), *Myth and Cosmos*. New York: Natural History Press.

Moore, H. (1986) *Space, Text and Gender: An Anthropological Study of the Marakwet of Kenya*. Cambridge: Cambridge University Press.

Morgan, L. H. (1965) *Houses and House-Life of the American Aborigines*. Chicago: University of Chicago Press. First published 1881.

Munn, N. (1972) Symbolic time in the Trobriands of Malinowski's era: an essay on the anthropology of time. Photocopy.

(1976) Gawan magic. Morgan Lectures, University of Rochester.

(1977) The spatiotemporal transformation of Gawa canoes. *Journal de la Société des Océanistes*. Tome 33 (mars–juin), 54–55:39–53.

(1983) Gawan kula: Spatiotemporal control and the symbolism of influence. In J. Leach and E. Leach (eds.), *The Kula: New Perspectives on Massim Exchange*. Cambridge: Cambridge University Press.

Nadel, S. (1954) *Nupe Religion*. London: Routledge and Kegan Paul.

(1957) *The Theory of Social Structure*. Melbourne: Melbourne University Press.

Panoff, M. (1977) Energie et vertu: Le travail et ses représentations en Nouvelle-Bretagne. *L'Homme* 17(2–3):7–21.

Parkin, D. (1982) *Semantic Anthropology*. A.S.A. Monograph 22. London: Academic Press.

Parsons, T. and E. Shils (1951) *Toward a General Theory of Action*. New York and Evanston: Harper and Row.

Patterson, M. (1974–5) Sorcery and witchcraft in Melanesia. *Oceania* 15, (2, 3): 132–60, 215–34.

Peirce, C. S. (1955) *Philosophical Writings of Peirce*. New York: Dover.

Pocock, D. (1966) The anthropology of time reckoning. *Contributions to Indian Sociology* 7:18–29.

Polanyi, K. (1968) *Primitive, Archaic, and Modern Economics*, G. Dalton (ed.). Garden City: Doubleday.

Poole, E. J. P. (1982) The ritual forging of identity. Aspects of person and self in

Bimin-Kuskusmin male initiation. In G. Herdt (ed.), *Rituals of Manhood. Male Initiation in Papua New Guinea*. Berkeley: University of California Press.

Pos, H. (1938) La notion d'opposition en linguistique. In *Onzième congrès international de psychologie, Paris, 1937*. Paris: Alcan.

Rabinow, P. and W. Sullivan (1979) The interpretive turn: emergence of an approach. In P. Rabinow and W. Sullivan (eds.), *Interpretive Social Science: A Reader*. Berkeley: University of California Press.

Read, K. E. (1959) Leadership and consensus in a New Guinea society. *American Anthropologist* 61:425–36.

Redfield, J. (1975) *Nature and Culture in the Iliad: The Tragedy of Hector*. Chicago: University of Chicago Press.

Ricoeur, P. (1979) The model of the text: Meaningful action considered as a text. In P. Rabinow and W. Sullivan (eds.), *Interpretive Social Science. A Reader*. Berkeley: University of California Press.

(1983) *Temps et récit*, Tome I. Paris: Editions du Seuil.

Roheim, G. (1950) *Psychoanalysis and Anthropology*. New York: International Universities Press.

Rubel, P. and A. Rosman (1978) *Your Own Pigs You May Not Eat: A Comparative Study of New Guinea Societies*. Chicago: University of Chicago Press.

Ruel, M. (1970) Were-animals and the introverted witch. In M. Douglas (ed.), *Witchcraft Confessions and Accusations*. London: Tavistock.

Sahlins, M. (1972) *Stone Age Economics*. Chicago: Aldine.

(1976) *Culture and Practical Reason*. Chicago: University of Chicago Press.

Sansom, B. (1972) When witches are not named. In M. Gluckman (ed.), *The Allocation of Responsibility*. Manchester: Manchester University Press.

Sartre, J. P. (1966) *Being and Nothingness*. New York: Washington Square Press (Pocket Books).

(1968) *Search for a Method*. New York: Random House.

Saussure, F. de. (1966) *Course in General Linguistics*. New York: McGraw-Hill.

Schutz, A. (1962) Collected Papers, I. *The Problem of Social Reality*. The Hague: Martinus Nijhoff.

Schwimmer, E. (1973) *Exchange in the Social Structure of the Orokaiva*. New York: St. Martin's Press.

Seligmann, C. G. (1910) *The Melanesians of British New Guinea*. Cambridge: Cambridge University Press.

Seligmann, C. G. and W. Strong (1906) Anthropological investigations in British New Guinea. *The Geographical Journal* 28(3):225–42, 347–69.

Silverstein, M. (1981) Metaforces of power in traditional oratory. Lecture read to the Department of Anthropology, Yale University.

Simmel, G. (1950) *The Sociology of Georg Simmel*. Translated by K. Wolff. Glencoe: The Free Press.

(1955) *Conflict and the Web of Group Affiliations*. New York: The Free Press.

(1971) *On Individuality and Social Forms*. Chicago: University of Chicago Press.

(1978) *The Philosophy of Money*. Translated by T. Bottomore and D. Frisby. London, Henley, and Boston: Routledge and Kegan Paul.

Singer, M. (1984) *Man's Glassy Essence. Explorations in Semiotic Anthropology*. Bloomington: Indiana University Press.

Smith, W. R. (1956) *The Religion of the Semites*. New York: Meridian Books. First published 1889.

Sperber, D. (1974) *Rethinking Symbolism*. Cambridge: Cambridge University Press.

Strathern, A. (1975) Veiled Speech in Mt. Hagen. In M. Block (ed.), *Political Language and Oratory in Traditional Society*. London: Academic Press.

(1981) Death as exchange: Two Melanesian cases. In S. Humphreys and H. King (eds.), *Mortality and Immortality. The Anthropology of Death*. New York: Academic Press.

(1982) Witchcraft, greed, cannibalism and death: Some related themes from the New Guinea Highlands. In M. Bloch and J. Parry (eds.), *Death and the Regeneration of Life*. Cambridge: Cambridge University Press.

Strathern, A. and M. Strathern (1971) *Self-Decoration in Mt. Hagen*. London: Duckworth.

Strathern, M. (1972) *Women in Between*. London: Seminar (Academic) Press.

(1981a) Culture in a netbag: The manufacture of a subdiscipline in anthropology. *Man* 16(4):665–88.

(1981b) Self interest and the social good: Some implications of Hagen gender imagery. In S. Ortner and H. Whitehead (eds.), *Sexual Meanings. The Cultural Construction of Gender and Reality*. Cambridge: Cambridge University Press.

Tambiah, S. (1968) The magical power of words. *Man* n.s. 3:175–208.

(1983) On flying witches and flying canoes: The coding of male and female values. In J. Leach and E. Leach (eds.), *The Kula: New Perspectives on Massim Exchange*. Cambridge: Cambridge University Press.

Tcherkézoff, S. (1983) *Le roi Nyamwezi, la droite et la gauche: Révision comparative des classifications dualistes*. Cambridge: Cambridge University Press.

Thompson, E. P. (1967) Time, work discipline and industrial capitalism. *Past and Present* (38):56–97.

Thornton, R. (1980) *Space, Time and Culture among the Iraqw of Tanzania*. New York: Academic Press.

Thune, C. (1980) The Rhetoric of Remembrance: Collective Life and Personal Tragedy in Loboda Village. Ph.D. diss. Princeton University.

Touraine, A. (1974a) Towards a sociology of action. In A. Giddens (ed.), *Positivism and Sociology*. London: Heinemann.

(1974b) The raison d'être of a sociology of action. In A. Giddens (ed.), *Positivism and Sociology*. London: Heinemann.

(1977) *The Self-Production of Society*. Chicago: University of Chicago Press.

Turner, T. (1979a) The Gê and Bororo societies as dialectical systems: A general model. In D. Maybury-Lewis (ed.), *Dialectical Societies: The Gê and Bororo of Central Brazil*. Cambridge, Mass.: Harvard University Press.

(1979b) Anthropology and the politics of indigenous peoples' struggles. *Cambridge Anthropology* 5(1):1–42.

(1980) The social skin. In J. Cherfas and R. Lewin (eds.), *Not Work Alone*. Beverly Hills: Sage Publications.

(1985) Dual opposition, hierarchy, and value: Moiety structure and symbolic polarity in Central Brazil and elsewhere. In J. Galey (ed.), *Différences, valeurs, hiérarchie*. Paris: Editions de l'Ecole des Hautes Etudes en Sciences Sociales.

(1984) Production, value and structure in Marx: New interpretations of the central concepts of Marxian Political Economy and some implications for anthropology. Paper prepared for the Annual Meeting of the American Anthropological Association, Denver, 1984.

Turner, V. (1967) *The Forest of Symbols*. Ithaca: Cornell University.

(1975) Symbolic studies. In B. Siegel et al. (eds.), *Annual Review of Anthropology*. Palo Alto: Annual Reviews Inc.

Tuzin, D. (1980) *The Voice of the Tambaran. Truth and Illusion in Arapesh Religion*. Berkeley: University of California Press.

Tyler, S. (1978) *The Said and the Unsaid: Mind, Meaning, and Culture*. New York: Academic Press.

Uberoi, J. Singh (1971) *Politics of the Kula Ring*. Manchester: Manchester University Press.

Wagner, R. (1986) *Symbols that Stand for Themselves*. Chicago: University of Chicago Press.

Weiner, A. (1976) *Women of Value, Men of Renown*. Austin: University of Texas Press.

(1978) The reproductive model in Trobriand society. *Mankind* 11(3):175–86.

(1979) Trobriand kinship from another view: the reproductive power of women and men. *Man* 14(2):328–48.

(1980) Reproduction: a replacement for reciprocity. *American Ethnologist* 7:71–85.

(1982) Plus précieux que l'or: Relations et échanges entre hommes et femmes dans les sociétés d'Océanie. *Annales* (2):222–45.

(1983) A world of made is not a world of born: Doing kula on Kiriwina. In J. Leach and E. Leach (eds.), *The Kula: New Perspectives on Massim Exchange*. Cambridge: Cambridge University Press.

(1985) Inalienable wealth. *American Ethnologist* 12(2):210–27.

Williams, R. (1977) *Marxism and Literature*. Oxford: Oxford University Press.

Willis, P. (1977) *Learning to Labor. How Working Class Kids Get Working Class Jobs*. New York: Columbia University Press.

Willis, R., ed. (1975) *The Interpretation of Symbolism*. London: Malaby Press.

Wilson, M. (1951) *Good Company*. Oxford: Oxford University Press. (Reference to Beacon Press edition, 1963.)

(1970) Witch-beliefs and social structure. In M. Marwick (ed.), *Witchcraft and Sorcery*. Middlesex: Penguin Books.

Young, M. (1971) *Fighting with Food*. Cambridge: Cambridge University Press.

(1983a) The Massim: An introduction. *The Journal of Pacific History* 18 (1–2):4–10.

(1983b) *Magicians of Manumanu: Living Myth in Kalauna*. Berkeley: University of California Press.

(1983c) Ceremonial visiting in Goodenough Island. In J. Leach and E. Leach (eds.), *The Kula: New Perspectives on Massim Exchange*. Cambridge: Cambridge University Press.

Zelenietz, M. (1981) Sorcery and social change: An introduction. In M. Zelenietz and S. Lindenbaum (eds.), *Sorcery and Social Change in Melanesia*. Special Issue, *Social Analysis* 8 (3–14).

Index

Nancy D. Munn is Professor of Anthropology at the University of
Chicago. She is author of *Walbiri Iconography: Graphic Representation and Cultural Symbolism in a Central Australian Society.*

Library of Congress Cataloging-in-Publication-Data

Munn, Nancy D., 1931–

The fame of Gawa: a symbolic study of value representation in a

Massim (Papua New Guinea) society / Nancy D. Munn.

Originally published: Cambridge; New York: Cambridge University

Press, 1986 (Lewis Henry Morgan Lectures; 1976)

Includes bibliographical references and index.

ISBN 0-8223-1270-0 (pbk.)

1. Massim (Papua New Guinea people)   2. Ceremonial exchange—

Papua New Guinea.   3. Values—Case studies.   4. Social change—

Case studies.   I. Title.

[DU740.42.M86   1982]   306' .089995—dc20   92-9614 CIP